Lecture Notes in Computer Science

Edited by G. Goos and J. Hartmanis

Advisory Board: W. Brauer   D. Gries   J. Stoer

Peter A. Fritzson (Ed.)

Automated and Algorithmic Debugging

First International Workshop, AADEBUG '93
Linköping, Sweden, May 3-5, 1993
Proceedings

Springer-Verlag

Berlin Heidelberg New York
London Paris Tokyo
Hong Kong Barcelona
Budapest

Series Editors

Gerhard Goos
Universität Karlsruhe
Postfach 69 80
Vincenz-Priessnitz-Straße 1
D-76131 Karlsruhe, Germany

Juris Hartmanis
Cornell University
Department of Computer Science
4130 Upson Hall
Ithaca, NY 14853, USA

Volume Editor

Peter A. Fritzson
Department of Computer and Information Science, Linköping University
S-581 83 Linköping, Sweden

CR Subject Classification (1991): D.2.5, F.3.1, D.2.4, D.2.6, I.2.2

ISBN 3-540-57417-4 Springer-Verlag Berlin Heidelberg New York
ISBN 0-387-57417-4 Springer-Verlag New York Berlin Heidelberg

Typesetting: Camera-ready by author
Printing and binding: Druckhaus Beltz, Hemsbach/Bergstr.
45/3140-543210 - Printed on acid-free paper

Preface

This volume contains a selection of the papers which were accepted for presentation at AADEBUG'93, the First International Workshop on Automated and Algorithmic Debugging, held in Linköping, Sweden, 3-5 May 1993.

The area referred to as automated debugging has seen major developments over the last decade. One especially successful area of automated debugging is algorithmic debugging which originated in logic programming but later has been generalized to concurrent languages, imperative languages, lazy functional languages, etc. Important advances have also been made in knowledge-based program debugging, and in approaches to automated debugging based on static and dynamic program slicing.

The goal of the workshop was to bring together researchers from different areas of automated debugging and different programming communities to exchange ideas and advance the state of the art of automated debugging. A total of 28 papers were submitted to the workshop of which 21 were selected for this volume. This is an unusually high acceptance rate, but both the program committee and the Lecture Notes editor judged that the average quality of the submitted papers was sufficiently high. Perhaps this is not uncommon for the first workshop to be arranged in a specialized area. An additional six papers of the submitted ones were only accepted for short presentations at the workshop, and are not present in this proceedings.

On behalf of the Program Committee, the Program Chairman would like to thank all those who submitted papers to AADEBUG'93. Thanks also go to the Program Committee and others who helped in reviewing and evaluating the papers. Also, special thanks to the invited keynote speaker, Professor Ehud Shapiro, who managed to come to the workshop despite a very busy schedule. Last but not the least, the effort of all those who helped in organizing the workshop in one way or another, in particular Henrik Nilsson and Gunilla Blom-Lingenhult, is gratefully acknowledged.

Linköping, September 1993   Peter Fritzson

Program Chairman: Peter Fritzson (Linköping University)

Program Committee:
    Gérard Ferrand   (University of Orléans and INRIA, France)
    Mireille Ducassé   (ECRC, Munich, Germany)
    Bogdan Korel   (Wayne State University, Detroit, USA)
    Mariam Kamkar   (Linköping University, Sweden)
    Jan Maluszynski   (Linköping University, Sweden)
    Jukka Pakki   (University of Jyväskylä, Finland)
    Luís Moniz Pereira   (Lisbon New University, Portugal)
    Steven P. Reiss   (Brown University, USA)
    Rudolph Seviora   (University of Waterloo, Canada)
    Nahid Shahmehri   (Linköping University, Sweden)
    Mary-Lou Soffa   (University of Pittsburgh, USA)

Local Organization:
    Henrik Nilsson
    Gunilla Blom-Lingenhult

Table of Contents

Slicing

Visualization and Graphical User Interfaces

Knowledge-Based Debugging and Trace-Based Debugging

Software Maintenance and Debugging of Logic Programs III

A pragmatic survey of automated debugging

Mireille Ducassé

European Computer-Industry Research Centre
Arabellastrasse 17, D - 81925 Munich, Germany
tel: +49 89 926 99 142, fax: +49 89 926 99 170
email: mireille@ecrc.de

Abstract. This article proposes a structuring view of the area of automated debugging. Nineteen automated debugging systems are analyzed. Thirteen existing automated debugging techniques are briefly evaluated from a pragmatic point of view. The three underlying strategies are identified, namely *verification with respect to specification, checking with respect to language knowledge* and *filtering with respect to symptom.*
The verification strategy compares the actual program with some formal specification of the intended program. The checking strategy looks for suspect places which do not comply with some explicit knowledge of the programming language. The filtering strategy assumes correct parts of the code which cannot be responsible for the error symptom.
Assertion evaluation and algorithmic debugging are the most promising verification techniques. Some intrinsic limitations of the checking strategy makes it only a complementary, though helpful, debugging support. The slicing technique should be included in any debugger.

1 Introduction

In the last 30 years, there have been numerous studies on automated debugging which have led to a number of techniques and systems. This number is relatively large (13 techniques listed below) and the trends are not obvious to a non expert observer. In the following we analyze existing automated debugging techniques and identify the strategies behind the proposed techniques. All the techniques can be sorted into 3 main strategies and this gives a structuring view of the area of automated debugging. We only examine *existing* systems. Although the systems mentioned in the following are research prototypes, they are running or have run, hence their authors had some practicability concerns in mind.

Among the reviewed systems there are two different categories: tutoring systems and diagnosis systems. On the one hand tutoring systems aim at correcting programs written by novice programmers. The debugged programs are usually small; the problems addressed by these programs are usually stereotyped; some sort of specification is in general given. On the other hand, diagnosis systems aim at locating code errors in programs written by experienced programmers. The debugged programs are in general large; the problems addressed by these programs are not necessarily well understood; specifications are very seldomly given. Tutoring and diagnosis systems have thus very different constraints and requirements, they usually develop different strategies but we will see that they also have common features. In each category the systems are listed in chronological order, below. For each system we first give the full name, then the abbreviation used in the rest of the paper if needed. We also give the target programming language, the place where the debugging system was developed and the most interesting reference.

The tutoring systems are: *Intelligent Program Analysis* (IPA), Lisp-like languages or PL/1, MIT, USA [25]; *Pudsy*, Pascal, University of Sussex, UK [21]; *Laura*, Fortran, University of Caen, France [1]; *Phenarete*, Lisp, University Paris VIII, France [34]; *Proust*, Pascal, Yale University, USA [10]; *Talus*, Lisp, University of Texas, USA [23]; and *Apropos*, Prolog, University of Edinburgh, UK [19].

The diagnosis systems are: *Debussi*, it is claimed to be independent of the programming language (the examples given are Lisp programs), MIT, USA [17]; *Focus*, Fortran and Ada, University of Maryland, USA [22]; *Program error-locating assistant system* (PELAS), Pascal, Wayne State University and Oakland University, USA [13]; *Algorithmic Program Debugging* (APD), Prolog, Yale University, USA [28]. This system has inspired many other systems. In the following we mention only those which differ significantly with respect to the debugging strategies and techniques; *Yoda*, Ada, University of California, USA [18]; *Preset*, Prolog, Tokyo Institute of Technology, Japan [31]; *Rational Debugging* (RD), Prolog, University of Lisbon, Portugal [24]; *Annalyzer*, Ada, Standford University, USA [20]; *Algorithmic Debugging with Assertion* (ADAss) Prolog, Polish Academic of Sciences, Poland and Linköping University, Sweden [7]; *Process state model debugger* (PSMD), Pascal-like languages, Purdue University, USA [2]; *Generalized Algorithmic Debugging Technique* (GADT), Pascal, Linköping University, Sweden [12] ; *Aspect*, CLU, MIT, USA [9].

This article exhibits 13 techniques and there are no signs that the problem is fully addressed. Each of the described technique has its limitation. The techniques have, then, to be compared and discussed. We provide a list of criteria to enable a uniform comparison and evaluate briefly each technique. The aim here is not to make a quantitative comparison, which would take too long, but to show the obvious limitations, to put each technique in perspective.

It is interesting to note (see the table at the end of the paper) that each system uses its own combination of a subset of techniques. There are usually little justification for why a particular combination is used. Our conclusion is that all possible techniques should be available so that the user can decide which combination to use. Therefore an automated debugger must be an *extendable environment* where all the automated techniques can be integrated.

In the following we discuss erroneous and suspect code. We introduce the three automated debugging strategies that we have identified, namely verification with respect to specification, checking with respect to language knowledge and filtering with respect to symptom. Then for each of the strategies we describe briefly the relevant techniques. A table at the end of the article summarizes the results.

2   Erroneous and suspect code

People sometime talk about code errors as if they were absolute and well defined concepts whereas they are, in general, only relative and ill-defined. Figure 1 shows the idealistic view of debugging. Initially the errors are hidden, the programmer has

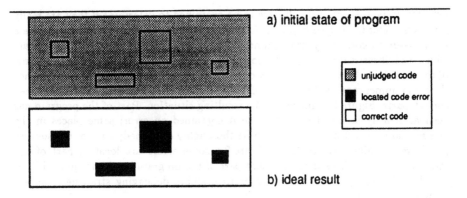

a) initial state of program

b) ideal result

Fig. 1. An idealistic view of debugging

not yet made any judgement about the program. Then at the end of the debugging session *all* the code errors are located and understood; the rest of the program is correct.

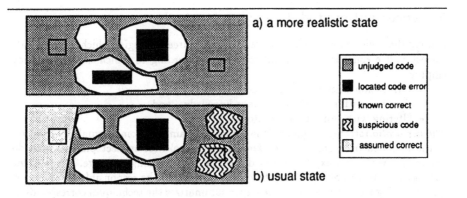

a) a more realistic state

b) usual state

Fig. 2. A more realistic view of debugging

The situation is, however, more subtle. Firstly, it is impossible to prove that all the errors in a program have been found. Hence there is no final state, but only intermediate states. This results in situations as illustrated by Figure 2.a. At a certain stage of debugging, some errors have been located and portion of text have been investigated and declared·correct. Part of the program is still not judged and some errors are still undetected. Secondly, errors are not absolute concepts. For example, depending on the point of view, a particular behavior of a program can be considered an error or a feature. Another example is a piece of code which breaks some company's convention, it may then be considered an error in that company while being considered correct in another place. Hence parts of the code can be detected to be suspect and still have to be examined to determine if they are really erroneous. Thirdly, it also happens that some parts of the examined program are a priori assumed correct by programmers. For example, when debugging a program which uses libraries it is in general a good strategy to assume the components of these libraries correct. However, they may contain the error which is searched for. Hence the programmer may have to backtrack on his assumption and examine the assumed correct parts. Figure 2.b illustrates the resulting situation. Part of the program has been arbitrarily assumed correct while it contained an error; some places in the program are suspect and still need to be thoroughly examined; some of the suspect parts are actually correct. As in Figure 2.a some errors are located, part of the program has been checked correct, and part of the program is still not judged

Therefore in the following, in order to evaluate debugging strategies, we will answer several questions:

⋄ how much of the program is still unjudged?

⋄ how much of the erroneous code is contained in the suspect part?

⋄ how much of the erroneous code is *not* contained in the suspect part

⋄ how much of the correct code is contained in the assumed correct code?

⋄ how much of the correct code is *not* contained in the assumed correct code?

Note that the survey of Shahmehri et al. uses user-oriented criteria and gives a complementary analysis of almost the same systems [27].

3   Three automated debugging strategies

Among the reviewed systems we have identified three strategies which approximate correct and erroneous code in different ways according to which knowledge they employ:

- verification with respect to specifications,
- checking with respect to language knowledge, and
- filtering with respect to symptom.

The *verification* strategy compares the actual program with some formal specification of the intended program. The *checking* strategy looks for suspect places which do not comply with some explicit knowledge of the programming language. The *filtering* strategy assumes correct parts of the code which cannot be responsible for the error symptom. Figure 6 at the end of the paper summarizes the techniques corresponding to these strategies. Strategies and techniques are described in the following sections.

Our classification of strategies is different from the classification made by Seviora [26]. Although Seviora also bases his classification on knowledge, he sorts the systems along "static" and "dynamic" strategies according to whether they use program source code *or* program execution traces. We do not consider program code and execution traces as knowledge but as *data* because they can be automatically obtained (at least for sequential programming languages) by mechanisms which are independent of the very program which is analyzed. The source code can be obtained by the language parser, and once a model of execution is designed and a tracers is implemented execution traces can be obtained for any program. Furthermore, programmers analyze both source and trace *jointly* and so do several of the techniques described in the following. Last, Seviora's classification does not consider specification as a taxonomy criterion. Specifications cannot be disregarded, it is realistic to assume that partial specifications can be obtained and they can help a lot. Then, whether or not a formal (partial) specification is used has a major influence on the potential debugging techniques.

4 Verification with respect to specifications

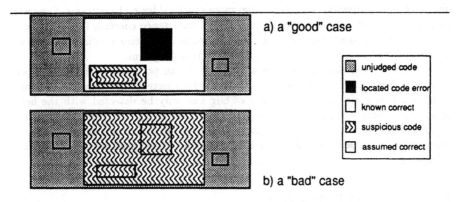

a) a "good" case

unjudged code	
located code error	
known correct	
suspicious code	
assumed correct	

b) a "bad" case

Fig. 3. An illustration of the verification strategy

The verification strategy is the only one which aims at fully automating the debugging process. Assuming that some formal specification [1] of the intended program is given, the verification strategy aims at comparing the specification and the actual program. The parts which are equivalent are assumed correct, the rest is suspect. Figure 3.a illustrates the result of a lucky verification. The unspecified part of the program is unjudged. Some errors are located and some suspect parts are detected which can very quickly lead to the location of the errors.

This sounds simple enough, but many technical problems arise. The first one is to get a complete and accurate specification. This is possible for tutoring systems and in very special cases of real-life programs, for example for well formalized application domains. For most programs, however, specifications are not provided. Furthermore, verification only detects inconsistencies between specification and actual code. As specifications can be incorrect, programmers have to check *both* specification and code in order to find the errors which led to the detected inconsistencies. Lastly, even if the specifications are correct, they may be so different from the actual implementation that the only result of the verification is to tell that the whole part of the program which has been specified is suspect, as illustrated by Figure 3.b.

As a matter of fact, most of the techniques developed so far can be applied only to toy programs. Each technique will be discussed in the following but here is a first overview. The tutoring systems initially used a program model as specification, which was easy enough to provide in such a context. However, the techniques used,

---

[1] In the following "specification" actually means "formal specification"

namely *symbolic execution* and *program transformation*, were impractical even for small programs. Later, still for the tutoring systems, it has been tried to provide algorithm models to represent the intended program in a way less sensitive to syntactical differences. The *algorithm recognition technique* is more satisfactory in the tutoring context but cannot be applied to real programs. A more promising trend is to rely on user-defined assertions which are more declarative and less sensitive to procedural differences. The first systems tried to *symbolically derive* assertions from the code and were quickly limited. Eventually, reducing the ambition of the verification and working on *partial* specification seem more practical for real programs. *Concrete evaluation* of assertions from actual executions, *consistency checking* between assertions and related aspects of the code, and *Algorithmic behavior verification* seem to be the only techniques which can be applied to real programs.

The verification strategy has an advantage: it can potentially detect all types of errors. For example it is the only strategy which may detect conceptual errors such as a wrong algorithm. This kind of bug can only be detected with the help of a specification of the intended program. But considering the costs of producing specifications and the cost of the related techniques this strategy can only be used marginally for real debugging. We are far from the initial goal of fully automatic debugging.

5 Verification techniques

The following techniques require that some sort of formal specification of the program is given. This specification may be partial.

Symbolic execution The intended program is represented by a model program. This technique uses a general theorem prover to formally verify the equivalence of the model program and the actual one. If the actual program and the model program are not equivalent the actual program is suspect.

This technique does not locate errors, it can only tell whether two pieces of programs are equivalent or not. It is anyway much too costly to be applied to real programs. Hence it is only suited to verify small program components. If the theorem prover is used appropriately the components of the program which are assumed correct really are.

Program transformation The intended program is represented by a model program. Both the model program and the student's program are transformed until either they match or diverge too much. The differences between the resulting transformed programs are suspect.

Due to intrinsic technical difficulties (how to choose the transformations, and when to stop transforming), this technique is not suited for real programs. Furthermore, as the error location is done in the transformed programs this technique is only acceptable if a history of transformations has been kept, which gives the location information to the user in terms of his original program (this is not the case in the reviewed systems). On the other hand, if a suspect part has already been located in the original program by another verification technique, program transformation can be a complementary technique to further check this suspect part.

Algorithm recognition The intended program is represented by a set of possible algorithms. The system then tries to match the possible algorithms to the actual source code. The closest algorithm is chosen to be the model program. The differences encountered between the closest algorithm and the actual program are suspect.

Besides the technical difficulty of designing a proper representation language for the algorithms, this technique has an important functional limitation. It is essential for accuracy that the set of possible algorithms is as complete as possible. Indeed, if the algorithm underlying the program source code is too different from the specified algorithms this technique will be totally incompetent. Yet, specifying just one algorithm can be difficult if the problem is not well known or the program is large. Therefore this technique is only suited for tutoring where the programs are small and solve stereotyped problems.

Symbolic derivation of assertions The intended behavior of the program is represented by symbolic assertions which specify the behavior of the program components. Then for each component of the actual program an assertion is symbolically derived using either symbolic evaluation or symbolic assertions attached to programming plans (see section 7). The derived assertion is compared to the specified one. If a difference is found the component is suspect.

Symbolic derivation is not practical for complex programs. Indeed, in the systems reviewed it has been used for small and simple programs written in simplified programming languages.

Concrete evaluation of assertion The intended behavior of the program is represented by assertions which specify the behavior of the program components. These assertions can be either symbolic or concrete. The latter give expected output(s) for a discrete set of given input(s). This technique is similar to the previous one, but the specified behavior is compared to the behavior derived by a *concrete* execution. A program component is executed and if the assertion derived by the execution is different from the specification the component is suspect.

This technique is less general than the previous one as it only partially verifies the program. It is, however, much more practical and can be applied to real programs, as discussed in [3].

Consistency checking with respect to assertions Some properties which should be verified by the code are specified by assertions, for example, types, modes or dependencies. Then this technique checks the consistency between these declarations and the actual code or its behavior. The parts of the program which do not conform are suspect.

The advantage of the techniques is that the specification is partial and can be incomplete. They hence have a better chance to be provided. The results are, however, equally partial and incomplete.

Algorithmic behavior verification This technique, also called "algorithmic debugging", aims at comparing the concrete behavior of a *whole* program against its specification, it assumes that there is a complete specification of the intended behavior. As in general it is impossible to have a complete formal specification of a program's behavior, it is actually assumed that the user can complement the formal specification and act as an "oracle". Algorithmic behavior verification, in its simplest form, runs an actual computation, then at each computation step the assertions derived from this computation are presented to the user who decides whether they hold. If the user answer all the questions an error is found, it is the part of the program whose behavior is incorrect and whose components all exhibit a correct behavior.

Algorithmic behavior verification is a promising technique. The current implementations, however, lack some user support. For example, the user may make a mistake while acting as an oracle. There must therefore be some sort of checking of his answers to validate the diagnosis of the algorithm.

6 Checking with respect to language knowledge

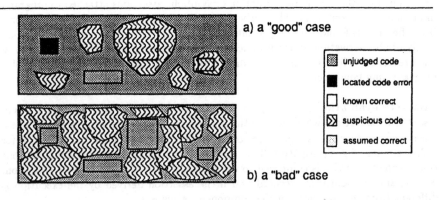

a) a "good" case

▨	unjudged code
■	located code error
□	known correct
▷◁	suspicious code
▧	assumed correct

b) a "bad" case

Fig. 4. An illustration of the language checking strategy

The checking strategy systematically parses programs and searches for language dependent errors. A part of a program is suspect either if it (or its behavior) does not conform to a well-formedness rule or if it (or its behavior) conforms to a stereotyped error rule. This strategy does not assume any code correct. Figure 4 illustrates the result of a lucky checking. Some errors are located, some suspect parts are detected which will quickly lead to the location of errors, few false alarms are given, few errors are undetected. To cover the missing errors one could think that only more checkings are needed. However some errors cannot be detected by a system which only uses language knowledge. Furthermore, there is no criterion to evaluate the completeness of the set of checkings. Therefore, there is no limit on the number of aspects to be checked. It can result in a situation as illustrated by Figure 4.b. None of the errors have been detected while most of the program is suspect with respect to several criteria. In such a case the programmer would have to analyze a lot of warnings for nothing.

This strategy, however, has an advantage: the rules used to detect errors also give some clues of what is wrong. Hence if a part of a program has already been detected to be erroneous, it might be worth running some checkings on this part. If the checkings find problems, they explain them and thus help programmers fix the related errors.

7 Checking techniques

Of the techniques presented in the following sections, the first one works on the program source code only, whereas the two others work on both the program source and behavior.

Plan recognition The knowledge of the language is represented by programming plans. Plans are "stereotypic methods for implementing goals (functional specifications) where the key elements have been abstracted and represented explicitly" [10]. The technique tries to recognize these plans in the program source code. The differences encountered between the closest plans and the actual program are suspect.

This technique is very similar to the algorithm recognition and has the same technical characteristics. Yet, because the knowledge used by the plan recognition depends only on the programming language, it can be used to locate suspect code even when no specification is available. Providing a set of reasonably complete programming plans is still a research topic, and the technical difficulties limit the size of the program which can be analyzed with this technique. In the reviewed systems plan recognition is applied only to small programs or small portions of programs.

Language consistency checking The knowledge of some aspects of the language is represented by consistency rules which model how these aspects should be implemented or should behave. These rules capture well-formedness knowledge which could not be encoded in the compiler. Some of the rules may assume that programming conventions are adhered to. This technique checks the program source (or less frequently the program behavior) against the consistency rules. The parts of the program which do not conform are suspect. The rules used to detect the errors provide some explanation of the mistake.

The larger the programs the more likely it is that they will deviate from stereotyped programming style even if coding standards are adhered to. Hence an important issue for this technique is to choose the sensitivity of the checkings: how much should a part of a program deviate from a rule to be suspected? If the technique is too sensitive it will be oversuspicious, if it is not sensitive enough it will miss many errors.

Stereotyped error recognition The knowledge of some stereotyped errors (related to the programming language) is represented by rules which model how these errors manifest themselves. This technique checks the program source and/or the program behavior against the bug rules. The parts of the program which conform to these rules are suspect. The rules used to detect the errors provide some explanation about the possible error.

Many error classifications have been proposed for example in [4, 11, 30, 29, 33, 18] but none of them provide a framework satisfactory enough to guide the design of an (almost) complete set of stereotyped errors. Errors are collected on a pragmatic basis only. Error recognition may be totally helpless to diagnose some errors and thus can only be used as a complementary technique.

8   Filtering with respect to a symptom

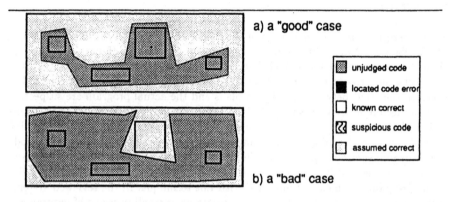

Fig. 5. An illustration of the filtering strategy

Once a symptom of error has been detected the filtering strategy assumes correct the parts of the program which cannot have produced the error symptom (or which are unlikely to produce it). This strategy does not suspect any code but aim at reducing the amount of code which has to be examined by users. Some techniques ensure that the code which is assumed correct does not contain the error which is searched. Figure 5.a illustrates the result of a lucky filtering. The errors which are searched are still in the part of the program which has to be examined, and this part has been significantly reduced. However if a heuristic filtering technique has been carelessly chosen the error which has produced the symptom can be assumed correct and most of the program can still have to be analyzed as illustrated by Figure 5.b.

Filtering focuses on locating the very error which has caused the error symptom, hence it is more accurate for diagnosis purposes than the other two strategies. Furthermore, with this strategy there is at most the whole program to be analyzed (as opposed to the checking strategy where *more* warnings can be generated than source code lines); there is very little information to give (as opposed to the specification of the verification strategy); and the techniques are not too costly. Hence, filtering should be systematically used as a preliminary step when a symptom of error is tracked. Even in the unlucky case where it does not help much, it does not cost much either.

9 Filtering techniques

The following techniques require that an error symptom has been detected.

Slicing This technique is a symptom-driven dependency analysis. So far, it addresses two symptoms: 'wrong valued output variable' and 'wrong control sequence'. It prunes out the parts of the program which the wrong value, respectively the wrong control sequence, does not depend on. What remains from the program is called a *slice*.

The slice can be computed symbolically using the program source only [32] or it can be computed on the particular program behavior which has exhibited the symptom under study [15]. Although the slice does not always contain the errors searched for (see a discussion in [14]), it is always informative.

Program mutation Program mutation can be used for any kind of symptom. It consists of changing small parts of a program and seeing whether the program still behaves incorrectly [6]. This technique is also called "constraint suspension" [5]. If a mutant does not eliminate the symptom then the parts of the program which have been changed to produce this mutant are assumed correct. A mutant may result from a change in the actual source code or a modification of the behavior of a program component.

This technique assumes that the program is "almost correct", hence it cannot be used to debug novice programs. The intrinsic difficulty is to choose the mutation transformation to avoid a combinatory explosion.

Heuristic filtering This technique consists of making a-priori hypotheses about parts of the program which may not have caused the detected symptom. It presumes that some parts of the actual program (behavior or source) are correct to restrict a-priori the search space for further investigations.

This technique is only acceptable if there is a possibility of backtracking over the assumption when further analysis does not succeed in finding the error.

10 Discussion

Practitioners may find the results of our analysis disappointing. The early systems were naively aiming at fully automatic debuggers. Even in the limited context of tutoring they could not meet their objectives. However, even if the developed techniques are often too costly to be used systematically on real life programs it would be a waste of resources to throw out the baby with the bath water. They are practical on small portions of code. They can be useful in some cases. When an error is hard to find, and that a programmer has already spent some time (may be days) on it, he is certainly happy to try a costly technique.

Practitioners may also object that many of the mentioned techniques require formal specification. How to specify a problem is in general not clear and programmers are not always ready to spend as much time specifying the problem as they spend programming it. There are, nevertheless, some problems which can be easily specified, an example is problems dealing with electrical circuits [16]. Furthermore, if an error is hard to find, or if the domain is critical (for example real time code for spatial shuttles) programmers may have enough resources to specify at least part of the problem. Then why a priori refuse to provide programmers with the appropriate techniques ?

11 Conclusion

In this article we have identified three main strategies for automated debugging. The verification strategy assumes that some program specifications are provided. The checking strategy uses explicit knowledge of the programming language. The filtering strategy uses data about the error symptom. We have identified 13 techniques which support these strategies. A summary of which strategies and techniques the reviewed systems use can be found in Figure 6. Assertion evaluation and algorithmic debugging are the most promising verification technique. Some intrinsic limitations of the checking strategy makes it only a complementary, though helpful, debugging support. The slicing technique should be included in any debugger.

The techniques are always insufficient to deal with certain cases. Among the techniques, those which can precisely locate errors are too costly or too verbose to be used on whole programs. On the other hand those which are practical can only roughly locate errors. However the three strategies are not incompatible but complementary. Indeed many systems combine different strategies according to the amount of knowledge they have, each step reinforcing the previous one. *Proust* and *Talus*, which are tutoring systems and hence can assume to be provided with a specification of the intended program, start with a verification of the program source which can check most of the program. Then to reduce the unjudged part *Proust* uses language-driven checking; *Talus* first uses symptom-driven filtering then again verification. *Yoda*, *RD*, *GADT*, and *PELAS* which are diagnosis systems, start with symptom-driven filtering. On the remaining program *RD*, *GADT*, and *PELAS* use verification while *Yoda* uses language-driven checking. In the summary table it is noticeable that not two lines are equal. There is not one unique way to combine the different techniques. It is most likely that there are more interesting combinations than what has been explored so far.

This survey shows that a fully automatic debugger is much beyond the state of the art. All the surveyed systems require the intervention of the programmer at some stage whether they reckon it or not. All the techniques, however are interesting if used in a proper context. An automated debugger can only be an *assistant*. However, the richness of the automated techniques developed so far let us believe that it could be a clever assistant. Hence an automated debugger should be a flexible *environment* providing high-level automated debugging tools which the user will apply as needed. As a first step towards this goal, our debugging system is an extendable debugging environment, where strategies and techniques can be easily programmed and integrated [8].

- Verification
  - **(se)** symbolic execution
  - **(pt)** program transformation
  - **(ar)** algorithm recognition
  - **(sd)** symbolic derivation of assertions
  - **(ce)** concrete evaluation of assertions
  - **(cc)** consistency checking wrt assertions
  - **(ab)** algorithmic behaviour verification
- Checking
  - **(pr)** plan recognition
  - **(lc)** language consistency checking
  - **(sb)** stereotyped bug recognition
- Filtering
  - **(sl)** slicing
  - **(m)** program mutation
  - **(hf)** heuristic filtering

	Verification							Checking			Filtering		
	se	pt	ar	sd	ce	cc	ab	pr	lc	sb	sl	m	hf
Tutoring systems													
Phenarete [34]								x	x				
Laura [1]		x											
IPA [25]	x		x	x									
Talus [23]	x		x		x								
Pudsy [21]				x				x					
Apropos [19]			x			x	x	x	x				
Proust [10]	x	x						x		x			x
Diagnosis systems													
Preset [31]								x	x				
Yoda [18]									x		x		
Focus [22]											x		x
Debussi [17]											x	x	x
PSMD [2]					x						x	x	
RD [24]						x					x		x
PELAS [13]						x					x		
GADT [12]						x					x		
Aspect [9]					x								
ADAss [7]				x	x								
Annalyzer [20]				x									
APD [28]			.			x							

Fig. 6. Summary of reviewed strategies and techniques

Acknowledgement Many thanks to Aileen Cunningham, Nabiel Elshiewy, Anna-Maria Emde, Bogdan Korel, Jacques Noyé, Thierry Le Provost and Pascal Van Hentenryck for fruitful comments on early drafts of the paper.

The author is partly supported by the ESPRIT Project 5291 CHIC

References

1. A. Adam and J.-P. Laurent. Laura, a system to debug student programs. *Artificial Intelligence*, 15(1,2):75–122, November 1980.

2. H. Agrawal and J.R. Horgan. Dynamic program slicing. *SIGPLAN Notices*, 25(6):246–256, June 1990. Proceedings of the ACM SIGPLAN'90 Conference on Programming Language Design and Implementation, White Plains, New York.

3. R.S. Boyer and J.S. Moore. An overview of automated reasoning and related fields: Program verification. *Journal of Automated Reasoning*, 1(1):17–23, 1985.

4. P. Brna, A. Bundy, H. Pain, and L. Lynch. Programming tools for Prolog environments. In J. Hallam and C. Mellish, editors, *Advances in Artificial Intelligence*, pages 251–264. J. Wiley and Sons, 1987. also published as DAI Research paper 302.

5. R. Davis. Diagnostic reasoning based on structure and behaviour. *Artificial Intelligence*, 1-3(24):347–410, December 1984.

6. R.A. DeMillo, W.M. McCracken, R.J. Martin, and J.F. Passafiume. *Software testing and evaluation*. Benjamin/Cumming, Menlo Park, 1987.

7. W. Drabent, S. Nadjm-Tehrani, and J. Maluszynski. The use of assertions in algorithmic debugging. In *Proceedings of the International Conference on Fifth Generation Computer Systems*, pages 573–581. ICOT, December 1988.

8. M. Ducassé and A.-M. Emde. Opium: a debugging environment for Prolog development and debugging research. *ACM Software Engineering Notes*, 16(1):54–59, January 1991. Demonstration presented at the Fourth Symposium on Software Development Environments.

9. D. Jackson. Aspect: An economical bug-detector. In *Proceedings of the 13th ICSE*, pages 13–22. IEEE, IEEE Computer Society Press, May 1991.

10. W.L. Johnson and E. Soloway. Proust: Knowledge-based program understanding. *IEEE Transactions on Software Engineering*, SE-11(3):267–275, March 1985.

11. W.L. Johnson, E. Soloway, B. Cutler, and S. Draper. Bug catalogue: I. Technical Report 286, Yale University, 1983.

12. M. Kamkar, N. Shahmehri, and P. Fritzson. Bug localization by algorithmic debugging and program slicing. In P. Deransart and J. Maluszynski, editors, *PLILP'90*, Lecture Notes in Computer Science, Linkoeping, Sweden, August 1990. Springer-Verlag.

13. B. Korel. PELAS- program error-locating assistant system. *IEEE Transactions on Software Engineering*, 14(9):1253–1260, September 1988.

14. B. Korel. Identifying faulty modifications in software maintenance. In P. Fritzson, editor, *Proceedings of the First Workshop on Automated and Algorithmic Debugging*, University of Linkoeping, Sweden, May 1993. Lecture Notes in Computer Sciences, Springer-Verlag.

15. B. Korel and J. laski. Dynamic program slicing. *Information Processing Letters*, 29(3):155–163, 1988.

16. K. Kuchcinski, W. Drabent, and J. Maluszynski. Automatic diagnosis of VLSI circuits using algorithmic debugging. In P. Fritzson, editor, *Proceedings of the First Workshop on Automated and Algorithmic Debugging*, University of Linkoeping, Sweden, May 1993. Lecture Notes in Computer Sciences, Springer-Verlag.

17. R.I. Kuper. Dependency-directed localization of software bugs. Technical report 1053, MIT, May 1989.
18. C.H. LeDoux. *A knowledge-based system for debugging concurrent software.* PhD thesis, University of California, Los Angeles, 1985.
19. C-K. Looi. Analysing novices' programs in a Prolog intelligent teaching system. In *Proceedings of the European Conference on Artificial Intelligence*, pages 314–319, Munich, August 1988.
20. D. Luckham, S. Sankar, and S. Takahashi. Two-dimensional pinpointing: Debugging with formal specifications. *IEEE Software*, 8(1):74–84, January 1991.
21. F.J. Lukey. Understanding and debugging programs. *Int. J. Man-Machine Studies*, 12(2):189–202, February 1980.
22. J.R. Lyle and M. Weiser. Automatic program bug location by program slicing. In *The Second International Conference on Computers and Applications*, Peking, June 1987.
23. W.R. Murray. *Automatic Program Debugging for Intelligent Tutoring Systems.* Research notes in Artificial Intelligence. Pitman, London, 1988.
24. L.M. Pereira. Rational debugging in Logic Programming. In *3rd Logic Programming Conference*, pages 203–210, London, July 1986.
25. G.R. Ruth. Intelligent program analysis. *Artificial Intelligence*, 7(1):65–85, 1976.
26. R.E. Seviora. Knowledge-based program debugging systems. *IEEE Software*, 4(3):20–32, May 1987.
27. N. Shahmehri, M. Kamkar, and P. Fritzson. Usability criteria for automated debugging systems. In P. Fritzson, editor, *Proceedings of the First Workshop on Automated and Algorithmic Debugging*, University of Linkoeping, Sweden, May 1993. Lecture Notes in Computer Sciences, Springer-Verlag.
28. E.Y. Shapiro. *Algorithmic Program Debugging.* MIT Press, Cambridge, MA, 1983.
29. J.C. Spohrer, E. Pope, M. Lipman, and W. Sack. Bug catalogue: II, III, IV. Research Report YALEU/CSD/RR #386, Yale University, Department of Computer Science, May 1985.
30. J.C. Spohrer, E. Soloway, and E. Pope. A goal/plan analysis of buggy Pascal programs. *Human-computer Interaction*, 1(2):163–207, 1985.
31. H. Takahashi and E. Shibayama. Preset - a debugging environment for Prolog. In *Logic Programming Conference*, pages 90–99, Tokyo, 1985.
32. M. Weiser. Program slicing. *IEEE Transactions on Software Engineering*, SE-10(4):352–357, July 1984.
33. H. Wertz. Stereotyped program debugging : an aid for novice programmers. *International Journal of Man-Machine Studies*, 16, 1982.
34. H. Wertz. *Automatic Correction and Improvement of Programs.* Artificial Intelligence, J. Campbell ed. Ellis Horwood, England, 1987.

Usability Criteria for Automated Debugging Systems

Nahid Shahmehri, Mariam Kamkar, Peter Fritzson

Department of Computer and Information Science
Linköping University, S-581 83 Linköping, Sweden
Email: {nahsh,marka,petfr}@ida.liu.se

Abstract. Much of the current discussion around automated debugging systems is centered around various technical issues. In contrast, this paper focuses on user oriented usability criteria for automated debugging systems, and reviews several systems according to these criteria. We introduce four usability criteria: *generality, cognitive plausibility, degree of automation* and *appreciation of the user's expertise*. A debugging system which is *general* is able to understand a program without restrictive assumptions about the class of algorithms, the implementation, etc. A *cognitively plausible* debugging system supports debugging according to the user's mental model, e.g. by supporting several levels of abstraction and directions of bug localization. A high *degree of automation* means that fewer interactions with the user are required to find a bug. A debugging system that *appreciates the user's expertise* is suitable for both expert and novice programmers, and has the ability to take advantage of the additional knowledge of an expert programmer to speed up and improve the debugging process. Existing automated debugging systems fulfill these user-oriented requirements to a varying degree. However, many improvements are still needed to make automated debugging systems attractive to a broad range of users.

1 Introduction

Debugging is one of the most demanding programming tasks. Thus it is important to develop computer support for this task, which is the aim of the current research on automated (really semi-automated) debugging systems. The currently existing prototype automated debuggers explore many ideas to improve and automate the debugging process. However, in order to make these systems practical and attractive for a broad range of users, we need to focus on the requirements of the user, his/her thought processes and mental modeling of the program behavior during debugging, etc. Only by adapting to the user's needs and way of thinking can we hope to make real progress in this area.

This paper is a step in the direction of more emphasis on user-oriented design and classification of automated debugging systems. We introduce four usability criteria in the next section: *generality, cognitive plausibility, degree of automation* and *appreciation of the user's expertise*. We also review a number of existing automated debugging systems and compare them according to these four criteria. Of the reviewed systems, *Pudsy* [AL80], *Proust* [JS85] *and Laura* [AL80] employ static (batch-oriented) debugging approaches, whereas *APD* [Sha82], *RD* [Per86] [PC89], *GADT* [Sha91] [FGKS91], *Focus* [Lyl84] [LW87], *PELAS* [Kor86] [Kor88] and *DEBUSSI* [Kup89] are based on interaction with the user.

The paper is organized as follows: Section 2 contains a description of the four usability criteria mentioned above, Section 3 presents an overview of some automated debuggers whereas Section 4 contains a discussion to what extend these systems fulfill our usability criteria. Finally, Section 5 presents conclusions.

2   Usability Criteria for Automated Debugging

In this section we briefly introduce four user-oriented usability criteria for automated debugging systems, namely *generality, cognitive plausibility, degree of automation* and *appreciation of the user's expertise.*

Generality

A debugging system which is *general* is able to understand a program without any previous assumptions about the program's algorithm or implementation, i.e. it should not be bound to a specific style of implementation. In addition its bug localization is not restricted to a specific type of bug.

Cognitive Plausibility

A model of debugging is *cognitively plausible* if it follows the user's mental model. One way to contribute to this goal is to provide support for several debugging levels or at least two abstraction levels: *abstract* and *detailed.* Another way is to provide flexibility in the direction of debugging, i.e. *top-down* vs. *bottom-up* and *forward* vs. *backward.*

The goal of *abstract* level debugging (related to abstract tracing [Duc91]) is to localize the bug in a small unit of program code (such as procedure, loop, etc.), i.e. *debugging unit,* while abstracting away certain implementation details. The size and structure of the debugging units are usually influenced by the syntax (or class) of the subject language, e.g. for functional languages a function may be a debugging unit. During abstract debugging the user is only interested in the overall behavior of the debugging units, i.e. their *functionality.* The user is not interested in details of program execution or the dependencies inside debugging units.

Detailed level debugging commences when the user has narrowed down the location of a bug to a certain debugging unit. At this stage the user usually follows the details of execution including the control and data dependencies inside the unit where the buggy instruction is found. An expert programmer usually starts a debugging session at an abstract level and terminates at a more detailed level.

To increase cognitive plausibility during abstract level debugging the debugging process may follow the execution sequence of the program (e.g. top-down, depth-first). This method is more suitable for *imperative* languages than *declarative* lazy functional languages. For detailed level debugging, i.e. debugging of a small piece of code, there is a choice between *forward* and *backward* debugging. The forward approach follows the execution order of the code. The backward method is based on the reverse execution order. The user who uses the backward approach examines the cause of an erroneous result in the previous execution steps.

Degree of Automation

Using the available knowledge about the program, the system should require the user to do as little work as possible. For instance, a static system should be able to use the knowledge it collects to make decisions about the program and the following interactions. Increasing the degree of automation will reduce the number of user interactions.

Appreciation of User Expertise

A debugging system should be suitable for both the novice and the expert programmer. Each of these groups of programmers should be able to (1) effectively transfer their knowledge to the debugger and (2) understand the system's messages. A system's capability to collect various types of knowledge from the user may be referred to as its *knowledge transfer capacity*.

The system should allow the expert programmer to voluntarily give additional knowledge about the debugged program, e.g. give clues to shortcuts to find the location of the bug. On the other hand, the responses required from a novice programmer should be very simple.

3   Overview of some Automated Debugging Systems

The tasks which may be performed by the automated debugging systems are *test generation, bug detection, bug localization, bug explanation* and *bug correction*. Systems that perform test generation and bug detection serve mainly for program testing purposes. Bug detection should be followed by bug localization which is the most common facility provided by today's automatic debuggers. Some debuggers even try to perform bug explanation and bug correction. Systems that provide the user with most of these functions turn out to be very complex and costly. The ideas behind such systems are influenced by program verification. They tend to check the total correctness of a program independently of any specific test case

Automated debugging systems use some kind of knowledge (see 1 and [DE88]) about the actual and intended program to perform the debugging task(s). Common combinations are: (1) *actual vs. intended input/output*, (2) *actual vs. intended implementation*, (3) *actual vs. intended program behavior*. It is notable that the actual implementation of a program may be present in any of these combinations. Other types of knowledge, such as knowledge of *common types of bugs*, may be used as an additional information source. The choice of knowledge is influenced by the aim of the debugging system and which task(s) it is supposed to perform.

The first two combinations: (1) *actual vs. intended input/output*, (2) *actual vs. intended implementation*, are used by program verifiers. Such systems check the correctness/incorrectness of a program against some kind of specification about the intended program. The intended implementation tends to be difficult to define for a large program. The application of the systems that use such knowledge, as in combination (2) above, is restricted to small classroom programs. Thus, they are classified as tutoring systems. Tutoring systems mostly serve for understanding rather than debugging.

The third combination, *actual vs. intended program behavior,* is used by general debuggers. Such systems primarily perform bug localization. Some systems are also able to perform bug explanation and bug correction to a limited extent.

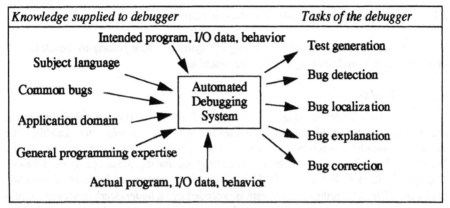

Knowledge supplied to debugger   *Tasks of the debugger*

Fig. 1. : Illustration of different types of the input supplied to and output by automatic debugging systems. None of the existing systems uses all knowledge types. The type of information produced by a debugger depends on the aim of the system.

The debugging strategies are strongly affected by the type of knowledge they employ. Naturally, the task they are aimed at defines what type of knowledge they should use. All of the knowledge types introduced in 1, except for the intended program behavior, may be defined *statically.* Once the knowledge is stored in a database, the automated debugging system is able to access the knowledge base without any need for user interaction.

Having an oracle database which can respond to queries about the intended program behavior could automate the entire debugging process for those systems which employ this type of information. This knowledge may exist in terms of formal specifications. However, due to the complex nature of such specifications and space requirements, it is difficult to define the total intended program behavior in advance.

One solution to this problem is to involve the user in the debugging process. The user is interrogated when some knowledge is needed about the intended behavior of part of a program. The user's response is treated as a partial specification for the program's intended behavior.

Systems which use knowledge of the intended program behavior supplied by the user in dialogue with the system, can be characterized as *interactive.* These systems are *semi-automated* rather than automated. However, the term *automated* is used to refer to such systems, as generally done in the literature [Kup89] [DE88] [Sevi87]. We use the term *static* in contrast to the term *interactive.* Systems that are characterized as static are constructed in such a way that the knowledge required by the system may be provided in advance without any need to interact with the user.

Here we divide debugging approaches into *interactive* and *static* strategies. Program verifiers and tutoring systems follow the static debugging strategy and general debugging systems use the interactive debugging strategy. Systems based on the interactive strategy are the most realistic systems, being more suitable for debugging real applications.

The next two sections describe some of the systems which use the static or interactive strategies respectively. Special attention is paid to systems based on the interactive debugging strategy.

3.1   Systems Based on the Static Debugging Strategy

In this section some automated debugging systems which belong to the classes of program verifiers and tutoring systems are described.

3.1.1   Pudsy

The *Program Understanding and Debugging System (Pudsy)* uses knowledge of the *actual implementation* of the program together with the *intended I/O* [Luk80]. The knowledge about the *programming language* and *programming expertise* is stored in a knowledge base. The actual implementation language for the subject program is Pascal. The specification of the intended I/O is given to the system in the form of *symbolic assertions*. The debugging of a program is preceded by an *understanding process*. *Pudsy* understands a program by analyzing it and generating an assertion about its actual I/O.

The debugging process consists of comparing the derived assertion (actual I/O) and the user-defined assertion (intended I/O). The discrepancies between the two assertions signal the existence of bugs. *Pudsy* then traces back from the differing parts to localize the bug.

Pudsy uses a *bottom-up* (or *code-driven*) approach for constructing the assertion about the intended I/O (or the specification). The knowledge about the programming language is stored in a knowledge base. The knowledge base also contains code patterns, called *schemas* and their corresponding assertions. *Pudsy* divides the program into useful units which are appropriate for analysis, i.e. *chunks* (see 2a). If a suitable schema is found for a chunk, an assertion is already available for it. Otherwise, the assertion is derived by symbolic evaluation of the chunk. The last chunk to be examined is the program itself (see 2b). A record of the assertion derivations is kept for debugging purposes.

The debugging process begins by comparing the derived assertion and the specification of the user defined assertion (see 2c). Some rewriting of the derived assertion may be needed in order to make it compatible to the specification. By backtracing the assertion derivation record and comparing it to the specification, the smallest differing assertion and its corresponding chunk are localized.

Pudsy automatically edits the localized bug and checks if the result is correct. This process goes on until the program is considered to be correct according to the specification.

Observations

The computational cost of the program-understanding part of *Pudsy* is very high. In addition *Pudsy* faces major difficulties when the derived assertion and the specification are to be compared. It is not easy to compare the two unless they are very similar. This leads to the fact that a bug may not be localized. In such cases *Pudsy* is only able to test a program. However, if *Pudsy* is able to compare the specification and the derived assertion, a bug is guaranteed to be localized. *Pudsy* is mainly suitable for small Pascal programs and is aimed at classroom application, although it is not classified as a tutoring system.

(a)

```
type arrayn=array[1..n] of integer;
procedure selectsort(var a:arrayn);
var i,j,min,temp: integer;
begin
    for i:=1 to n-1 do begin
        min:=i;
        for j:=i+1 to n do
            if a[j]>a[min] then min:=j;
        temp:=a[min];
        a[min]:=a[i];
        a[i]:=temp
    end;
end;
```

Chunk 1 { Chunk 2 { ... }

(b) **Assertion derived for Chunk2:** (Input:-a, i, Output:-min)
a[min]=MAX(DV2=i, n) a[DV2];
Assertion derived for Chunk1: (Input:-a, Output:-a)
$FORALL$DV2(1,n-1)(a[DV2]=MAX(DV1=DV2, n) a[DV1]);

(c) **User specification for the whole program:**
$FORALL$DV2(1,n-1)($FORALL$DV1(DV2,n)(a[DV2]<= a[DV1]));

Fig. 2. : Pudsy finds the inconsistencies between the user assertion and the assertion derived from the student program. (a) A small buggy Pascal program divided into two chunks. (b) The assertions derived for the chunks. The assertion for chunk2 denotes that output min is such that a[min] is the maximum of array elements with indices in 1..n. The second assertion denotes that a[DV2] is always the maximum of array elements with indices between DV2.. n, i.e. the array is sorted in descending order. (c) The specification defined by the user. It denotes that the array should be sorted in ascending order. In other words: for all DV2≤DV1, a[DV2] ≤ a[DV1]. (This figure is from [Sevi87])

3.1.2 Laura

Laura is a tutoring system for debugging student programs written in FORTRAN [AL80]. Given the *actual* and *intended implementations, Laura* localizes the bugs and performs *bug explanations*. Knowledge of the *programming* and *application domain* is hard-coded in the system. The intended implementation is a program written by the teacher, i.e. supposedly a correct program. The actual program is written by individual students. *Laura* translates both programs into internal graph representations. The graphs represent the computational process implied by the programs. Then a number of program transformations are applied to the graphs in order to increase their similarity. Mismatch between the graphs is a sign of bug existence.

Laura aims at performing bug localization and bug explanation. In order to do so, the *model program*, i.e. the teacher's program and the *student program* go through a standardization process. The first step of standardization consists of transforming both programs into intermediate flow graphs. The second step consists of a number of systematic graph transformations, such as variable separation and composition.

At this stage the primary goal of *Laura* is to check the correctness of the student program. Now, it tries to match the two graphs by binding corresponding variables, nodes and arcs between them. During this process several additional transformations may be necessary. Node splitting, node/subgraph permutation and node elimination are examples of these transformations.

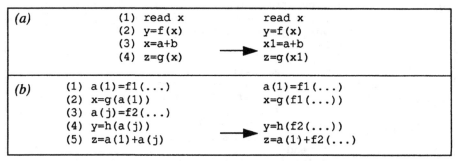

Fig. 3. : (a) Variable separation. Variable x in statement (2) is renamed as $x1$, and subsequently the reference to the value of variable x in statement(4) is replaced by a reference to variable $x1$. (b) Composition transformation. $a(1)$ in statement (2) is substituted by its corresponding expression value, i.e. $f1(...)$. $a(j)$ in statements (4) and (5) are substituted by $f2(...)$. Statement (3) is eliminated.

If the goal of matching the two graphs entirely does not succeed, *Laura* tries to reach another goal, namely bug detection. This process is similar to the previous one, except that minor mismatches are accepted as erroneous subgraphs. Thus, *Laura* may go on with the bug detection process in other parts of the graphs. After this process, if there are any major mismatches between the two graphs, *Laura* prints out the corresponding subgraphs as suspicious parts which may contain bugs.

Observations

Laura, like *Pudsy*, suffers from the high computational cost of detailed analysis during the repeated program transformations. The largest program that has been debugged by *Laura* is a thirty line program.

The program transformations in *Laura* are in the opposite direction of program optimization, thus increasing the size of the programs. These transformations may also cause a great deal of change to the structure of a program. Since the bug explanation in *Laura* is presented in terms of the transformed programs, they may be hard to understand. A severe limitation of *Laura* is that the program to be debugged must implement the same algorithm as the model program. *Laura* itself is implemented in 7000 lines of Fortran.

3.1.3 Proust

The *Program Understander for Students (Proust)* is a knowledge-based tutoring system [JS85]. The system is implemented in T which is a dialect of LISP. It uses knowledge about the *intended* and *actual implementation* of the program. Knowledge about the *programming language, programming expertise* and *common bug types* is available in a knowledge base. *Proust* performs *bug localization, explanation* and *correction*.

The intended implementation is given to the system by the teacher in terms of a problem description. The actual implementation is a student program written in Pascal. The aim of the system is to match the problem description with the student program. The description and the knowledge available to *Proust* potentially define a set of correct programs. Thus, the system is not practically usable outside very limited domains. *Proust* uses the knowledge base to find the closest implementation to the student's program. Differences are explained to the student in text form, using the knowledge about bugs.

Problem descriptions in *Proust* consist of programming *goals*, i.e. principal requirements that must be satisfied, and sets of *data objects*, i.e. the data that the program must manipulate.

The following problem statement is given to *Proust* in terms of goals and objects as in 4:

Write a program that reads in a sequence of positive numbers, stopping when 99999 is read. Compute the average of these numbers. Do not include the 99999 in the average. Be sure to reject any input that is not positive.

```
((Define-Program Average)
 (Define-Object ?New)
 (Define-Object ?Sentinel (Value 99999))
 (Define-Goal (Sentinel-Controlled-Input
                   ?New ?Sentinel))
 (Define-Goal (Input-Validation ?New (> ?New 0)))
 (Define-Goal (Output (Average ?New))))
```

Fig. 4. : The problem description in Proust is in terms of goals and data objects. Names affixed with "?" are pattern variables.

Each goal has a corresponding goal-definition in the knowledge base. Each goal-definition contains a list of various *plans*. Each plan is a possible implementation of the goal and has a corresponding plan-definition in the knowledge base. Assume that the plan Sentinel-Process-Read-While is in the list of plans for the goal Sentinel-Controlled-Input in 4. The plan-description of this plan is illustrated in 5.

```
(Plan-Definition Sentinel-Process-Read-While
    Constants    (?Stop)
    Variables    (?Input)
    Template     ((SUBGOAL (Input ?Input))
                 (WHILE (<> ?Input ?Stop)
                        (BEGIN
                         ?*
                         (SUBGOAL (Input ?Input))))))
```

Fig. 5. : Plan-definition of Sentinel-Process-Read-While for implementing the goal Sentinel-Controlled-Input of 4.

Given the problem description, *Proust* tries to understand the student program. It has a top-down (problem-driven) approach. *Proust* selects one goal from the problem description. It then retrieves a list of plans from its knowledge base and tries to match the individual plans with the components of the student program. Since the plans in turn may contain subgoals, this process is recursive.

Once the first goal has been matched, *Proust* selects another goal from the problem description and proceeds to match its plans against the student program. This process continues until all goals are satisfied. When a plan cannot be matched exactly against a piece of student program, a bug has been localized. In many cases, knowledge of common types of bugs, i.e. *bug rules*, helps explain the bug. In such cases *Proust* even suggests bug corrections.

Observations

The computational cost of detailed analysis is high due to the matching process. The system cannot be used for large programs, since it must search through deep and often bushy goal-plan trees. In order for *Proust* to recognize a wider range of programs, there must exist a large variety of plans which in turn will increase the computational cost even more. If a particular plan is not in the knowledge base, *Proust* is not able to analyze the corresponding program code.

In those cases where *Proust* succeeds in localizing bugs, it provides the student with a better understanding of the program design. This is due to the problem-driven approach of *Proust*. However, *Proust* can account only for those legal plan-program differences it knows about. A correct implementation that cannot be transformed to match a plan is, by default, buggy. Thus, the system raises false alarms in similar cases.

3.2 Systems based on Interactive Debugging Strategies

Debugging systems that interact with the user to collect knowledge about the intended program behavior follow an interactive debugging strategy. The actual program may exist in the form of its *actual implementation* and/or *behavior*.

The common characteristics for these systems can be described as follows. They aim at restricting the amount of information that a user has to examine to localize the bug. In order to do so, they interrogate the user to obtain information about the intended behavior of program components. Thus, as the system collects more knowledge of the intended behavior, the suspect program component is reduced in size. This process goes on until a bug is localized. Ducassé and her colleagues refer to this strategy as *filtering* [DE88]. Systems of this class use several different techniques for debugging.

3.2.1 Algorithmic Program Debugging

We recall the description of the *Algorithmic program debugger (APD)* from [Sha82]. *APD* uses the knowledge of the *actual I/O* and *actual behavior*. The user, though a *passive* participant in the debugging process, supplies the system with the *intended behavior*. The passive participant means that the debugging system is the one which initiates an interaction and the user can not influence the debugging process except for the responses she/he gives in response to system initiative. The system performs *bug localization* and *bug correction* according to the available knowledge.

The actual implementation is a *side-effect-free* and *loopfree* Prolog program. The user calls the debugger together with the suspect procedure call and the actual I/O. *APD* re-executes the suspect procedure call and keeps a trace of its *actual behavior* in an *execution tree*. Bug localization in *APD* is performed by inspecting the traced execution tree. The system interacts with the user about the intended program behavior. By comparing the intended and actual behavior the system is able to localize the bug at the procedure level. Once an erroneous procedure is identified, *APD* performs a number of user queries to be able to suggest a correction to the procedure.

The system has three diagnosis algorithms for three types of bugs: *wrong solution, missing solution* and *nontermination. Wrong solution* occurs when the output value of a procedure is incorrect. *Missing solution* refers to the case when there are missing values in the output of a procedure. *Nontermination* happens when a program execution enters an infinite loop.

(a)
```
isort([X|Xs],Ys) ← isort(Xs,Zs),insert(X,Zs,Ys).
isort([],[]).
insert(X,[Y|Ys],[Y|Zs])← Y > X, insert(X,Ys,Zs).
insert(X,[Y|Ys],[X,Y|Ys]) ← X ≤ Y.
insert(X,[],[X]).
```

(b)

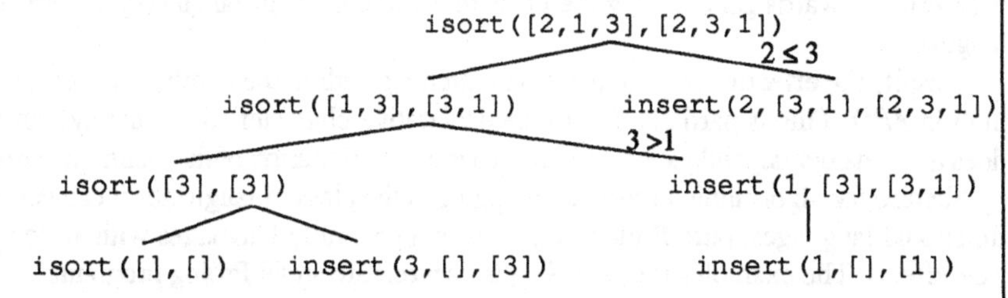

```
                              isort([2,1,3],[2,3,1])
                          ⁀‾‾‾‾‾‾‾‾‾‾‾‾‾‾‾‾‾⌐ 2≤3
           isort([1,3],[3,1])          insert(2,[3,1],[2,3,1])
        ⁀‾‾‾‾‾‾‾‾‾‾‾‾‾‾‾‾⌐ 3>1
  isort([3],[3])                            insert(1,[3],[3,1])
 ⁀‾‾‾‾‾⌃‾‾‾‾‾⌐                                      |
isort([],[])  insert(3,[],[3])             insert(1,[],[1])
```

(c)
```
Query: isort([],[])? yes
Query: insert(3,[],[3])? yes
Query: isort([3],[3])? yes
Query: insert(1,[],[1])? yes
Query: insert(1,[3],[3,1])? no
insert(1,[3],[3,1]) ← 3>1, insert(1,[],[1])
```

Fig. 6. : (a) An example of a buggy logic program for insertion sort. The condition $y>x$ in the definition of procedure insert should be $x>y$. (b) The trace execution tree for the call `isort([2,1,3],X)` which has returned $X= [2,3,1]$. (c) A dialogue between the system and the user during the bug localization process. The bottom-up single-stepping search method is applied in this example.

Shapiro presents two possible search methods, *bottom-up single-stepping* and *divide-and-query*. The example of 6a illustrates an erroneous insertion sort algorithm[1] defined in Prolog. The call `isort([2,1,3])` has returned the wrong result `[2,3,1]`. 6b illustrates the corresponding trace execution tree for this call statement. 6c shows the sequence of interactions between the system and the user. The bottom-up single-stepping method is used in this example. However, the divide-and-query method improves the search process and reduces the number of user queries.

Debugging the missing solution bug proceeds in a similar way. In this case, since the buggy procedure is non-deterministic, the debugger asks the user to supply all known solutions to intermediate results.

---

1. The same insertion sort algorithm was presented in Pascal to describe the basic principles of algorithmic debugging, see Figure 1-1.

Nontermination is debugged in several ways. First, the program can be run with bounds on space or time on the assumption that exceeding these bounds implies that the program does not terminate. Also, *well-founded orderings* can be defined on a procedure. An example of this ordering is that consecutive calls to a *divide-and-conquer* procedure have decreasing parameter size.

Observations

APD is implemented in Prolog. The system is based on a *declarative debugging* method which helps the user to concentrate on the *abstract behavior* of execution of individual procedures. During the debugging, the questions the system asks the user are at an abstract level regarding the input/output behavior of program units. The user should hopefully be able to answer the questions without any need to investigate the program code. This type of debugging may not suit all classes of languages. *GADT*, for example, is an effort towards generalizing the ideas to a wider class of languages, i.e. imperative languages.

Despite the effective bug localization search algorithm, the number of user queries is high in *APD*. This is partially due to the declarative characteristic of the system which does not consider dependencies within a program. A limitation of the technique presented by Shapiro for algorithmic program debugging is the class of languages it can debug, i.e. functional languages, pure Prolog programs and generally languages without loops and side-effects. The examples given in Shapiro's work are small Prolog programs.

An improvement to Shapiro's work is reported by Drabent and his colleagues [Drabetal88]. They have extended *APD*'s query language in order to reduce the number of user queries. The user may answer a query by giving a partial specification about the intended behavior, i.e. an *assertion*. Their system is implemented in Prolog and the assertions are Prolog programs.

3.2.2   Rational Debugging

The *Rational Debugger for Logic Programs (RD)* was introduced by Pereira [Per86] [PC89]. *RD* uses the knowledge of the *actual I/O* and *actual behavior*. The user, through a *passive* participant in the debugging process, supplies the system with the *intended behavior*. The system performs *bug localization* and *bug explanation* according to the available knowledge.

RD is a debugger which was basically designed for logic programs. Pereira has generalized the work to debug Prolog programs, thus handling side-effects [PC89]. The system uses the knowledge about the actual implementation in terms of the program code. The bug localization in *RD* is performed by inspecting existing dependencies in the execution tree through backtracking. The system's knowledge during this process consists of the dependencies on the execution trace and the knowledge collected by performing user queries.

RD is an algorithmic debugger which is a descendant of *APD* for debugging Prolog programs. The system is based on the *operational semantics* of Prolog. The knowledge primarily needed by *RD* consists of the actual program's source code and the knowledge about *dependencies* in the program. The system creates this knowledge during program execution using knowledge about Prolog's operational semantics.

RD deals with the cases *missing solution* and *wrong solution*. The strategy for *nontermination* does not provide great improvements compared to Shapiro's method described earlier. The intended input and output parameter data for a procedure call is supplied by the user. In the case of *wrong solution*, the user has to point out the erroneous component of the goal as well. The specific knowledge required for the *missing solution* case is the position of the missing answer. The system collects this information by interacting with the user.

The system analyzes the execution tree backwards from the bug symptom. The difference between RD and *APD* is their analysis method. *RD* applies the knowledge of the program's term dependencies to localize the bug, a technique which eliminates some irrelevant components of the program from being examined.

The system collects missing knowledge of the intended behavior incrementally. The systems asks questions about the correctness of a goal and expects a *"yes"* or *"no"* answer from the user. The system may require that the user points out the erroneous term causing a wrong goal. *RD* may also ask the user to check whether a goal is *admissible* or *solvable*. Intuitively an admissible goal is one which is textually correct with the right argument types and a solvable goal is one which should have a solution according to the intended program semantics. Some other types of query may demand the user to point out an erroneous term.

More recently *RD* has been extended to deal with side-effects in Prolog programs. The extended method is based on collecting a suspect set according to the description above. The details of handling the suspect set during the bug localization is not described thoroughly [PC89]. The main characteristic of the method is the backward analysis of the term dependencies. Prolog programs may have a self modifying effect. This effect is obtained using *assert* or *retract*. The side-effects inside a procedure are also added to the suspect set of a procedure. The process goes on until a bug is localized.

Observations

RD follows the ideas of *APD*, i.e. algorithmic debugging. The bug localization process in *RD* is more effective than *APD*, due to its dependency-based analysis approach.

The extended system deals with side-effects caused by Prolog programs. The key question here is whether this system performs declarative debugging. More generally, is declarative debugging suitable for languages which allow self-modifying programs? The position taken in the GADT approach is that self-modifiable code goes against the principles of declarative debugging, since the truth of a partial specification $P(X)=Y$ for $X=X'$ and $Y=Y'$ may differ at various execution positions.

3.2.3   GADT - Generalized Algorithmic Debugging Technique

GADT, the *Generalized Algorithmic Debugging Technique* [Sha91] [FGKS91], is a generalization of basic algorithmic debugging as introduced by Shapiro in his *APD* system. GADT is the first algorithmic debugging method based on the principle of declarative debugging which can handle debugging of programs written in an *imperative language* including *loops* and *side-effects*.

The generalized algorithmic debugging method uses *program transformation* and *program flow analysis* techniques to transform the subject program to a largely side-effect-free internal form which is used for bug localization. Thus, this algorithm defines two views of a program: (1) *the user view* which is the original program with side-effects and (2) *the transformed view* which is the transformed side-effect-free version of the original program. Transparent program debugging is supported by maintaining a mapping between these two views. The bug localization algorithm works on the transformed version, whereas user interactions are defined in terms of the user view.

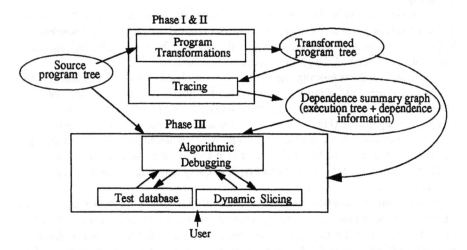

Fig. 7. The functional structure of the generalized algorithmic debugging system when integrated with interprocedural dynamic slicing and test database lookup. Arrows denote information transfer.

Program slicing, a data flow analysis technique, can be used to focus the search process during bug localization with algorithmic debugging. Given a variable at a certain point in the program, program slicing will compute the set of all statements whose execution might have contributed to the variable's current value. Thus the slicing technique will extract a subset (or slice) of the program. The slicing is applied each time the user of the algorithmic debugger is questioned by the debugger provided the user can point out an erroneous data value. It eliminates the parts of the execution tree which are independent of the erroneous value, and thus irrelevant for finding the bug.

Other extensions to GADT are *test database lookup* [FGKS91], to avoid questions to the user regarding already tested units, and a two-level architecture for debugging that includes both *global level* and *local level* debugging. Global level bug localization refers to the process of examining the overall behavior of larger pieces of program code whereas local bug localization is suitable for more restricted pieces of program code.

Observations

The GADT system has so far been applied to rather small Pascal programs (4 pages) although work is in progress to gain experience on using it for more realistic examples. Currently the main limitation of the system is that it cannot deal with pointer-related side effects. GADT is implemented in 8000 lines of Pascal and C, and is integrated with the incremental Pascal compiler and programming environment of the DICE [Frit83] system.

3.2.4 Focus

Focus is a debugging system for automatic bug localization [Lyl84] [LW87]. The knowledge *Focus* requires is the *actual I/O* and *implementation*. Although the user has to supply the system with very little knowledge of the *(detailed) intended behavior*, the user is still an active partner during debugging.

A typical example of the information the user gives to the system is: The value of variable *x* at program position *p* is incorrect. *Focus* employs this knowledge to analyze the actual implementation. Those parts of the program which *may* contain the bug are presented to the user. This means that the program statements that had absolutely nothing to do with the bug are removed from the user's sight.

Focus is based on the *slicing/dicing* techniques which follow *backward* execution dependencies in a program [Lyl84] [LW87]. The dependencies in a program consist of *control* and *data dependencies*. Data dependencies are between *variable instances*, i.e. between *variables at certain program positions*.

The *Static program slicing* technique, introduced by Weiser [Wei82] [Wei84], is based on a static analysis of possible control and data dependencies among program variables. The *static slice* of a program is computed from a program position with respect to a variable (possibly with an erroneous value). The slice will, possibly, be a smaller program which contains all the statements that somehow may have affected the value of the variable at that position. This slice denotes all possible computations of the value of this variable at the given program position.

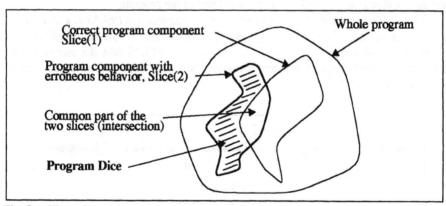

Fig. 8. : Illustration of the slicing/dicing technique. Two slices are taken on a correct and on an erroneous value of two variables respectively. Dicing confines the location of a bug to a small area of code, i.e. Slice(2)-Intersection(Slice(1), Slice(2)).

The main idea behind *program dicing* is to isolate those parts of a program which behave correctly and those which behave erroneously into two slices. The code obtained by taking the intersection of the two slices has the property that it is correct code, although it also belongs to a code area with erroneous behavior. Removing this intersected part from the erroneous code leaves a smaller piece of code which is buggy, i.e. a *dice*. This is illustrated in 8 in terms of sets and set operations.

The correctness of the dicing technique relies on the following three restrictive assumptions: (1) all incorrectly computed variables have been identified, (2) a variable whose computation depends on an incorrectly computed variable will also have incorrect values, and (3) there is exactly one bug in the program.

Observations

The slicing technique has been used in many applications, see e.g. [Kam93]. However, using the static slicing technique as the only debugging aid is not so useful, since the static slice of a variable in practice may turn out to be quite large. Later work on dynamic slicing techniques has attempted to overcome this weakness [Kor86] [Kor88] [AH90] [KSF92] [Kam93]. The dicing technique increases the power of the static slicing technique, but due to the assumptions mentioned above it is quite restrictive.

The slicing/dicing process is language-independent. *Focus* can be fully automatized by using a test-generating tool and an oracle. The oracle contains the knowledge about the intended program behavior, i.e. the intended value of variables at different program positions. The test results can be checked against the *oracle* at the cost of a huge oracle. The FOCUS system is implemented in C for Fortran and Ada programs.

3.2.5 PELAS

The bug localization in the *Program Error-Locating Assistant System (PELAS)* is carried out by using knowledge of the *actual implementation* and the *(detailed) actual program behavior* [Kor86] [Kor88]. The user plays a *passive* role in the bug localization process by answering the system queries about the program's *intended behavior*. The system localizes the cause of a bug to a small part of the program.

The knowledge of the actual implementation is represented in *PELAS* as a *dependency network* (a variant of dependency graph). The knowledge of the actual behavior is obtained by collecting the program's *execution trace*. *PELAS* asks the user questions about the detailed intended program behavior. The user's responses are in the form of "*yes*" or "*no*" answers.

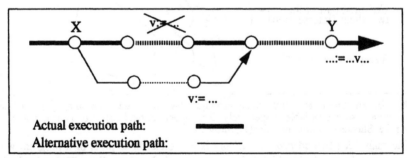

Fig. 9. :Illustration of a potential dependency as defined by PELAS. In this example, instruction X has a potential dependency on instruction Y, since v is used in Y, there is no definition of v in the actual execution path, but there is a definition of v in an alternative execution path which was not executed during the current execution.

PELAS, like *Focus*, performs bug localization by studying the dependencies in the actual implementation. In most cases the system is able to localize the bug to a statement. In some other cases, such as a missing statement, a small section of program code is localized as the source of the bug.

The system identifies three types of dependencies between program instructions, *data dependency, control dependency,* and *potential dependency:* the potential dependency is defined between two instructions x and y, such that x is a test instruction, x and y are both in the actual execution path, there exists a variable *v* which is referenced in y but not defined in the execution path between *x* and *y*, and there is a definition of *v* in an alternative execution path from *x* to *y*. This type of dependency is illustrated in 9.

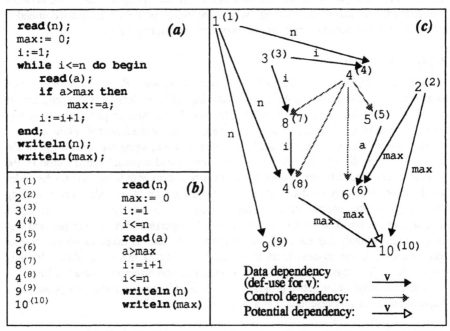

Fig. 10. : (a) An example program. (b) The execution trace of the program on a given input. Each execution of an instruction is uniquely identified by the instruction number x and execution position p in the form $x^{(p)}$. (c) The dependency network based on the execution tree and the static dependency information of the program.

PELAS constructs a dependency network which represents the described dependencies between the executed program instructions. The knowledge used in the construction consists of the *execution trace* and some *static dependency* information. 10 contains an example program, an execution trace of the same program on some input and finally a dependency network constructed for this execution.

PELAS localizes bugs by backtracing through the dependency network, starting at the observed incorrect program output. Each backtracing step acts to localize the bug to previous point backward in the network. Backtracing iterates until a single faulty program instruction has been found. A hypotheses set is employed to keep track of the suspect instructions. This set is updated during the backward analysis of the dependency network.

In the case of *missing instructions*, the system takes a *dynamic slice* of the program with respect to the current execution. The computation of the dynamic slice begins at the observed incorrect program output.

Observations

The dependency network guides the debugger to focus on the relevant program components which have been executed. *PELAS* is implemented in Pascal and can debug programs in a subset of Pascal. There are two major restrictions in the system. The first is the restricted subject language - it is quite small and does not include procedure calls. This restriction makes the system unsuitable for debugging larger programs. The second restriction is the large number of user queries for real sized program.: Since the network construction and analysis is based on the detailed execution trace (i.e. detailed intended behavior), the number of queries will be very high for larger programs.

3.2.6 DEBUSSI

DEBUSSI, Dependency-Directed Localization of Software Bugs, is a system which localizes program bugs by reasoning about the logical dependencies in the program, its *actual* and *intended behavior* [Kup89]. The user has a *passive* participation in *bug localization* in supplying the system with knowledge about the *intended behavior*.

The system constructs a so called *dependency graph*, using the knowledge of the source program, the execution trace of the program and a partial specification of the program's intended behavior. This graph is a proof system with basic facts on the nodes which do not have any predecessors and deduced facts on other nodes. The reasoning component of the system called *Cake* detects a program bug by discovering a contradiction in the dependency graph. *DEBUSSI* cooperates with *Cake* to perform bug localization by analyzing the dependency graph. The user is asked to provide partial specifications, if the system finds it necessary. *DEBUSSI* has some ability for bug explanation. The subject language for the system is a side-effect-free subset of Lisp.

The knowledge of the actual program is in terms of its control and data dependencies. Kuper refers to this representation as a *plan diagram* (see 11c).

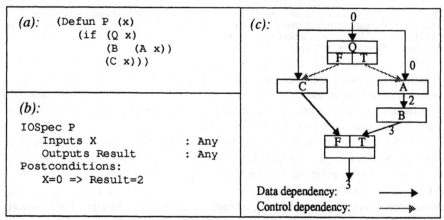

Fig. 11. : (a) Definition of a function *P* in Lisp. (b) The partial specification of the intended program behavior. (c) The plan diagram annotated with the input/output behavior of an execution of function *P*.

The knowledge required for bug localization in *DEBUSSI* is implemented as a dependency graph. The data dependency information, the actual behavior and the partial specifications are represented as logical predicates. For instance, the data dependence between the input value of function *B* and the output value of function *A* (see 11a) is denoted by the predicate: *Input(B)=Output(A)*. Deduction of these predicates is carried out by *Cake*. 12 illustrates part of the dependency graph for the example plan diagram of 11c.

The existence of a bug in the program is characterized by a contradiction between the program's specification and its actual behavior. This contradiction is reported to *DEBUSSI*.

DEBUSSI forms an initial set of suspects through *dependency analysis*, starting at the contradicting predicates.This set is updated during the dependency analysis, until a bug is localized. The user may be asked to give additional information to the system. Some of the suspects will be conditional statements, or *splits*, in the control flow of the program. In *split analysis DEBUSSI* retracts the definition of a control flow split and then asks the reasoning system to rederive the contradiction. If the contradiction can be demonstrated without the definition of a particular control flow split, *DEBUSSI* can conclude that the split is not a cause of the bug.

DEBUSSI repeatedly performs dependency analysis, split analysis and querying until the suspect set contains either one suspect or none. If one suspect remains, and it corresponds to a call to a language primitive such as *CAR* in LISP, then the system concludes that the bug is due to an incorrect use of that primitive. If the one suspect represents a call to a user-defined function, then *DEBUSSI* attempts to localize the bug to some point within that function call. If after this attempt *DEBUSSI* is unable to localize the bug and ends with no suspects, then it concludes that the bug is at some undetermined place within the enclosing function call. The empty suspect set may also be due to the existence of multiple bugs, which *DEBUSSI* is unable to handle.

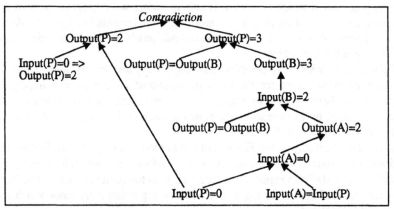

Fig. 12. : Part of an example dependency graph in DEBUSSI. The interior nodes are the derived predicates. The arrows are drawn from premises to conclusions.

Observations

DEBUSSI is a debugging assistant tool which can perform bug localization for *side-effect-free* programs. Run-time information and static dependencies are employed for the purpose of dependency-directed analysis.

The analysis component of *DEBUSSI* focuses on function calls rather than individual statements. The abstraction level achieved with this method is advantageous both for interactions with the user and for saving the trace information. However, due to the nature of Lisp, where all primitive operations are expressed as function applications, the level of abstraction is not particularly high. Thus the saved trace information may still be voluminous. The use of split analysis may reduce the number of user queries.

The system relies on the *single fault* assumption and is suitable even for debugging partially implemented programs. *DEBUSSI* localizes bugs to function *calls* rather than to function *definitions*.

4 Discussion and Comparison of some Automated Debugging Systems

Several automated debugging systems have been described in this paper. *Pudsy, Proust and Laura* employ static approaches, whereas, *APD, RD, GADT, Focus, PELAS* and *DEBUSSI* are based on interactive approaches.

Four user-oriented criteria for comparing automated debugging systems were introduced in the beginning of this paper. These are *generality, cognitive plausibility, degree of automation* and *appreciation of user expertise*. The last three criteria are mostly relevant to interactive systems. Below we discuss the debugging systems mentioned in the overview in terms of these criteria.

4.1 Generality

A debugging system which is *general* is able to understand a program without any previous assumptions about the program's algorithm or implementation, i.e. it should not be bound to a specific style of implementation. Additionally its bug localization is not restricted to a specific type of bug.

APD primarily handles two types of errors: *insufficiency* and *incorrectness*. *DEBUSSI* handles both types of errors for the class of functional languages. For imperative languages most of these errors belong to the class of incorrectness. GADT and PELAS handle errors caused by incorrectness. In principle there is, however, no obstacle for handling errors caused by insufficiency.

Focus and *DEBUSSI* rely on the single fault assumption. *Focus* goes even further with assumptions: a previous reliable test and exposure of all variables which have erroneous values. *APD* and *GADT* can support bug localization in the presence of multiple bugs. The searching method applied in the bug localization algorithm determines which bug among several is localized.

Proust and *Laura* have the limitation that they require a model of the intended implementation. Thus they are not general enough to debug arbitrary programs. *Pudsy* is general, though it is more suitable for debugging small programs. For larger programs *Pudsy* performs mostly bug detection.

The debugging process in GADT and similar systems (*APD, RD, Focus, PELAS* and *DEBUSSI*) is not based on any ad hoc assumptions about the subject program. Thus, they fulfill the generality requirement.

The language covered by *DEBUSSI* restricts the program to be side-effect-free. *APD* is also restricted to the class of pure functional languages and logic programs. *RD* handles Prolog programs with side-effects. However, the system is not able to declaratively debug programs in the presence of side-effects. This is because side-effects in Prolog programs may modify the program code during execution. *PELAS* also handles side-effects in a program, though it does not consider programs with procedures and procedure calls. GADT is suitable for imperative languages with side-effects. However, there is no treatment of the side-effects caused by pointer variables. Although there exist programming languages without pointers, e.g. Fortran, this is still a major shortcoming in this system.

4.2 Cognitive Plausibility

As mentioned before, *cognitive plausibility* is a property of a debugging systems which adapts to the user's mental model of the debugging process. This can be provided to a certain extent if the system can support several levels of abstraction, (e.g. module level, procedure level, statement level), and also allow flexibility in the search direction during bug localization, e. g. forward, backward, top-down, bottom-up, etc.

Abstract level debugging

The bug localization in *APD, RD, GADT* and *DEBUSSI* is performed at an *abstract* level, since all systems consider procedures as units for debugging. The final suspect unit in *APD* and *RD* is a (Prolog) procedure. *DEBUSSI* terminates the debugging by pointing out either an erroneous application of a primitive function call or a non-primitive function body. The unit for bug location in GADT is either a procedure or a loop. The bug is localized to an instance of a debugging unit.

Detailed level debugging

APD and *RD* lack the *detailed* level debugging that is expected to take place after the abstract level. The need for such a step has not been discussed in reference to these systems. *DEBUSSI* provides bug localization at the abstract level of functions. However, since the subject language of this system is side-effect-free LISP programs and the elements of a program are function applications, the debugging will be at a *detailed* level. GADT is extensible to contain *detailed* level debugging which is described in chapter 4 of [Sha91] and in [FAS92].

PELAS is based on *detailed* level debugging, which increases the number of queries during bug localization. The system does not cover debugging of programs in the presence of procedures and procedure calls. For larger programs, it is difficult for the user to respond to the debugger's queries at the detailed level.

Search method and direction

GADT has a top-down depth-first method for traversing the execution trace for examining the program's correctness at the abstract level. This approach helps the user to connect the execution semantics of the program with the (declarative) specification of the program components. *APD* has a divide-and-query method for the doing the same job. This search method is more effective than the one applied in GADT, though it is not as close to the user's cognitive process. This matter may not be as important for a logic program as for a program written in an imperative language. The reason is that logic programs are declarative descriptions of problems. *RD* follows the *backward* direction of the term dependencies on the program's execution tree. In the presence of side-effects, the knowledge of the context in which the side-effect occurs helps the user a great deal in understanding the program's actual behavior. It is not clear what type of search method is applied in *RD* for following the dependencies and how much connection is made between the side-effects and the context which causes them. *DEBUSSI* constructs a dependency graph according to the existing dependencies and partial specifications of the subject program. Then it heuristically employs a number of search methods for analyzing this graph, e.g. binary search and single stepping.

4.3 Appreciation of User Expertise

Automatic debugging systems are influenced by the methods which programmers choose to use. Some systems, such as Focus [Lyl84] [LW87], are based on active user participation. Such systems provide the information required by the user and leave the main bug localization process to the user. It could be argued that these systems do not have a high degree of *cognitive plausibility*. The reason is that the user has to choose the slicing/dicing variable(s) irrespective of her/his degree of experience, which is difficult. Other systems, such as *APD* [Sha82], *DEBUSSI* [Kup89] and GADT, take control of bug localization. They require additional information from the user for bug localization. The user has a passive role in the debugging process in such systems. In order to take advantage of the user's knowledge and experience, the latter systems should be flexible enough to adapt the debugging to the user's degree of experience.

APD and *PELAS* interact with the user expecting only *"yes"* or *"no"* responses, although the suggestion of using partial specifications in algorithmic program debugging was mentioned by Shapiro [Sha82]. *DEBUSSI, RD* and GADT have higher knowledge transfer capacity, since they allow the user also to define partial specifications in terms of assertions about the program. In such systems it is possible to save the partial specifications and reuse them. *RD* and GADT also allow the user to point out a certain output variable (and even input variable in *RD*) in a call statement and claim that its value is wrong. This additional feature keeps the hypothesis suspect set at a reasonable size, which in turn makes bug localization faster. The user of GADT is not permitted to point out an input value as erroneous.

4.4   Degree of Automation

The interactive automated systems combine the user's knowledge with advanced techniques. Through this combination a high degree of debugging automation is achieved. *DEBUSSI* and GADT are the ones with the widest capacity for employing the user's knowledge. *RD, DEBUSSI, PELAS* and GADT use some kind of backward analysis technique to follow the program dependencies. *DEBUSSI* uses the dependency-directed analysis technique for bug localization, while *PELAS* employs the dynamic slicing technique. *RD* employs term dependency and backtracking.

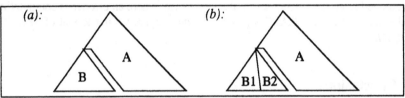

Fig. 13. : (a) An execution tree which mainly consists of two components A and B. (b) The computation of B is performed by the two components B1 and B2. In this example B1 and B2 are illustrated as separate subtrees. In practice they might be overlapping.

In order to compare the power of the techniques used in these systems, let us assume that the debugging process begins with an investigation of a suspect set. Each element of this set is a hypothetical source of a bug. The analysis technique used by a system reduces this set until this set can not be further reduced. Then the location of the bug is restricted to this set. The power of a debugger may be evaluated in terms of the ability to reduce the suspect set after each elementary bug localization step, i.e. the *power of reduction*.

A rough comparison between some systems based on usability criteria

	Pudsy	Laura	Proust	APD	RD	GAD T	Focus	PELA S	Debus si
Generality				Yes	Yes	Yes	Yes (Single fault)	Yes (No procs)	Yes (Single fault)
Cognitive Plausibility				Partial	Partial	High		Partial	High
Degree of Automation	Full (when applic.)	Partial (when applic.)	Partial (when applic.)	Partial	Semi (> than partial)	Semi	Semi to High	Low	Partial
Appreciation of User Expertise		Partial		Partial	Yes	Yes	Partail	Partial	Partial

The power of reduction in *PELAS* and *DEBUSSI* may be illustrated by the example of 13a. For the sake of simplicity, the execution tree is illustrated by the two components *A* and *B*. Both components are initially in the suspect set. Assume that the system queries the user about the correctness of the computation related to *B*. If the user's answer denotes that *B* is correct, then *B*'s corresponding subtree is removed from the suspect set. In the alternative case, *A*'s corresponding subtree is removed from the suspect set. In the latter case, the component *A* is the largest component removed from the suspect set.

RD and GADT provide an additional power of reduction. *RD* employs a dependency technique for more effective bug localization which could be compared to the interprocedural dynamic slicing technique used in GADT. Both of the systems allow the user to point out one or more of the parameters of a procedure call which has/have an erroneous value. This case is illustrated in 13b. The computation of *B* is performed by means of *B1* and *B2*. Thus, when the system asks the user about the correctness of B, the user can point out *B1*'s computation as erroneous. In this case the components *A* and *B2* are removed from the suspect set. In the worst case, where an erroneous computation is not dividable, *RD*'s and GADT's power of reduction are similar to that of *PELAS* and *DEBUSSI*.

5 Conclusions

Automated debugging systems help the user with one or several tasks in program understanding, verifying or debugging. Prior to debugging, static (batch-oriented) systems need to have exhaustive knowledge that they *might* need for debugging. Current static systems have not yet managed to be general enough to debug arbitrary program.s Interactive systems are more realistic, since they incrementally collect information about a program's *intended behavior* on a *need-to-know* basis. Whether these systems are useful in practise is largely determined by the extent that they fulfil our four usability criteria. All current systems are prototypes with various restrictions, but progress in this area might lead to practically useful systems within the next ten years.

6 References

[AL80]   Anne Adam and Jean-Pierre Laurent. Laura, A System to Debug Student Programs. *Artificial Intelligence*, 15(1):75-122, November 1980.

[DE88]   Mireille Ducassé and Anna-Maria Emde. A Review of Automated Debugging Systems: Knowledge, Strategies, and Techniques. In Proc. of the 10:th International Conference on Software Engineering, 1988. IEEE Press.

[Duc91]]   Mireille Ducassé. Abstract views of Prolog executions in Opium. In Proc. of the International Logic Programming Symposium, San Diego, Oct. 1991, pp 18-32. ed V. Saraswat and K. Ueda, MIT Press.

[Duc93]   Mireille Ducassé. A Pragmatic Survey of Automated Debugging. In Proc. of AADEBUG'93 - 1:st International Workshop on Automated and Algorithmic Debugging, Linköping University, Linköping, Sweden, May 1993.

[DNTM88]   Wlodek Drabent, Simin Nadjm-Tehrani, and Jan Maluszynski. The Use of Assertions in Algorithmic Debugging. In *Proceedings of the FGCS Conference*, pages 573-581, Tokyo, Japan, 1988.

[FGKS91]   Peter Fritzson, Tibor Gyimothy, Mariam Kamkar, and Nahid Shahmehri. Generalized Algorithmic Debugging and Testing. In *Proceedings of the ACM SIGPLAN'91*, pages 317-326, Toronto, Ontario, Canada, June 1991. Also accepted to LOPLAS, and as report LiTH-IDA-R-90-42.

[Fri83b]   Peter Fritzson. Symbolic Debugging Through Incremental Compilation in an Integrated Environment. *The Journal of Systems and Software*, 3:285–294, 1983.

[FAS92]   Peter Fritzson, Mikhail Auguston, Nahid Shahmehri: *Using Assertions in Declarative and Operational Models for Automated Debugging*, Accepted (1992) for publication in the Journal of Systems and Software.

[How82]   William E. Howden. Weak Mutation Testing and Completeness of Test Sets. *IEEE Transactions on Software Engineering*, SE-8(4):371–379, 1982.

[JS85]   W. Lewis Johnsson and Elliot Soloway. Proust: Knowledge-Based Program Understanding. *IEEE Transactions on Software Engineering*, 11(3):267–275, March 1985. Also reprinted in C. Rich and R. C. Waters editors, Readings in Artificial Intelligence and Software Engineering, Morgan Kaufman, 1986.

[Kam93]   Mariam Kamkar. *Interprocedural Dynamic Slicing with Applicationsto Debugging and Testing*. Ph.D. Thesis No. 297, Department of Computer Science, Linköping University, April 1993.

[Kor86]   Bogdan Korel. *Dependence-Based Modelling in the Automation of Error Localization in Computer Programs*. PhD thesis, Oakland University, 1986.

[Kor88]   Bogdan Korel. Pelas- Program Error-Locating Assistant System. *IEEE Transactions on Software Engineering*, 14(9):1253–1260, 1988.

[KSF90]   Mariam Kamkar, Nahid Shahmehri, and Peter Fritzson. Bug Localization by Algorithmic Debugging and Program Slicing. In *Proceedings of the International Conference on Programming Language Implementation and Logic Programming, PLILP'90*, pp. 60–74, Linköping, Sweden, Aug. 1990. LNCS 456, Springer-Verlag.

[KSF92]   Mariam Kamkar, Nahid Shahmehri and Peter Fritzson. Interprocedural Dynamic Slicing. In *Proc. of PLILP'92*, pp 370-384, Leuven, Belgium Aug 1992. LNCS 631. Earlier version as Tech. Report LiTH-IDA-R-91-20, June 1991.

[Kup89]   Ron I. Kuper. Dependency-Directed Localization of Software Bugs. Technical report, Artificial Intelligence Laboratory, May 1989. AI-TR 1053.

[Luk80]   F. J. Lukey. Understanding and Debugging Programs. *International Journal on Man-Machine Studies*, 12(2):189–202, February 1980.

[LW87]   James R. Lyle and Mark Weiser. Automatic Program Bug Location by Program Slicing. In *The 2:nd IEEE Symposium on Computers and Applications*, pages 877–883, Beijing(Peking), China, June 1987.

[Lyl84]   James R. Lyle. *Evaluating Variations on Program Slicing for Debugging*. PhD thesis, University of Maryland, December 1984.

[PC89]   Luis Moniz Pereira and Miguel Calejo. Algorithmic Debugging of Prolog Side-Effects. In *Fourth Portuguese Conference on Artificial Intelligence*. Springer-Verlag, 1989.

[Per86]   Luis Moniz Pereira. Rational Debugging in Logic Programming. In *Third Logic Programming Conference*, pages 203–210, London, England, July 1986.

[Rut76]   G. R. Ruth. Intelligent Program Analysis. *Artificial Intelligence*, 1(7), 1976.

[Sev87]   Rudolph E. Seviora. Knowledge-Based Program Debugging Systems. *IEEE Software*, 4(3):20–32, May 1987.

[Sha82]   E. Y. Shapiro. *Algorithmic Program Debugging*. MIT Press, May 1982.

[Sha91]   Nahid Shahmehri: *Generalized Algorithmic Debugging*. Ph.D. thesis, Linköping University, Dec 1991.

[Wei82]   Mark Weiser. Programmers use Slices when Debugging. *Communications of the ACM*, 25(7):446–452, July 1982.

[Wei84]   Mark Weiser. Program Slicing. *IEEE Transactions on Software Engineering*, Se-10(4):352–357, July 1984.

The Notions of Symptom and Error
in Declarative Diagnosis of Logic Programs

Gérard Ferrand

Université d'Orléans * and INRIA
LIFO, Département d'Informatique, BP 6759
F-45067 Orléans cedex 2, France
ferrand@univ-orleans.fr

Abstract. The aim of this paper is to explain, in a tutorial style, the notions of symptom and error, and the relation between symptom and error, in declarative diagnosis of logic programs. The emphasis is on the declarative nature of these notions (they do not depend on a particular computational behaviour). Our framework is not a logical formalism but an inductive formalism.

1 Introduction

The aim of this paper is to explain, in a tutorial style, the notions of symptom and error, and the relation between symptom and error, in declarative diagnosis of logic programs.

From an intuitive viewpoint, we call *symptom* the appearance of an anomaly during the execution of a program. For example in logic programming a symptom can be a "wrong answer" but, because of the relational nature of logic programming, it can be also a "missing answer". An anomaly is relative to *expected properties* of the program.

Symptoms are caused by *errors* in the program. *Diagnosis* is error localization when a symptom is given. Symptoms can be produced by testing. Error diagnosis can be seen as a first step in *debugging*, a second step being error correction.

Declarative Error Diagnosis was introduced in Logic Programming by Shapiro (*Algorithmic Program Debugging* [20]). *Declarative* means that the user has no need to consider the computational behaviour of the logic programming system, he needs only a declarative knowledge of the expected properties of the program ([20, 15, 16, 9, 8]).

Declarative diagnosis has been studied in a framework which is wider than classical logic programming : Concurrent logic programming ([14]), deductive data bases ([22])... Extensions of Shapiro's method have also been studied for imperative languages and functional languages ([18, 12]).

For a *declarative diagnoser system*, the input must include at least (1) the actual *program*, (2) the *symptom* and (3) some information on the *expected se-mantics* of the program. This information on the expected semantics can be given

---

* This work was supported also in part by CNRS.

by the programmer during the diagnosis session or it can be specified by other means but, in any case, from a conceptual viewpoint, this information is given by an *oracle*. An important problem in algorithmic debugging is the need for optimizations in the search for the error and in the interaction with the oracle.

This paper is not a survey on declarative diagnosis, it is concentrated only on the notions of symptom (here "wrong answer" or "missing answer") and error, and on the relation between them. At first a clear understanding of the relation between symptom and error (the symptom "caused" by the error) is useful for specifying the semantics of diagnoser programs. Moreover the emphasis here is on the *declarative* nature of these notions : They do not depend on a particular computational behaviour. It is the reason why they can be used in various domains (where the semantics is described by a rule-based formalism in a logic programming style) even if an actual execution is not PROLOG-like.

In this paper the emphasis is also on the level of abstraction of these notions and on their *inductive* nature. These notions have been first defined for definite programs (so without negation) by Shapiro ([20]) using essentially an inductive framework : on the one hand least fixpoint, i.e. *induction*, for the relation between incorrectness symptom and incorrectness, on the other hand greatest fixpoint, i.e. *co-induction*, for the relation between insufficiency symptom and insufficiency. For normal programs (so with negation) Lloyd ([15, 16]) has extended definitions and results in a framework where the declarative semantics of a program is defined by its Clark's completion. But there are many ways to see the logical meaning of a program, especially with negation ([21]) and Clark's semantics is not always the one which is considered for normal programs.

In this paper we study the notions of symptom and error without reference to a particular logic, but in an inductive framework which is more natural to define these notions and to understand the relation between them. This inductive framework has also a logical meaning, in a partial or three-valued logic, it is Fitting's semantics ([11, 23]) but it is outside the scope of this paper. It is a natural extension of the inductive framework where these notions were defined for definite programs.

To be more precise, on the one hand we have a *program P* which semantics is formalized by a set of literals $M(P)$ in an inductive framework and on the other hand we have *expected* properties which are also formalized by a set of literals S. The notion of *symptom* is based in the comparison of $M(P)$ with S. Another advantage of this approach is that the expected properties (formalized by S) are not necessarily a complete specification for the program. So this framework can be applied to situations where we are only interested in some properties of some predicates defined by the program.

Afterwards, we show how this abstract framework can be applied to symptoms effectively produced by an actual execution, when the computation is formalized by an operational semantics such as SLD resolution ([15]).

From a purely theoretical viewpoint, seeing that definite programs are normal programs, we could consider from the start normal programs. But for pedagogical reasons we begin with definite programs and we explain basic ideas in this framework. It is the main part of the paper. The last part is devoted to programs with negation. In this part the formalism is somewhat more involved.

Our formalization could use sets of literals with variables ([9, 4, 7]) but here, to be simpler while keeping the emphasis on main ideas, we consider only sets of ground atoms.

The paper is organized as follows : In section 2 we recall basic results on induction, co-induction and definite programs. In section 3 we define abstract notions of symptom and error. In sections 4 and 5 we apply this framework to study symptoms and error for definite programs. In section 6 we study symptoms and errors for normal programs. Section 7 is a conclusion.

2   Induction, Co-induction and Definite Programs

We start with a very small example.

Example 1. Let P be the logic program defined by the two clauses :
$rev([\,], L, L) \leftarrow$
$rev([H|B], A, L) \leftarrow rev(B, [H|A], L)$

We are going to consider that P defines a set of atoms (atomic formulas) $M^+(P)$ which will be a set-theoretical formalization of the (ground, positive) declarative semantics of P. For example, in practice, if we ask the *question* $rev([a, b], [\,], L)$ we have the *answer* $L = [b, a]$, and this will be represented by the fact that the atom $rev([a, b], [\,], [b, a])$ is in $M^+(P)$. The following tree ("proof tree") is a good way to understand this fact

$$rev([a, b], [\,], [b, a])$$
$$|$$
$$rev([b], [a], [b, a])$$
$$|$$
$$rev([\,], [b, a], [b, a])$$

From an intuitive viewpoint, a proof tree is only made of clause instances pasted together, here the 3 clause instances :
$rev([a, b], [\,], [b, a]) \leftarrow rev([b], [a], [b, a])$
$rev([b], [a], [b, a]) \leftarrow rev([\,], [b, a], [b, a])$
$rev([\,], [b, a], [b, a]) \leftarrow$
and the root of the proof tree is an instance of the question.

This notion of proof tree is not an operational notion, the definition of the tree is not the same thing as a particular way to compute the tree.

With this example we have stressed the *inductive* nature of $M^+(P)$. An *inductive definition* is merely a set of rules (Aczel [1]). To be more precise :

Definition 1. A *rule* on a set H is a pair denoted by $h \leftarrow B$ where $h \in H$ and $B \subseteq H$. h is the *head* and B is the *body* of the rule. The rule is *finitary* if its body is a finite set.

We say that a rule $h \leftarrow \emptyset$ is a *fact* and it is also denoted by $h \leftarrow$

Let $\mathcal{R}$ be a set of rules on H. The *operator associated with* $\mathcal{R}$ is the function T defined as follows :

$T : 2^H \rightarrow 2^H$ i.e. $T(I)$ is defined for any $I \subseteq H$ and $T(I) \subseteq H$.

$T(I)$ is defined by : for any $h \in H$, $h \in T(I)$ iff there is a rule in $\mathcal{R}$ the head of which is h and the body is $\subseteq I$.

It is easy to see that T is *monotonic* i.e. $T(I) \subseteq T(J)$ if $I \subseteq J$. (Conversely, because of the very general definition of a rule, each monotonic operator is associated with a set of rules).

Definition 2. We say that $I \subseteq H$ is *closed* by T (and by $\mathcal{R}$) if $T(I) \subseteq I$ i.e. for each rule, if the body is included in I then the head is in I.

The *set* which is *inductively defined by* T (and by $\mathcal{R}$) is the least set closed by T. It will be denoted by *ind(T)* (and *ind(\mathcal{R})*).

(Notice that such a set exists because it is the intersection of all the sets closed by T. If there is no fact in $\mathcal{R}$ then *ind(T)* is the empty set).

We see each *definite program* (set of definite clauses, so without negation) as an inductive definition. To be more precise, given a first-order language, H is the Herbrand base i.e. the set of the ground atoms. Given a definite program P, the rules are all the ground instances of the clauses of P (with any clause instance $a_0 \leftarrow a_1, \cdots, a_n$ we associate the rule $a_0 \leftarrow \{a_1, \cdots, a_n\}$).

In this context *ind(T)* will be denoted also by $M^+(P)$. It is our formalization of the (ground, positive) *declarative semantics* of P.

The link with the logical viewpoint is merely that : I is closed iff I is a Herbrand model of P, so *ind(T)* is the least Herbrand model of P. (It is also the set of all the ground atoms which are logical consequences of P). (see [15, 2]).

There is also a *dual* view of inductive definitions (it can be seen directly but in fact it is sufficient to apply the previous notions to the monotonic operator T' defined by $T'(I) = H - T(H - I)$). In Logic Programming, this dual view is useful for *negative* information.

Definition 3. We say that $I \subseteq H$ is *supported* by T (and by $\mathcal{R}$) if $I \subseteq T(I)$ i.e. each member of I is the head of a rule the body of which is included in I.

The *set* which is *co-inductively defined by* T (and by $\mathcal{R}$) is the greatest set supported by T.

It will be denoted by *coind(T)* (and *coind(\mathcal{R})*).

With each *inductive definition* a *proof method by induction* is associated : What can be proved by induction is that each member of *ind(T)* satisfies some property. From an abstract viewpoint what can be proved is that *ind(T)* $\subseteq S$ for some set S. Since *ind(T)* is the least set closed by T, we have

Theorem 4. *If S is closed by the monotonic operator T then ind(T) $\subseteq S$.*

So the *proof method by induction* consists in proving that S is closed by T, i.e. $T(S) \subseteq S$, i.e. that, for each rule, if the body is included in S then the head is in S (in particular that $h \in S$ for each fact $h \leftarrow$).

Example 2. Let P be the definite program of the previous example. We have $l_2 = reverse(l_1)$ for each atom $rev(l_1, [\,], l_2)$ in $M^+(P)$ where l_1 is a list. This is because, in $M^+(P)$, each atom $rev(l_1, l_2, l_3)$ satisfies the following property $\mathcal{P}(l_1, l_2, l_3)$: if l_1 and l_2 are lists then l_3 is a list and $l_3 = reverse(l_1) + l_2$ (+ stands for concatenation).

This is easy to prove by induction, here $S = \{rev(l_1, l_2, l_3) | \mathcal{P}(l_1, l_2, l_3)\}$ is $S_1 \cup S_2$ with
$S_1 = H - \{rev(l_1, l_2, l_3) | l_1 \text{ and } l_2 \text{ are lists}\} = \{rev(l_1, l_2, l_3) | l_1 \text{ or } l_2 \text{ are not lists}\}$
$S_2 = \{rev(l_1, l_2, l_3) | l_1, l_2, l_3 \text{ are lists and } reverse(l_1) + l_2 = l_3\}$

In a dual way, there is a *proof method by co-induction* :

Theorem 5. *If S is supported by the monotonic operator T then $S \subseteq coind(T)$.*

So what can be proved by co-induction is that $S \subseteq coind(T)$ for some set S. The proof method consists in proving that S is supported by T i.e. $S \subseteq T(S)$, i.e. that each member of S is the head of a rule the body of which is included in S.

In fact $ind(T)$ is not only the least I such that $T(I) \subseteq I$, it is also the least I such that $T(I) = I$ i.e. the *least fixpoint* of T.

In the dual way $coind(T)$ is not only the greatest I such that $I \subseteq T(I)$, it is also the *greatest fixpoint* of T.

So $ind(T) \subseteq coind(T)$, and $ind(T) = coind(T)$ iff T has only one fixpoint.

All these results are consequences of Knaster-Tarski theorem (see Lloyd [15]), but can be easily proved by induction and co-induction.

There is also a *"constructive"* approach to $ind(T)$: If each rule in $\mathcal{R}$ is *finitary*, by defining $T \uparrow 0 = \emptyset$ and $T \uparrow (n+1) = T(T \uparrow n)$, $ind(T)$ is the limit (union) of the $T \uparrow n$ (n integer ≥ 0). If the rules are not finitary, integers are not sufficient and transfinite ordinals are necessary. There is also a dual approach to $coind(T)$. We do not enter into details (it is more than what is needed here).

Definition 6. Let us suppose that each rule in $\mathcal{R}$ is *finitary*. A *proof tree* for $\mathcal{R}$ is a *finite* tree where each node is (an occurrence of) a member of H and such that, for each node h, if its children are $b_1, \cdots, b_n$ then $h \leftarrow \{b_1, \cdots, b_n\}$ is a rule of $\mathcal{R}$; such a rule is said to be *in the proof tree*. (In particular if h is a *leaf* of the proof tree then $h \leftarrow$ is a fact of $\mathcal{R}$).

Of course the set of the proof trees could be inductively defined and it is easy to prove

Theorem 7. *Let us suppose that each rule in $\mathcal{R}$ is finitary. Then, for each $h \in H$, $h \in ind(T)$ iff h is the root of a proof tree.*

(If the rules are not finitary well-founded infinite trees are necessary).

Note 8 on the operational semantics : SLD resolution + Finite Failure. SLD resolution (see [15]) can be considered as an operational semantics to compute *positive* information. The set of atoms proved by SLD resolution is $M^+(P) = ind(T)$.

Finite Failure (see [15]) is another operational notion and has a formalization by a set of atoms, the *finite failure set* of P, which is included in $H - (coind(T))$.

So if the atom a is in the *finite failure set* of P, $a \notin M^+(P)$ (since $ind(T) \subseteq coind(T)$) but the converse is not valid (because in general $ind(T) \neq coind(T)$).

Finite Failure can be considered as an operational semantics to compute *negative* information : The *negation* of a is proved if a is in the *finite failure set* of P (Negation as Failure, see [15]).

3 Symptoms and Errors for Inductive Definitions

Given on the one hand a set of rules $\mathcal{R}$ on H and on the other hand a set $S \subseteq H$, let us suppose that we are expecting $ind(T) \subseteq S$ but that actually we see an $h \in ind(T)$ such that $h \notin S$. Such an h is a *symptom* which shows that something goes wrong in $\mathcal{R}$. Necessarily there is a rule $h' \leftarrow B$ in $\mathcal{R}$ with $B \subseteq S$ and $h' \notin S$ (otherwise by *induction* we would have $ind(T) \subseteq S$). The existence of such rules $h' \leftarrow B$ explains that $ind(T) \nsubseteq S$ i.e. the appearance of symptoms. So such a rule $h' \leftarrow B$ can be considered as an *error* in $\mathcal{R}$. So we have

Definition 9. A *symptom* of $\mathcal{R}$ (and of T) wrt S is a member of $ind(T)$ which is not in S. ("No symptom" means $ind(T) \subseteq S$).

An *error* of $\mathcal{R}$ (and of T) wrt S is a rule $h \leftarrow B$ in $\mathcal{R}$ such that $B \subseteq S$ and $h \notin S$. ("No error" means $T(S) \subseteq S$ i.e. S closed by T).

Theorem 10. *If there is a symptom then there is an error.*

A relation of *"causality"* between an error and a symptom can be expressed with the notion of *proof tree* : It is easy to see that each symptom is the root of a proof tree in which there is a rule which is an error. This error can be seen as a "cause" of the symptom.

From the dual viewpoint : Let us suppose that we are expecting $S \subseteq coind(T)$ but that actually we see an $h \in S$ such that $h \notin coind(T)$. We call such an h a *co-symptom*. Necessarily there is a $h' \in S$ such that there is no rule $h' \leftarrow B$ with $B \subseteq S$, i.e. $h' \notin T(S)$ (otherwise by *co-induction* $S \subseteq coind(T)$). We call this h' a *co-error*.

Definition 11. A *co-symptom* of $\mathcal{R}$ (and of T) wrt S is a member of S which is not in $coind(T)$. ("No co-symptom" means $S \subseteq coind(T)$).

A *co-error* of $\mathcal{R}$ (and of T) wrt S is a member of S which is not in $T(S)$, i.e. a member h of S such that there is no rule $h \leftarrow B$ with $B \subseteq S$. ("No co-error" means $S \subseteq T(S)$ i.e. S supported by T).

Theorem 12. *If there is a co-symptom then there is a co-error.*

4 Symptoms and Errors for Definite Programs

We apply the notions of the previous section to definite programs. Let us suppose that we are expecting that each answer produced by the definite program P satisfies some property, i.e. that each atom of $M^+(P)$ satisfies some property. From an abstract viewpoint we are expecting $M^+(P) = ind(T) \subseteq S$ for some set S which is a set-theoretical formalization of an expected property.

The following definitions are equivalent to Shapiro's ones ([20]) :

Definition 13. An *incorrectness* of P wrt S is an *error* of T wrt S.

An *incorrectness symptom* of P wrt S is a *symptom* of T wrt S.

Such a symptom is a formalization of a *wrong answer* (wrt S) produced by P.

Of course in practice such a set S is not effectively available, it is only an abstraction which is a theoretical mean to explain the principles without needless details. The concept of *oracle* (Shapiro [20]) is useful to describe the way by which a diagnoser system can get knowledge on the expected properties formalized by S, but this is outside the scope of this paper.

Moreover let us emphasize that the expected properties, which are here formalized by S, are not necessarily a complete specification for P. In other terms it is not necessarily expected that $S = M^+(P)$. In general it is only expected that $M^+(P) \subseteq S$.

Example 3 (continuation). Let us take as expected property the same set S as in the previous example, but let us put a bug in the second clause of the program :
$rev([\ ], L, L)$
$rev([H|B], A, L) \leftarrow rev(B, A, L)$ (the bug is A instead of $[H|A]$ in the body)

Then $rev([a, b], [\ ], [\ ])$ is an (incorrectness) symptom and the clause instance $rev([b], [\ ], [\ ]) \leftarrow rev([\ ], [\ ], [\ ])$ is an incorrectness ("cause" of the symptom). It is clearly seen in the proof tree

$$rev([a, b], [\ ], [\ ])$$
$$|$$
$$rev([b], [\ ], [\ ])$$
$$|$$
$$rev([\ ], [\ ], [\ ])$$

From the dual viewpoint : The following definitions are equivalent to Shapiro's ones ([20]) :

Definition 14. An *insufficiency* (or *uncovered atom*) of P wrt S is an *co-error* of T wrt S.

An *insufficiency symptom* of P wrt S is a *co-symptom* of T wrt S.

Example 4. See the examples below, where the notion of *insufficiency symptom* is related to the operational notion of *finite failure*.

Right now we can state the following comparisons between :

- (i) $S = M^+(P) = ind(T) = least\ fixpoint(T)$
- (ii) no error (no incorrectness and no insufficiency)
  i.e. $S = T(S)$ i.e. S is a *fixpoint* of T
- (iii) no symptom
  i.e. $least\ fixpoint(T) = ind(T) \subseteq S \subseteq coind(T) = greatest\ fixpoint(T)$

We have $(i) \Rightarrow (ii) \Rightarrow (iii)$. It's easy to see that each converse $\Leftarrow$ is not valid.

Note 15 on finite failure and insufficiency symptom. Let us consider an actual execution, the computation being formalized by SLD resolution + Finite Failure (see note 8). From an intuitive viewpoint, let us suppose that we are expecting that each atom satisfying the property formalized by S is computed, i.e. we are expecting that $S \subseteq M^+(P)$. But let us suppose that we have a *missing answer* because of a *finite failure*, i.e. that we have an atom $a \in S$ (*expected answer*) but that a is also in the *finite failure set* of P (so actually a *missing answer*). This atom a is actually a symptom that something goes wrong. Since the finite failure set of P is included in $H - (coind(T))$, our atom a is a particular case of *insufficiency symptom*.

Example 5. Let us take
  $S = \{rev(l_1, l_2, l_3) | l_1, l_2, l_3\ are\ lists\ and\ reverse(l_1) + l_2 = l_3\}$
If we have forgotten the first clause of the previous examples, we have only :

$rev([H|B], A, L) \leftarrow rev(B, [H|A], L)$

Then $rev([a, b], [\ ], [b, a]$ is an *insufficiency symptom* (expected but finite failure) and $rev([\ ], [b, a], [b, a])$ is an *insufficiency*. See the tree

$$rev([a, b], [\ ], [b, a])$$
$$|$$
$$rev([b], [a], [b, a])$$
$$|$$
$$rev([\ ], [b, a], [b, a])$$

(It's a "partial proof tree" which cannot be completed but we do not formalize this notion here).

This example is simple but too particular, it does not show all the relevance of the notion of insufficiency.

Example 6. Again $S = \{rev(l_1, l_2, l_3) | l_1, l_2, l_3\ are\ lists\ and\ reverse(l_1) + l_2 = l_3\}$
but now the program is
$rev([\ ], L, L)$
$rev([H|B], A, L) \leftarrow rev(B, [H], L)$ (the bug is $[H]$ instead of $[H|A]$ in the body)

Then $rev([a, b, c], [\,], [c, b, a])$ is an *insufficiency symptom* and $rev([b, c], [a], [c, b, a])$ is an *insufficiency*.

We can clearly understand this on the "partial proof tree"

$$rev([a, b, c], [\,], [c, b, a])$$
$$|$$
$$rev([b, c], [a], [c, b, a])$$
$$|$$
$$rev([c], [b], [c, b, a])$$
$$|$$
$$rev([\,], [c], [c, b, a])$$

We see why the atom $rev([a, b, c], [\,], [c, b, a])$ is an insufficiency symptom : It is in the finite failure set, because of the atom $rev([\,], [c], [c, b, a])$ which is instance of no clause head of P. But it is not this atom $rev([\,], [c], [c, b, a])$ which explains the symptom. Its explains why there is a finite failure, but *finite failure* is a property of P *alone* while *symptom* and *error* depend also on the expected properties of P i.e. depend on P *and* S *together*. In fact it is the atom $rev([b, c], [a], [c, b, a])$ which is the insufficiency because this atom is expected (i.e. it is in S) but it is the head of no clause instance the body of which is expected (i.e. included in S). So it is in $S - T(S)$ i.e. it is a co-error or insufficiency. If we want to correct the program, we have to get rid of this insufficiency. *The failure was caused by the first clause of the program but the insufficiency is not here.* We have to modify P in such a way that $rev([b, c], [a], [c, b, a])$ is the head of a clause instance the body of which is in S ...

Remark. Note that with the same S and P, $rev([a, b, c], [\,], [c])$ is an incorrectness symptom, $rev([c], [b], [c]) \leftarrow rev([\,], [c], [c])$ being an incorrectness :

$$rev([a, b, c], [\,], [c])$$
$$|$$
$$rev([b, c], [a], [c])$$
$$|$$
$$rev([c], [b], [c])$$
$$|$$
$$rev([\,], [c], [c])$$

5 Incorrectness and Insufficiency Symptoms of Definite Programs as Positive and Negative Symptoms

On the one hand there is a link of "causality" between incorrectness and incorrectness symptom and on the other hand a link of "causality" between insufficiency and insufficiency symptom. But for *normal programs* (i.e. with negation, next section) such a separation will not be valid any longer. It will not be possible to distinguish these two kinds of links any longer because any interaction will be possible through negations between symptom and error. A uniform framework will be necessary. It is useful to see what is this uniform framework right now for *definite* programs.

A *literal* is an atom *(positive literal)* or the negation $\neg a$ of an atom a *(negative literal)*. The following *notations* will be useful :
For $J \subseteq H$, let $\overline{J} = H - J$ i.e. the set of the atoms which are not in J, and let $\neg J = \{\neg a | a \in J\}$ i.e. the set of the negations of atoms in J. So $H \cup \neg H$ is the set of the ground literals.
For each $I \subseteq H \cup \neg H$, let $I^+ \subseteq H$ and $I^- \subseteq H$ defined by $I = I^+ \cup \neg I^-$.

To sum up the previous section :

Incorrectness and incorrectness symptom are defined wrt a set S' which is a formalization of some expected properties. An incorrectness symptom of P wrt S' is a member of $M^+(P) = ind(T)$ which is not in S'. In the example 3, S' is the set : $S = \{rev(l_1, l_2, l_3) | if\ l_1, l_2\ are\ lists\ then\ l_3 = reverse(l_1) + l_2\}$.

Insufficiency and insufficiency symptom are defined wrt a set S'' which is a formalization also of some expected properties. An insufficiency symptom of P wrt S'' is a member of S'' which is not in $coind(T)$. In the examples 5 and 6, S'' is the set : $S = \{rev(l_1, l_2, l_3) | l_1, l_2, l_3\ are\ lists\ and\ l_3 = reverse(l_1) + l_2\}$.

S' and S'' are used in dual ways : $ind(T) \subseteq S'$ iff *no incorrectness symptom*, $S'' \subseteq coind(T)$ iff *no insufficiency symptom*. $T(S') \subseteq S'$ iff *no incorrectness*, $S'' \subseteq T(S'')$ iff *no insufficiency*.
In any case the notion of symptom is based on the comparison of some set which represents the semantics of P ($ind(T)$ or $coind(T)$) with some set which represents expected properties (S' or S''). The idea now is merely to consider that the *declarative semantics* of a program has a *positive* part (set of atoms) and a *negative* part (set of negative literals), that the *positive* part is defined by using $ind(T)$ and the *negative* part by using $coind(T)$, and that the *expected properties* have also a *positive* part, defined by using S' and a *negative* part defined by using S''. To be more precise, we use the following *notations* :

$S = S' \cup \neg \overline{S''}$ i.e. $S^+ = S'$ and $S^- = \overline{S''}$.
S is a uniform formalization of some *expected properties*.

$M^-(P) = \overline{coind(T)}$ and $M(P) = M^+(P) \cup \neg M^-(P)$.

So we have consistent notations :
$M(P)^+ = M^+(P) = ind(T)$ and $M(P)^- = M^-(P) = \overline{coind(T)}$.
$M(P)$ is a uniform formalization of the *declarative semantics* of P.

It is easy to check that the inclusion $M(P) \subseteq S$ means exactly : *no incorrectness symptom wrt S' and no insufficiency symptom wrt S''*.

Now to achieve our uniform framework we are going to show that $M(P)$ itself can be directly defined by induction, by a suitable monotone operator Ψ (i.e. $ind(\Psi) = M(P)$). So it is possible to apply to this inductive definition the concepts of section 3, and the notion of symptom is easy to recognize right now :

A *symptom* wrt S is a *literal* $l \in M(P) - S$ so there are two kinds of symptoms :

A *positive symptom* wrt S is an atom $a \in M^+(P) - S^+ = M^+(P) - S'$, i.e. an *incorrectness symptom* wrt S',

A *negative symptom* wrt S is a negative literal $\neg a$ with $a \in M^-(P) - S^- = S'' - coind(T)$ i.e. the negation $\neg a$ of an *insufficiency symptom* a wrt S''.

The notion of *error* cannot be recognized without precising the inductive definition i.e. the monotone operator Ψ. But we are going to see that this notion of error fits with the previous notions of *incorrectness* and *insufficiency*.

It remains to give the right monotonic operator Ψ. To define it we still use the previous operator T :

Let $\Psi : 2^{(H \cup \neg H)} \to 2^{(H \cup \neg H)}$ defined by :

for $I \subseteq H \cup \neg H$, $\Psi(I) = \Psi^+(I) \cup \neg\Psi^-(I) \subseteq H \cup \neg H$, where :

$$\Psi^+(I) = T(I^+)$$

for each $a \in H$, $a \in \Psi^-(I)$ iff, for each clause instance $h \leftarrow B$ of a clause of P such that $a = h$, $B \cap I^- \neq \emptyset$.

It is an easy exercise to check that $\Psi^-(I) = \overline{T(\overline{I^-})}$, that Ψ is monotonic and that $ind(\Psi) = M(P)$.

For $S = S' \cup \neg \overline{S''}$, it is easy to check that :

$\Psi(S) \not\subseteq S$ is equivalent to $(T(S') \not\subseteq S')$ or $(S'' \not\subseteq T(S''))$, so

there is an *error* of Ψ wrt S

iff

there is an *incorrectness* of P wrt S' or there is an *insufficiency* of P wrt S''

To explicit a set of rules associated with the monotone operator Ψ is outside the scope of this paper (some of them are not finitary, [3, 5, 4]) but it is possible to define such a set of rules satisfying the following conditions :

There are two kinds of rules, the *positive rules* and the *negative rules*.

The *positive rules* are exactly the *ground instances* of the clauses of P i.e. the set of rules associated with the monotonic operator T from the beginning. Such a rule is an *error* of Ψ wrt S iff it is an *incorrectness* of P wrt S'.

Each *negative* rule has a head which is a *negative literal.* Such a rule with the head $\neg a$ is an *error* of Ψ wrt S iff a is an *insufficiency* of P wrt S''. In that case $a \in S''$ but $a \notin T(S'')$ i.e. for each clause instance $a \leftarrow B$ there is an atom $a' \in B$ such that $a' \notin S''$. The body of the negative rule is a formalization of the family composed of all these a' so it may be infinite. We keep only the head $\neg a$ i.e. we consider only the finite information a which is an insufficiency (also called *uncovered* atom). We do not enter into details here ([4]).

Note 16 on the operational semantics. Let us define a set-theoretical formalization, denoted by $SLDNF(P)$, of the operational semantics SLD resolution + Negation as Failure (in this section P is a definite program).

Let $SLDNF(P) = M^+(P) \cup \neg (finite\ failure\ set(P))$.

Since $(finite\ failure\ set(P)) \subseteq \overline{coind(T)}$, we have $SLDNF(P) \subseteq M(P)$.

A literal which is effectively proved but not expected is a symptom which is in $SLDNF(P)$, but the notion of symptom and error, and the link between symptom and error, are easier to understand when $SLDNF(P)$ is embedded in the abstract inductive semantics $M(P)$.

6 Symptoms and Errors for Normal Programs

In this section P is a *normal program* i.e. a set of *normal clauses* $a \leftarrow l_1, \cdots, l_n$ where a is an *atom* and $l_1, \cdots, l_n$ *literals*. We are going to extend the notions and results of the previous section to normal programs.

6.1 Inductive Semantics for a Normal Program

We now define for a normal program P an abstract declarative semantics $M(P)$ which is a set of literals. We give for $M(P)$ an inductive definition i.e. a monotonic operator Φ such that $M(P) = ind(\Phi)$. We need some preliminaries :

For $J \subseteq H$ let $T_J : 2^H \rightarrow 2^H$ defined by :

for $J' \subseteq H$, $T_J(J') \subseteq H$, and, for each $a \in H$, $a \in T_J(J')$ iff there is a ground instance of a clause of P the head of which is a and the body is $\subseteq J' \cup \neg J$ (i.e. each atom of the body is in J' and each negative literal of the body is the negation of an atom in J).

T_J is monotonic (if P is a definite program, T_J is merely the operator T of the previous sections).

Remark. With this monotonic operator an obvious *set of rules* is associated : take all the ground instances of the clauses of P where the negative literals $\neg a$ satisfy $a \in J$, and discard these negative literals.

These rules are finitary, so we can use a notion of (finite) proof tree : For each atom a, $a \in ind(T_J)$ iff a is the root of a proof tree. It is more intuitive to consider that the rules are exactly ground clause instances (with their negative literals) and to consider also these negative literals $\neg a$, $a \in J$, as facts). So in these proof trees there are two kinds of *leaves* : *positive leaves* which are instances of facts of P as previously when P was a definite program, but there are also *negative leaves* $\neg a$ where $a \in J$.

Let $\Phi : 2^{(H \cup \neg H)} \to 2^{(H \cup \neg H)}$ defined by :

for $I \subseteq H \cup \neg H$, $\Phi(I) = \Phi^+(I) \cup \neg \Phi^-(I) \subseteq H \cup \neg H$ where :

$\Phi^+(I) = ind(T_{I^-})$ and $\Phi^-(I) = \overline{coind(T_{\overline{I^+}})}$.

It is an exercise to check that Φ is monotonic.

Let $M(P) = ind(\Phi)$.

Obviously, if P is a definite program, $M(P)$ is exactly the $M(P)$ of the previous section (since $T_J = T$, $\Phi(I) = M(P)$ does not depends on I).

In fact, $M(P)$ is *Fitting's model* ([11, 23]). But we do not enter into details of Fitting's semantics, in particular partial or three valued logic are outside the scope of this paper.

Remark. There is another equivalent inductive definition for Fitting's model :
$M(P) = ind(\Psi)$ where Ψ is defined by :
for $I \subseteq H \cup \neg H$, $\Psi(I) = \Psi^+(I) \cup \neg \Psi^-(I) \subseteq H \cup \neg H$ where :

$\Psi^+(I) = T_{I^-}(I^+)$ and $\Psi^-(I) = \overline{T_{\overline{I^+}}(\overline{I^-})}$.

$\Psi^-(I)$ can be seen from another viewpoint : The *opposite* of a literal l is the literal $-l$ defined by : $-a = \neg a$ and $-\neg a = a$ if a is an atom. Then, for each $a \in H$, $a \in \Psi^-(I)$ iff, for each clause instance $h \leftarrow B$ of a clause of P such that $a = h$, there is a $l \in B$ such that $-l \in I$. If P is a definite program, Ψ is the same as the operator Ψ of the previous section.

Remark. Since $M(P) = ind(\Phi)$, it is the least fixpoint of Φ, so ($M(P)$ being denoted by M to be shorter) $M = \Phi(M)$ i.e. $M^+ = ind(T_{M^-})$ and $\overline{M^-} = coind(T_{\overline{M^+}})$.
So, as when P was a definite program, the atoms of M^+ are exactly the roots of *proof trees* but now with a notion of proof tree in which we can see *negative leaves* $\neg a$ ($a \in M^-$). From an intuitive viewpoint these $\neg a$ ($a \in M^-$) behave as "negative facts".

Note 17 on the operational semantics SLDNF resolution. Let
$SLDNF(P) = SLDNF^+(P) \cup \neg SLDNF^-(P)$ the set of literals proved by SLDNF resolution (see Lloyd [15]), $SLDNF^+(P)$ and $SLDNF^-(P)$ being sets of atoms. In particular, for an atom a, $a \in SLDNF^-(P)$ iff a has a finitely failed SLDNF-tree, i.e. $\neg a$ is proved by SLDNF resolution.

$SLDNF(P)$ is embedded in $M(P)$ i.e. $SLDNF(P) \subseteq M(P)$ (soundness of SLDNF resolution wrt Fitting's semantics, given without proof, see [11, 13]). It is especially significant in our framework.

Example 7. Let P be the following normal program (it is a normal version of an example used by Lloyd [15] §18) :
$subset(L_1, L_2) \leftarrow \neg nsubset(L_1, L_2)$
$nsubset(L_1, L_2) \leftarrow member(X, L_1), \neg member(X, L_2)$
$member(X, [X|L]) \leftarrow$
$member(X, [H|L]) \leftarrow member(X, L)$

The atoms $subset([a], [a, b])$ and $\neg nsubset([a], [a, b])$ are in $SLDNF(P)$ hence are in $M(P)$.

6.2 Symptoms

The notion of *symptom* is based on the comparison of $M(P)$ with a set S which is a set-theoretical representation of the *expected properties* : It is expected that $M(P) \subseteq S$. A *symptom* is a literal which shows that something goes wrong, it is a literal in $M(P)$ which is *not expected* i.e. a literal $\in M(P) - S$.

In order to compare S with $M(P) = M^+(P) \cup \neg M^-(P)$ and motivated by the previous notions and results when P was a definite program, we choose to represent the *expected properties* by two sets of atoms S', S'' such that

$$S = S' \cup \neg \overline{S''} \quad \text{(i.e. } S^+ = S', S^- = \overline{S''}).$$

Notice the particular case $S' = S''$. In such a case, for each atom a, $a \in S^+$ or $a \in S^-$ i.e. the *expected properties* are *completely specified*.

An example is when $S' = S'' =$ the set of the atoms true in some *intended interpretation*. It is the case for Lloyd's approach ([15, 16]), which is based on the logical semantics of Clark's completion and SLDNF resolution.

But our framework is more flexible. As suggested by the examples we are not compelled to specify expected properties for all the atoms. In our examples, with a suitable S' we are discarding badly typed atoms (when some terms are not lists). So this framework has some links with a declarative view of *rational debugging* ([19]) and with other views on the relations between types and intended meaning ([17]). We do not enter into details here ([4]).

Notice also that here to have $S^+ \cap S^- \neq \emptyset$ is not an anomaly since an atom in $S^+ \cap S^-$ is an atom in $S' - S''$ (see badly typed atoms in our examples). It is the reason why $S = S^+ \cup \neg S^-$ cannot always be seen as a *model* in a logical sense, even in a partial or three valued logic. We do not need here a semantic in a formal logic, we have only set-theoretical inductive notions.

Definition 18. A *positive symptom* of P wrt S' is an atom in $M^+(P) - S'$.

A *negative symptom* of P wrt S'' is a negative literal $\neg a$ such that $a \in M^-(P) \cap S''$.

A *symptom* of P wrt S', S'' is a *positive symptom* of P wrt S' or a *negative symptom* of P wrt S'' (so the symptoms are the literals in $M(P) - S$).

Lemma 19. *If there is a symptom of P wrt S', S'' then there is a symptom of $T_{\overline{S''}}$ wrt S' or there is a co-symptom of $T_{\overline{S'}}$ wrt S''.*

Proof. By the definition of $M(P) = ind(\Phi)$, $\Phi(S) \subseteq S \Rightarrow M(P) \subseteq S$.
But $\Phi(S) \subseteq S \Leftrightarrow ind(T_{\overline{S''}}) \subseteq S'$ and $S'' \subseteq coind(T_{\overline{S'}})$.
So, if there is a *symptom* of P wrt S', S'' then $ind(T_{\overline{S''}}) \not\subseteq S'$ or $S'' \not\subseteq coind(T_{\overline{S'}})$.

6.3 Errors

Now we use Lloyd's terminology ([15, 16]).

Definition 20. An *incorrect clause instance* of P wrt S', S'' is an error of $T_{\overline{S''}}$ wrt S', i.e. an instance $h \leftarrow B$ of a clause of P such that $h \notin S'$, each atom of B is in S' and each negative literal $\neg a$ of B satisfies $a \notin S''$.

An *uncovered atom* for P wrt S', S'' is a co-error of $T_{\overline{S'}}$ wrt S'', i.e. an atom $a \in S''$ for which there is no $h \leftarrow B$ instance of a clause of P such that $a = h$, each atom of B is in S'' and each negative literal $\neg a$ of B satisfies $a \notin S'$.

Notice that, if P is a *definite program*, an *incorrect clause instance* of P wrt S', S'' is exactly an *incorrectness* of P wrt S' and an *uncovered atom* for P wrt S', S'' is exactly an *insufficiency* of P wrt S'' In section 4, P was a definite program and we had, on the one hand incorrectness "cause" of incorrectness symptom, on the other hand insufficiency "cause" of insufficiency symptom. Now this separation is not possible any longer, because "causality" can go through negations. We have only :

Theorem 21. *If there is a symptom of P wrt S', S'' then there is an incorrect clause instance of P wrt S', S'' or an uncovered atom for P wrt S', S''.*

Proof. By lemma 19 and the theorems of section 3.

Remark. An equivalent statement of this theorem is the following :
A *sufficient condition* for $M(P) \subseteq S' \cup \neg \overline{S''}$ is the conjunction of the two following conditions (i) and (ii) :
(i) For each instance $h \leftarrow B$ of a clause of P, if each atom of B is in S' and each negative literal $\neg a$ of B satisfies $a \notin S''$, then $h \in S'$.
(ii) For each atom $a \in S''$ there is an instance $h \leftarrow B$ of a clause of P such that $a = h$, each atom of B is in S'' and each negative literal $\neg a$ of B satisfies $a \notin S'$.

Example 8. Let S', S'' defined by :
$S'' = S''_{subset} \cup S''_{nsubset} \cup S''_{member}$ with

$S''_{subset} = \{subset(l_1, l_2) | l_1, l_2 \text{ lists and } l_1 \subseteq l_2\}$
$S''_{nsubset} = \{nsubset(l_1, l_2) | l_1, l_2 \text{ lists and } l_1 \not\subseteq l_2\}$
$S''_{member} = \{member(x, l) | l \text{ list and } x \in l\}$

$S' = S'_{subset} \cup S'_{nsubset} \cup S'_{member}$ with

$S'_{subset} = \{subset(l_1, l_2) | if\ l_1, l_2\ lists\ then\ l_1 \subseteq l_2\}$
$S'_{nsubset} = \{nsubset(l_1, l_2) | if\ l_1, l_2\ lists\ then\ l_1 \nsubseteq l_2\}$
$S'_{member} = \{member(x, l) | if\ l\ list\ then\ x \in l\}$

but with the following program P (normal version of an example used by Lloyd [15] §19)

$subset(L_1, L_2) \leftarrow \neg nsubset(L_1, L_2)$
$nsubset(L_1, L_2) \leftarrow member(X, L_1), \neg member(X, L_2)$
$member(X, [X|L]) \leftarrow$
$member(X, [H|L]) \leftarrow member(H, L)$

We see that $subset([b], [a, b]) \in SLDNF^-(P)$ (finite failure) but this atom is also in S'' so $\neg subset([b], [a, b])$ is a negative symptom wrt S''.

$nsubset([b], [a, b]) \in SLDNF^+(P)$ but this atom is not in S' so it is a positive symptom wrt S'.

$member(b, [a, b]) \in SLDNF^-(P)$ (finite failure) but this atom is in S'' so $\neg member([b], [a, b])$ is a negative symptom wrt S''.

Here $member(b, [a, b])$ is an uncovered atom wrt S', S''.

It is possible to express accurately a relation of "causality" between an error (incorrect clause instance or uncovered atom) and a symptom by using generalized proof trees ([4]).

Lloyd ([15, 16]) described such a relation in the SLDNF framework. We could do the same as suggested by the previous example. This effort would be useful especially for designing an error diagnoser but this is outside the scope of this paper.

Moreover the note 16 can be extended to this general framework.

7 Conclusion

This inductive formalism for the declarative semantics of a program, combined with the flexibility of the set-theoretical representation of the expected properties, give a good level of abstraction to express the notions of symptom and error for logic programs. It is a basis for a study of declarative diagnosis of various systems with various operational semantics. The semantics of diagnoser (meta)programs can be clarified by describing connections between symptoms and error through proof trees ([20, 16, 4]).

There is a duality between program diagnosis and program proving. This inductive framework has some analogies with another inductive framework which was used for the validation of program wrt the well-founded semantics ([10]). The links between the two frameworks are studied in ([4]).

References

1. P. Aczel. *An Introduction to Inductive Definitions.* Handbook of Mathematical Logic, J. Barwise (Ed) C.7, 739-782, Noth Holland, 1977.
2. K.R. Apt. *Logic programming.* Handbook of Theoretical Computer Science, J. Van Leeuween (Manag. Ed) Vol 2, Chapt 10, 493-574, Elsevier 1990.
3. M. Bergere, G. Ferrand. *Inductive semantics and declarative approach of error diagnosis.* ICLP'91 Preconference Workshop on Logic Programming Semantics and non Classical Logics, Paris 1991.
4. M. Bergere, G. Ferrand. (to appear)
5. M. Bergere. *Approche declarative du diagnostic d'erreurs pour la Programmation en logique avec negation.* Thesis, Orleans 1991.
6. P. Deransart, G. Ferrand. *Advanced tutorial on proof methods and declarative diagnosis in Logic Programming.* ICLP'89.
7. P. Deransart, J. Maluszynski. *A Grammatical View of Logic Programming.* MIT Press (to appear).
8. W. Drabent, S. Nadjm-Tehrani, J. Maluszynski. *Algorithmic Debugging with Assertions.* META'88 365-378, 1988.
9. G. Ferrand. *Error diagnosis in Logic programming : an adaptation of E.Y. Shapiro's method.* Journal of Logic programming, 4:177-198, 1987.
10. G. Ferrand, P. Deransart. *Proof method of partial correctness and weak completeness for normal logic programs.* Proc. Joint International Conference and Symposium on Logic Programming, MIT Press, 1992.
11. M. Fitting. *A Kripke-Kleene semantics for logic programs.* Journal of Logic programming, 2:295-312, 1985.
12. P. Fritzson, T. Gyimothy, M. Kamkar, N. Shahmehri. *Generalized Algorithmic Debugging and Testing.* Proc. ACM SIGPLAN'91 Conference on Programming Language Design and Implementation, Toronto, 1991, SIGPLAN Notices Vol 26, Nb 6, June 1991.
13. K. Kunen. *Negation in Logic Programming.* Journal of Logic programming, 4:289-308, 1987.
14. Y. Lichtenstein, E. Shapiro. *Abstract Algorithmic Debugging.* Proc. Joint International Conference and Symposium on Logic Programming, 512-530, MIT Press, 1988.
15. J. W. Lloyd. *Foundations of Logic Programming.* 2nd ed, Springer Verlag, 1987.
16. J. W. Lloyd. *Declarative Error Diagnosis.* New Generation Computing, 5:133-154, 1987.
17. L. Naish. *Types and intended meaning.* in *Types in Logic programming* 189-216, F. Pfenning (Ed), MIT Press 1992.
18. H. Nilsson, P. Fritzson. *Algorithmic Debugging of Lazy functional languages.* PLILP'92, LNCS 631, 1992.
19. L.M. Pereira. *Rational Debugging in Logic Programming.* 3th ICLP 203-210, LNCS 225.
20. E.Y. Shapiro. *Algorithmic Program Debugging.* ACM Distinguished Dissertation Series. MIT Press 1982.
21. J.C. Shepherdson. *Negation in Logic Programming.* Foundations of Deductive Databases and Logic Programming, J. Minker (Ed), Morgan Kaufmann Publishers, 1988, 19-88.
22. O. Shmueli, S. Tsur. *Logical Diagnosis of LDL Programs.* New generation Computing, 9 (1991) 277-303.

23. V. Thibau, J.P. Delahaye. *Programming in three-valued logic*. Theoretical Computer Science, vol 78: 189-216, 1991.
24. M. Van Emden, R. Kowalski. *The semantics of predicate logic as a programming language*. Journal of the ACM, 23(4): 733-742, 1976.

Debugging by Diagnosing Assumptions

Luís Moniz Pereira, Carlos Viegas Damásio, José Júlio Alferes

CRIA, Uninova and DCS, U. Nova de Lisboa*
2825 Monte da Caparica, Portugal
{lmp | cd | jja}@fct.unl.pt

Abstract. We present a novel and uniform technique for normal logic program declarative error diagnosis. We lay down the foundations on a general approach to diagnosis using logic programming, and bring out the close relationship between debugging and fault–finding.

Diagnostic debugging can be enacted by contradiction removal methods. It relies on a simple program transformation to provide a contradiction removal approach to debugging, based on revising the assumptions about predicates' correctness and completeness.

The contradiction removal method is justified in turn in terms of well–founded semantics. The loop detection properties of well–founded semantics will allow in the future for a declarative treatment of otherwise endless derivations. The debugging of programs under well–founded semantics with explicit negation is also foreseen.

Here, we apply our techniques to finite SLDNF derivations, whose meaning coincides with the well–founded model, for which our contradiction removal method and algorithm is sound and complete. Several examples illustrate the algorithm at work.

1 Introduction

It is clear that fault-finding or diagnosis is akeen to debugging. In the context of Logic, both arise as a confrontation between theory and model. Whereas in debugging one confronts an erroneous theory, in the form of a set of clauses, with models in the form of input/output pairs, in diagnosis one confronts a perfect theory (a set of rules acting as a blueprint or specification for some artifact) with the imperfect input/output behaviour of the artifact (which, if it were not faulty, would behave in accordance with a theory model).

What is common to both is the mismatch. The same techniques used in debugging to pinpoint faulty rules can equally be used to find the causes, in a perfect blueprint, which are at odds with artifact behaviour. Then, by means of the correspondence from the blueprint's modelization to the artifact's subcomponents whose i/o behaviour they emulate, the faulty ones can be spotted.

Declarative debugging then is essentially a diagnosis task, but until now its relationship to diagnosis was unclear or inexistent. We present a novel and uniform technique for normal logic program declarative error diagnosis by laying

* We thank JNICT and Esprit BR project Compulog 2 (no 6810) for their support.

down the foundations on a general approach to diagnosis using logic programming. By so doing the debugging activity becomes clarified, thereby gaining a more intuitive appeal and generality. This new view may beneficially enhance the cross–fertilization between the diagnosis and debugging fields. Additionally, we operationalize the debugging process via a contradiction removal (or abductive) approach to the problem. The ideas of this work extend in several ways the ones of [4].

A program can be thought of as a theory whose logical consequences engender its actual input/output behaviour. Whereas the program's intended input/output behaviour is postulated by the theory's purported models, i.e. the truths the theory supposedly accounts for.

The object of the debugging exercise is to pinpoint erroneous or missing axioms, from erroneous or missing derived truths, so as to account for each discrepancy between a theory and its models. The classical declarative debugging theory [4] assumes that these models are completely known via an omniscient entity or "oracle". In a more general setting, that our theory accounts for, these models may be only partially known and the lacking information might not be (easily) obtainable. By hypothesizing the incorrect and missing axioms that are compatible with the given information, possible incorrections are diagnosed but not perfected, i.e. sufficient corrections are made to the program but only virtually. This process, of performing sufficing virtual corrections is at the kernel of our method.

From the whole set of possible diagnoses we argue that the set of minimal ones is the expected and intuitive desired result of the debugging process. When the intended interpretation (model) is entirely known, then a unique minimal diagnosis exists which identifies the bugs in the program. Whenever in the presence of incomplete information, the set of minimal diagnoses corresponds to all conceivable minimal sets of bugs; these are exactly the ones compatible with the missing information; in other words, compatible with all the imaginable oracle answer sequences that would complete the information about the intended model. It is guaranteed one of these sets pinpoints bugs that justify the disparities observed between program behaviours and user expectations. Mark that if only one minimal diagnosis is obtained then, at least part of the bugs in the program were sieved, but more may persist.

Diagnostic debugging can be enacted by the contradiction removal methods introduced in [8]. Indeed, a simple program transformation affords a contradiction removal approach to debugging, on the basis of revising the assumptions about predicates' correctness and completeness, just for those predicates and goals that support buggy behaviour. We shall see this transformation has an effect similar to that of turning the program into an artifact specification with equivalent behaviour, whose predicates model the components, each with associated abnormality and fault–mode literals. When faced with disparities between the expected and observed behaviour, the transformed program generates, by using contradiction removal methods, all possible virtual corrections of the original program This is due to a one-to-one mapping between the (minimal) diagnoses of the original program and the (minimal) revisions of the transformed one.

These very same methods can be applied to the updating of knowledge bases with integrity constraints represented as logic programs. By only partially transforming the program the user can express which predicates are liable to retraction of of rules and addition of facts. The iterative contradiction removal algorithm of [8] ensures that the minimal transactions thus obtained do satisfy the integrity constraints.

These ideas on how debugging and fault-finding relate are new, the attractiveness of the approach being its basis on logic programs. In the same vein that one can obtain a general debugger for normal logic programs irrespective of the program domain, one can aim at constructing a general fault-finding procedure, whatever the faulty artifact may be, just as long as it can be modelled by logic programs not confined to being normal logic programs, but including more expressive extensions such as explicit negation.

However we must go a long way until this ultimate goal can be achieved. The current method applies only to a particular class of normal logic programs where the well–founded model [11] and SLDNF–resolution [3] coincide in meaning. The debugging of programs under well–founded semantics with explicit negation [5] is also foreseen, where new and demanding problems are yet to be solved. The loop detection properties of well–founded semantics will allow for a declarative treatment of otherwise endless derivations.

In the subsequent section we clearly state to what programs our method is applicable. The next two sections briefly review, respectively, our work in two-valued contradiction removal and Lloyd's rendering of classical declarative error diagnosis. In section 5 we describe the diagnostic debugging theory and enounce its attending theorems. In section 6 we present the above mentioned program transformation. A debugging algorithm is also produced. Finally, the relationship between debugging and diagnosis is displayed via a simple logical circuit. Proofs are omitted for brevity but can be found in an extended version of this paper.

2 Scope of Application

Given a first order language *Lang*, a (normal) logic program is a set of rules of the form:

$$H \leftarrow B_1, \ldots, B_n, not\ C_1, \ldots, not\ C_m \quad (m \geq 0, n \geq 0)$$

where $H, B_1, \ldots, B_n, C_1, \ldots, C_m$ are atoms in *Lang*. H is an alternative representation of rule $H \leftarrow$. Each logic program rule stands for all its ground instances wrt *Lang*. Given program P we denote by $\mathcal{H}_P$ (or sometimes $\mathcal{H}$) its Herbrand base.

We here examine the problem of declarative error diagnosis, or debugging, for the class of normal logic programs where SLDNF-Resolution can be used to finitely compute *all* the logic consequences of these programs, i.e. SLDNF-Resolution gives the complete meaning of the program. In the sequel we designate this particular class of programs as source programs.

By considering only source programs, we guarantee that the well-founded model (WFM) is total[2] and equivalent to the model computed by SLDNF-Resolution. In [9] Przymusinsky showed that SLDNF-Resolution is sound wrt to well–founded semantics.

Well–founded semantics plays an important rôle in our approach to declarative debugging. Indeed, on the one hand, by considering only source programs, it is guaranteed that the WFM is total and equivalent to the model computed by SLDNF-Resolution. Thus, for these programs is indifferent to consider the WFM or Clark's completion semantics (which characterizes SLDNF).

On the other hand, we intend to further develop this approach, and then deal with the issue of debugging of programs under WFS. By using WFS, loop problems are avoided. Conceivably, we could so debug symptoms in loop–free parts of a normal program under SLDNF, even if some other parts of it have loops.

Last, but not least, the basis of our declarative debugging proposal consists in applying a contradiction removal method we've defined for programs under WFS, to a transformed (object) programs require extending the class of normal logic programs with integrity rules of the form:

$$\bot \leftarrow B_1, \ldots, B_n, not\ C_1, \ldots, not\ C_m \quad (m \geq 0, n \geq 0)$$

where $B_1, \ldots, B_n$, $C_1, \ldots, C_m$ are atoms. Contradictory programs are those where $\bot$ belongs to the program model M_P. Programs with integrity rules are liable to be contradictory.

3 How to Revise your Assumptions

First we present a rephrased review of some results of [8], that will be of use in order to obtain a declarative error diagnosis theory of source programs by virtue of a contradiction removal process exercised over a transformed version of them.

Example 1. Consider $P = \{a \leftarrow not\ b; \bot \leftarrow a\}$. Since we have no rules for b, $not\ b$ is true by Closed World Assumption (CWA) on b. Hence, by the second rule, we have a contradiction. We argue the CWA may not be held of atom b as it leads to contradiction.

The first issue in contradiction removal is to define exactly which negative literals $not\ A$ alone, true by CWA, may be *revised* to false by adding A. Contradiction removal is achieved by adding to the original program the complements[3] of some revisable literals.

Definition 1 (Revisables). The revisables of a program P are a subset of $NoRules(P)$, the set of literals of the form $not\ A$, with no rules for A in P.

---

[2] A well-founded model is total iff all literals are either true or false in it.

[3] The complement of atom L is $not\ L$, and of literal $not\ L$ is L.

Definition 2 (Positive assumptions of a program). A set A of atoms is a set of positive assumptions of program P if for every $a \in A$, $not\ a$ is a revisable.

Definition 3 (Revised program wrt positive assumptions). Let A be a set of positive assumptions of P. The revised P wrt A, $Rev(P, A)$, is the program $P \cup A$.

Definition 4 (Violation of an integrity rule by a program). An integrity rule $\bot \leftarrow B_1, \ldots, B_n, not\ C_1, \ldots, not\ C_m$ is violated by program P iff

$$P \models B_1, \ldots, B_n, not\ C_1, \ldots, not\ C_m.$$

Definition 5 (Revision of a set of integrity rules). A program revision to satisfy a set of integrity rules S in P is a (possibly empty) set of positive assumptions A s.t. $Rev(P, A)$ does not violate any integrity rule in S.

Definition 6 (Revision of a program). A set of positive assumptions A is a **revision** of P iff $Rev(P, A) \not\models \bot$, i.e. A is a revision of the set of all integrity rules of P.

Example 2. Consider contradictory program P:

$$
\begin{array}{ll}
a \leftarrow not\ b,\ not\ c. & \bot \leftarrow a,\ a'. \\
a' \leftarrow not\ d. & \bot \leftarrow b. \\
c \leftarrow e. & \bot \leftarrow d,\ not\ f.
\end{array}
$$

Intuitively literals $not\ b$, $not\ d$ and $not\ e$ are true by CWA, entailing a and a', and thus $\bot$ via violation of the integrity rule $\bot \leftarrow a, a'$.

The revisions of the above program are $\{e\}$, $\{d, f\}$, $\{e, f\}$ and $\{d, e, f\}$. The minimal ones are $\{e\}$ and $\{d, f\}$.

Next we identify which subsets of the revisables support contradiction via violation of some of the integrity rules, in the sense that the revision of elements from each such subsets (i.e. adding the corresponding positive assumptions) definitely eliminates the introduction of $\bot$ via those integrity rules that were being violated. But the revision may introduce fresh contradiction now via distinct, newly violated, integrity rules. If that is the case, then the revision process is just simply iterated. We are interested only in the overall minimal revisions.

To do so, we first define support in the WFM; informally a support set of literal L is the set of nodes in a derivation for L:

Definition 7 (Support set of a literal). Support sets of literal L true in the well–founded model M_P of a program P are denoted by $SS(L)$, always exist, and are obtained as follows:

1. When L is an atom, then for each rule $L \leftarrow \mathcal{B}^4$ in P such that $\mathcal{B}$ is true in M_P, each $SS(L)$ is formed by the union of $\{L\}$ with some $SS(B_i)$ for each $B_i \in \mathcal{B}$. There are as many $SS(L)$ as ways of making true some rule body for L.

---

[4] $H \leftarrow \mathcal{B}$ is alternative rule notation, where set $\mathcal{B}$ is the set of literals in its body.

2. When L is a *not A* literal:
   (a) if no rules exist for A in P then the single support set of L is $\{not\ A\}$.
   (b) if rules for A exist in P then choose from each rule with non-empty body a single literal whose complement is true in M_P. For each such multiple choice there are several $SS(not\ A)$, each formed by the union of $\{not\ A\}$ with an SS of the complement of every literal of a multiple choice. There are as many $SS(not\ A)$ as minimal ways of making false all rule bodies for A.

The revisables on which contradiction rests are those in some support of $\bot$:

Definition 8 (Assumption set of $\bot$ wrt revisables). An assumption set of $\bot$ wrt revisables R is any set $AS(\bot, R) = SS(\bot) \cap R$, of negative literals, for some $SS(\bot)$.

Definition 9 (Hitting set). A hitting set of a collection of sets C is a set formed by the union of one non-empty subset from each $S \in C$. A hitting set is minimal iff no proper subset is a hitting set for C. If $\{\} \in C$ then C has no hitting sets.

We revise programs (resp. minimally) by revising the literals of (resp. minimally) hitting sets:

Definition 10 (Contradiction removal set). A contradiction removal set of P wrt revisables R is a minimal hitting set of the collection of all assumption sets $AS(\bot, R)$ supporting $\bot$.

A program is not revisable if $\bot$ has a support set without revisable literals.

Based on the above, we have devised an iterative algorithm to compute the minimal revisions of a program P wrt to revisables R, and shown its soundness and completeness for finite R. The algorithm is a repeated application of an algorithm to compute contradiction removal sets.[5]

The algorithm starts by finding out the $CRSs$ of the original program plus the empty set of positive assumptions (assuming the original program is revisable, otherwise the algorithm stops after the first step). To each CRS there corresponds a set of positive assumptions obtained by taking the complement of their elements. The algorithm then adds, non-deterministically and one at a time, each of these sets of assumptions to the original program. One of three cases occurs: (1) the program thus obtained is non-contradictory and we are in the presence of one minimal revising set of assumptions; (2) the new program is contradictory and non-revisable (and this fact is recorded by the algorithm to prune away other contradictory programs obtained by it); (3) the new program

---

[5] [10] gives an "algorithm" for computing minimal diagnosis, called DIAGNOSE (with a bug corrected in [2]). DIAGNOSE can be used to compute $CRSs$, needing only the redefinition of the function Tp refered there. Our Tp can be built from a top-down derivation procedure adapted from [7, 6].

is contradictory but revisable, and this very same algorithm is iterated until we finitely attain one of the two other cases. For the formal description see Alg. 1.

The sets of assumptions employed to obtain the revised non-contradictory programs are the minimal revisions of the original program. The algorithm can terminate after executing only one step when the program is either non-contradictory, or contradictory but non-revisable. It can be shown this algorithm is (at least) NP-complete [1].

Algorithm 1 (Minimal revisions of a program).

Input: A possibly contradictory program P and a set R of revisables.

$$AS_0 := \{\{\}\}$$
$$Cs := \{\}$$
$$i := 0$$
repeat
   $AS_{i+1} := \{\}$
   for each $A \in AS_i$
    if $\neg \exists C \in Cs : C \subseteq A$
     if $Rev(P, A) \models \bot$
      if $Rev(P, A)$ is revisable
       for each $CRS_j(R)$ of $P \cup A$
        Let $NAs := A \cup not\, CRS_j(R)$
        $AS_{i+1} := AS_{i+1} \cup \{NAs\}$
       endfor
      else
       $Cs := MinimalSetsOf(Cs \cup \{A\})$
      endif
     else
      $AS_{i+1} := AS_{i+1} \cup \{A\}$
     endif
    endif
   endfor
   $AS_{i+1} := MinimalSetsOf(AS_{i+1})$
   $i := i + 1$
until $AS_i = AS_{i-1}$.

Output: AS_i, the collection of all minimal revisions of P wrt R.

Example 2 (cont). The integrity rule $\bot \leftarrow a, a'$ is violated. By adding to P any of the sets of assumptions $\{b\}$, $\{d\}$, or $\{e\}$, this rule becomes satisfied.

Program $Rev(P, \{e\})$ is non-contradictory: thus $\{e\}$ is a revision of P. But $Rev(P, \{b\})$ and $Rev(P, \{d\})$ still entail $\bot$, respectively violating integrity rules $\bot \leftarrow b$ and $\bot \leftarrow d, not\, f$. In $Rev(P, \{b\})$ integrity rule $\bot \leftarrow b$ cannot be satisfied:

$\{b\}$ is not a revision. In $Rev(P, \{d\})$ integrity rule can be satisfied by adding to $\{d\}$ the assumption f, to obtain also the revision $\{d, f\}$ (cf. Fig. 1).

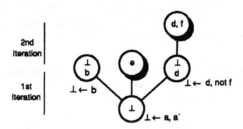

Fig. 1. Revision of example 2.

In [8] we apply these techniques to solve a rather general class of diagnosis problems.

4 Declarative Error Diagnosis

Next we present the classical theory of declarative error diagnosis, following mainly [4], in order to proceed to a different view of the issue.

It would be desireable that a program gave all and only the correct answers to a user's queries. Usually a program contains some bugs that must be corrected before it can produce the required behaviour.

Let the meaning of a logic program P be given by the normal Herbrand models for $comp(P)$, Clark's completion of P. Let the ultimate goal of a program be for its meaning to respect the user's intended interpretation of the program.

Definition 11 (Intended interpretation [4]). Let P be a program. An intended interpretation for P is a normal Herbrand interpretation for $comp(P)$.

Definition 12 (Program correct wrt intended interpretation [4]).
A logic program P is correct wrt to an intended interpretation I_M iff I_M is a model for $comp(P)$.

Errors in a terminating logic program manifest themselves through two kinds of symptoms (we deliberately ignore here the question of loop detection).

Definition 13 (Symptoms). Let P be a logic program, I_M its intended interpretation, and A an atom in the Herbrand base of P.

- if $P \vdash_{SLDNF} A$ and $A \notin I_M$ then A is a *wrong solution* for P wrt I_M.

– if $P \not\vdash_{SLDNF} A$ and $A \in I_M$ then A is a *missing solution* for P wrt I_M.

Of course, if there is a missing or a wrong solution then the program is not correct wrt its intended interpretation, and therefore there exists in it some bug requiring correction. In [4] two kinds of errors are identified: uncovered atoms and incorrect clause instances. As we deal with ground programs only, we prefer to designate as incorrect rules the latter type of error.

Definition 14 (Uncovered atom). Let P be a program and I_M its intended interpretation. An atom A is an uncovered atom for P wrt I_M iff $A \in I_M$ but for no rule $A \leftarrow W$ in P, $I_M \models W$.

Definition 15 (Incorrect rule). Let P be a program and I_M its intended interpretation. A rule $A \leftarrow W$ is incorrect for P wrt I_M iff $A \notin I_M$ and $I_M \models W$.

Theorem 1 (Two types of bug only [4]). *Let P be a program and I_M its intended interpretation. P is incorrect wrt I_M iff there is an uncovered atom for P wrt to I_M or there is an incorrect rule for P wrt to I_M.*

Thus, if there is a missing or a wrong solution there is, at least, an uncovered atom or an incorrect rule for P.

Example 3. Let P be the (source) program with model $\{not\ a, b, not\ c\}$:

$$a \leftarrow not\ b. \quad b \leftarrow not\ c.$$

Suppose the intended interpretation of P is $I_M = \{not\ a, not\ b, c\}$, i.e. b is a wrong solution, and c a missing solution for P wrt I_M. The reader can check, c is an uncovered atom for P wrt I_M, and $a \leftarrow not\ b$ is an incorrect rule for P wrt I_M.

5   What is Diagnostic Debugging?

We now know, from the previous section (cf. theorem 1), that if there is a missing or a wrong solution then there is, at least, an uncovered atom or an incorrect rule for P. In classical declarative error diagnosis the complete intended interpretation is always known from the start. Next we characterize the situation where only partial knowledge of the intended interpretation is available but, if possible or wanted, extra information can be obtained. To formalise this debugging activity we introduce two entities: the user and the oracle.

Definition 16 (User and Oracle). Let P be a source program and I_M the intended interpretation for P. The user is identified with the limited knowledge of the intended model that he has, i.e. a set $U \subseteq I_M$. The oracle is an entity that knows everything, that is, knows the whole intended interpretation I_M.

By definition, the user and the oracle share some knowledge and the user is not allowed to make mistakes nor the oracle to lie. The user has a diagnosis problem and poses the queries and the oracle helps the user: it knows the answers to all possible questions. The user may coincide with the oracle as a special case.

Our approach is mainly motivated by the following obvious theorem: if the incorrect rules of a program[6] are removed, and a fact A for each uncovered atom A is added to the program, then the model of the new transformed program is the intended interpretation of the original one.

As justified in section 2, our approach uses the well–founded semantics to identify the model of programs.

Theorem 2. *Let P be a source program and I_M its intended interpretation. If $WFM(P) \neq I_M$, and*

$$Unc = \{ \quad A \quad : \ A \text{ is an uncovered atom for } P \text{ wrt } I_M\}$$
$$InR = \{A \leftarrow B: \ A \leftarrow B \text{ is incorrect for } P \text{ wrt } I_M\}$$

then $WFM((P - InR) \cup Unc) = I_M$.

Example 4. Consider the source program P

$$a \leftarrow not\ b. \quad b \leftarrow not\ c.$$

The $WFM(P)$ is $\{not\ a, b, not\ c\}$. If $I_M = \{not\ a, not\ b, c\}$ is the intended interpretation, then c is an uncovered atom for P wrt I_M, and $a \leftarrow not\ b$ is an incorrect rule for P wrt I_M. The WFM of the new program,

$$b \leftarrow not\ c. \quad c.$$

obtained by applying the transformation above, is I_M.

The user may have only limited knowledge of the intended interpretation.

Definition 17 (Diagnosis). Let P be a source program, U a set of literals of the language of P, and D the pair $\langle Unc, InR \rangle$ where $Unc \subseteq \mathcal{H}_P$, $InR \subseteq P$.
D is a diagnosis for U wrt P iff

$$U \subseteq WFM((P - InR) \cup Unc).$$

Example 4 (cont). The diagnoses for $U = \{not\ a, c\}$ wrt P are:

$$
\begin{array}{llll}
D_1 = \langle\{b,c\}, & \{\} & \rangle & D_5 = \langle\{c\}, \quad \{a \leftarrow not\ b\} \quad \rangle \\
D_2 = \langle\{b,c\}, & \{a \leftarrow not\ b\} & \rangle & D_6 = \langle\{c\},\{a \leftarrow not\ b;\ b \leftarrow not\ c\}\rangle \\
D_3 = \langle\{b,c\}, & \{b \leftarrow not\ c\} & \rangle & \\
D_4 = \langle\{b,c\},\{a \leftarrow not\ b;\ b \leftarrow not\ c\}\rangle &
\end{array}
$$

Each one of these diagnoses can be viewed as a virtual correction of the program. For example, D_1 can be viewed as stating that if the program is corrected so

---

[6] In this section program means source program, unless stated otherwise.

that b and c become true, by adding them as facts say, then the literals in U also become true. Another possibility is to set c true and correct the first rule of the original program. This possibility is reflected by D_5.

However some of these diagnoses are redundant: for instance in D_6 there is no reason to consider the second rule wrong; doing so is redundant.

This is even more serious in the case of D_3. There the atom b is considered uncovered and all rules for b are considered wrong.

Definition 18 (Minimal Diagnosis). Let P be a source program and U a set of literals. Given two diagnosis $D_1 = \langle Unc_1, InR_1 \rangle$ and $D_2 = \langle Unc_2, InR_2 \rangle$ for U wrt P we say that $D_1 \preceq D_2$ iff $Unc_1 \cup InR_1 \subseteq Unc_2 \cup InR_2$.

D is a minimal diagnosis for U wrt P iff there is no diagnosis D_1 for U wrt P such that $D_1 \preceq D$. $\langle \{\}, \{\} \rangle$ is called the empty diagnosis.

Example 4 (cont). The minimal diagnoses for $U = \{not\ a, c\}$ wrt P are D_1 and D_5 above.

Obviously, if the subset of the intended interpretation given by the user is already a consequence of the program, we expect empty to be the only minimal diagnosis: i.e. based on that information no bug is found:

Theorem 3. *Let P be a source program, and U a set of literals. Then $U \subseteq WFM(P)$ iff the only minimal diagnosis for U wrt P is empty.*

A property of source programs is that if the set U of user provided literals is the complete intended interpretation (the case when the user knowledge coincides with oracle's), a unique minimal diagnosis exists. In this case the minimal diagnosis uniquely identifies all the errors in the program and provides one correction to all the bugs.

Theorem 4. *Let P be a source program and I_M its intended interpretation. Then $D = \langle Unc, InR \rangle$, where*

$$Unc = \{ \quad A \quad : A \text{ is an uncovered atom for } P \text{ wrt } I_M \}$$
$$InR = \{ A \leftarrow B : A \leftarrow B \text{ is incorrect for } P \text{ wrt } I_M \}$$

is the unique minimal diagnosis for I_M wrt P.

The next lemma helps us show important properties of minimal diagnosis:

Lemma 5. *Let P be a source program, and U_1 and U_2 sets of literals. If $U_1 \subseteq U_2$ and if there are minimal diagnosis for U_1 and U_2 wrt P then there is a minimal diagnosis for U_1 wrt P contained in a minimal diagnosis for U_2 wrt P.*

Let us suppose the set U provided by the user is a proper subset of the intended interpretation. Then it is expectable that the errors are not imediately detected, in the sense that several minimal diagnoses may exist. The next theorem guarantees that at least one of the minimal diagnoses finds an error of the program.

Theorem 6. *Let P be a source program, I_M its intended interpretation, and U a set of literals. If $U \subseteq I_M$ and if there are minimal diagnosis for U wrt P then there is a minimal diagnosis $\langle Unc, InR \rangle$ for U wrt P such that for every $A \in Unc$, A is an uncovered atom for P wrt I_M, and for every rule $A \leftarrow B \in InR$, $A \leftarrow B$ is incorrect for P wrt I_M.*

As a special case, even giving the complete intended interpretation, if one single minimal diagnosis exists then it identifies at least one error.

Corollary 7. *Let P be a source program, I_M its intended interpretation, and U a set of literals. If there is a unique minimal diagnosis $\langle Unc, InR \rangle$ for U wrt P then for every $A \in Unc$, A is an uncovered atom for P wrt I_M, and for every rule $A \leftarrow B \in InR$, $A \leftarrow B$ is incorrect for P wrt I_M.*

In a process of debugging, when several minimal diagnoses exists, queries should be posed to the oracle in order to enlarge the subset of the intended interpretation provided, and thus refine the diagnoses. Such a process must be iterated until a single minimal diagnosis is found. This eventually happens, albeit when the whole intended interpretation is given (cf. theorem 4).

Example 4 (cont). As mentioned above, minimal diagnoses for $U = \{not\ a, c\}$ wrt P are $D_1 = \langle \{b, c\}, \{\} \rangle$ and $D_5 = \langle \{c\}, \{a \leftarrow not\ b\} \rangle$.

By theorem 6, at least one of these diagnoses contains errors. In D_1, b and c are uncovered. Thus, if this is the error, not only literals in U are true but also b. In D_5, c is uncovered and rule $a \leftarrow not\ b$ is incorrect. Thus, if this is the error, b is false.

By asking about the truthfulness of b one can, in fact, identify the error: e.g. should the answer to such query be *yes* the set U is augmented with b and the only minimal diagnosis is D_1; should the answer be *no* U is augmented with *not b* and the only minimal diagnosis is D_5.

The issue of identifying disambiguating oracle queries is dealt with in the next section.

In all the results above we have assumed the existence of at least one minimal diagnosis. This is guaranteed because:

Theorem 8. *Let P be a source program, I_M its intended interpretation, and U a finite set of literals. If $U \subseteq I_M$ and $U \not\subseteq WFM(P)$ then there is a non-empty minimal diagnosis $\langle Unc, InR \rangle$ for U wrt P such that, for every $A \in Unc$, A is an uncovered atom for P wrt I_M, and for every rule $A \leftarrow B \in InR$, $A \leftarrow B$ is incorrect for P wrt I_M.*

6 Diagnosis as Revision of Program Assumptions

In this section we show that minimal diagnosis are minimal revisions of a simple transformed program obtained from the original source one. Let's start with the program transformation and some results regarding it.

Definition 19. The transformation Υ that maps a source program P into a source program P' is obtained by applying to P the following two operations:

- Add to the body of each rule $H \leftarrow B_1, \ldots, B_n, \text{not } C_1, \ldots, \text{not } C_m$ in P the literal $\text{not incorrect}(H \leftarrow B_1, \ldots, B_n, \text{not } C_1, \ldots, \text{not } C_m)$.
- Add the rule $p(X_1, X_2, \ldots, X_n) \leftarrow \text{uncovered}(p(X_1, X_2, \ldots, X_n))$ for each predicate p with arity n in the language of P.

It is assumed predicate symbols *incorrect* and *uncovered* don't belong to the language of P.

It can be easily shown that the above transformation preserves the truths of P: the literals $\text{not incorrect}(\ldots)$ and $\text{uncovered}(\ldots)$ are, respectively, true and false in the transformed program. The next theorem captures this intuitive result.

Theorem 9. *Let P be a source program. If L is a literal with predicate symbol distinct from incorrect and uncovered then $L \in WFM(P)$ iff $L \in WFM(\Upsilon(P))$.*

Example 4 (cont). By applying transformation Υ to P we get

$$a \leftarrow \text{not } b, \text{not incorrect}(a \leftarrow \text{not } b) \; . \quad a \leftarrow \text{uncovered}(a).$$
$$b \leftarrow \text{not } c, \text{not incorrect}(b \leftarrow \text{not } c) \; . \quad b \leftarrow \text{uncovered}(b).$$
$$c \leftarrow \text{uncovered}(c).$$

The reader can check that the WFM of $\Upsilon(P)$ is

$$\{\text{not } a, b, \text{not } c, \text{not uncovered}(a), \text{not uncovered}(b), \text{not uncovered}(c),$$
$$\text{not incorrect}(a \leftarrow \text{not } b), \text{not incorrect}(b \leftarrow \text{not } c) \quad \}$$

A user can employ this transformed program in the same way he did with the original source program, with no change in program behaviour. If he detects an abnormal behaviour of the program, in order to debug the program he then just explicitly states what answers he expects:

Definition 20 (Debugging transformation). Let P be a source program and U a set of user provided literals. The debugging transformation $\Upsilon_{debug}(P, U)$ converts the source program P into an object program P'. P' is obtained by adding to $\Upsilon(P)$ the integrity rules $\bot \leftarrow \text{not } a$ for each atom $a \in U$, and $\bot \leftarrow a$ for each literal $\text{not } a \in U$.

Our main result is the following theorem, which links minimal diagnosis for a given set of literals wrt to a source program with minimal revisions of the object program obtained by applying the debugging transformation.

Theorem 10. *Let P be a source program and U a set of literals from the language of P. The pair $\langle Unc, InR \rangle$ is a diagnosis for U wrt P iff*

$$\{\text{uncovered}(A) : A \in Unc\} \cup \{\text{incorrect}(A \leftarrow B) : A \leftarrow B \in InR\}$$

is a revision of $\Upsilon_{debug}(P, U)$, where the revisables are all the not incorrect$(\ldots)$ and not uncovered$(\ldots)$ literals.

The proof is trivial and it is based on the facts that adding a positive assumption *incorrect* has an effect similar to removing the rule from the program, and adding a positive assumption *uncovered*(A) makes A true in the revised program. The integrity rules in $\Upsilon_{debug}(P, U)$ guarantee that the literals in U are "explained".

For finite U, algorithm 1 can be used to compute the minimal diagnosis for the buggy source program.

Theorem 11 (Correctness). *Let P be a source program, I_M its intended interpretation, and U a finite set of literals. Algorithm 1 is sound and complete wrt the minimal revisions of $\Upsilon_{debug}(P, U)$, using as revisables all the not incorrect($_-$) and not uncovered($_-$) literals.*

Corollary 12. *Let P be a source program, I_M its intended interpretation, and U a finite set of literals. If $U \subseteq I_M$ and $U \not\subseteq WFM(P)$ then there is a non-empty minimal revision R of $\Upsilon_{debug}(P, U)$, using as revisables all the not incorrect($_-$) and not uncovered($_-$) literals, such that for every uncovered(A) $\in R$, A is an uncovered atom for P wrt I_M, and for every incorrect($A \leftarrow B$) $\in R$, $A \leftarrow B$ is incorrect for P wrt I_M.*

From all minimal revisions a set of questions of the form "What is the truth value of $< AN\ ATOM >$ in the intended interpretation ?" can be compiled. The oracle answers to these questions identify the errors in the program.

Definition 21 (Disambiguating queries). Let $D = \langle Unc, InR \rangle$ be a diagnosis for finite set of literals U wrt to the source program P, I_M its intended interpretation, and let (the set of atoms)

$$Query = (Unc \cup Atom_{InR}) - U$$

where $Atom_{InR}$ is the set of all atoms appearing in rules of InR.

The set of disambiguating queries of D is:

$$\{What\ is\ the\ truth\ value\ of\ A\ in\ I_M?\ |\ A \in Query\}$$

The set of disambiguating queries of a set of diagnoses is the union of that for each diagnosis.

Now the answers to the disambiguating questions to the set of all diagnoses, given by the oracle, can be added to the current knowledge of the user, i.e. atoms answered true are added to U, and for atoms answered false their complements are instead. The minimal diagnoses of the debugging transformation with the new set U are then computed and finer information about the errors is produced. This process of generating minimal diagnoses, and of answering the disambiguating queries posed by these diagnoses can be iterated until only one final minimal diagnosis is obtained:

Algorithm 2 (Debugging of a source program).

1. Transformation $\Upsilon(P)$ is applied to the program.
2. The user detects the symptoms and their respective integrity rules are inserted.
3. The minimal diagnosis are computed. If there is only one, one error or more are found and reported. Stop[7].
4. The disambiguating queries are generated and the oracle consulted.
5. Its answers are added in the form of integrity rules.
6. Goto 3.

Example 4 (cont). After applying Υ to P the user detects that b is a wrong solution. He causes the integrity rule $\bot \leftarrow b$ be added to $\Upsilon(P)$ and provokes a program revision to compute the possible explanations of this bug. He obtains two minimal revisions: $\{uncovered(c)\}$ and $\{incorrect(b \leftarrow not\ c)\}$.

Now, if desired, the oracle is questioned:

– What is the truth value of c in the intended interpretation ? Answer: true.

Then the user (or the oracle...) adds to the program the integrity rule $\bot \leftarrow not\ c$ and revises the program. The unique minimal revision is $\{uncovered(c)\}$ and the bug is found.

The user now detects that solution a is wrong. Then he adds the integrity rule $\bot \leftarrow a$ too and obtains the only minimal revision, that detects all the errors.

$$\{incorrect(a \leftarrow not\ b), uncovered(c)\}$$

7 Debugging via Fault Finding and vice–versa

Here we illustrate with an example the close relationship between debugging and fault finding.

Example 5. Consider the circuit of figure 2.

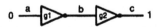

Fig. 2. A two inverters circuit.

We model them with the program:

---
[7] We conjecture that termination occurs, in the worst-case, after the first time the oracle is consulted, i.e. the algorithm stops either the first or second time it executes this step.

$$\begin{array}{ll}
\text{inv}(G,I,1) \leftarrow \text{node}(I,0),\ \text{not ab}(G). & 1 \\
\text{inv}(G,I,0) \leftarrow \text{node}(I,1),\ \text{not ab}(G). & 2 \\
\text{inv}(G,\_,0) \leftarrow \text{node}(I,\_),\ \text{fault\_mode}(G,s0). & 3 \\
\text{inv}(G,\_,1) \leftarrow \text{node}(I,\_),\ \text{fault\_mode}(G,s1). & 4 \\
\text{node}(b,B) \leftarrow \text{inv}(\ g1,\ a,\ B\ ). & 6 \\
\text{node}(c,C) \leftarrow \text{inv}(\ g2,\ b,\ C\ ). & 7 \\
\perp \quad\quad \leftarrow \text{fault\_mode}(\ G,\ s0\ ),\ \text{fault\_mode}(\ G,\ s1\ ). & 8 \\
\text{node}(a,0). & 9 \\
\perp \quad\quad \leftarrow \text{node}(c,0). & 10 \\
\perp \quad\quad \leftarrow \text{not node}(c,1). & 11
\end{array}$$

Rules 1-2 model normal inverter behaviour. Rules 6-7 specify the circuit topology. Rules 3-4 model two fault modes: one expresses the output is stuck at 0, and the other that it is stuck at 1, whatever the input may be (although it must exist). According to rule 8 the two fault modes are mutually exclusive. Rule 9 establishes the input as 0. Rule 11 specifies the observed output is 1, and that it must be explained (i.e. proved) on pain of contradiction. Rule 10 specifies that the expected output 0 does not obtain, and so is not to be proven. Let the revisables be *ab* and *fault_mode*.

Explanation is to be provided by finding the revisions of revisables that added to the program avoid contradiction. Indeed, contradiction ensues if all CWAs are assumed.[8]

The following expected minimal revisions are produced by algorithm 1:

$$\{ab(g1),\ fault\_mode(g1, s0)\}\ \{ab(g2),\ fault\_mode(g2, s1)\}$$

Consider next that we make the fault model only partial by, withdrawing rule 4. So that we can still explain all observations, we "complete" the fault model by introducing rule 5 below, which expresses that in the presence of input to the inverter, and if the value to be explained is not equal to 0 (since that is explained by rule 3), then there is a missing fault mode for value V. Of course, *missing* has to be considered a revisable too.

$$\begin{array}{ll}
\text{inv}(G,\_,V) \leftarrow \text{node}(I,\_),\ \text{not equal}(V,0),\ \text{missing}(G,V). & 5 \\
\text{equal}(V,V). & 12
\end{array}$$

Now the following expected minimal revisions are produced:

$$\{ab(g1),\ fault\_mode(g1, s0)\}\ \{ab(g2),\ missing(g2, s1)\}$$

The above fault model "completion" is a general technique for explaining all observations reporting the missing fault modes. In fact, we are simply debugging the fault model according to the methods above: we've added a rule

---

[8] Comments: In rules 3-4, not ab(G) is absent (but could be added) because we presuppose, for simplicity, that the revision of a *fault_mode* to true implicitly signals an abnormality. Rule 8 is not strictly necessary since fault model rules 3-4 already make the fault modes incompatible.

that detects and provides desired solutions not found by the normal rules, just as in debugging. But also solutions not explained by other fault rules: hence the not equal(V,0) condition. The debugging equivalent of the latter would be adding a rule to "explain" that a bug (i.e. fault mode) has already been detected (though not corrected). Furthermore, the reason $node(I, \_)$ is included in 5 is that there is a missing fault mode only if the inverter actually receives input. The analogous situation in debugging would be that of requiring that some predicate must actually ensure some predication about goals for it (e.g. type checking) before it is deemed incomplete.

The analogy with debugging allows us to debug artifact specifications in fault finding. Indeed, it suffices to employ the techniques of the previous section. By adding $not\ incorrect(\ldots, G)$ instead of $not\ ab(G)$ in rules, revisions will now inform us of which rules possibly produce wrong solutions that would explain bugs. Of course, we now need to add $not\ incorrect(\ldots, G)$ to all other rules, but during diagnosis they will not interfere if we restrict the revisables to just those for the original rules. With regard to uncovered atoms, we've seen in the previous paragraph that it would be enough to add an extra rule for each predicate.

References

1. M. R. Garey and D. S. Johnson. *Computers and Intractability.* Freeman and Co., 1979.
2. R. Greiner, B. A. Smith, and R. W. Wilkerson. A correction to the algorithm in reiter's theory of diagnosis. *Artificial Intelligence*, 41:79–88, 1989.
3. J. W. Lloyd. *Foundations of Logic Programming.* Symbolic Computation. Springer–Verlag, 1984.
4. J. W. Lloyd. Declarative error diagnosis. *New Generation Computing*, 5(2):133–154, 1987.
5. L. M. Pereira and J. J. Alferes. Well founded semantics for logic programs with explicit negation. In B. Neumann, editor, *Proc. ECAI'92*, pages 102–106. John Wiley & Sons, 1992.
6. L. M. Pereira, J. J. Alferes, and C. Damásio. The sidetracking principle applied to well founded semantics. In *Proc. Simpósio Brasileiro de Inteligência Artificial SBIA'92*, pages 229–242, 1992.
7. L. M. Pereira, J.N. Aparício, and J. J. Alferes. Derivation procedures for extended stable models. In *Proc. IJCAI-91.* Morgan Kaufmann, 1991.
8. L. M. Pereira, C. Damásio, and J. J. Alferes. Diagnosis and debugging as contradiction removal. In L. M. Pereira and A. Nerode, editors, *2nd Int. Ws. on Logic Programming and NonMonotonic Reasoning.* MIT Press, 1993.
9. T. Przymusinski. Every logic program has a natural stratification and an iterated fixed point model. In *8th Symp. on Principles of Database Systems.* ACM SIGACT-SIGMOD, 1989.
10. R. Reiter. A theory of diagnosis from first principles. *Artificial Intelligence*, 32:57–96, 1987.
11. A. Van Gelder, K. A. Ross, and J. S. Schlipf. The well-founded semantics for general logic programs. *Jouranel of ACM*, pages 221–230, 1990.

Debugging Logic Programs Using Specifications

Yuh-jeng Lee[1]* and Nachum Dershowitz[2]**

[1] Computer Science Department, Naval Postgraduate School
Monterey, CA 93943, U.S.A.
[2] Department of Computer Science, University of Illinois
1304 W. Springfield Ave., Urbana, IL 61801, U.S.A.

Abstract. We show how executable specifications may be used to generate test cases for bug discovery, locate bugs when test data cause a program to fail, and guide deductive and inductive bug correction.

1 Introduction

Logic programming has gained in popularity in recent years. This style of programming, using Horn clauses to express procedural information, allows one to reason easily about the effects of executing program statements.

We present a methodology for reasoning about the relationship between logic programs and their specifications, to help debug erroneous programs. To allow for debugging, the specifications must describe the relationships between the values of input and output variables. Since Horn clauses are a powerful subset of first-order logic, a program's specifications can oftentimes be written in Prolog itself and executed by the Prolog interpreter or compiler directly. (Whereas specifications are intended to emphasize clarity and simplicity, in implementing programs, efficiency is a major consideration.)

The debugger follows the pattern of Shapiro's ([12]). We focus on the use of executable specifications to generate test cases for bug discovery, locate bugs when test data cause a program to fail, and guide deductive and inductive bug correction ([3]). We also ask that specifications provide information on the well-founded ordering of input arguments for recursive procedures. (A well-founded ordering $\succ$ is a transitive and irreflexive binary relation on elements of a set S such that the S has no infinite descending sequences.) The ordering specifies, for each recursive call, which arguments should be decreasing. This is used for detecting looping.

Programs, for our purposes, are presumed to obey their Horn clause declarative semantics, i.e., extra-logical features, such as cuts, clause order, and subgoal order, may affect efficiency and termination, but not correctness. We also presume that specifications faithfully reflect the intended requirements of a program. To obtain the desired effect, it is sometimes necessary to use impure features, i.e., non-logical control structures, of Prolog.

---

* Research supported in part by the U. S. Naval Postgraduate School and the U. S. Army Artificial Intelligence Center.
** Research supported in part by a Meyerhoff Visiting Professorship at the Weizmann Institute of Science and by the U. S. National Science Foundation under Grants CCR-90-07195 and CCR-90-24271.

More expressive languages, like EQLOG ([5]) or RITE ([6]), which use equational Horn clauses, may be even more suited to the kind of program manipulations advocated here.

Other work on declarative debugging includes [4, 10, 7, 2, 11, 1, 8, 9].

2   Using Executable Specifications

Executable specifications of a program not only serve to check the output, but also generate useful test cases for that program, provided that axioms for primitive predicates are supplied. The information contained in specifications regarding the expected output behavior is indispensable for checking the correctness of the results of program execution, while test cases help reveal instances of incorrect output.

We assume that the properties of each procedure in the program have been described in the program's specifications, which detail the relationships between program variables. In other words, they define all legal input/output pairs for each procedure. To check for termination, we also need a well-founded ordering under which successive input values to recursive procedures are intended to form a descending sequence. Any unspecified procedures are presumed correct and terminating.

A program is *(partially) correct* with respect to its specification if each clause of the program can be proved from the specifications and given domain facts by first-order reasoning. If we can find an atomic formula that follows logically from the program (and domain facts), but which cannot be proved from the specifications (and domain facts), then we have shown that the program is *incorrect* with respect to the given specifications.

A program is *complete* with respect to its specifications if each clause of the specification follows from the program and domain facts. If we can find an atomic formula that follows from the specifications (and domain facts) which can not result from executing the program, then that formula is "uncovered" and the program is *incomplete*.

If during a computation, the program generates an infinite sequence of procedure calls, it is *nonterminating*. Otherwise, it is said to *terminate*.

We test for correctness and completeness by checking a program's computation results against its specifications, for a sequence of test inputs. Of course, finding no instances of incorrectness or incompleteness does not prove correctness and completeness. *Termination* is tested for by routines that compare the inputs with respect to the specified well-founded ordering whenever a procedure is invoked.

To generate test cases for a given goal, we first run the specifications of that goal to obtain a pair consisting of an input along with its expected output. We then use only the input value to run the goal on the program to be debugged. If the execution fails, goes into a loop, or returns an incorrect output value, then this test case has shown us that there is at least one bug in the program. In other words, a test case consisting of a correct input/output pair can be used to discover bugs should they cause the program to fail to compute the correct answer. If one of the predicates in the specifications of a program is defined in the form of a "generator", then we can generate alternate test cases by utilizing Prolog's built-in backtracking facility.

3   Bug Location

When a Prolog program does not compute correct results, it may be that the program contains incorrect clauses, is incomplete in defining certain relationships between program variables, or has an infinite procedure invocation sequence.

We constructed a meta-interpreter which executes programs, diagnoses errors according to the specifications of programs, and locates and reports bugs. Figure 1 summarizes the algorithm in pseudo-Prolog code.

```
execute( (Goal1, Goal2), Message ) :-
    execute( Goal1, Msg_Goal1 ),
    if Msg_Goal1 = ok( Goal1 )
        then execute( Goal2, Message )
        else Message = Msg_Goal1
execute( Goal, ok(Goal) ) :-
    system( Goal ), call( Goal )
execute( Goal, looping(Goal) ) :-
    not decreasing( Goal )
execute( Goal, Message ) :-
    not system( Goal ),
    clause( Goal, Subgoals ),
    execute( Subgoals, Msg_Subgoal ),
    if Msg_Subgoal = ok( Subgoals )
        then if spec( Goal )
                then Message = ok( Goal )
                else Message = incorrect( (Goal :- Subgoals) )
        else Message = Msg_Subgoal
execute( Goal, uncovered(Goal) ) :-
    spec( Goal )
```

Fig. 1. Algorithm for Automated Bug Location

The procedure *execute(Goal, Message)* serves two functions: goal reduction and bug location. The first clause deals with conjunctive goals. If the first conjunct executes correctly, the remaining conjuncts will be tried in order; otherwise, it just returns the error found to the top level. The second clause executes built-in primitives directly. The next three clauses detect bugs of nontermination, incorrect clauses, and uncovered goals, respectively.

The procedure first checks if the input variables violate the well-founded ordering defined in the specification of the procedure that covers the goal. To accomplish this, the parameters to each recursive call are recorded (asserted) during computation. If such is the case, we have an instance of a looping goal.

If the input cannot cause an infinite sequence of procedure calls, the interpreter will proceed to check if the program can actually complete the computation on the given input. It first finds a clause whose head can be unified with *Goal* and then recursively executes the subgoals in the body of that clause. If a bug is found in the body of a clause, it will be returned to the top level (for subsequent correction). If all the subgoals complete successfully, then all the output variables in *Goal* will be instantiated. The interpreter then checks if the output value is correct with respect to the specifications of *Goal*. If not, then we have found an incorrect clause.

If the goal fails because there is no clause in the program that covers it for the given input data (i.e., no unifying clause or a subgoal fails in every unifying clause), then, provided *Goal* is satisfiable according to the specifications, the program must be incomplete and we have an instance of an uncovered goal.

4 Bug Correction

Bug correction requires reasoning with knowledge of the domain and intended algorithm, the semantics of the programming language and the input/output specifications. Some automatic debugging systems use information stored in their system's knowledge base for bug correction by matching (maybe partially) and replacing the buggy program with the established code fragments. In our case, we have only the knowledge contained in the specifications of the individual procedures, plus some heuristics that suggest possible causes of errors. Deductive and inductive corrective measures are employed.

If a clause $p(x, y) :- p_1, ..., p_n$ returns an incorrect output y' on input x', we execute the specification of p with goal $p(x', Y)$, to get a correct output y''. If $p(x', y'')$ is covered by another clause in the program, then the incorrect clause should presumably have failed for this input. We, therefore, attempt to find extra conditions to prevent computation for input x', by trying to construct a proof that the right hand side of the clause implies the left hand side. If the proof fails because of some missing conditions, we add them as subgoals to the clause. (In the worst case, we can always add the subgoal **fail** to the clause. Although this might be too strong a fix and might result in some other goals becoming uncovered, we will see below how to deal with any uncovered goals.)

If the atom $p(x', y'')$ is only covered by the incorrect clause, then we proceed to add conditions that preclude computation of the wrong answer y', with input x', as above, or an inductive approach may be taken. If $p(x', y'')$ is not covered by any clause, then the fix proceeds in different directions, depending on whether $p(x', y'')$ can be unified with the head of the incorrect clause. If the head does unify, but some of the subgoals fail for y'', then we presume that the incorrect clause should cover the goal $p(x', y)$ and compute y'' instead of y'. In this case, we can combine fixes for the uncovered goal, $p(x', y'')$, and the incorrect clause that computes the erroneous solution $p(x', y')$. We check, for $p(x', y'')$ (i.e., under the current input and *correct* output), which of the subgoals in the clause fail with the output constrained to be y''. After identifying any such incorrect subgoals, we try to fix them by either applying a heuristic rule or an inductive method. We rearrange, replace, delete, or add new variables within subgoals until the original incorrect clause computes $p(x', y'')$ correctly, as in the refinement method of [12].

The last possibility is that $p(x', y'')$ cannot be unified with the head of the incorrect clause, nor is it covered by other clauses in the program. In this case, we assume that the incorrect clause we have identified should cover this goal. Accordingly, the only way to correct the bug is to first fix (i.e., weaken) the clause head so that it is unifiable with $p(x', y'')$. The methods described above can then be used to fix any incorrect subgoals.

To find subgoals that correct a faulty clause, we modify the approach of [13]. Our (incomplete) prover employs the following rules, in which G (possibly with a subscript) represents a goal, H (possibly with a subscript), an hypothesis, $\wedge$, $\vee$, and $\neg$ stand for logical "and", "or", and "not", respectively, $H \rightarrow G$" for "if H then G", and "$A \Leftarrow B$" for "to prove A, it is sufficient to prove B".

Rule 1. $H \rightarrow G_1 \wedge G_2 \;\; \Leftarrow \;\; (H \rightarrow G_1) \wedge (H \rightarrow G_2)$
Rule 2. $H \rightarrow G_1 \vee G_2 \;\; \Leftarrow \;\; (H \rightarrow G_1) \vee (H \rightarrow G_2)$
Rule 3. $(H_1 \vee H_2) \rightarrow G \;\; \Leftarrow \;\; (H_1 \rightarrow G) \wedge (H_2 \rightarrow G)$
Rule 4. $H \rightarrow (G_1 \rightarrow G_2) \;\; \Leftarrow \;\; (H \wedge G_1) \rightarrow G_2$
Rule 5. $(H_1 \rightarrow H_2) \rightarrow G \;\; \Leftarrow \;\; (\neg H_1 \rightarrow G) \wedge (H_2 \rightarrow G)$
Rule 6. $\neg H \rightarrow \neg G \;\; \Leftarrow \;\; G \rightarrow H$
Rule 7. $\neg H_1 \wedge H_2 \rightarrow \neg G \;\; \Leftarrow \;\; G \wedge H_2 \rightarrow H_1$

We replace a goal with its definition, as given in the goal's specification:

Rule 8. $H \rightarrow G \;\; \Leftarrow \;\; H \rightarrow G'$, if $G = G'$.

A logical simplifier is invoked after each reduction step and performs tasks such as removing nested conjunctions, duplicate goals, and tautologies. Also, domain facts can be used to replace a goal with something equivalent.

We use transitivity of implication:

Rule 9. $H \rightarrow G \;\; \Leftarrow \;\; H \rightarrow G'$, if $G' \rightarrow G$.

In particular, if the head of a correct program clause matches the goal, we can replace the goal with the subgoals obtained from that clause. Also, when a specific domain fact is known, it can be used to strengthen a goal.

Similarly, domain facts may be used to weaken hypotheses:

Rule 10. $H \rightarrow G \;\; \Leftarrow \;\; H' \rightarrow G$, if $H \rightarrow H'$.

An effort was also made to build in some domain knowledge about lists and inequalities so that it can employ a bit of common sense when reasoning about programs.

The proof process terminates when the original goal is reduced to **true**, in which case the clause is proved correct; when the original set of hypotheses (that is, the subgoals in the body of the clause) is reduced to **false**, meaning that there are conflicting subgoals in the clause, and that the clause is vacuously correct; when the goal is reduced to a subset of the hypotheses, in which case the implication is also established; or when the original goal is reduced to primitives and hypotheses, in which case those goals not appearing as hypotheses are added as subgoals to the original clause. In the latter case, we have identified those missing subgoals which will make the clause correct.

Once we identify an incorrect subgoal, we can correct it using either a heuristic rule or an inductive method, besides using the deductive methods outlined above.

We employ heuristics meant to correct certain commonly made, easily corrected, errors. For example, one of the rules is to swap the variables if there are only two variables in the subgoal. Other rules include moving a simple variable to a different position, replacing simple variables with more complicated terms, deleting seemingly redundant variables, and adding free variables that have appeared elsewhere in the same clause.

When the heuristic rules cannot correct the errors in a subgoal, a general inductive strategy is employed with the hope of fixing the bugs. This is done by applying some refinement operations on terms within the subgoals. For example, we can try to unify two free variables, or unify a compound term with variables appearing elsewhere in the same clause.

It should be noted that all heuristic fixes will be tested immediately after the changes are made; and if the fixes cannot correct the errors, all the changes will be undone.

To remedy the problem of an uncovered goal, we first check if the goal can be unified with the head of a clause. If indeed such a clause exists, then we presume that it should cover this goal. Since the original clause might be useful for other goals, instead of modifying the clause directly, we make local changes on a copy. We locate the subgoal that causes this clause to fail and either try to fix it inductively (by rearranging, replacing, deleting, or adding variable within the subgoal) or eliminate the offending subgoal entirely and use deductive means to correct it, if necessary.

When there is no clause whose head unifies with the uncovered goal, we use the specifications to synthesize a new clause. This can be done by using the uninstantiated goal as the clause head and the specifications as the clause body, simplifying the resulting clause as much as possible, or by an inductive method such as that in [12], using the specifications to guide the search. We can also fix a clause head so that it can be unified with the uncovered goal, and then debug the subgoals in the clause.

When the input to a procedure call violates the well-founded ordering defined for that procedure, a likely cause is that the input argument of the call is too general. For example, it may contain an irrelevant variable that does not appear in either the clause head or other subgoals of the same clause. Other possibilities are that some variables are missing or that the order of arguments is wrong. In any of these cases, what we have is a clause that contains a looping call caused by incorrect arguments. We try to fix the offending subgoal, using the same inductive method as for fixing incorrect subgoals. Alternatively, we can weaken it and employ deductive techniques to ensure that the well-founded condition is met.

It is also possible that a subgoal that would preclude the looping case is missing (and that the goal is covered by another clause). This can be treated in the same way as an incorrect clause.

5 The Constructive Interpreter

We integrated the functions of test case generation, bug discovery, bug location, and bug correction into an automated debugging environment, called the *Constructive Interpreter*. Its structure is described in Fig. 2 in pseudo-Prolog code. Upon receiving a goal, the interpreter first examines the input variables. If the input is symbolic (partially uninstantiated), then by executing the specifications of the procedure,

```
interpret( Goal )  :-
    spec( Goal ),
    freeze_input_variables( Goal, Goal' ),
    execute( Goal', Message ),
    if Message ≠ ok(Goal')
        then fix_bug( Message )
```

Fig. 2. The Constructive Interpreter

the interpreter will generate test cases. If the input variables are instantiated, then running the specifications on the given input checks if the input values are satisfiable. Once the legality of the input is established or a legal test input generated, the interpreter proceeds to execute the program on the input. Note that the interpreter will "freeze" the variables at this point, treating them as constants so that they will not be changed by the Prolog system. If execution completes successfully, the interpreter returns correct output values. In the case of symbolic input, the user can continue to generate alternate test cases and execute the program on different inputs. If the execution ever fails, that is, if the program contains an incorrect, incomplete, or nonterminating procedure, then the interpreter returns a diagnostic message with the location. Bug-fixing routines will then be invoked to correct the bug that has been identified and located.

Procedure $fix\_bug(Message)$ implements the bug correction heuristics discussed in Section 4.

This interpreter is constructive in the sense that it assumes an active role during the debugging process and actually tries to complete the construction of the program being debugged, all with very little user involvement. It consists of the three major components: test case generator, bug locator, and bug corrector. The test case generator executes specifications to either generate test input or verify the satisfiability of user-supplied input. The bug locator also carries out the computation. It has a run-time stack that records all the procedure invocations. This information and the specified well-founded ordering are used to check against looping. The execution is simulated to perform depth-first search and backtracking upon failure. A message stack is maintained during execution, and an error message is recorded whenever an error occurs. The bug corrector contains three main procedures, dealing with three different kind of errors respectively. In addition to performing error analysis and suggesting fixes, they all have access to the deductive theorem prover and inductive subgoal refiner.

In the remainder of this section, we illustrate the integrated functions, including test case generation, bug location, and correction, of the *Constructive Interpreter*. Our experimental implementation is able to generate test cases that reveal errors and locate bugs for all the sorting examples in [12].

Consider the quicksort program in Fig. 3, with the specifications in Fig. 4. The specifications say that $qsort(X,Y)$ holds if Y is sorted and Y is a permutation of X, that $part(L,E,X,Y)$ holds if Y is the list obtained by removing elements of X from L and E is greater than all the elements in X and smaller then all the elements in Y, and that $append(X,Y,Z)$ is true if Z is the combination of lists X and Y, in their

$$qsort([X|L], L0) :- part(L, X, L1, L2), \; qsort(L1, L3), \; qsort(L2, L4),$$
$$append([X|L3], L4, L0)$$
$$part([X|L], Y, L1, [X|L2]) :- part(L, Y, L1, L2)$$
$$part([X|L], Y, [X|L1], L2) :- X \leq Y, \; part(L, Y, L1, L2)$$
$$part([\,], X, [X], [\,])$$
$$append([X|L1], L2, [X|L3]) :- append(L1, L2, L3)$$
$$append([\,], L, L)$$

Fig. 3. A Buggy Quicksort Program

$$spec(qsort(X, Y)) :- ordered(Y), \; perm(X, Y)$$
$$spec(part(L, E, X, Y)) :- rm\_list(X, L, Y), \; gt\_all(E, X),$$
$$lt\_all(E, Y)$$
$$spec(append(X, Y, Z)) :- length(X, N), \; front(N, Z, X),$$
$$rm\_list(X, Z, Y)$$
$$wfo(qsort(X, Y), \; qsort(U, V)) :- shorter(X, U)$$
$$wfo(part(X, A, B, C), \; part(Y, D, E, F)) :- shorter(X, Y)$$
$$wfo(append(X, A, B), \; append(Y, C, D)) :- shorter(X, Y)$$

Fig. 4. Specifications for the Quicksort Program

original order. The predicate *wfo* specifies the well-founded ordering for sequences of input values. For procedures *qsort*, *part*, and *append*, the number of elements in the input list should decrease with each recursive call. The predicates *perm*, *ordered*, *rm_list*, *gt_all*, *lt_all*, and *shorter* can be defined as standard Prolog procedures, as in Fig. 5.

Invoking the debugger on the symbolic goal $qsort(U, V)$ generates a test case $qsort([\,], X)$ which it tries to satisfy. It discovered that this goal should have a solution $qsort([\,], [\,])$ according to the specification of *qsort*, but cannot get it from the program supplied. It then The debugger uses the specification for *qsort* to synthesize the clause $qsort([\,], [\,]):-ordered([\,]), perm([\,], [\,])$ to cover that goal. Since the body of this clause can be reduced to *true*, the debugger added a unit clause to the program (by asserting it to the database).

The debugger generates a one element list $qsort([x], X)$ as its next test input. (Note that the generated input, $[x]$, contains a Skolem constant x.) This time, it finds an incorrect clause in the procedure *part*, because partitioning an empty list should result in two empty sublist, so the result of $parti([\,], x, X, Y)$ should be $part([\,], x, [\,], [\,])$ instead of $part([\,], x, [x], [\,])$. After further analysis, the debugger concludes that $part([], X, [X], []):-true$ is incorrect. Since it can not fix the head, it retracts the clause. After synthesizing a clause that covers $part([\,], x, [\,], [\,])$, the debugger reexecutes all the test goals generated so far to make sure the changes do not destroy anything. (Note that there is no way a correctly synthesized clause can cause a problem; retracting an incorrect clause, however, can cause some goals to become uncovered.)

$$ordered([\,])$$
$$ordered([X])$$
$$ordered([X1, X2|Xs]) :- lt(X1, X2),\ ordered([X2|Xs])$$

$$perm([\,],[\,])$$
$$perm([X|Xs], Ys) :- del(X, Ys, Zs),\ perm(Xs, Zs)$$
$$del(X, [X|Xs], Xs)$$
$$del(X, [Y|Xs], [Y|Ys]) :- del(X, Xs, Ys)$$

$$rm\_list([\,], Y, Y)$$
$$rm\_list([H|T], Y, Z) :- remove(H, Y, YY),\ rm\_list(T, YY, Z)$$
$$remove(A, [A|T], T)$$
$$remove(A, [H|T], [H|U]) :- remove(A, T, U)$$

$$gt\_all(E, [\,])$$
$$gt\_all(E, [H|T]) :- E > T,\ gt\_all(E, T)$$

$$lt\_all(E, [\,])$$
$$lt\_all(E, [H|T]) :- E < T,\ lt\_all(E, T)$$

$$front(N, Z, X) :- append(X, Y, Z),\ length(X, N)$$
$$shorter(X, Y) :- length(X, Lx),\ length(Y, Ly), Lx < Ly$$

Fig. 5. Some Utility Procedures

The next test case generated is $qsort([0, 1], X)$. Unlike the previous two test cases, the goal $qsort([0, 1], X)$ is solved directly by the clauses currently in the program. Continuing with $qsort([1, 0], X)$ results in the location of an incorrect clause in the procedure *part*. A trace of the procedures shows that the correct solution to $part([0], 1, X, Y)$ can be obtained from the other clause of *part*. Thus, this incorrect clause should have failed, but did not because of a missing subgoal. The corrected clause is $part([X|Y], Z, U, [X|W]) :- Z <= X, part(Y, Z, U, W)$.

Rechecking the previous goal $qsort([1, 0], X)$, the instance $qsort([1, 0], [1, 0])$ $:- part([0], 1, [0], [\,]),\ qsort([0], [0]),\ qsort([\,], [\,]),\ append([1, 0], [\,], [1, 0])$ is found false. That is, $qsort([X|W], U) :- part(W, X, U1, V1),\ qsort(U1, Y),\ qsort(V1, Z),\ append([X|Y], Z, U)$ contains an incorrect subgoal $append([X|Y], Z, U)$. The local fix is $qsort([X|Y], Z) :- part(Y, X, W, X1),\ qsort(W, Z1),\ qsort(X1, V1),\ append(Z1, [X|V1], Z)$.

Up to this point, all the bugs in the original program have been detected and corrected. If we now continue to debug the program, the debugger will keep on generating arbitrarily long lists as test input without reporting an error. We would be led to believe, in this case, that the program is correct with respect to its specifications.

6 Conclusion

In this work, we have explored a distinctive feature of logic programming, namely the ability to use logic for both specification and computation. We have shown how user-supplied executable program specifications are used to define the intended behavior of a program and to generate test cases for bug discovery. We have employed the execution mechanism of a Prolog machine to locate bugs, using specifications to validate computation results. We have also devised heuristics to analyze bugs and suggest fixes, and used deductive theorem proving and inductive synthesis to mechanize the bug correction process, again with the help of specifications.

References

1. Paul Brna, Alan Bundy, and Helen Pain. A framework for the principled debugging of Prolog programs: How to debug non-terminating programs. In D. R. Brough, editor, *Logic Programming: New Frontiers*, chapter 2, pages 22–55. Intellect, Oxford, 1992.
2. W. Drabent, S. Nadjm-Tehrani, and J. Maluszynski. Algorithmic debugging with assertions. In *Proceedings of a Workshop on Meta-Programming in Logic Programming*, Bristol, June 1988.
3. Nachum Dershowitz and Yuh-jeng Lee. Deductive debugging. In *Proceedings of the Fourth IEEE Symposium on Logic Programming*, pages 298–306, San Francisco, CA.
4. Gérard Ferrand. Error diagnosis in logic programming, an adaptation of E. Y. Shapiro's method. Technical Report 375, Institut National de Recherche en Informatique et en Automatique, Le Chesnay, France, March 1985.
5. Joseph A. Goguen and José Meseguer. EQLOG: Equality, types, and generic modules for logic programming. In D. DeGroot; G. Lindstrom, editor, *Logic Programming: Relations, Functions, and Equations*. Prentice Hall, Englewood Cliffs, NJ, 1986.
6. N. Alan Josephson and Nachum Dershowitz. An implementation of narrowing: The RITE way. In *Proceedings of the IEEE Symposium on Logic Programming*, pages 187–197, Salt Lake City, UT, September 1986.
7. J. W. Lloyd. Declarative error diagnosis. *New Generation Computing*, 5:133–154, 1987.
8. L. Naish. Declarative debugging of lazy functional programs. Report 92/6, Department of Computer Science, University of Melbourne, Australia, 1992.
9. H. Nilsson and P. Fritzson. Algorithmic debugging for lazy functional languages. In M. Bruynooghe and M. Wirsing, editors, *Proceedings of the Fourth International Symposium on Programming Language Implementation and Logic Programming*, pages 385–399, Leuven, Belgium, August 1992. Available as Vol. 631 of Lecture Notes in Computer Science, Springer-Verlag.
10. L. M. Pereira. Rational debugging in logic programming. In *Proceedings of the Third International Conference on Logic Programming*, pages 203–210, London, United Kingdom, July 1986. Available as Vol. 225, Lecture Notes in Computer Science, Springer-Verlag.
11. L. M. Pereira and M .C. Calejo. A framework for Prolog debugging. In *Proceedings of Fifth International Conference and Symposium on Logic Programming*, Seattle, August 1988.
12. Ehud Y. Shapiro. *Algorithmic Program Debugging*. MIT Press, Cambridge, MA, 1983.
13. Douglas R. Smith. Derived preconditions and their use in program synthesis. In *Proceedings of the Sixth Conference on Automated Deduction*, pages 172–193, New York, NY, June 1982.

Model-Based Diagnosis Meets
Error Diagnosis in Logic Programs
(Extended abstract)*

Luca Console[1], Gerhard Friedrich[2], Daniele Theseider Dupré[3]

[1] Dipartimento di Matematica e Informatica – Università di Udine
Via Zanon 6, 33100 Udine, Italy
[2] Christian Doppler Laboratory for Expert Systems
Technische Universität Wien
Paniglgasse 16, A-1040 Vienna, Austria
[3] Dipartimento di Informatica – Università di Torino
Corso Svizzera 185, 10149 Torino, Italy

A lot of attention has been paid in the last years in the logic programming community to the design of automatic declarative error diagnosers (after Shapiro's seminal work [10]). Such diagnosers are declarative in the sense that they do not need any understanding of the computational behavior of the program but they need to know only the intended interpretation of the program (the set of answers that the program should compute). Information on such an intended behavior is obtained querying an oracle, usually corresponding to the user.

Automated diagnosis has always been (and still is) an important research area (and source of new problems and methodologies) in the Artificial Intelligence Community [11]. In particular, Model-based diagnosis (MBD), an innovative approach of diagnosis, emerged in the 80's. MBD concentrates on the problem of isolating faults of physical systems, starting from a model of the structure (components and their connections) and function (or behavior) of the system and a set of observations indicating an abnormal behavior [7]. A system is faulty if the observed behavior of the system contradicts the behavior predicted by assuming that all of its components are correct. Making assumptions about faulty components of the modeled system allows explaining the deviation of the observed behavior from the predicted one; thus the faulty components can be isolated (see figure 1). Depending on the notion of explanation, two formal characterizations of diagnosis have been proposed in the literature, namely the *consistency-based* [5, 9, 6, 4] and the abductive one [8, 2, 3]. In the former case a diagnosis is a (minimal) set of abnormality assumptions (assumptions about the abnormal behavior of some components) such that the observations are consistent with the assumption that all the other components are acting correctly; in the latter case a diagnosis is a (minimal) set of abnormality assumptions which

---

* This work has been partially supported on the Italian part by MURST 40% and on the Austrian part by the Austrian Industries. The extended version of this abstract appears in the Proceedings of the 13th International Joint Conference on Artificial Intelligence (IJCAI '93), published by Morgan Kaufmann.

is not only consistent but also implies (covers) the observations.

The goal of our work is to use MBD techniques to diagnose logic programs (and suggest corrections). If a formal, complete specification of the procedures in the program to be debugged were available, it could be used as the model in figure 1, where the program to be diagnosed is considered as the actual system. Since such an assumption is not realistic, we introduced a different analogy: the program to be diagnosed (whose structure and behavior is known in detail) is technically used in the same way as the model is used in MBD; the clauses of the program are regarded as components which may be correct or abnormal. In contrast, the role of the observations is technically played by the information available on the user's model of the intended behavior of the program.

Given a set of assertions about the intended behavior of the program (a set of expected answers and a set of undesired ones), the goal is to determine the bugs by comparing the actual program behavior with such assertions. In the same way as a system is faulty when assuming that all its components are correct is in contradiction with the observed behavior, a program is faulty when assuming that all its clauses are correct is in contradiction with the assertions on the intended behavior. The goal is to remove such a discrepancy, isolating a set of clauses which are not correct and must be fixed. This amounts to determining a set of clauses to be removed and, possibly, a set of clauses to be added such that the resulting modified program is in accordance with the assertions (see figure 2). In particular, given such a framework, the goal of our work is twofold:

- Using the formal machinery of MBD to characterize the alternative ways of modifying the program (removing clauses and adding new clauses) in order to match the available information on its expected behavior. This corresponds to characterizing all the ways of fixing the program. Notice that, as it is common in MBD, each diagnosis may involve more than one fault (i.e. more than one clause to be removed or added).
- Given a notion of "leading" diagnoses (diagnoses which are more likely than the others), devising an algorithm that can generate all the solutions in increasing order of preference.

The first goal is quite different from traditional algorithmic debugging, whose aim is at querying the user until a fault (one at a time) is isolated.

The definitions we introduced are adapted from the classical ones in consistency-based and abductive diagnosis, and in the reasoning process we appeal to the same machinery. An interesting aspect of our approach (which, up to now, has been completely developed only for definite logic program) is that not only we isolate the set of clauses to be fixed but we also provide repair information. A diagnosis in our approach is formed by two strictly related parts:

1. A set of clauses of the original program to be removed.
2. A set of predicates for which a new definition has to be added. For each predicate p in such a set, we also provide constraints on such a definition. Two types of constraints are provided for each p: the lowest bound of its extension

(i.e. the set of ground instances of p that must be true in the modified program in order to be in accordance with the available information on the intended behavior of the program) and the upper bound of its extension (i.e. the set of ground instances that must be necessarily false).

The two parts are related in the sense that the set of clauses to be added depends on the set of clauses that are removed. These two sets can be computed using the machinery of model-based diagnosis.

The approach we have proposed has some advantages with respect to other error diagnosers. First of all, we look at the program and at all the 'observations' globally and thus we are able to characterize the whole set of diagnoses (possibly involving multiple faults), accounting for available information on the expected behavior of the program rather than looking at one execution tree for one wrong or missing clause instance at a time. Moreover, the use of MBD techniques and the notion of leading diagnoses can provide a more focused interaction with the user; for example, if one diagnosis is much more likely than all the others, we simply output it without asking new information. More generally, we can include in our approach techniques similar to those used in MBD, e.g. for selecting what should be asked to the user to discriminate at best between the available candidates or for focusing the reasoning process.

The interested reader is referred to the full paper [1] for the precise definitions and the description of the algorithm for computing diagnoses, as well as for a comparison of our approach with related ones .

References

1. L. Console, G. Friedrich, and Theseider Dupré. Model-based diagnosis meets error diagnosis in logic programs. In *Proc. 13th IJCAI*, Chambery, 1993.
2. L. Console, D. Theseider Dupré, and P. Torasso. A theory of diagnosis for incomplete causal models. In *Proc. 11th IJCAI*, pages 1311–1317, Detroit, 1989.
3. L. Console and P. Torasso. A spectrum of logical definitions of model-based diagnosis. *Computational Intelligence*, 7(3):133–141, 1991. Also in [7].
4. J. de Kleer, A. Mackworth, and R. Reiter. Characterizing diagnoses and systems. *Artificial Intelligence*, 56(2–3):197–222, 1992. Also in [7].
5. J. de Kleer and B.C. Williams. Diagnosing multiple faults. *Artificial Intelligence*, 32(1):97–130, 1987. Also in [7].
6. Gerhard Friedrich and Wolfgang Nejdl. MOMO — Model-based diagnosis for everybody. In *Proc. IEEE Conf. on AI Appl.*, Santa Barbara, 1990. Also in [7].
7. W. Hamscher, L. Console, and J. de Kleer. *Readings in Model-Based Diagnosis.* Morgan Kaufmann, 1992.
8. D. Poole. Normality and faults in logic-based diagnosis. In *Proc. 11th IJCAI*, pages 1304–1310, Detroit, 1989. Also in [7].
9. R. Reiter. A theory of diagnosis from first principles. *Artificial Intelligence*, 32(1):57–96, 1987. Also in [7].
10. E. Shapiro. *Algorithmic Program Debugging.* MIT-Press, 1983.
11. P. Struss. Knowledge-based diagnosis: an important challenge and touchstone for AI. In *Proc. 10th ECAI*, pages 863–874, Vienna, 1992.

Towards Declarative Debugging of Concurrent Constraint Programs

Markus P.J. Fromherz

Xerox PARC, 3333 Coyote Hill Road, Palo Alto, CA 94304
fromherz@parc.xerox.com

Abstract. The concurrent constraint (cc) framework [17] describes a family of concurrent programming languages that use constraints for the synchronization of processes. In this paper, we describe an approach to the declarative debugging of cc programs. We develop the concept of observable and specified behaviors of cc processes, define incorrect processes based on differences between these behaviors, and present a top-down debugging algorithm for the detection of incorrect processes in finite computations. We also investigate the meaning of behaviors in infinite computations. This allows us to define a debugging algorithm for partial computations (prefixes of infinite computations) that can search for an incorrect process as soon as a wrong behavior is observed.

1 Introduction

The concurrent constraint (cc) framework as introduced by Saraswat [17] describes a family of concurrent programming languages. Their common characteristics is the use of constraints for the synchronization of processes. Constraints can be *tell* constraints, which are added to a global constraint store, or *ask* constraints, which test whether a constraint is entailed by the constraint store. Ask constraints also block a process until their variables are sufficiently constrained by the store. Ask and tell operations are independent of the underlying constraint system. Further characteristics of cc languages are the and-parallel execution of processes, and the indeterminate, or-parallel selection of process clauses to be executed.

Due to their concurrent nature, and even more due to the additional work that is done by the underlying constraint solver during computations, cc programs can be difficult to debug. The cc framework, however, gives these programs a declarative semantic model that makes them amenable to algorithmic debugging.

Algorithmic debugging is a debugging theory that takes into account both the computed and the intended behaviors of a program; given a computation, program errors can be found by comparing these behaviors on a semantical level [20, 16, 11, 5, 2]. One important instance of this idea is declarative debugging, where only the declarative meaning of expressions is considered.

Algorithmic debugging has also been applied to concurrent logic programming. Huntbach presents a debugging algorithm for Parlog programs [7]. Lloyd and Takeuchi develop a framework for the declarative debugging of GHC programs [12, 21], and present single-stepping and divide-and-query algorithms for the debugging of wrong answers and deadlocks. Lichtenstein and Shapiro describe Concurrent Algorithmic Debugging, a general top-down algorithm for FCP programs [8], which also allows one to debug programs with various abstractions applied [9]. More recently, a similar framework has been applied in the context of Temporal Debugging [4, 3]. Finally, a related problem is the debugging of programs written in lazy functional languages, were the lazy evaluation of expressions introduces a kind of coroutining [15, 14].

Our work can be seen as an extension of the above work in two ways. First, we present a semantic model and a corresponding declarative debugging algorithm for concurrent *constraint* programs. Our foundation will be the cc framework. Second, we address the fact that in the future concurrent (constraint) programs will often define reactive processes that have no finite computation, and thus do not allow to record and debug a finite computation tree. Among the above approaches, only Temporal Debugging can deal with infinite computations.

This paper is structured as follows. In the next section, we present a basic cc language and its computational model. In Section 3, we develop the concepts of observable, computed, and specified behaviors of cc processes. In Section 4, we define incorrectness in computations and programs, and present a debugging algorithm for finite computations. In Section 5, we revisit our view of behaviors in the light of partial computations (finite prefixes of infinite computations). This allows us to restate the debugging algorithm for infinite computations. We see this work as the groundwork for more sophisticated debugging algorithms for cc programs and outline further issues in the conclusion.

2 Syntax and Computational Model of Basic cc Programs

Several instances of the cc framework have been designed and implemented, differing mainly in the underlying constraint system [17, 18, 6]. Table 1 defines a basic, backtracking-free cc language. This will be the language used in this paper. The difference to a particular cc language instance is that we make no requirements about the constraint system, and we assume a simple syntax. The former serves the generality of our approach, while the latter simplifies our arguments. However, programs in a more powerful syntax can be rewritten in this syntax by simple program transformation.

The computation of a cc program can be seen as a sequence of states $\langle A, s \rangle$. Such a state is a pair of processes A and constraint store s.[1] A constraint store is a set of constraints. Table 2 defines the transition rule that determines the

---

[1] In this paper, we will use *process* for a set of clauses with the same heads, and *process instance* to refer to a running version of a process. Starting a process spawns a process instance which may then start other processes. There will be no further distinction between processes and their instances, and in particular, we will use the same variables to refer to both.

Table 1. Abstract syntax of a basic cc language

Syntax. The main object of a cc program is a process defined by a set of clauses $H::C_1 : C_2 \to G$ with same heads H. A clause further consists of ask constraints C_1, tell constraints C_2, and body G. Variables appearing in clause heads are implicitly all-quantified; variables appearing in bodies only are implicitly existentially quantified. Programs are defined as follows.

$\quad$ *Program* $P ::= H::C : C \to G \mid P$. P (Clause, Composition)
$\quad$ *Processes* $G ::= H \mid G, G$ $\qquad$ (Process Start, Conjunction)
$\quad$ *Constraints* $C ::= c \mid C, C$ $\qquad$ (Basic Constraint, Conjunction)
Process Start $H ::= p(X_1, \ldots, X_n)$

A clause without ask constraints can be written as $H::C_2 \to G$, a clause that does not start processes as $H::C_1 : C_2$ respectively $H::C_2$. The syntax of the constraints c depends on the underlying constraint system.

---

transformation of states. For reasons of simplicity in the subsequent arguments, variable substitutions are assumed to be defined as tell constraints.

A *finite computation* is the sequence $\langle A_i, s_i \rangle \longrightarrow \ldots \longrightarrow \langle A_f, s_f \rangle$: the computation starts with process(es) A_i and initial store s_i and quiesces when no transition rule is applicable with final store s_f. A_f is either empty (written as ()), or a set of processes which cannot be executed.

Consider the following sample program, which contains an error in the definition of max/3. (In our examples, we assume a simple cc language with equality and disequality constraints only.)

```
eval(X,Y,Z) :: true -> value(X,Y), rating(Y,Z).

value(X,Y) :: M=2 -> max(X,M,Y).

rating(Y,Z) :: Y>1,Y<5 : Z = low.
rating(Y,Z) :: Y>4 : Z = high.

max(X,Y,Z) :: X>=Y : Z=X.
max(X,Y,Z) :: X<Y : Z=X.
```

Two possible computation sequences are as follows. Note that the second one exhibits unexpected behavior in that rating(Y,Z) cannot be executed.

```
Computation sequence for <eval(X,Y,Z), {X=3}>:
<eval(X,Y,Z), {X=3}>
<(value(X,Y),rating(Y,Z)), {X=3}>
<(max(X,M,Y),rating(Y,Z)), {X=3,M=2}>
<rating(Y,Z), {X=3,M=2,Y=3}>
<(), {X=3,M=2,Y=3,Z=low}>
```

Table 2. Computational model of the basic cc language

Transition rule. For the above defined language, there is only one transition to be defined, namely the *Call* transition. It is defined as follows.

$$\langle (H_1, \ldots, H_k, \ldots, H_n), s \rangle \longrightarrow \langle (H_1, \ldots, H_{k-1}, G_1, \ldots, G_m, H_{k+1}, \ldots, H_n), s \cup C_2 \rangle$$

The *Call* transition is applicable if store s is consistent, and if for some k there is a program clause $K = H_k::C_1 : C_2 \rightarrow G_1, \ldots, G_m$ such that $s \vdash C_1$. Variables in K have to be renamed so that K and $(H_1, \ldots, H_n)$ share only the variables in H_k.

With store s and the conjunction of constraints C, $s \vdash C$ means that s entails all constraints in C, and $s \cup C$ is a new store where the constraints of C are added to s. Entailment and consistency are defined by the underlying constraint system. Note that adding the tell constraints C_2 to the store may result in an inconsistent store, in which case the computation halts.

```
Computation sequence for <eval(X,Y,Z), {X=1}>:
<eval(X,Y,Z), {X=1}>
<(value(X,Y),rating(Y,Z)), {X=1}>
<(max(X,M,Y),rating(Y,Z)), {X=1,M=2}>
<rating(Y,Z), {X=1,M=2,Y=1}>
```

For a detailed account of the semantic foundation of concurrent constraint programming, see [19].

3 The Behavior and Specification of Processes

We will define the correctness of processes in terms of the correspondence between their behavior and their specification. This corresponds to comparing the real and intended semantics of logic programs [20, 11, 10], and to comparing the (declarative abstraction of) processes and the intended process space of concurrent logic programs [8, 9].

3.1 Process Behavior

The set of abstract *behaviors* of a process H is defined in terms of the initial and final stores of its computation:

$$B(H) = \{ \langle s, t \rangle : \text{whenever process } H \text{ is started with store } s,$$
$$\text{the computation quiesces with store } t \}.$$

A few remarks on this definition of behavior are in order. In the literature, the term behavior is usually associated with a sequence of ask and tell operations. In this paper, we will require the observation of abstract behavior only. Consequently, all definitions assume programs to be determinate. The main reason is that, with indeterminate programs, different processes may show the same abstract behaviors, but lead to different context behaviors when used in different contexts (Brock-Ackerman anomaly [1]). This sofar seems to preclude declarative debugging of indeterminate programs using abstract behavior only. (We will return to this problem in Section 6.) Finally, in this and the next sections, for the purpose of simplicity, we will pretend that process behavior can be completely described by pairs of initial and final stores. This will be extended in Section 5.

For our purposes, we are only interested in the observable behavior of processes. We define the *observable* subset of a constraint store with respect to a process H as the projection of the store wrt. the variables that appear in the definition of H, i.e. all constraints that do not contain those variables are removed. (We talk about the observable subset of a constraint store when it is clear from the context with respect to which process the store is observable. In this paper, we will usually reduce the observable constraint set even further to those about variables in the head of H only.) Then, the set of *observable behaviors* $B_o(H)$ of process H is defined as the projection from $B(H)$ that contains only the observable subsets of the initial and final stores.

Finally, the *computed behavior* of a process instance H is the actual behavior that was computed in a given computation involving H. For example, the computed observable behaviors (or observed behaviors, or just observations) for rating(Y,Z) in the above computations are $\langle \{Y = 3\}, \{Y = 3, Z = \text{low}\} \rangle$ and $\langle \{Y = 1\}, \{Y = 1\} \rangle$, respectively. One might argue that only the final store is computed. However, as discussed in Section 5, the initial store may evolve as well, and we will need this more general notion of computed behavior.

The set of *specified behaviors* (or the *specification*) $S(H)$ of a process H simply is the set of expected observable behaviors:

$$S(H) = \{\langle s, t \rangle: \text{whenever process } H \text{ is started with store } s,$$
$$\text{the computation is expected to quiesce with store } t\}.$$

3.2 Computation Revisited

Given the computed behavior of processes, we can define a computation as a tree instead of a sequence. This will be beneficial later on, as we aspire a top-down debugging algorithm. A finite *computation tree* is a tree where nodes represent process instances and subnodes are processes started by these. The nodes are labeled with $\langle H, b_H \rangle$, where H is the process instance with computed observable behavior b_H. The computation tree for process H started with store s_H is rooted in $\langle H, \langle s_H, t_H \rangle \rangle$ and has as subtrees a computation tree for each process started by H. Leaves of this tree denote processes that either did not start other processes, or that cannot be executed.

There is a straightforward transformation from states of the computation sequence $\langle A_i, s_i \rangle \longrightarrow \ldots \longrightarrow \langle A_f, s_f \rangle$ to nodes in the computation tree. For each *Call* transition for H_k from state $\langle (H_1, \ldots, H_k, \ldots, H_n), s \rangle$ in the sequence, there is a node $\langle H_k, \langle s_{H_k}, t_{H_k} \rangle \rangle$ in the tree, where s_{H_k} is the observable subset of s, and t_{H_k} is the observable subset of s_f. For each process H in A_f (if any), there is a leaf node $\langle H, \langle s_H, s_H \rangle \rangle$ in the tree, where s_H is the observable subset of s_f.

Consider again the two computations given above. The corresponding computation trees are as follows. (In our simple tree representation, each line represents a node, the indentation denotes the level in the tree, and all nodes of a certain level with no nodes of lower level in between are subnodes of the node above the first of these nodes. The constraints present in the initial stores are not repeated in the final stores, but instead represented by "...", i.e. $\langle \{X = 3\}, \{\ldots, Y = 3\} \rangle$ is equivalent to $\langle \{X = 3\}, \{X = 3, Y = 3\} \rangle$.)

```
Computation tree for <eval(X,Y,Z), {X=3}>:
<eval(X,Y,Z), <{X=3},{...,Y=3,Z=low}>>
   <value(X,Y), <{X=3},{...,Y=3}>>
      <max(X,M,Y), <{X=3,M=2},{...,Y=3}>>
   <rating(Y,Z), <{Y=3},{...,Z=low}>>

Computation tree for <eval(X,Y,Z), {X=1}>:
<eval(X,Y,Z), <{X=1},{...,Y=1}>>
   <value(X,Y), <{X=1},{...,Y=1}>>
      <max(X,M,Y), <{X=1,M=2},{...,Y=1}>>
   <rating(Y,Z), <{Y=1},{...}>>
```

4 Declarative Debugging of cc Programs

As a process is started, it might give a wrong answer, or miss an answer. The purpose of the debugging algorithm is to start from such an error and find an incorrect process that causes the error. We will now formalize the concepts of incorrect answer, incorrect process, and incorrect program.

4.1 Wrong Answers and Incorrect Processes

The *wrong answers* of process H with respect to $S(H)$ are the computed observable behaviors $B_o(H) \backslash S(H)$. The *missing answers* of process H with respect to $S(H)$ are the missing behaviors $S(H) \backslash B_o(H)$.

Note that here we treat constraint stores as sets of syntactical objects. This means that, with determinate programs, every missing answer has a wrong answer as counterpart. In other words, answers with missing constraints appear as wrong answers.

A process H is called *correct* with respect to $S(H)$ if for every node $\langle H, b_H \rangle$ in the computation tree, this is either a leaf node and b_H in $S(H)$, or whenever for all subnodes $\langle G, b_G \rangle$ b_G is in $S(G)$, then b_H is in $S(H)$. Otherwise, H is *incorrect* with respect to $S(H)$.

Let S be the set of sets $S(H)$ of the processes H defined in program P, called the specification of program P. A program P is called *correct* with respect to its specification S if the root of every computation tree of P is $\langle H, b_H \rangle$ and b_H is in $S(H)$. Otherwise, the program is *incorrect*. The following connection between incorrect program and incorrect process follows the usual argument line for top-down debuggers [10, 8].

Theorem. Given are a program P and its specification S. If P is incorrect with respect to S, then P contains a process H that is incorrect with respect to $S(H)$.

Proof. Suppose $\langle H, b_H \rangle$ is the root of a computation tree such that the computation returned a wrong answer, i.e. b_H is not in $S(H)$.

If the tree contains the single node $\langle H, b_H \rangle$, process H must be incorrect.

If the root has subnodes $\langle G, b_G \rangle$, then either all b_G are in their respective specifications $S(G)$, and thus process H is incorrect. Otherwise, at least one behavior b_G of a subnode is not in its specification $S(G)$, and by induction there is an incorrect process in the computation subtree with root node $\langle G, b_G \rangle$. $\square$

4.2 The Debugging Algorithm

The above argumentation suggests a top-down debugging algorithm which starts at the root of a computation tree and descends recursively. The algorithm is given a computation tree for a process instance that returned a wrong answer; the output of the algorithm is an incorrect process. We also require an oracle which knows whether the computed behavior of a process instance is in the specification of its process. Note that we require only knowledge about observable ("local") behavior.

The debugging algorithm proceeds as follows, starting with the root node of the computation tree.

> If the current node $\langle H, b_H \rangle$ is a leaf, return H;
> else for all subnodes $\langle G, b_G \rangle$, ask the oracle whether b_G is in $S(G)$:
> > if all are, return H,
> > else choose a subnode $\langle G, b_G \rangle$ where b_G is not in $S(G)$ and iterate.

Since the user typically has to act as the oracle, one measure of usefulness of the algorithm is the number of queries asked. The top-down algorithm effectively uses information from the computation to guide the search for the incorrect process. The various ways how the query complexity can be further optimized [20, 13] are beyond the scope of this paper.

As an example, consider a program for the generation of prime numbers. Its input is a stream of number (e.g., coming from a generator), and its output is a stream of prime numbers. All the prime numbers up to the largest number in the input stream are returned.

```
sift(Ns,Ps) ::
    Ns=[P|Ns1] : Ps=[P|Ps1] -> filter(Ns1,P,Ns2), sift(Ns2,Ps1).
sift(Ns,Ps) :: Ns=[] : Ps=[].

filter(In,N,Out) :: In=[] : Out=[].
filter(In,N,Out) ::
    In=[X|In1], 0=\=X mod N : Out=[X|Out1] -> filter(In1,N,Out1).
filter(In,N,Out) ::
    In=[X|In1], 0=:=X mod N : Out=[X|Out1] -> filter(In1,N,Out1).
```

When starting process **sift(Ns,Ps)** with store **Ns=[2,3,4,5]**, the computation quiesces with observable store **{Ns=[2,3,4,5],Ps=[2,3,4,5]}**. As 4 is no prime number, and thus $\langle \{Ns = [2,3,4,5]\}, \{Ns = [2,3,4,5], Ps = [2,3,4,5]\}\rangle$ is not in the expected behavior, the debugging algorithm is started on the original goal. The following is a log of the debugging session. (Readability could be enhanced by substituting variables that have simple equality constraints, but the following representation is more general.)

```
Debugging <sift(Ns,Ps), {Ns=[2,3,4,5]}>:

Wrong <filter(Ns1,P,Ns2), <{Ns1=[3,4,5],P=2},{...,Ns2=[3,4,5]}>> ? yes.
Wrong <filter(Ns1',P,Ns2'), <{Ns1'=[4,5],P=2},{...,Ns2'=[4,5]}>> ? yes.
Wrong <filter(Ns1'',P,Ns2''), <{Ns1''=[5],P=2},{...,Ns2''=[5]}>> ? no.

Incorrect process at
  <filter(Ns1',P,Ns2'), <{Ns1'=[4,5],P=2},{...,Ns2'=[4,5]}>>.
```

In this case, the last clause of **filter/3** can be identified as being incorrect.

5 Concurrent Debugging of Partial Computations

The above debugging algorithm assumes that a finite computation tree is available. However, concurrent programs often define reactive processes which are not necessarily finite. In order to be able to diagnose incorrect processes in such programs, we have to relax some of the assumptions made above. In particular, we will allow constraint stores in behaviors to evolve, and we will show how "partial" stores can be used to declaratively identify incorrect procedures. This is a different approach than that of Temporal Debugging, where the timing of operations is taken into account [4, 3].

5.1 Observations in Partial Computations

With reactive processes, it no longer makes sense to talk about initial and final stores; instead we will call them input and output stores. An *input store* wrt. process H is a constraint store that contains constraints on variables in H that have been told outside of H. An *output store* wrt. H is a constraint store that contains constraints on variables in H that have been told by process H, or by subprocesses of H. (An output store thus does not contain the input store as a subset.)

Informally, input and output stores are justified as follows. When we start process **sift(Ns,Ps)** with input store **{Ns=[2,3|Ns1']}**, the output store will be **{Ps=[2,3|Ps1']}**. This is, however, no final store. Instead, the input store is allowed to *evolve* in that we can add constraints about **Ns1'**. Suppose we add constraint **Ns1'=[4,5|Ns1'']**, i.e. the evolved observable input store of **sift(Ns,Ps)** is **{Ns=[2,3,4,5|Ns1'']}**. Once the computation has quiesced again, the output store (given a correct program) will be **{Ps=[2,3,5|Ps1'']}**.

The obvious reason why input stores are allowed to evolve is that the behavior of processes can be defined without regard as to when input constraints have been added to the input store. Declaratively, the behavior of sift/2 is the same, whether started with the initial but evolving input store, or with the evolved input store. The behavior of processes is therefore redefined:

$$B(H) = \{(s, t): \text{whenever process } H \text{ is running with evolved input store } s,$$
$$\text{the computation quiesces with output store } t\}.$$

The definitions of observable, computed, and specified behavior are adapted accordingly.

We will not restrict ourselves to finite computations, though. We can observe the abstract behavior of a process, i.e. its input and output stores, at any time during a computation. As constraint operations are monotonous, such an observation $\langle s_H, t_H \rangle$ for process H has the following property: there exists a behavior $\langle S_H, T_H \rangle$ in $B_o(H)$ such that $S_H = s_H$, and t_H is entailed by T_H. Furthermore, if s_H does no longer evolve, t_H will eventually become T_H. Observations are usually associated with the time when they are made.

Behavior observations lead to partial computation trees. A *partial computation tree* is a computation tree at some time T such that for all node labels $\langle H, b_H \rangle$, b_H is an observation for H at time T.

As an example, consider the above program for prime number filtering, and the following additional process (where integers(I,Ns) generates a stream of integers Ns starting at I).

```
primes(Ps) :: I=2 -> integers(I,Ns), sift(Ns,Ps).
```

When starting primes(Ps) with the empty store, a potential partial computation tree during the computation is as follows.

```
Partial computation tree for <primes(Ps), {}> at time 7:

<primes(Ps), <{},{Ps=[2|Ps1]}>>
  <integers(I,Ns), <{I=2},{Ns=[2,3,4,5|Ns1''']}>>
  <sift(Ns,Ps), <{Ns=[2,3,4,5|Ns1''']},{Ps=[2|Ps1]}>>
    <filter(Ns1,P,Ns2), <{Ns1=[3,4,5|Ns1'''],P=2},{Ns2=[3,4|Ns2'']}>>
      <filter(Ns1',P,Ns2'), <{Ns1'=[4,5|Ns1'''],P=2},{Ns2'=[4|Ns2'']}>>
    <sift(Ns2,Ps1), <{Ns2=[3,4|Ns2'']},{}>>
```

Note that the notion of evolving input constraint stores solves another limitation of fixed initial stores: with initial stores, the behavior of processes that exchange incomplete messages and wait for answers before they continue cannot be described properly. (One example is a producer-consumer pair where the producer waits for an acknowledgement for each item produced.)

5.2 The Debugging Algorithm

We redefine the concepts of wrong answer, incorrect process, and incorrect program for partial computations. The two major differences are that we allow evolving constraint stores, and that we make no statements about the correctness of processes and programs. The correctness of processes and programs in infinite computations can only be defined with respect to some point in time, since an infinite computation may always run longer and return a wrong answer.

An observation $\langle s_H, t_H \rangle$ is a *wrong answer* of process H with respect to $S(H)$ if there is no specified behavior $\langle S_H, T_H \rangle$ in $S(H)$ such that when $S_H = s_H$, t_H is entailed by T_H.

A process H is called *incorrect* with respect to $S(H)$ if for some node $\langle H, b_H \rangle$ in the partial computation tree, b_H is a wrong answer of H with respect to $S(H)$, and this is either a leaf node, or for all subnodes $\langle G, b_G \rangle$, b_G is not a wrong answer. (Note that although some of the process instances G might still produce wrong answers, the point is that none of them contributed to the wrong answer of H.)

Let the specification S of program P be the set of sets $S(H)$ of the processes H in P. A program P is called *incorrect* with respect to its specification S if some partial computation tree of P contains a node $\langle H, b_H \rangle$ such that b_H is a wrong answer of H with respect to $S(H)$.

As for finite computation trees, we can show that given a program P and its specification S, if P is incorrect with respect to S, then P contains a process H that is incorrect with respect to $S(H)$. The proof is essentially the same using the new definitions, except that we can start with any partial computation tree rooted at a node with wrong answer.

The new debugging algorithm is given a partial computation tree for a process instance that returned a wrong answer; the output of the algorithm is an incorrect process. The main change is the new definition of wrong answers.

5.3 Spy Points

One interesting aspect of this debugging algorithm is of course that we do not have to wait until a wrong behavior can be observed at the root of the computation tree. In the partial computation tree shown above, the root node does not show a wrong behavior yet. We can, however, attached *spy points* to suspected processes in order to continually make observations. As soon as a wrong answer is observed, the computation can be stopped and the current partial computation tree can be used for debugging. This scheme can also cut down on the number of queries, since we will start debugging at the node were the observation was made instead of at the top.

A typical scenario for the use of spy points might be to place them on processes with complex constraints. While we may often have difficulties to interpret the constraints in a process definition, we might find the abstract behavior easier to understand. It is in those cases that spying on processes is most useful.

Given our definition of wrong answer, an observation $\langle s_H, t_H \rangle$ is not a wrong answer if there is no specified behavior $\langle S_H, T_H \rangle$ in $S(H)$ such that $S_H = s_H$. However, if we make such an observation for a suspected and spied upon process, we know that there is another process that returned a wrong answer (which was propagated to s_H), and we can use this information for placing new spy points.

Consider again the above program. Assume that we already suspect filter/3 for giving wrong answers and therefore want to observe its behavior. When starting primes(Ps) with the empty store, we can see how the computation tree grows and the node behaviors evolve. In particular, a spy point on filter/3 leaves the following trace for the first process instance up to time 7. (The number in front of each line shows the time; the indentation actually corresponds to that in the computation tree, and each line stands for a change in the observed behavior. The times do not really matter, but help to understand the evolution of behaviors with respect to other behaviors in the computation tree.)

```
Spying filter/3 ...

5    filter(Ns1,P,Ns2): <{Ns1=[3|Ns1'],P=2},{}>
6                    -> <{Ns1=[3,4|Ns1''],P=2},{Ns2=[3|Ns2']}>
7                    -> <{Ns1=[3,4,5|Ns1'''],P=2},{Ns2=[3,4|Ns2'']}>
```

This trace shows how the input store of filter/3 evolves as the generator continues to produce numbers. One can also observe the output store; in particular, from time 7 on, this instance of filter/3 shows a wrong answer. We can stop the computation and start debugging at this node.

6   Conclusion and Future Work

In this paper, we have discussed the concept of process behavior in the concurrent constraint framework, both for finite computations and finite prefixes of infinite computations. Our top-down algorithm for declarative debugging of determinate cc programs allows to find incorrect processes in such computations, based on the observable and specified behaviors of processes. Based on this work, we hope to make progress in the following areas.

Our approach provides a framework for the debugging of cc programs without regard to the underlying constraint system, but we have yet to test the usability of the algorithm for complex constraint systems. We expect, for example, that the incorrectness of process behavior will be more difficult to determine, and that suitable abstractions will be needed in order to simplify queries to the user.

Current debuggers for concurrent logic languages do not diagnose missing answers given an indeterminate program. In fact, only an exhaustive execution of the program, where the process scheduler is cooperating and exercises all possible process clauses, will reveal these missing answers. In addition, the definition of process behavior has to be extended in that an input store and a *set* of possible output stores for that input store together define the behavior of a process. Finally, the debugging algorithm has to be given a missing answer to search for an incorrect process that inhibits that answer. It is not clear how useful the debugging of missing answers would be, since missing answers of indeterminate concurrent programs cannot be observed in the first place, and since answers may always be missing due to a particular (unfair) scheduling strategy.

However, the limitation to abstract behavior (input/output store pairs only) is more severe. As the Brock-Ackerman anomaly shows, we cannot even debug wrong answers in indeterminate programs: it is possible that a process gives a wrong answer because of an incorrect subprocess, but that the abstract behavior of that subprocess is correct [1]. Ideally, for the (declarative) debugging of indeterminate programs, we would like to extend the notion of behavior only slightly without expecting a full temporal representation. An adaptive approach as in [9] is a possible solution.

Obviously, our approach could benefit from a visual representation of computation trees [4, 3, 15]. In particular, we consider the presentation of spied-upon behaviors as changing nodes in a partial computation tree (instead of as traces).

Finally, diagnosis of timing errors is not possible with our approach, as we abstract to the declarative behavior of processes. Although we are usually not concerned about the temporal behavior of processes, timing information can sometimes be used to reduce the number of queries [3]. This optimization should be possible by suitably extending our framework.

Acknowledgments

The author would like to thank Vijay Sarawat, Ken Kahn and Ehud Shapiro for helpful discussions and comments on earlier versions of this paper.

References

1. J. D. Brock and W. B. Ackerman. Scenarios: A model of non-determinate computation. In J. Díaz and I. Ramos, editors, *Int. Colloquium on Formalization of Programming Concepts*, number 107 in Lecture Notes in Computer Science, pages 252–259. Springer-Verlag, April 1981.
2. W. Drabent, S. Nadjm-Tehrani, and J. Maluszynski. Algorithmic debugging with assertions. In *META'88, Proc. Workshop on Meta-Programming in Logic Programming*, pages 365–378, Bristol, June 1988.
3. Y. Feldman. *Animation of Concurrent Computation*. PhD thesis, The Weizmann Institute of Science, Rehovot, Israel, 1993.
4. Y. Feldman and E. Shapiro. Temporal debugging and its visual animation. In V. Saraswat and K. Udea, editors, *Proc. of the 1991 Logic Programming Int. Symposium*, pages 3–17. MIT Press, 1991.
5. G. Ferrand. Error diagnosis in logic programming, an adaptation of E. Y. Shapiro's method. *Journal of Logic Programming*, 4:177–198, 1987.
6. P. Van Hentenryck, V. A. Saraswat, and Y. Deville. Constraint processing in cc(FD). Technical report, Brown University, 1992.
7. M. Huntbach. Algorithmic Parlog debugging. In *Proc. IEEE Symposium on Logic Programming*, San Francisco, September 1987.
8. Y. Lichtenstein and E. Shapiro. Concurrent algorithmic debugging. Technical Report CS87-20, Dept. of Applied Math. and Computer Science, Weizmann Inst. Rehovot, Israel, December 1987.

9. Y. Lichtenstein and E. Shapiro. Abstract algorithmic debugging. In R. A. Kowalski and K. A. Bowen, editors, *Proc. of the Fifth Int. Conf. and Symposium*, pages 512–530. MIT Press, 1988.

10. J. W. Lloyd. Declarative error diagnosis. *New Generation Computing*, (5):133–154, 1987.

11. J. W. Lloyd. *Foundations of Logic Programming*. Springer-Verlag, Berlin, Heidelberg, second edition, 1987.

12. J. W. Lloyd and A. Takeuchi. A framework for debugging GHC. Technical Report TR-186, ICOT, Institute for New Generation Computer Technology, Tokyo, 1986.

13. L. Naish. Declarative diagnosis of missing answers. Technical Report 88/9, Univ. of Melbourne, Dept. of Computer Science, 1988.

14. L. Naish. Declarative debugging of lazy functional programs. Technical Report 92/6, Univ. of Melbourne, Dept. of Computer Science, 1992.

15. H. Nilsson and P. Fritzson. Algorithmic debugging for lazy functional languages. Technical Report 92-17, Dept. of Computer and Information Science, Linköping University, Linköping, Sweden, 1992. Also in Proc. PLILP'92, Springer-Verlag, LNCS, Leuven, Belgium, Aug. 1992.

16. L. M. Pereira. Rational debugging in logic programming. In *Proc. 3rd Int. Conf. on Logic Programming*, pages 203–210, London, 1986. Springer-Verlag, LNCS 225.

17. V. A. Saraswat. *Concurrent Constraint Programming Languages*. Logic Programming Series. MIT Press, Cambridge, MA, 1993.

18. V. A. Saraswat, K. M. Kahn, and J. Levy. Janus: A step towards distributed constraint programming. In *Proc. of the North American Conf. on Logic Programming*, Cambridge, MA, October 1990. MIT Press.

19. V. A. Saraswat, M. Rinard, and P. Panangaden. Semantic foundations of concurrent constraint programming. Technical Report SSL-90-86, Xerox PARC, Palo Alto, CA, October 1990.

20. E. Y. Shapiro. *Algorithmic Program Debugging*. ACM Distinguished Dissertation Series. MIT Press, Cambridge, MA, 1982.

21. A. Takeuchi. Algorithmic debugging of GHC programs and its implementation in GHC. In E. Shapiro, editor, *Concurrent Prolog*, volume 2, chapter V, pages 180–196. MIT Press, Cambridge, MA, 1987. Also in [22].

22. A. Takeuchi. *Parallel Logic Programming*, volume 2. Wiley, 1992.

Hierarchy in Testing Distributed Programs*

Sridhar Alagar and *S. Venkatesan*
Computer Science Program, EC 31
University of Texas at Dallas
Richardson, TX 75083
{sridhar,venky}@utdallas.edu

Abstract

Testing distributed programs, a problem of theoretical and practical significance and closely related to debugging, is more involved than testing sequential programs because of the presence of multiple points of control, the asynchronous communication medium, and the inherent concurrency. This paper develops a hierarchical approach, consisting of three levels, to dynamic testing of distributed programs. Several problems arising in these levels are computationally hard. In certain restricted cases, the second and the third levels are easier to handle. Several important issues are considered and distributed algorithms are presented. Some of the techniques presented in level 2 and level 3 are useful for debugging distributed programs also.

Keywords

Distributed Algorithm, Global States, Input space, Distributed test cases, Predicate-based testing, Message Complexity.

1   Introduction

Distributed systems are harder to program and test than the sequential systems [7] for the following reasons. First, they consist of a varying number of processes executing in parallel. Second, a process may update its variables independently or in response to the actions of another process. Third, problems specific to the development of distributed applications are not suitably reflected by known programming languages and software engineering environments [19]. As distributed computing systems are used in many critical environments, it is extremely important that programs running on them be correct. Testing distributed programs is a challenging task of great significance. In this paper, we present a hierarchical approach for testing distributed programs. Figure 1 shows the three levels of the hierarchy.

Level 1 of the hierarchy deals with the selection of input data from the input space. Conventional testing criteria like path testing, branch testing, and statement testing can be extended for distributed programs also. In general, even the statement testing criterion is intractable [24], since such a scheme must generate input data that will ensure certain groups of statements are executed. Taylor and Kelly [24] have proposed a lesser criterion which is feasible but less

---

*This research was supported in part by NSF under Grant No. CCR-9110177, by the Texas Advanced Technology Program under Grant No. 9741-036, and by a grant from Alcatel Network Systems.

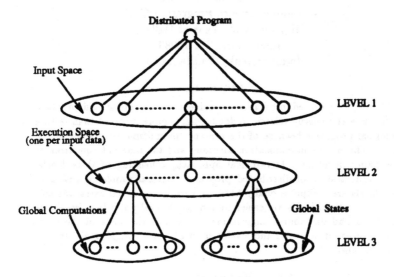

Figure 1: Hierarchy in testing distributed programs

effective. The contribution of the paper is only to level 2 and level 3. We discuss about the issues in level 1 for the sake of completeness.

Level 2 of the hierarchy addresses the question of non-determinism due to the random message delays of the communication medium. The execution of a distributed program for a fixed input data is not unique. An error may not be revealed in one execution. Thus we need to test several executions. At this level, for a single input data selected from the input space in Level 1, *different execu-tions* are produced. We present a distributed algorithm for producing different executions for a fixed input data. Also, we show that the role of non-determinism due to the communication is drastically reduced in (1) distributed programs that run on unidirectional rings with FIFO channels and (2) distributed programs whose fundamental steps involve associative function computation.

Level 3 of the hierarchy involves testing a particular execution selected from the execution space in Level 2. To achieve a comprehensive testing strategy, the states of the processes cannot be tested independently; "global states" have to be tested. A single execution chosen from the execution space in Level 2 may consist of a large number of global states and may correspond to several *global computations*. We propose three criteria, namely, testing all global computa-tions, testing all global states, and predicate based testing. Testing all global computations is effective, but infeasible. Testing all global states is adequate, but it may be difficult to perform. Predicate based testing is feasible, but may be less effective.

The organization of the paper is as follows. We present the system model and definitions in Section 2. Certain issues related to selecting test data (Level 1) are discussed in Section 3. In Section 4, we consider the problem of generating different executions for a given input data (Level 2). Issues related to Level 3 of the testing hierarchy are considered in Section 5. Section 6 concludes the paper.

2   Model and Definitions

A distributed system is a collection of processes connected by a set of communication links. The links are bidirectional. Communication links take an arbitrary but finite amount of time to deliver the messages (i.e., the links are asynchronous). The communication between the processes is by message passing only.

Let $P = \{P_1, \ldots, P_n\}$ be the set of processes. An event e in a process P_i is an action (or a sequence of actions) that changes the state of P_i. An event may be (i) a send event resulting in sending of a message, or (ii) a receive event resulting in receiving of a message, or (iii) an internal event where the process executes a series of instructions (but no message receipt or sending is involved). The kth event of P_i is denoted by e_k^i. The computation is assumed to be event driven — a process receives a message, processes it, sends messages (possibly zero) to other processes, and waits for the next message.

The partial order *happens before*, denoted by →, defined by Lamport [12] is used to express the causality between two events. To determine the causality between any two events, we use the vector clock introduced by Fidge [8] and Mattern [17]. Let C^i be the vector clock maintained by P_i, and C_k^i be the value of C^i after executing e_k^i. Whenever a process sends a message, it *timestamps* the message by appending the current (updated) clock value to it. The following operations are performed on the clock C^i by P_i when it executes an event e.

1. For each event e, P_i first increments the ith component of its clock, i.e., $C^i[i] = C^i[i] + 1$.

2. If e is a receive event and T is the time stamp of the message, $\forall j, C^i[j] = max(C^i[j], T[j])$.

An example is shown in Figure 8 in the Appendix.

We say that $C_k^i < C_l^j$ if $\forall x, C_k^i[x] \leq C_l^j[x]$. It is easy to show that $e_k^i \to e_l^j$ iff $C_k^i < C_l^j$. Events e_k^i and e_l^j are *consistent*, if $C_k^i[i] \geq C_l^j[i]$ and $C_l^j[j] \geq C_k^i[j]$. (Intuitively, e_k^i does not depend on any event of P_j that occurs after e_l^j, and e_l^j does not depend on any event of P_i that occurs after e_k^i.) A *cut* is a collection of events with one event from every process. A cut $< e_{k_1}^1, \ldots, e_{k_n}^n >$ is a *consistent cut* if for all i, j and $i \neq j$, $e_{k_i}^i$ and $e_{k_j}^j$ are consistent. A *global state* is a collection of the local states of all the processes [5]. For every cut $< e_{k_1}^1, \ldots, e_{k_n}^n >$, there is a unique global state $< s_{k_1}^1, \ldots, s_{k_n}^n >$ where $s_{k_i}^i$ is the state of P_i after executing $e_{k_i}^i$ (and for every global state, there is a unique cut). A global state $< s_{k_1}^1, \ldots, s_{k_n}^n >$ is a *consistent global state* if its corresponding cut is a consistent cut. A consistent global state is a state of the distributed system that could have been observed by an external observer.

We assume that our model is capable of *reproducing execution*, i.e., the behavior of each process during the first execution and during subsequent executions of a distributed program is identical. Reproducible execution is needed in generating *different runs* (§ 4.1) and in *predicate based* testing (§ 5.3). Several algorithms exist for reproducible execution and the reader is referred to [10, 13, 25] for details .

3 Selecting Input Data (Level 1)

In a distributed program for each read statement executed by a process, a value must be chosen and given. Thus, an *input data* for a distributed program is a set of sequences of input values, one sequence per process, such that when a process needs data, the next value from the sequence associated with that process is given.

In the sequential case, the traditional program based testing is based on the flow graph model of a program. In this graph, a program statement or a block is represented by a node and the flow of control from one statement (block) to another statement (block) is represented by an edge between the corresponding nodes [11]. Based on the flow graph, various testing criteria – like path testing, branch testing and statement testing, to name a few – are defined. These criteria form a hierarchy based on their effectiveness in testing. Path testing, which is at the top of the hierarchy, involves testing all paths that the control could take in a program and is clearly the most complete testing methodology. However, the number of paths may be infinite, and this strategy is impractical. Statement testing is less effective but practical.

Taylor and Kelly [24] extend the flow graph model to concurrent programs. They define several criteria and establish a hierarchy among these criteria. (Note that the hierarchy proposed by Taylor and Kelly is based on the flow graph model of the program and is different from the hierarchy proposed by us which is inherent in dynamic testing of distributed programs.) The technique at the top of hierarchy, all paths, is the most effective but it is not practical. Even the restricted statement testing criterion is impractical for concurrent programs. The added difficulty is due to the multiple number of processes. To bypass this difficulty, they restrict the criterion further, by choosing nodes that require closer examination. This criterion is less effective, but feasible. Further research is needed (i) for finding new criteria that include the communication medium and (ii) for developing strategies to meet the criteria.

4 Coping with Communication Medium (Level 2)

In a sequential program the input determines the output. But, in a distributed program, the output of a process not only depends on the input data but also on

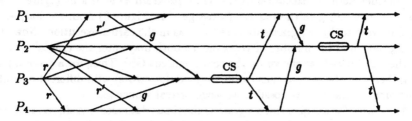

Figure 2: Execution 1 of mutual exclusion program

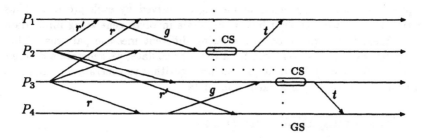

Figure 3: Execution 2 of mutual exclusion program

the sequence of the messages received by it. A different message arrival sequence may produce a different result for the same input data. Also, for a given input data, an error in a distributed program may not be revealed in a particular execution while the error may be revealed in a different execution. We illustrate this point with an example.

Consider a voting-based distributed mutual exclusion program. Every process has one vote. A process trying to enter its critical section must get a majority of votes from the other processes. (For simplicity, we do not consider deadlocks and livelocks.) Assume that in an implementation, a process trying to enter its critical section waits for exactly half the number of votes instead of waiting for more than half the number of votes (due to typing error). We consider two executions; one reveals this error and the other does not reveal it.

Figure 2 represents one execution of the mutual exclusion program outlined above. Initially, processes P_2 and P_3 try to enter the critical section. P_2 broadcasts a request vote message (message r' in Figure 2), P_3 broadcasts a request vote message (message r), and both of them wait for the votes. P_1 and P_4 receive the request from P_3 first, hence they send their votes to P_3 (messages g). Since P_3 gets half the number of votes, it enters its critical section (denoted as CS in the Figure). P_2 has only one vote (its own vote), so it does not enter its critical section. After leaving its critical section, P_3 returns the votes (messages t). Now, P_1 and P_4 grant their votes to P_2, and P_2 enters its critical section.

Consider another execution of the same program as shown in Figure 3. In this execution, P_1 gets the request (message r' in Figure 3) from P_2 first, so it sends its vote to P_2. P_4 grants its vote to P_3 as in the earlier execution. Now, P_2 and P_3 have half the number of votes, hence both may enter the critical section "at the same time" (as shown by the consistent cut GS). Thus, for a given input data, there may be several runs (some may exhibit errors) with different outputs depending on the several possible message arrival sequences.

A test case for a sequential program is the input data alone. A *distributed test case* is a collection of values such that the behavior of the distributed system is identical for each run of the distributed test case [25]. Thus a test case for distributed systems is a collection of initial values (input data) to each of the processes and the sequence of messages received by each process. Thus, generating test cases for distributed programs involves generating input data, as in sequential programs, and considering different message patterns. (Note that by generating a different run for a fixed input data, we generate a different distributed test case.) We next present an algorithm to generate different runs (distributed test cases) for a fixed input data.

4.1 Producing Different Runs

Let the distributed program be executed once, and $E_i = < e_1^i e_2^i \ldots >$ be the sequence of consecutive events of P_i. E_i is a *process run* for process P_i. $E = \{E_1, \ldots, E_n\}$ is a *run* of the distributed system.

For a process P_i, a process run E_i' is *different* from a process run E_i if the sequence of messages received by P_i in the two process runs E_i' and E_i are different (even if the input data is same for E_i and E_i'). Unless mentioned otherwise, the term "different run" means a different run for the same input data. A run $E' = \{E_1', \ldots, E_n'\}$ of a distributed system is *different* from a run $E = \{E_1, \ldots, E_n\}$ if and only if there exists at least one process P_i such that E_i' is different from E_i. Let $recv(m)$ denote the receive event initiated by the receipt of message m, and let $send(m)$ be the event that involves the sending of m.

Lemma 1 *Let E be a run (of the distributed system) for a given input data and let $M_i = < m_1, m_2, \ldots >$ be the sequence of messages received by P_i during process run $E_i \in E$. There is a process run E_i', for the same input data, different from E_i if and only if there are two consecutive messages m_{t-1} and m_t received by P_i in E_i such that $recv(m_{t-1}) \not\rightarrow send(m_t)$ in E.*

Proof: See Appendix.

Lemma 1 holds when the links are not FIFO. If the links are FIFO, the FIFO condition must be included.

FIFO condition: *If two messages, m_1 and m_2, received by process P_i are sent by the same process P_j connected to P_i by a bidirectional FIFO communication link, then $send(m_1) \rightarrow send(m_2) \Leftrightarrow recv(m_1) \rightarrow recv(m_2)$.*

Lemma 2 *Let E be a run (of the distributed system) for a given input data. Assume that the links are FIFO. Let $M_i = < m_1, m_2, \ldots >$ be the sequence of messages received by P_i during process run $E_i \in E$. There is a process run E'_i, for the same input data, different from E_i if and only if there are two consecutive messages m_{t-1} and m_t received by P_i in E_i such that (i) $recv(m_{t-1}) \nrightarrow send(m_t)$ in E, and (ii) $send(m_{t-1})$ and $send(m_t)$ are events on two different processes in E.*

Proof: (sketch) It follows from Lemma 1 and the FIFO condition. See [2] for a more complete proof. ∎

Lemmas 1 and 2 are very significant. To produce a different run, we need to check only consecutive receive events to see if they can be swapped as opposed to checking every pair of receive events. Thus, the number of pairs checked for swapping is linear in the number of receive events. (The number of pairs checked is quadratic if all pairs are considered.) We now explain the algorithm to produce *different runs*. For the sake of brevity we say that two messages, m_k and m_l, received by P_i in E_i can be *permuted* if $recv(m_k) \nrightarrow send(m_l)$ in E. During the first run, in addition to the data required for reproducible execution, process P_i stores the vector clock value of $recv(m)$ and the timestamp of m for every message m received by P_i. First, P_i checks whether there are two consecutive messages received by it that can be permuted. Several processes may be able to permute two messages. So a leader is elected (by the user or by executing a leader election algorithm), and the leader will permute two messages. If there is no process that can permute two message receives, then there is no other run. Algorithm *Different Runs* of Figure 4 is executed by every process after the completion of one run E.

The number of possible test cases for a fixed input data may be large, and we do not have an upper bound. But, there are certain class of programs for which the number of test cases is unique.

Theorem 1 *For a fixed input data, the run in a unidirectional network with FIFO links is unique.*

Proof: A process can receive a message from only one process and since the links are FIFO, it follows from Lemma 2 that the run is unique. ∎

It is clear from Theorem 1 that testing distributed programs in unidirectional rings is simpler than in other networks since the input data alone determines the behavior of the processes in unidirectional rings (and a distributed test case consists of only the input data). A similar result applies to distributed programs that are based on *associative function*. Many of the distributed algorithms such as algorithms for breadth first search, shortest paths, maximum flow, maximum matching, sorting, median finding, and constructing snapshots use associative functions [21] for reducing the message complexity. The details are not provided for brevity. The reader is referred to [2] for more details.

It is interesting to note that the idea behind the algorithm for producing different runs can used for reproducing executions efficiently. Reproducing an execution is an important strategy for debugging distributed programs as the bugs in a given run may have to be reproduced many times to trace their cause. An independent work by Netzer and Miller [20] uses ideas similar to ours for reproducing an execution optimally.

---

begin

    $k \leftarrow$ the number of messages received by P_i in E_i; *permute* $\leftarrow$ *false*.

    for $t = 1$ **to** $k - 1$ **do**

        if $recv(m_t) \not\to send(m_{t+1})$ **then** (*use vector clock for checking*)

            permute $\leftarrow$ *true*; exit loop.

    if (*permute* = *true*) **and** (P_i is the leader) **then**

        (*P_i can become leader only if it can permute. *)

        (i) Reproduce execution E_i till messages m_t and m_{t+1} are received.

        (ii) Process m_{t+1} before processing m_t and broadcast

        REP_OVER message.

    else Reproduce execution till REP_OVER message is received and

        continue normal execution.

end.

Figure 4: Algorithm *Different Runs* for P_i

---

5   Testing a run (Level 3)

Sequential programs are tested by running the test cases and by comparing the (intermediate and) final states with the expected values. Testing a distributed program is complicated because of the presence of multiple processes. Testing the local states of all of the processes in isolation is insufficient; we need to test the global states. The necessity of testing global states is illustrated with an example. Consider again the execution of the mutual exclusion program shown in Figure 3. In the consistent global state GS (denoted by the dotted line in the Figure) both P_2 and P_3 are in their critical section which is clearly an error. We cannot detect errors of this nature by testing the local states of the processes alone. Also, it is not sufficient to test the final global state alone, since the errors occurring in the intermediate global states may not be detected.

Mattern [17] has shown that the set of all global states of a given execution (run) forms a lattice. The lattice for the execution shown in Figure 8 in Appendix is shown in Figure 9 in Appendix. A point in a lattice represents a global state. Two global states G and G' are connected by a directed edge if G' can be reached from G by executing one event in any of the processes. There is a path from a global state G to G' in the lattice if G' is reachable from G by executing several events. Finally, a path from the initial global state to the final global state represents one *global computation* and is a possible computation of the system. Note that there may be several paths from the initial global state to the final global state depending on the relative order in which the events take place within the processes.

5.1 Testing all Global Computations

Each path from an initial global state to the final global state (of a lattice) represents a global computation that could have been observed by an external observer. One way to test a distributed program is to test all possible paths from the initial global state to the final global state in the lattice. This corresponds to testing all the global computations of an execution. Clearly, this technique can ensure correctness, but, in the worst case, the number of paths may be exponential in the number of global states. Hence, this criterion is not feasible in all cases.

5.2 Testing all Consistent Global States

In this technique, we test all consistent global states instead of testing all possible paths. If every possible global state is tested for correctness, then we can ensure that the distributed program, for the given run, does not exhibit a "bad state". Unfortunately, the worst-case number of global states may be exponential in the number of processes. For a given number of events (on all processes), the number of global states may not be high when large number of messages are transmitted since messages create dependencies, hence all the consistent global states may be tested. The reader is referred to [6] for generating all possible global states of a given run. The number of global states is very high when the number of messages transmitted is low. In this case we have to settle for a lesser criterion like predicate based testing.

5.3 Predicate based testing

Given a run and a predicate Φ, we test the run by asking the question "Does there exist a global state where the predicate Φ holds ?" This question is posed as POSSIBLY(Φ) in [6, 26] and as weak predicates in [9]. If Φ represents an error condition, then POSSIBLY(Φ) represents a possible occurrence of an error. For example, if the distributed program implements a solution to the mutual exclusion problem, then "$\Phi = (P_1$ is in critical section$) \wedge (P_2$ is in critical section$)$" denotes an error. Global predicates have been used in [6, 9, 16, 26] for testing and debugging. Also, predicate based testing is useful in detecting whether any *safety* property of the specification is violated.

The predicates may be constructed using the specification of the distributed program with some input from the implementation group. To thoroughly test the program, sufficient number of predicates covering all aspects of specification and implementation must be constructed. We do not discuss methods for constructing predicates since they are specific to the application program. As in [9], we consider only conjunctive predicates where each conjunct is any boolean expression using constants and variables of a single process. Thus, a conjunctive predicate may be represented as $C_1 \wedge C_2 \wedge \ldots \wedge C_n$, where conjunct C_i is any

1. Let f_i be the index of the first event of S_i and l_i be the index of the last event of S_i. Process P_i broadcasts l_i.

2. Wait till l_j values sent by each P_j is received and locally stored in P_i.

3. Let x_i be the index of the *latest* event of P_i such that $C^i_{x_i}[j] \leq l_j$ for each j. ($C^i_{x_i}[j]$ is the jth component of the vector clock of P_i associated with event x_i.) Clearly, such an event of P_i exists since the first event of P_i satisfies this property.

4. If x_i is earlier than f_i, then POSSIBLY(Φ) is false. If $x_i = f_i$ or x_i occurs later than f_i for each process P_i, then POSSIBLY(Φ) is true.

Figure 5: Algorithm POSSIBLY(Φ)

boolean expression involving constants and variables local to process P_i only. We next present a distributed algorithm for evaluating POSSIBLY(Φ).

Testing POSSIBLY(Φ)

An event may be the result of the execution of several statements or subprograms, and several variables may be updated in an event. Note that no messages are sent or received during any part of an event except in the beginning, and each action that results in sending a message or receiving a message marks the beginning of a new event. if the conjunct C_i becomes true at any time t of execution of the program at process P_i, then P_i marks the event that occurs during time t. Clearly, the marked events of P_i represent those events during which C_i becomes true at least once. Since C_i refers to variables of P_i only, no messages are needed in marking events.

The events are marked on-line by all of the processes and, when the distributed computation terminates, the (off-line) predicate based testing process begins. Each process merges consecutive marked events into a maximal sequence of marked events. Let S_i be a maximal sequence of consecutive marked events of P_i. Clearly, within each event of S_i, C_i becomes true at least at one point during that event. The event immediately before the first event of S_i and the event immediately after the last event of S_i are unmarked events. If $C_i = \phi$, then S_i contains all events of P_i. The following theorem gives a method for testing POSSIBLY(Φ).

Theorem 2 *Let S_i be the single maximal sequence of consecutive marked events of P_i. POSSIBLY(Φ) is true if and only if there is a consistent cut GS of n events with exactly one marked event of S_1, one marked event of $S_2, \ldots,$ one marked event of S_n.*

Proof: See [2]. ∎

Testing POSSIBLY(Φ) is equivalent to checking if there exists a consistent global state such that each component of the global state represents a process

---

1. For each process P_i, S_i is set to the last sequence of marked events of P_i.

2. Run the algorithm of Figure 5. If the algorithm halts and determines that POSSIBLY(Φ) is true, halt.

3. Otherwise, there exists at least one process P_j such that x_j is earlier than f_j. For each such process P_j, remove the current S_j from consideration and set S_j to the sequence of marked events of P_j that occurs just before the currently removed S_j.

4. If there exists a process P_k such that all of the sequence of marked events of P_k have been removed in step (3), stop and declare POSSIBLY(Φ) to be false.

5. Go to step (2).

Figure 6: POSSIBLY(Φ) with multiple marked sequences

---

state that occurs within a marked event. If no event of P_i is marked, then POSSIBLY(Φ) is false. A formal description is presented in Figure 5.

Theorem 3 *Algorithm POSSIBLY(Φ) of Figure 5 is correct.*

Proof: See [2]. ∎

There may be more than one marked group at each process. In this case, we proceed as shown in the algorithm of Figure 6.

Message complexity: Each process broadcasts two numbers and $O(n)$ messages are used in broadcasting one number. Thus, $O(n^2)$ messages are sufficient for determining POSSIBLY(Φ) if each process has one marked sequence. Otherwise, the message complexity is $O(kn^2)$ where k is the total number of marked sequences in all of the processes.

Detecting POSSIBLY(Φ) is an important technique for debugging distributed programs. A programmer may want to stop the execution when an error occurs (breakpoint) to analyse the cause of the error. The algorithm POSSIBLY(Φ) can be used to stop the execution in a global state where the bug appears.

6 Conclusions

Related Work
Taylor and Kelly [24] and Carver and Tai [4] propose a program based static analysis technique for testing concurrent programs (ADA and CSP). Our method is for asynchronous distributed programs, based on events and global states, and is dynamic in nature. Our algorithm for producing *different runs* is different from the perturbation technique described in [27] for testing protocols. There a

process' behavior can be represented by a directed graph(Finite State Machine), whereas our model is more powerful than a FSM. Also, we do not know the behavior of a process a-priori. The possibility of receiving a different message is determined only by the causality relation "happened before".

The concept of evaluating global predicates used in the third level of our technique has been used by Miller and Choi [18], Spezialetti [22], Spezialetti and Kearns [23], Cooper and Marzullo [6], Marzullo and Neiger [16], and Manabe and Imase [15] for debugging, and by Venkatesan and Dathan [26] and Garg and Waldecker [9] for testing distributed programs. Our technique uses vector clocks of Fidge and Mattern [8, 17] for global predicate detection, is more efficient and decentralized than the techniques of [6, 9, 16], and is similar in spirit to Venkatesan and Dathan's [26] method for detecting global predicates which requires $O(n^3)$ messages. Our algorithm uses $O(n^2)$ messages, but the technique of [26] does not use vector clocks while our algorithm uses vector clocks.

Concluding Remarks

It is well known that program testing is very difficult and is undecidable in the general case. Testing distributed programs is harder than testing sequential programs due to the asynchrony and combinatorial explosion of state space.This paper develops a hierarchical approach, consisting of three levels, to dynamic testing of distributed programs. At the first level, input data is selected. The second level deals with selecting different runs for an input data. An execution of the distributed program is tested for correctness at the third level. Though our methodology is not a complete one, we believe that it must be a part of any comprehensive testing scheme.

There is no way to generate a finite number of distributed test cases which will "expose" all errors. Further research is needed to find reasonable criteria for selecting distributed test cases. Testing all paths in a lattice, and enumerating and testing all global states are infeasible. Thus, we have chosen a lesser criterion like predicate base testing. More study is required in this direction, both from theoretical and empirical point of view, and what we have provided is just a starting point. Different approaches such as (1) placing restrictions on the type of distributed programs, (2) probabilistic approaches, (3) combining the methods used in software testing and verification as done by Lloyd and Kearns [14], and using ideas from distributed debugging [1, 3] are future directions for research. We are working on these and related problems.

Acknowledgements

We thank the anonymous referees for their valuable suggestions and comments.

References

[1] AHUJA, M., KSHEMKALYANI, A., AND CARLSON, T. A basic unit of computation in distributed systems. In *Proceedings of the Tenth International Conference on Distributed Computing Systems* (1990), IEEE, pp. 12–19.

[2] ALAGAR, S., AND VENKATESAN, S. Hierarchy in testing distributed programs. Computer Science Technical Report UTDCS-8-92, The University of Texas at Dallas, September 1992.

[3] BATES, P., AND WILEDON, J. High-level debugging of distributed systems: The behavioral abstraction approach. *Journal of Systems and Software 3*, 4 (1983), 255–264.

[4] CARVER, R., AND TAI, K. Static analysis of concurrent software for deriving synchronization constraints. In *Proceedings of the Eleventh International Conference on Distributed Computing Systems* (1991), IEEE, pp. 544–551.

[5] CHANDY, K., AND LAMPORT, L. Distributed snapshots: Determining global states of distributed systems. *ACM Trans. Comput. Syst. 3*, 1 (1985), 63–75.

[6] COOPER, R., AND MARZULLO, K. Consistent detection of global predicates. *Sigplan Notices* (1991), 167–174.

[7] FAGERSTROM, J. Design and test of distributed applications. In *Proceedings of the Tenth International Conference of Software Engineering* (1988), pp. 88–92.

[8] FIDGE, J. Timestamps in message passing systems that preserve the partial ordering. In *Proceedings of the 11th Australian Computer Science Conference* (1988), pp. 55–66.

[9] GARG, V., AND WALDECKER, B. Detection of unstable predicates in distributed programs. In *Proceedings of the International Conference on Foundations of Software Technology and Theoretical Computer Science* (1992), Springer Verlag.

[10] GOLDBERG, A., GOPAL, A., LOWRY, A., AND STROM, R. Restoring consistent global computation of distributed computations. *Sigplan Notices* (1991), 144–154.

[11] HOWDEN, W. E. A survey of dynamic analysis methods. In *Tutorial: Software Testing and Validation Techniques*, E. Miller and W. Howden, Eds., second ed. IEEE Computer Society Press, 1981, pp. 209–231.

[12] LAMPORT, L. Time, clocks, and the ordering of events in a distributed system. *Commun. ACM 21*, 7 (1978), 558–565.

[13] LEBLANC, T., AND MELLOR-CRUMMY, J. Debugging parallel programs with instant replay. *IEEE Transactions on Computers C-36*, 4 (1987), 471–482.

[14] LLOYD, W., AND KEARNS, P. Using tracing to direct our reasoning about distributed programs. In *The 11th IEEE International Conference on Distributed Computing Systems* (1991), pp. 552–559.

[15] MANABE, Y., AND IMASE, M. Global conditions in debugging distributed programs. *Journal of Parallel and Distributed Computing* (1992), 62–69.

[16] MARZULLO, K., AND NEIGER, G. Detection of global state predicates. In *Distributed Algorithms Proceedings of 3rd International Workshop.* Springer-Verlag, 1991, pp. 254–272.

[17] MATTERN, F. Virtual time and global states of distributed systems. In *Parallel and Distributed Algorithms: Proceedings of the International Workshop on Parallel and Distributed Algorithms*, M. Cosnard et. al., Ed. Elsevier Science Publishers B. V., 1989, pp. 215–226.

[18] MILLER, B., AND CHOI, J.-D. Breakpoints and halting in distributed programs. In *The 8th IEEE International Conference on Distributed Computing Systems* (1988), pp. 316–323.

[19] MUHLHAUSER, M. Software engineering for distributed applications: The design project. In *Proceedings of the Tenth International Conference on Software Engineering* (1988), pp. 93–101.

[20] NETZER, R. H. B., AND MILLER, B. P. Optimal tracing and replay for debugging message-passing parallel programs. In *Supercomputing* (1992), pp. 502–511.

[21] RAMARAO, K., AND VENKATESAN, S. Distributed problem solving in spite of process failures. In *Proceedings of the 11th Symposium on Reliable Distributed systems* (1992), pp. 164–171.

[22] SPEZIALETTI, M. *A generalized approach to monitoring distributed computations for event occurrences.* PhD thesis, University of Pittsburgh, Pittsburgh, Pennsylvania, 1989.

[23] SPEZIALETTI, M., AND KEARNS, P. Simultaneous regions: A framework for the consistent monitoring of distributed computations. In *Proceedings of the Ninth International Conference on Distributed Computing Systems* (1989), IEEE, pp. 61–68.

[24] TAYLOR, R., LEVINE, D., AND KELLY, C. Structural testing of concurrent programs. *IEEE Trans. Softw. Eng. 18*, 3 (1992), 206–215.

[25] VENKATESAN, S. Reproducible execution of distributed programs. Computer Science Technical Report UTDCS-8-91, The University of Texas at Dallas, 1991.

[26] VENKATESAN, S., AND DATHAN, B. Testing and debugging distributed programs distributively. In *Proceedings of Thirtieth Annual Allerton Conference on Communication, Control and Computing* (1992).

[27] WEST, C. General technique for communications protocol validation. *IBM Journal of Research and Development 22*, 4 (1978), 393–404.

Appendix

Proof for Lemma 1

($\Rightarrow$) <u>Given:</u> E and E' are different process runs. Let $S = \{e'_{k_1}, \ldots, e'_{k_n}\}$ be a set of events such that e'_{k_j} is an event in E'_j (of process P_j) and e'_{k_j} is the earliest event of E'_j that differs from its corresponding event e_{k_j} in E_j. Note that the first event in E'_j, for all j, is the first event in E_j since the input data is same for both the runs.

Fact 1: There exists an event $e'_{k_y} \in S$ such that $e'_{k_z} \not\to e'_{k_y}$ for all $z \neq y$. (That is, no event of $e'_{k_z} \in S$ happens before/precedes e'_{k_y}.)

Since our model is event driven (where an event e is determined solely on its previous event and, if e is a receive event, on the contents of the message received), e'_{k_y} is a receive event. Now, choose $i = y$ ($P_i = P_y$). Let $recv(m') = e'_{k_i}$ and $recv(m_q) = e_{k_i}$ where m_q is a message received by P_i in E_i (See Figure 7). Since $e'_{k_i} \neq e_{k_i}$, $m' \neq m_q$. Now, there exists a message $m_t \in M_i$ such that $m' = m_t$ and $t > q$. (Recall that e'_{k_i} is the earliest event in E'_i that differs from e_{k_i} in E_i and, from Fact 1, e'_{k_i} is not preceded by any other event of S.) Clearly, m_t is received before m_q in E'_i. Therefore, $recv(m_q) \not\to send(m_t)$ in E. (Call this **Claim 1**.) Now, for any r ($q \leq r < t$), $recv(m_q) \to recv(m_r)$ in E_i. This implies that $recv(m_{t-1}) \not\to send(m_t)$ in E_i (otherwise $recv(m_q) \to send(m_t)$, contradicting Claim 1 that was proved before).

($\Leftarrow$) Clearly, during E'_i message m_t can be received before m_{t-1} by P_i yielding a different process run. ∎

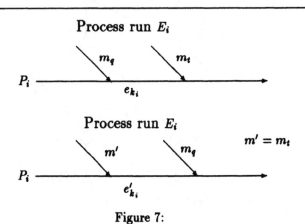

Figure 7:

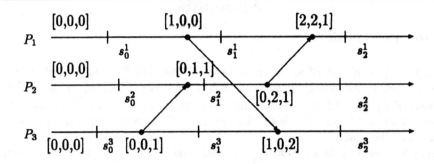

Figure 8: *The initial clock value of all three processes is* $[0,0,0]$. *When* P_1 *sends its first message to* P_3, P_1 *changes its clock value to* $[1,0,0]$ *(by operation 1) and timestamps it with* $[1,0,0]$. *On receiving this message,* P_3 *changes its clock value to* $[1,0,2]$ *(by operation 2).*

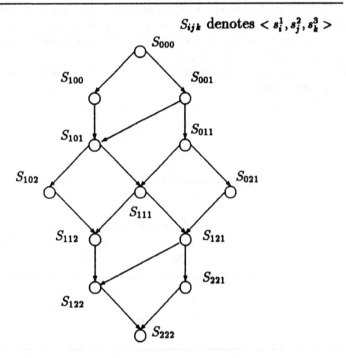

Figure 9: Lattice for the execution shown above.

Lazy Algorithmic Debugging: Ideas for Practical Implementation

Henrik Nilsson and Peter Fritzson

Programming Environments Laboratory
Department of Computer and Information Science
Linköping University, S-581 83 Linköping, Sweden
E-mail: henni@ida.liu.se, paf@ida.liu.se

Abstract. Lazy functional languages have non-strict semantics and are purely declarative, i.e. they support the notion of referential transparency and are devoid of side effects. Traditional debugging techniques are, however, not suited for lazy functional languages since computations generally do not take place in the order one might expect. Since *algorithmic debugging* allows the user to concentrate on the declarative aspects of program semantics, and will semi-automatically find functions containing bugs, we propose to use this technique for debugging lazy functional programs. Our earlier work showed that this is a promising approach. However, the current version of our debugger has severe implementational problems, e.g. too large trace size and too many questions asked. This paper suggests a number of techniques for overcoming these problems, at least partially. The key techniques are *immediate strictification* and *piecemeal tracing*.

1 Introduction

Debugging has always been a costly part of software development, and several attempts have been made to provide automatic computer support for this task [14]. The algorithmic debugging technique, introduced by Shapiro [16], was the first attempt to lay a theoretical framework for program debugging and to take this as a basis for a partly automatic debugger.

Algorithmic debugging is a two phase process: an execution trace tree is built at the procedure/function level during the first (trace) phase. This tree is then traversed during the second (debugging) phase. Each node in the tree corresponds to an invocation of a procedure or function and holds a record of supplied arguments and returned results. Once built, the debugger basically traverses the tree in a top-down manner, asking, for each encountered node, whether the recorded procedure or function invocation is correct or not. If not, the debugger will continue with the child nodes, otherwise with the next sibling. A bug has been found when an erroneous application node is identified where all children (if any) behaved correctly.

Algorithmic debugging was first developed in the context of Prolog. In previous research by our group, the algorithmic debugging method has been generalized to a class of imperative languages and its bug finding properties improved by integrating the method with program slicing [15][4][8][7].

Within the field of lazy functional programming, the lack of suitable debugging tools has been apparent for quite some time. We feel that traditional debugging techniques (e.g. breakpoints, tracing, variable watching etc.) are not particularly well suited for the class of lazy languages since computations in a program generally do not take place in the order one might expect from reading the source code [3].

Algorithmic debugging, however, allows a user to concentrate on the declarative semantics of an application program, rather than its operational aspects such as evaluation order. During debugging, the user only has to decide whether or not a particular function applied to some specific arguments yields a correct result. Given correct answers from the user, the debugger will determine which function that contains the bug. Thus, the user need not worry about why and when a function is invoked, which suggests that algorithmic debugging might be a suitable basis for a debugging tool for lazy functional languages. Obviously, there must be a visible bug symptom for this technique to work.

In our previous work [12], support for algorithmic debugging was added to an existing compiler for a small lazy functional language and an algorithmic debugger was implemented. The language, called Freja [11], is essentially a subset of Miranda[1] [18]. It is based on graph reduction and implemented using a G-machine approach [1][2][5][6][13]. The system was successfully applied to a number of small examples, thus showing the relevance of algorithmic debugging for lazy functional programming.

However, as we gained experience from using the system, a number of problems became apparent. Firstly, storing the complete trace is impractical for any but the smallest of problems. Secondly, the number of questions asked by the debugger for realistic programs are too large. Finally, the questions asked were often big and complex, involving large data structures and unevaluated expressions.

In order to alleviate the last problem, a technique which we term *strictification* was introduced. This technique is concerned with hiding the lazy evaluation order, thus giving the user an as strict impression of lazy execution as possible. This reduces the number of unevaluated expressions involved in questions posed to the user which tends to make them easier to understand and answer.

This leaves the first two, rather severe, problems. We don't believe that an algorithmic debugger will be practically usable unless they are addressed in a satisfactory manner. Thus, in this paper, we outline a number of possible approaches for overcoming these problems, at least to some extent.

We are only aware of two other algorithmic debuggers for lazy functional languages, both inspired by our earlier efforts and developed at the University of Melbourne, Australia. The first is for a functional language which is implemented by transformation into Prolog. The debugger itself is also written in Prolog [10]. The other is an attempt to implement a debugger similar to ours but in a more systematic way within a general monitoring framework [17][9]. However, within that framework, strictification seems to be difficult to implement.

The rest of this paper is organized as follows. First, the need for special "lazy" debugging tools is justified in section 2. Lazy algorithmic debugging and strictification

---

1. Miranda is a trademark of Research Software Ltd.

is then described in section 3. In section 4 the current implementation and its problems are overviewed. Sections 5 presents a number of ideas to alleviate these problems and in section 6 conclusions are given.

2   The Need for Lazy Debugging Tools

Consider the following functional program, where foo is a function that clearly must not be applied to the empty list:

```
foo xs = 0, if hd xs < 0
         = hd xs, otherwise;

fie xs = (foo xs):fie (tl xs);

main = fie [-1];
```

The problem is that there is no termination condition in the recursive function fie, which means that fie eventually will apply foo to the empty list since main applies fie to the *finite* list [-1]. Suppose that we have strict semantics. Then we would get an execution trace tree as shown in Fig. 1.

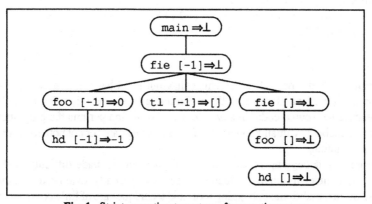

Fig. 1. Strict execution trace tree after run-time error.

In the rightmost branch, we see how the application of hd to the empty list provoked a run-time error, represented by the symbol ⊥ ("bottom"). At this point, we simply have to follow the edges from the leaf node towards the root, which in practice is easily achieved by inspecting the run-time stack, in order to find out that the problem is that fie has applied foo to [].

Now suppose that we had had lazy semantics instead. We would then get an execution tree as shown in Fig. 2. Applying the same technique as above to this tree would not give any insight as to what the problem might be: foo is applied to an expression that will evaluate to the empty list, that is for sure, but which function applied foo to that expression? There is no recollection of this in any of the execution tree records on the path from the node that caused the error to the root node, which are the only records available to a conventional debugger in the form of the run-time stack.

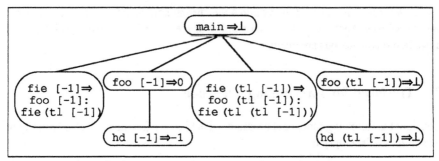

Fig. 2. Lazy execution trace tree after run-time error.

The presence of (partially) evaluated expressions in the lazy execution tree should also be noted. In general, these may become very large and complicated, even if they only denote very simple values, thus making it even harder for a user to get a clear understanding of what is going on.

We could also try to do a conventional trace on the lazy execution:

```
Entering fie:
    xs = [-1]
Leaving fie, result is:
    (foo [-1]):(fie (tl [-1]))
Entering foo:
    xs = [-1]
...
```

Apparently, `fie` did not call `foo`! This behaviour is probably not in agreement with the programmer's mental model of the execution process, and it is at least not obvious from reading the source code. In any case, lazy evaluation permits the programmer to largely forget about evaluation order, so there is a strong case for not bothering him with it during debugging.

To sum up, debugging of lazy functional programs is made difficult by delayed evaluation, counter-intuitive evaluation order and partially evaluated expressions. Because of this, traditional debugging tools and techniques are of little or no use. Hence "lazy" debugging tools, that address the above mentioned problems and that conceptually fit into a lazy framework, are needed.

3   Lazy Algorithmic Debugging

In this section, we describe how algorithmic debugging may be applied to programs written in lazy functional languages. The reasons that algorithmic debugging is interesting in the context of lazy functional languages are that it frees the user from concerns regarding evaluation order, lets him concentrate on the declarative aspects of the program and that it semi-automatically will locate the erroneous function.

3.1 The Basic Approach

Basic algorithmic debugging [16] may readily be used for lazy functional languages since functions *are* side-effect-free. We do have to regard the execution environment of a function as belonging to its input parameters, though, since a function may contain references to *free variables*.

However, while gaining experience in using the debugger, the fact that arguments to functions in general are partially evaluated expressions soon proved to be a major problem: the user is usually concerned with the values that these expressions represent, details of the inner workings of the underlying evaluation machinery is often of little or no interest. Furthermore, the questions that the debugger asked were frequently textually very large and difficult to interpret [12].

This suggests that we should replace unevaluated expressions by the values they represent, wherever possible, in order to give the user an impression of strict evaluation, which probably is closer to the user's mental model of the evaluation process anyway. We will refer to technique of giving an impression of strict evaluation (if possible) as *strictification* from now on.

However, Strictification is, as illustrated in the following subsection, not as straight forward as it first might appear: not only must values be substituted for expressions wherever possible, but the actual structure of the execution tree has to be changed as well. Otherwise, there is no longer any guarantee that the bug will be found.

3.2 Why Substitution of Values for Expressions Is Not Enough

Suppose that strictification was implemented in the obvious way, i.e. before asking whether a function application yielded a correct result or not, any unevaluated expressions that occur in the arguments or in the result of the application are replaced by the results of evaluating the expressions in case they are known to the debugger (i.e. were needed at some point during the execution). This of course has to be done recursively should the results themselves contain any unevaluated subexpressions [2]. The user will then see a version of the function application which is as strict as possible given a particular execution trace.

Unfortunately, the debugging algorithm is then no longer guaranteed to find the bug, as illustrated below (the function add is incorrect).

```
dbl x = add x x;

add x y = x * y;
```

---

2. This could also be implemented in a more efficient way by keeping pointers from the execution tree to the graph representation of the unevaluated expressions. Due to the nature of graph reduction, these pointers would at the end of the execution refer to graphs representing the expressions in their most evaluated form, which is the most we can hope for under lazy evaluation unless we are going to change the semantics of the language by forcing further evaluation, something a debugger should not do and that could change a terminating program into a non-terminating one.

```
main = dbl 3;
```

If no strictification is performed, evaluating main would yield an execution tree as depicted in Fig. 3. The debugger quickly concludes that the bug must be in the function add since applying add to 3 and 3 yields something erroneous and since that node has no children.

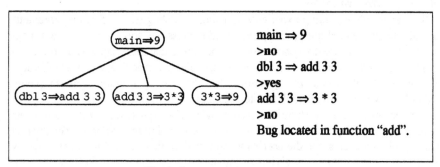

main $\Rightarrow$ 9
>**no**
dbl 3 $\Rightarrow$ add 3 3
>**yes**
add 3 3 $\Rightarrow$ 3 * 3
>**no**
Bug located in function "add".

Fig. 3. Lazy execution trace tree.

Now, suppose that we did substitute values for expression wherever possible in the tree above and then tried to do algorithmic debugging. The result is shown in Fig. 4. When asked whether main should evaluate to 9 the user answers no and the debugger proceeds to the first child node and asks whether dbl 3 should evaluate to 9 or not. Since the intention is that dbl should double its argument the user again answers no. Now, since this node has no children, the debugger will come to the conclusion that the bug is within the function dbl, which is wrong.

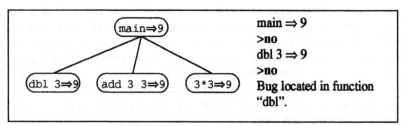

main $\Rightarrow$ 9
>**no**
dbl 3 $\Rightarrow$ 9
>**no**
Bug located in function "dbl".

Fig. 4. Incorrectly strictified execution trace tree.

The problem is that in doing the substitutions (in this case first substituting 3*3 for add 3 3 and then 9 for 3*3) we are effectively pretending that these computations take place at an earlier point in time than is actually the case, but this is not reflected in structure of the execution tree. A correctly strictified tree and the resulting debugging interaction may be seen in Fig. 5. Note how the nodes involved in the substitution have become child and grand child of the dbl 3 node.

3.3   Correct Strictification

A correct way of doing strictification can be derived from the following two observations:

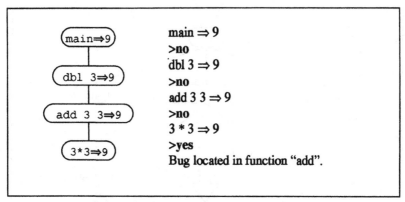

Fig. 5. Correctly strictified execution trace tree.

- Performing a substitution of a result for an expression in one of the arguments of a function application, corresponds to evaluation of the expression in question *before* entering the function (precisely what happens in a strict language). Thus, a new node should be inserted in the execution tree to the left of the node corresponding to the function application.
- Performing a substitution of a result for an expression in the result of a function application, corresponds to evaluation of the expression in question *during* the invocation of the function (again as in a strict language). Thus, the node corresponding to the function application should be given a new child (inserting it to the right of its siblings will do).

These transformations should be applied recursively, i.e. the new nodes must themselves be strictified. The process is depicted in Fig. 6 for a simple case. Grey nodes represent computations that have taken place elsewhere, e1, e2 and e3 are expressions.

However, there is no need to actually perform these transformations on the execution tree; it is sufficient to ask the questions during the debugging phase in such an order as if the transformation had been performed. This is how strictification is implemented in the current debugger.

4 The Current LADT System

In this section we will give a brief overview of the current system, LADT (Lazy Algorithmic Debugging Tool). The main features of LADT are outlined and the major problems with the current implementation are discussed.

4.1 Main Features

LADT is written in C and presently runs on Sun SPARC stations. It consists of two major parts: routines that perform the tracing and build the execution trace tree, and

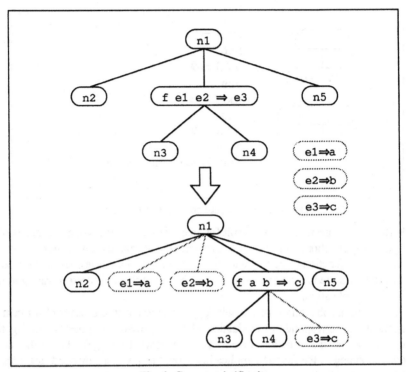

Fig. 6. Correct strictification.

routines that perform the actual debugging. The whole debugger is linked with the code output by the Freja compiler, thus forming a single executable.

As mentioned above, strictification is currently performed during the debugging phase, i.e. after a complete execution trace tree reflecting the lazy evaluation has been built. The structure of the tree is however not changed, only the order in which questions are asked is.

It might well be the case that a user is unwilling to give a definite answer to a question. LADT then allows him to postpone the question by giving the answer "maybe". Debugging will then continue with the children of the node in question. Should a bug be found among these, then the better. Otherwise the user will eventually be faced with the deferred question again. Hopefully, he should now be confident enough to give a decisive answer.

In order to reduce the number of questions asked, the debugger keeps a record over all questions and answers asked so far. Thus, the same question never has to be asked twice. There is also a simple assertion facility whereby the user may assert the correctness of a particular function. Questions regarding this function will then be suppressed.

Obviously, a debugger must be able to cope with programs that terminate in an abnormal manner. For an algorithmic debugger, this means that it will be left with an incomplete trace tree. LADT deals with this situation by patching the tree into a consistent state before the actual debugging starts in the case of a run-time error. This is done by inserting nodes representing the value ⊥ wherever there is a branch missing in the tree.

In the case of a program that actually is non-terminating, the user has to interrupt the program by pressing Ctrl-C. This is then interpreted as a normal run-time error and dealt with as outlined above.

The debugger also handles interactive programs without problem. This is because I/O is managed without resorting to side effects. In Freja, as in many other lazy functional languages, input is made available as a list of characters which is supplied as the sole argument to the main function in the program. Due to the lazy semantics, no input actually has to be available until it is used, and thus it is possible to write interactive programs.

LADT has so far been used to debug a number of small programs, e.g. a program for calculating prime numbers, as well as a somewhat larger expression evaluator, consisting of some 250 lines of Freja code. Some of the found "bugs" were artificially introduced into the programs, whereas others were real bugs, inadvertently introduced during implementation of the test programs. Further details on LADT may be found in Nilsson and Fritzson [12].

4.2 Problems

The current LADT implementation has two severe problems that make it difficult or impossible to apply to real, large programs. The main one is the size of the trace tree: currently every single reduction is recorded, which means that the size easily could reach hundreds of megabytes. The situation is akin to running a lazy functional program without garbage collection. Also, building the tree takes a long time. Though we have not done any extensive measurements, execution seemed to be slowed down by two or three orders of magnitude when doing tracing.

Now, it certainly would be possible to keep the trace on secondary storage, even if tracing (as well as strictification) then would become even more expensive. Indeed, one might even argue that the sizes of primary memories within a not too distant future will be large enough to accommodate traces of such sizes. However, the fundamental problem is that there is *no upper bound* on the size of trace, and that problem remains however we store the trace.

The other big problem is that far too many questions are asked. This makes LADT a very tedious debugging tool to use, especially since a large number of the questions are irrelevant. It might well be the case that a user can see exactly what is wrong in a result returned from function. If this information could be conveyed to the debugger, many irrelevant questions could in principle be discarded.

5 Ideas for Practical Implementation

Despite the problems with current implementation, we feel that this approach to debugging is basically sound and promising in the context of lazy functional languages.

In this section, a number of ideas for dealing with the above problems and extending the basic approach are suggested, with the aim of making algorithmic debugging for lazy functional languages practical.

The ideas are summarized in the list below and then explained further in the following subsections.

- *Thin tracing*: If it is known beforehand that some functions or modules are correct (e.g. library routines), it should not be necessary to trace everything, thereby reducing the size of the trace as well as the number of questions asked.
- *Piecemeal tracing*: Do not store the entire trace at once. Instead, parts of the trace can be constructed as and when they are needed by rerunning the program that is being debugged.
- *Immediate Strictification*: Instead of building a lazy execution trace tree and applying strictification on it afterwards, a strictified tree could be built directly.
- *Slicing*: If the user is able to be more specific as to what is wrong, rather than just saying that *something* is wrong, it ought to be possible to make use of this information to reduce the number of questions asked by applying program slicing.
- *A smarter user interface*: It is often the case that the details of large data structures are of no interest in answering questions. Thus it would be beneficial to be able to suppress such details.

5.1   Thin Tracing

Currently, LADT records every single reduction that takes place during execution. Quite a few of these are applications of language primitives and library functions which may reasonably be assumed to behave correctly. Thus the user should not be asked about the behaviour of such functions, in which case there seems to be little point in tracing such applications in the first place.

Furthermore, large systems are usually built modularly, so it is not unreasonable to assume that it frequently will be the case that there are a large number of well tested, trusted modules and a few, new "prime suspects" when a bug manifests itself.

So under a *thin tracing* scheme, only a subset of the reductions would be traced, based on assumptions regarding the correctness of certain modules. Clearly, this will also reduce the number of questions that are asked and the time taken to build the tree. However, not having the entire trace at our disposal, means that strictification cannot be performed as it is currently done, i.e. during the debugging phase. Therefore, a new approach to strictification must be adopted in order to use thin tracing.

There is also a more subtle problem as to what is meant by a function being "correct". For a first-order function it is obvious: a function is correct if it computes the expected result for whatever arguments it is applied to. During debugging, this means that a user no doubt would indicate that an application of the function is correct, and the entire branch in the execution trace tree emerging from that point may thus be cut away.

But for a higher-order function that takes another function as an argument, it would be a rather bold claim that the result is correct for arbitrary arguments: the supplied function is effectively behaviour that has been abstracted out of the higher-order function, and claiming that the higher-order function produces the correct result when some arbitrary behaviour is being plugged back in cannot be justified. It is only possible to say that the higher-order function uses the supplied function in the intended way.

For our purposes, this means that the branch in the execution trace tree corresponding to the application cannot be cut away. The question about the application of the higher-order function could of course be suppressed, but if the node has many children, then more questions would be asked on average than if the question had not been suppressed.

On the other hand, if it is known that the function that is supplied as an argument is correct as well, then the application could be treated as in the first-order case. This suggests that some simple "correctness calculation" should be performed on higher-order applications.

5.2   Piecemeal Tracing

Even if it is possible to substantially reduce the size of the trace using thin tracing, there is still no guaranteed upper bound on the size of the trace tree. Indeed, as long as the trace for a whole execution is going to be stored, there can be no general, fixed such upper bound.

An interesting alternative would then be to store only so much trace as there is room for. Debugging is then started on this first piece of trace. If this is enough to find the bug, then all is well. Otherwise, the program to be debugged is re-executed, and the next piece of the trace is captured and stored. Re-executing the program is not a problem since pure functional programs are deterministic, but any input to the program must obviously be preserved and reused. We will refer to such a tracing scheme as *piecemeal tracing* from now on.

The question is then how to select the piece of the trace to be stored in a sensible way. Just storing reductions as they happen until the trace storage is full would not be very useful since it may then happen that a very deep but narrow piece of the tree is captured. If the top reduction actually is correct, the program would have to be rerun immediately to get the next piece of the trace. It would be better if trace corresponding to the next *n* questions, regardless of what the answers to these questions will be, could be stored.

This leads to the idea of introducing a distance measure on the nodes in the tree based on the number of questions that would have to be answered in order to get from one node to another (if this is possible, otherwise the measure is undefined). We term this measure the *query distance* and the idea is illustrated in Fig. 7. The nodes are labelled with their query distance from the root node and the grey arcs are labelled with the answer that would take a user from one node in the execution trace tree to the other during algorithmic debugging.

Given a cache for execution trace tree nodes, piecemeal tracing can be performed as follows. Suppose that a particular node in the trace tree has been reached during debugging and that it is found that more trace is needed to proceed. Call this particular node the current node.

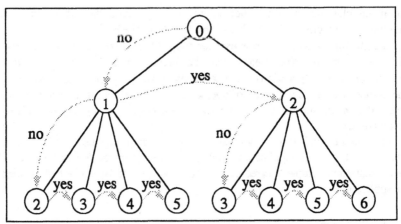

Fig. 7. Query distances from the root node.

Now the entire program is re-executed. (There is a good reason for re-executing the *entire* program as will become clear in the next subsection.) Only nodes reachable from the current node, i.e. nodes for which the query distance is defined relative to the current node, are stored in the cache. When the cache is full, nodes with the largest query distance relative to the current node are thrown out in favour of nodes with a smaller query distance. Then nodes corresponding to the next *n* questions will be in the cache when the tracing is completed, where *n* depends on the size of the cache.

Thus, an arbitrary upper bound may be imposed on the trace size, but obviously, the larger the size of a cache, the fewer times the program will have to be rerun. The piecemeal tracing scheme makes it possible to trade space for time as is appropriate for any specific implementation. However, as is the case with thin tracing, the entire trace is no longer available during debugging, which means that strictification cannot be performed as it is currently done. This problem is addressed in the next subsection.

5.3 Immediate Strictification

In the current LADT system, a lazy execution trace tree reflecting the real order in which reductions take place is built during the trace phase. Strictification is performed afterwards, during the debugging phase, by recursively substituting values for expressions while asking for confirmation, as described in subsection 3.3.

This means that the debugger is effectively redoing work that has already been done during execution of the program that is being debugged. Also, due to the way graph reduction works, some strictification opportunities are missed by LADT which means that only approximative strictification is achieved [12]. Furthermore, doing strictification afterwards is only possible if the entire trace, containing every single reduction, is available to the debugger. Thus thin and piecemeal tracing cannot be integrated with the current debugger.

As observed in passing in subsection 3.2, it would not be necessary to perform any substitutions at all if we kept pointers from the execution trace tree to the corresponding pieces of graphs, since these would be in their most evaluated form once the execution was completed. Not only would it then not be necessary to have access to the complete trace during debugging, but it would also solve the problem with approximative strictification. But, as explained in the aforementioned subsection, correct strictification also requires the structure of the execution tree to be changed. So is it possible to build a tree with the correct, i.e. strict, structure directly, during tracing rather than afterwards?

Indeed this seems to be possible. The basic idea is that whenever a *redex* (reducible expression) is *created* during the execution of code corresponding to a function, a node referring to this redex is also inserted at the appropriate place in the execution trace tree. Since a strict language would not create the redex for later evaluation, but *evaluate it directly*, the "appropriate place" is as a child node of the node corresponding to the current function invocation. The key observation is that the creation of a redex in the lazy case corresponds to strict evaluation of that expression.

The redexes also has to be tagged with pointers referring back to the corresponding nodes in the execution trace tree so that this node can be found once the redex is reduced. Having this back pointer is also convenient during garbage collection since pointers in the execution trace tree then must be updated when pieces of graph are moved around. We will therefore in the following assume that there is a single pointer from the execution tree to any graph node (and vice versa). This means that once a reduction has taken place, any piece of graph that has reached its final form is copied into the execution trace tree. However, there are several design options here and it might be better not to copy anything, leaving it where it is.

The above also explains why the entire program should be re-executed during piecemeal tracing: it is only after completing the execution that each piece of graph will be in its most evaluated form. If we tried to only re-evaluate a particular function application, we would not know when to stop since we would not know which parts of the result that actually were going to be used later on (assuming that the result is a list for example).

Hopefully, the following example should give a feeling for what we are trying to achieve. Suppose that we were to execute the following (bug free) program:

```
sqr x = x * x;
main = sqr (1 + 2);
```

Fig. 8 shows the corresponding lazy execution tree, i.e. it reflects the order in which the reductions actually happens, while Fig. 9 shows the strict tree, i.e. the tree that we are trying to construct using immediate strictification.

First, main is invoked. It builds two redexes: 1+2 and sqr (1+2). Thus nodes corresponding to these are inserted into the execution trace tree, in the order in which they are created. Note how the sqr node refers to the 1+2 node so that there is only one pointer from the execution tree to each redex. Since the result of main is the result of the latter redex, the result field of the tree node for main points at the tree node for sqr in order to preserve the single pointer property. The situation is shown in Fig. 10.

The next thing that happens, as can be seen from the lazy execution tree, is that the sqr function is invoked to reduce sqr (1+2) to (1+2)*(1+2). This means that

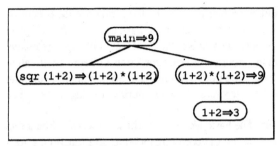

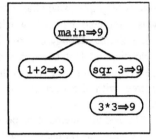

Fig. 8. Lazy execution trace tree.   **Fig. 9.** Strict execution tree.

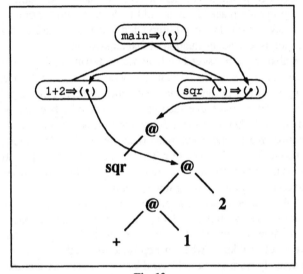

Fig. 10.

sqr has built a new redex, so the corresponding node is inserted into the execution tree. This is depicted in Fig. 11. Since the result of sqr (1+2) is the result of (1+2)*(1+2), the result field of the sqr execution tree node has been redirected to the new node.

Then 1+2 is reduced to 3. This creates no new redexes, but the result of the reduction is copied into the tree, see Fig. 12. Finally, 3*3 is reduced to 9. Again, no new redexes are created so it only remains to copy the result into the tree, see Fig. 13. Compare the resulting strictified tree with the strict tree in Fig. 9.

5.4 Slicing

Obviously, the more information the user is able to supply the system with per question, the fewer questions the system has to ask in order to locate the bug. For example, if a user indicates that a particular element in a list is not what it is supposed to be, the system can disregard any computations that are not relevant for the production of this

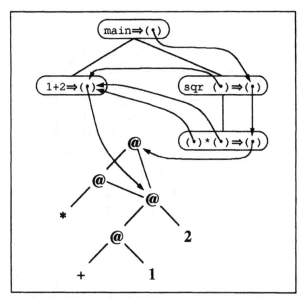

Fig. 11.

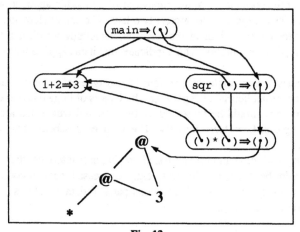

Fig. 12.

particular element. This technique is a variation of *program slicing* [19][20] and it could reduce the number of questions asked during algorithmic debugging considerably.

The approach that seems to be the most suitable is dynamic slicing, since dynamic slices are more precise than are static ones [7]. Perhaps something similar to what Kamkar has done could be used [8][7]. Amongst other things, this would require keeping track of data dependencies, i.e. which node in the execution tree that corresponds to the function application that computed a certain value. Note, however, that some such information would be present in the strictified tree "for free" if

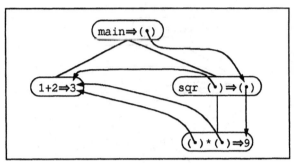

Fig. 13.

strictification is performed as outlined in the previous subsection. Thus, it might be possible to do a coarse, approximative, but yet useful, slicing without much extra effort.

5.5 A Smarter User Interface

Even if strictification helps in making the questions asked by the debugger easier to understand and answer, they are still large if large data structures are involved. Frequently, the details of such structures are not important when it comes to answering questions about the correctness of the behaviour of a function application. As a trivial example, consider the function to append two lists. The actual elements in the list are not important for the behaviour of the function, something which is reflected by the polymorphic type of the function which indicates that it can append lists of any specific type.

This suggests that it might be possible to use type information and other static properties to construct heuristics regarding which parts of large data structures that are interesting and thus should be presented to the user, and which that are not and thus should be suppressed, at least initially. The gain of a scheme like this could be considerable.

By building a window and pointer based graphic user interface, the usability of the debugger would be further enhanced, e.g. suppressed subcomponents could be expanded by clicking on them and erroneous parts of data structures could easily be marked for computing a slice.

6 Conclusions

This paper has argued that algorithmic debugging is a suitable technique for debugging lazy functional programs. Experience from work with the current LADT implementation supports this claim. However, as it stands, LADT cannot be considered to be a practically usable system, mainly due to the prohibitively large trace size for any real world problem and because far to many questions has to be answered during debugging.

In this paper, we have suggested a number of techniques to alleviate these and other problems. *Thin tracing* should be used so that only relevant applications are traced. By using *piecemeal tracing*, the debugger can handle traces of arbitrary size at the expense of re-executing the program when more trace is needed.

Since both thin tracing and piecemeal tracing means that strictification cannot be performed during the debugging phase, as is currently the case, a method for building a strictified tree directly during the trace phase, *immediate strictification*, was suggested.

Finally, it was argued that the debugger should employ *dynamic slicing* to reduce the number of questions asked and that heuristics based on type information and other statically inferable properties should be used to perform sensible pretty printing of questions to reduce their size.

If all these techniques can be successfully integrated, we believe that a practically useful algorithmic debugger for lazy functional languages could be built.

References

[1] Lennart Augustsson. A compiler for lazy ML. In *Proceedings of the 1984 ACM Conference on LISP and Functional Programming*, pages 218–227, August 1984.

[2] Lennart Augustsson. *Compiling Lazy Functional Languages part II*. PhD thesis, Department of Computer Science, Chalmers University of Technology, December 1987.

[3] Lennart Augustsson. Personal communication on the lack of suitable debugging tools for lazy functional languages, November 1991.

[4] Peter Fritzson, Tibor Gyimothy, Mariam Kamkar, and Nahid Shahmehri. Generalized algorithmic debugging and testing. In *Proceedings of the 1991 ACM SIGPLAN Conference*, pages 317–326, Toronto, Canada, June 1991. A revised version to appear in ACM LOPLAS (Letters of Programming Languages and Systems).

[5] Thomas Johnsson. Efficient compilation of lazy evaluation. In *Proceedings of the 1984 ACM SIGPLAN Symposium on Compiler Construction*, pages 58–69, June 1984. Proceedings published in SIGPLAN Notices, 19(6).

[6] Thomas Johnsson. *Compiling Lazy Functional Languages*. PhD thesis, Department of Computer Science, Chalmers University of Technology, February 1987.

[7] Mariam Kamkar. *Interprocedural Dynamic Slicing with Applications to Debugging and Testing*. PhD thesis, Department of Computer and Information Science, Linköping University, S-581 83, Linköping, Sweden, April 1993.

[8]   Mariam Kamkar, Nahid Shahmehri, and Peter Fritzson. Interprocedural dynamic slicing. In M. Bruynooghe and M. Wirsing, editors, *Programming Language Implementation and Logic Programming*, volume 631 of *Lecture Notes in Computer Science*, pages 370–384, Leuven, Belgium, August 1992.

[9]   Amir Shai Kishon. *Theory and Art of Semantics Directed Program Execution Monitoring*. PhD thesis, Yale University, May 1992.

[10]   Lee Naish. Declarative debugging of lazy functional programs. Research Report 92/6, Department of Computer Science, University of Melbourne, Australia, 1992.

[11]   Henrik Nilsson. Freja: A small non-strict, purely functional language. MSc dissertation, Department of Computer Science and Applied Mathematics, Aston University, Birmingham, England, September 1991.

[12]   Henrik Nilsson and Peter Fritzson. Algorithmic debugging for lazy functional languages. In M. Bruynooghe and M. Wirsing, editors, *Programming Language Implementation and Logic Programming*, volume 631 of *Lecture Notes in Computer Science*, pages 385–399, Leuven, Belgium, August 1992.

[13]   Simon L. Peyton Jones. *The Implementation of Functional Programming Languages*. Prentice Hall, 1987.

[14]   Rudolph E. Seviora. Knowledge-based program debugging systems. *IEEE Software*, 4(3):20–32, May 1987.

[15]   Nahid Shahmehri. *Generalized Algorithmic Debugging*. PhD thesis, Department of Computer and Information Science, Linköping University, S-581 83, Linköping, Sweden, 1991.

[16]   Ehud Y. Shapiro. *Algorithmic Program Debugging*. MIT Press, May 1982.

[17]   Robert Sturrock. Debugging systems for lazy functional programming languages. Honours dissertation, Department of Computer Science, University of Melbourne, Australia, November 1992.

[18]   David A. Turner. Miranda: A non-strict functional language with polymorphic types. In *Proceedings of the IFIP International Conference on Functional Programming Languages and Computer Architecture, FPCA'85*, number 201 in Lecture Notes in Computer Science, Nancy, 1985.

[19]   Mark Weiser. Programmers use slices when debugging. *Communications of the ACM*, 25(7):446–452, July 1982.

[20]   Mark Weiser. Program slicing. *IEEE Transactions on Software Engineering*, 10(4):352–357, July 1984.

The Location of Errors
in Functional Programs

Jonathan E. Hazan* and Richard G. Morgan

Artificial Intelligence Systems Research Group
School of Engineering and Computer Science
University of Durham, DH1 3LE, UK
e-mail: J.E.Hazan@durham.ac.uk

Abstract. Programmers using imperative languages have a number of well-established debugging tools available to them; functional programmers have few, if any, tools available. Many of the tools and techniques developed for debugging functional programs are based on those for imperative programming and lack a theoretical basis relevant to functional programming. In addition, the techniques used are typically very time-consuming. A theoretical foundation on which to base the study of errors and debugging in functional programming is presented in this paper. Using this theoretical foundation, a set of program transformation schemes has been developed which facilitate the location of the type of error which results in an evaluation-time error message and the termination of evaluation. A brief description of the practical experience obtained using the tool is also presented.

1 Introduction

In a strongly typed functional programming language such as Miranda[1] [10], many errors are caught by the typechecking system before the program is executed. Errors remaining after typechecking are caused by functions which behave differently from the way expected by the programmer. These errors may manifest themselves in several different ways; an error may cause an incorrect value to be returned by the program, or may cause non-termination of the evaluation of the program. Another type of error causes evaluation to terminate and an error message to be printed out. In Miranda for example, an attempt to evaluate the head of an empty list with the function **hd** will cause **hd** to terminate evaluation.

The goal of debugging is to find the function which contains the error and to fix it. Conventionally, finding errors in functional programs has meant conducting thorough searches through the program until the erroneous function is detected. There are several methods for carrying out searches. Most of them employ the programmer's knowledge of how the functions in the program fit

---

* The author is supported by a grant from the Science and Engineering Research Council of Great Britain.

[1] Miranda is a trademark of Research Software Limited.

together. Using these methods is straightforward for small programs; however with larger programs there will be many occurrences of common functions like hd being used by different functions. This will mean that there are a large number of paths through the program leading to the function which gave the error message, which in turn leads to a great deal of time and effort being required to analyze the program.

In this paper we shall present a new theoretical framework on which to base the study of errors and debugging in functional programming. We shall describe a set of program transformations which use this framework to facilitate the detection of erroneous functions and lessen the reliance on the programmer's intuition in the debugging process. This is done by providing the static path which led to the error message as part of the error message itself. This information reduces the search space in which the programmer must search for the error.

2   Existing Debugging Tools

Debugging tools which have been devised for functional programming languages can be divided into two categories—those which involve altering the implementation of the language in order to provide debugging information and those which are written in the language itself, requiring no knowledge of the implementation.

Tools in the first category include systems developed by Toyn and Runciman [9]. These systems are environments (i.e. language interpreters) for a language with eager evaluation and a language with lazy evaluation. Both of these environments provide a facility for displaying snapshots of a computation at the time of failure, or when the program is interrupted. These snapshots consist of a list of the reduction steps involved in the evaluation of the program. This allows the programmer to examine the uses and arguments of each function in order to find why the error occurred.

Other debugging methods in this category include a hypertext system for tracing the evaluation of programs written in a lazy language [3] and a method for the "lazy debugging" of lazy functional programs [8]. The system described in [8] makes available at run-time the whole of the reduction history in terms of the source program, allowing tracing systems to be written.

Also in this category are the algorithmic debugging tools which have been produced for functional languages. Although algorithmic debugging tools may be implemented for Prolog without modifying the language implementation, this is not the case for the strongly-typed lazy functional languages currently in common use, as the typechecking system precludes the writing of meta-interpreters. Algorithmic debugging is an important technique which was developed for PRO-LOG by Shapiro [7] with the aim of reducing the effort involved in debugging by partially automating the process and also by reducing the search space for the error. It is a *declarative* debugging technique, which means that it concentrates on the algorithm itself rather than the operational behaviour of the program. Algorithmic debugging has recently been applied to lazy functional programming by Nilsson and Fritzson [5] and also by Naish [4]. Algorithmic debugging relies on the concept of an *oracle* which can determine whether or not the result of the application of a function is correct. The oracle can be either a program, a previous (correct) version of the program being debugged or a human; in the case of [5], the oracle is the programmer.

Hall and O'Donnell argue in [6] that the second category of debugging tools are more flexible, extensive and portable than those of the first category. By implementing the debugging tool in the language in which the programs to be debugged are written, little or no knowledge of the implementation of the language is required. This means that it is not necessary to have access to the source code of the language implementation in order to write debugging tools. In [6], two debugging tools are presented. The first prints out a full trace of the program, showing function parameters and values. The second is an interactive tool for examining and altering intermediate results of the computation.

Many of the approaches taken to the debugging of lazy functional programs have borrowed heavily from debugging tools and techniques for imperative languages. However, much of the debugging information available in an imperative language implementation is not present in lazy functional language implementations. For example, a common feature of imperative language debuggers (such as dbx) is the facility to display a stack dump of the sequence of procedures called during execution. Lazy functional language implementations have no equivalent of the imperative stack; recording such information could be costly. The concept of single-stepping, also a common feature of imperative language debuggers, causes problems when applied to functional programming. With lazy evaluation, functions may be evaluated in an unexpected order, or not at all. This also causes problems with program tracing—how does one represent a partially evaluated argument or function result? With program tracing and snapshots, much unwanted and irrelevant information is output. In addition, many of the tools and techniques developed so far lack a theoretical framework to support them. This is one of the problems we shall address in this paper.

3 Framework

3.1 Specifications and Incorrect Functions

Since we will be judging the correctness of a function against its specification, it is necessary to clarify what we mean by the specification of a function.

The assumption is made that an oracle (in this case the programmer) can always be relied upon to determine whether or not a function returned a correct value. Each function has a specification associated with it. This specification is what the programmer intended the behaviour of the function to be. The specification can be explicitly stated, either as a comment in the program or in a separate document. In many cases however, the programmer may consider the function definition itself to be sufficiently simple or self-explanatory not to require an explicit specification. Even so, we assume that the programmer has in mind a particular behaviour for the function, and this can be considered an intended specification.

We are thus only concerned with the intended specifications of functions, and it is these we shall be referring to when we mention specifications in the rest of this document.

A function is *incorrect* if its behaviour is different from the behaviour described by its specification.

3.2 Debugging

In the testing of a program, expressions which evaluate incorrectly are identified. The goal of debugging is to find the incorrect functions which caused the wrong values to be produced[2] and to fix them. In this paper, we shall concentrate on the issue of finding the bug. A function which produces a wrong value may be doing so either because its definition is incorrect or because it is making use of another incorrect function. We are thus interested in the dependency graph of the program. The presence of mutually recursive functions introduces cycles into the dependency graph; this complicates matters because with mutually recursive functions it is impossible to say which one is further down the dependency graph. We shall therefore conduct our discussion in terms of *recursion groups* (or simply *groups*). A recursion group is a strongly connected component of the dependency graph. This means that a recursion group is a set of mutually recursive functions. The dependency graph between groups is thus acyclic. A recursion group may also consist of a single function which is not mutually recursive with any other functions. A recursion group is incorrect if one or more of the functions in the group is incorrect.

We need to define two relations in order to discuss dependency: *directly depends* and *depends*. A recursion group r directly depends on a recursion group s (which we shall write as $r > s$) iff a function belonging to r contains a reference to a function from s. In terms of the dependency graph, r directly depends on s iff r is connected to s (i.e. there is an arc on the dependency graph leading from r to s). r depends on s (written $r \overset{*}{>} s$) iff s can be reached from r; the *depends* relation is defined by:

$$r \overset{*}{>} s \Leftrightarrow r > s \lor (\exists t . r \overset{*}{>} t \land t \overset{*}{>} s)$$

Some examples of the dependency relations are given in Figure 1.

3.3 Minimal Incorrect Groups

If r and s are incorrect groups and $r \overset{*}{>} s$, we should examine s first for incorrectness because it may be the cause of the incorrectness of r. It is not possible for r to be responsible for the incorrectness of s, although it may be using s in an incorrect manner according to the specification of s. This is essentially similar to

---

[2] Debugging can also be the improvement of the space or time efficiency of a program; however this type of debugging will not be addressed in this paper.

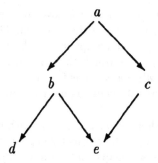

Fig. 1. In this dependency graph, the following relations hold: $a > b$, $a > c$, $b > d$, $b > e$, $c > e$, $a \overset{*}{>} d$ and $a \overset{*}{>} e$

the concept of incorrectness which underlies the technique of algorithmic debugging. When searching for an incorrect group it is therefore sensible to examine functions lower down the dependency graph first. It follows that there will be an incorrect group which does not use any other incorrect groups. This group is a *minimal incorrect group* (MIG). If r and s are both groups and the predicate *incorrect(t)* is true iff the group t is an incorrect group, the MIG property can be defined as follows:

$$MIG(r) \Leftrightarrow incorrect(r) \wedge \neg \exists s . (incorrect(s) \wedge r \overset{*}{>} s)$$

4 Finding an MIG—Existing Approaches

The goal of debugging is to find the MIGs in a program and correct them in order to correct the behaviour of the program. We shall concentrate on the finding of MIGs rather than their correction. If the program is large, this requires searching in a very large search space, so finding an MIG can be a non-trivial problem. In this section, methods will be examined for finding MIGs in a program. The discussion in the remainder of this paper is restricted to programs which contain *exception errors*. An exception error is an error which results in termination of evaluation and the output of an error message.

4.1 Intuition-based Search

This is the simplest approach to searching. It involves the programmer examining functions for incorrectness based on intuition. This may take a great deal of time if the programmer's choice of function is wrong, but if the programmer has made a good choice of function, the search will be shorter. This method depends on the programmer's expertise and knowledge of the program.

4.2 Directed Search

There are two types of directed search—top-down and bottom-up.

- The top-down search starts at the top-level expression. This is the expression which initiates the evaluation of the program. The search then proceeds by examining all the recursion groups which the top-level expression directly depends on, and all groups which those groups directly depend on, and so on. The search stops when a group is found which satisfies the condition that all of the groups it directly depends on are correct. This must by definition be an MIG.
- The bottom-up search starts at the group which produced the error message and checks all the groups which directly depend on it, and the groups which directly depend on those groups, and so on. It stops when it finds an incorrect group and then proceeds in a top-down manner from this group, searching the groups it directly depends on.

The problem with these approaches to searching for an MIG is that although they are more systematic and methodical than random searching, they involve searching a large number of functions. In algorithmic debugging, the directed search is automated. In the implementation of algorithmic debugging for lazy functional programming given in [5], the programmer is guided through the evaluation tree of the program as opposed to the dependency graph. This can still lead to a very large number of functions being searched. In the next section, a method of cutting down this search space is introduced, based on examining the dependency graph of the program.

5   A New Approach to Finding MIGs

This method uses a combination of the top-down and bottom-up approaches to searching. To narrow down the search space, searching is restricted to a particular set of *static paths* for as long as possible.

5.1   Static Paths

A *static path* between two recursion groups r_1 and r_n is a list of groups $[r_1, r_2, \ldots, r_n]$ such that $r_x > r_{x+1}$ for $1 \leq x < n$. For example, in Figure 1 two possible static paths between a and e are $[a, b, e]$ and $[a, c, e]$.

The search is initially restricted to the set of static paths from the group which is made up of the top-level expression (the *top-level group*) to the group which gave the error message (the *exception group*). We shall call these paths *exception paths*. Searching proceeds in either a top-down or a bottom-up manner. The search will stop when an MIG is found; however it is possible that there will be no MIGs on the exception path which is being searched. It will therefore be necessary to continue the search using the top-down method described in Section 4.2. The next section addresses the problem of identifying the group from which to start the top-down search.

5.2   Minimal Path Incorrect Groups

Given an exception path containing incorrect groups, there will be ah incorrect group on this path below which there are no other incorrect groups. This is the *minimal path incorrect group* (MPIG). If *path* is the set of groups on the exception path, then:

$$MPIG(r) \Leftrightarrow incorrect(r) \wedge r \in path \wedge \neg\exists s.(s \in path \wedge incorrect(s) \wedge r \overset{.}{>} s)$$

The MPIG is either an MIG or it is not an MIG. If the MPIG is not an MIG, it will depend on another incorrect function which is not in *path*.

For example, in Figure 2, *a* is the top-level expression and *j* is the group which is giving the error message. Possible static paths are $[a, b, d, g, j]$, $[a, b, e, g, j]$ and $[a, c, f, h, j]$. Suppose the initial choice of path to examine is $[a, b, d, g, j]$. A case where the MPIG is the MIG would be if *a*, *b* and *d* were incorrect groups. The MPIG is *d*, which must also be an MIG because there are no incorrect groups below it on and it does not lie on any other paths. A case where the MPIG is not an MIG is when the incorrect groups are *a*, *b* and *e*. The MPIG is *b*, but the MIG lies on path $[a, b, e, g, j]$.

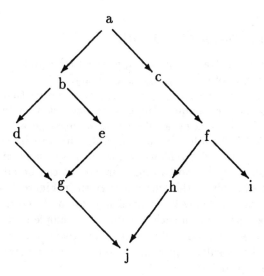

Fig. 2.

5.3   Searching for an MPIG

Using this knowledge, we can devise a search strategy. An exception path is chosen. Searching on this exception path can be done either in a top-down manner, starting at the beginning of the path and working forwards until an incorrect group is found followed by a correct group, or it can be done in a bottom-up manner by starting at the end of the path and working towards the beginning until an incorrect group is found. Once an MPIG has been found, a top-down search is performed from the MPIG as described in Section 4.2, examining each group which the MPIG depends on until an MIG is found.

This approach is an improvement on the top-down and bottom-up methods given in Section 4.2 as it narrows down the search space. The remaining problem lies in selecting the best static path to search first.

5.4 Distinguished Path

A possible choice of exception path is the one which gave rise to the error. This is the static path followed by evaluation of the top-level expression which led from the top-level group to the exception group. We shall call this path the *distinguished path*. An MPIG x is on an exception path p. This path p is not the distinguished path, but coincides with the distinguished path. x is on the part of p which coincides with the distinguished path. x will thus either depend on, or be the same as the MPIG d on the distinguished path itself. If x depends on d then the search space for d will be reduced since it is included in the search space of x.

5.5 Finding the Distinguished Path

We take the source code transformation approach to this problem—no knowledge of the implementation of the language is necessary.

The program is transformed in such a way as to ensure that all static paths through the program are unique. The dependency graph of the program thus becomes a tree. By associating a different error message with each exception path, the distinguished path can be identified. This can be done by creating a duplicate group with a different name each time the same group appears on more than one static path—no two different groups can be allowed to use the same group. An example of this method is given in Figure 3 which shows the tree produced by transforming the dependency graph of Figure 2.

Transforming a program in such a manner is a simple task. However in the worst case the transformation could result in an exponential increase in the size of the program. The resulting program might even be too large to be handled by the language implementation.

A different approach is to distinguish between the same group being used on different paths by adding an extra parameter to the functions in the group. Every group is altered in this manner and each time a group is used, a unique group identifier is appended to the parameter. The parameter thus contains a representation of the path taken to reach the group. The value of the parameter will be unique for each different static path. At the point at which the error message is produced, the value of the parameter will be the distinguished path. If the value of the parameter is incorporated into the error message, it will be possible to tell which static path was followed. This method of transformation is

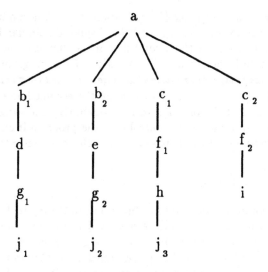

Fig. 3. The dependency graph transformed into a tree.

equivalent to creating duplicate functions. Passing an extra parameter to each function involves a much smaller increase in the size of the program than creating duplicate functions. There will however be an increase in evaluation time.

6 Translation Schemes for Finding the Distinguished Path

In this section, we present some translation schemes for printing out the distinguished path as part of a run-time error message produced by the **error** function. The distinguished path can then be used to find the MPIG and hence an MIG. The translation schemes add an extra parameter, the distinguished path, to the left-hand side of a function definition, and transform the right-hand side to add the extra parameter when the function is used.

6.1 The Function "error"

Before we describe the transforms, it is important to introduce the Miranda function **error**. This function takes a single parameter. When it is evaluated, it causes evaluation of the program to halt and its parameter to be output. It is normally used when a function is given a value for which no sensible value can be returned. An example of its use is in the list tail function **tl**, which can be defined using pattern-matching as:

```
tl (x : xs) = xs
tl []       = error "tl []"
```

If tl is passed the parameter [], evaluation of the program will halt, and the message "program error: tl []" will be displayed. Similar behaviour could be produced by leaving out the second line of the definition altogether. In this case, if tl [] were to be evaluated, evaluation of the program would halt and the message "program error: missing case in definition of tl" would be displayed. It is better however to include the second line of the definition, as it alerts the user of the function to the possibility of passing a bad value. It also gives the programmer more control over the program if error messages are inserted into functions rather than leaving it to the interpreter to generate them.

6.2 Translation Schemes

The schemes require a new Miranda function (addfunc) to be added to each script. The function addfunc takes a path and a function name. It works out the recursion group to which the function belongs and returns the path with the name of the group added. In addition, the translation schemes require a function *recgroup* which takes a function name and returns the set of functions which make up the recursion group of which that function is a member. *builtins* is the set of pre-defined Miranda functions and identifiers. Throughout the translation schemes, path is a new identifier which is not in the current scope; f and g are function names; $v_1, \ldots, v_n$ are variables and *identifier* is a Miranda identifier. Function type declarations must be removed from the script; they could be altered to include the type of the extra parameter, but they are not required in a Miranda script so it is easier to remove them in the process of translation.

$$\mathcal{TD}[\![f\ v_1, \ldots, v_n\ =\ RHS]\!] \equiv$$
$$f\ \text{path}\ v_1, \ldots, v_n\ =\ \mathcal{TRHS}[\![RHS]\!](f, \{v_1, \ldots, v_n\}) \qquad (1)$$

$$\mathcal{TRHS}[\![R\ \text{where}\ LD_1; \ldots; LD_n]\!](f, formals) \equiv$$
$$\mathcal{TE}[\![R]\!](f, formals)\ \text{where}\ \mathcal{TLD}[\![LD_1]\!](f, formals);$$
$$\ldots; \mathcal{TLD}[\![LD_n]\!](f, formals); \qquad (2)$$

$$\mathcal{TRHS}[\![R]\!](f, formals) \equiv$$
$$\mathcal{TE}[\![R]\!](f, formals) \qquad (3)$$

$$\mathcal{TLD}[\![g\ v_1, \ldots, v_n\ =\ R]\!](f, formals) \equiv$$
$$g\ \text{path}\ v_1, \ldots, v_n\ =\ \mathcal{TRHS}[\![R]\!](g, formals \cup \{v_1, \ldots, v_n\}) \quad (4)$$

$$\mathcal{TE}[\![\text{error}\ xs]\!](f, formals) \equiv$$
$$\text{error}\ (xs\ \text{++}\ ":\ path:\ "\ \text{++}\ path) \qquad (5)$$

$$\mathcal{TE}[\![e_1\ e_2]\!](f, formals) \equiv$$
$$\mathcal{TE}[\![e_1]\!](f, formals)\ \mathcal{TE}[\![e_2]\!](f, formals) \qquad (6)$$

$$\mathcal{TE}[\![identifier]\!](f, formals)$$
$$\equiv identifier,$$
$$\text{if}\ identifier \in recgroup(f)$$

$$\lor\ identifier \in formals$$
$$\lor\ identifier \in builtins \tag{7}$$
$$\equiv identifier\,(\texttt{addfunc}\ identifier\ \texttt{path}),$$
$$otherwise \tag{8}$$

In Formula 1 the translation scheme $T\mathcal{D}$ transforms a function definition. It inserts the path parameter as the new first parameter to the function, and transforms the right-hand side of the function using $T\mathcal{RHS}$. The parameters to $T\mathcal{RHS}$ are the name of the function and the set of its formal parameters.

In Formula 2 $T\mathcal{RHS}$ transforms the right-hand side of a function definition containing **where** clauses – each subdefinition must be translated separately by $T\mathcal{LD}$. Formula 3 translates right-hand sides which do not contain **where** clauses.

$T\mathcal{LD}$ translates local definitions (Formula 4). The only relevant difference between local definitions and non-local definitions is that the formal parameters of the function of which the local definitions are a part are in scope in the local definitions. Apart from this, the right-hand sides of local definitions can be translated in the same way as those of non-local definitions. The formal parameters of the parent function must therefore be included in the set of formal parameters that is passed to $T\mathcal{RHS}$.

$T\mathcal{E}$ translates expressions. Formula 8 uses **addfunc** to identify the recursion group of function *identifier* and add this recursion group to the path. Formula 5 deals with the case when the expression contains the function **error**. We want to pass the path to **error** in order for it to be displayed as part of the error message when evaluation of the program is halted. We also want to include the original error message. Formula 6 deals with function application. e_1 and e_2 are both expressions and must be translated separately as such. Formula 7 leaves unchanged identifiers which should not be translated. If *identifier* is a member of the latest recursion group to be added to the path, it should not be added to the path as it is a recursive function or a function which is mutually recursive with other functions. Variables (formal parameters) should not be translated or added to the path. The main reason for not translating formal parameters which are functions is that they do not form part of the static path. There is however another reason. Consider the case of **apply**, a simple higher order function:

```
apply f x = f x
```

The variable **f** is clearly a function, as it is being applied to **x** on the right-hand side. Should **f** be translated on the right-hand side of **apply**? The definition of the function which is being passed to **apply** as parameter **f** has been translated to include the extra path parameter. It is possible that although this function is being used by **apply** as a function with only one parameter, it is in fact a curried function of more than one parameter which has been supplied with its other parameters before being used by **apply**. Figure 4 gives an example of such a function. It is thus not possible to supply **f** with the extra path parameter in the definition of **apply**, as it may already have been supplied.

```
times x y = x * y            times path x y = x * y

foo x y = apply (times x) y   foo path x y
                               = apply (addfunc "apply" path)
                                 (times (addfunc "times" path) x) y
```

Fig. 4. Translating curried functions. The originals appear on the left, with their translations on the right.

6.3 Example

An example Miranda script is shown in Appendix A. The script was written by an undergraduate as part of a larger program to perform map colouring which was set as an exercise. None of the functions are mutually recursive, although the script does contain recursive functions. addcol takes two parameters: a map and a colouring scheme, and returns the colouring scheme with one extra region coloured. When the expression go is evaluated, it attempts to use addcol to produce a new colouring scheme given the map and the colouring scheme defined in the script. However during evaluation, the script terminates with the exception error "program error: hd []".

The transformations were applied to the script to give the script shown in Appendix B. The translated script has been formatted to aid readability. This script contains a %include directive which includes the script stdenv.new which contains selected functions from the Miranda standard environment to which the transformations have been applied. The translated standard environment functions have the same names as the original functions but are prefixed by e_ (e.g. hd becomes e_hd).

When go is evaluated, the error message "program error: hd []: path: hd lookup will_clash clash addc addcol" is produced. This tells us the distinguished path. The dependency graph of the script is shown in Figure 5. Using a top-down directed search, the MIG (will_clash) can be found by searching nine functions. With a bottom-up directed search, the MIG can be found in five steps. However, searching along the distinguished path yields the MIG in six steps when the search begins at the top of the path, or three steps if the search begins at the bottom.

7 Implementation

An implementation of a distinguished path translation tool has been developed in Miranda. The tool takes the original source file, translates it and places it in a new file, leaving the original unaltered. This implementation has been designed for use with large Miranda programs and thus incorporates facilities for handling programs made up of a number of modules. These facilities include a UNIX make-

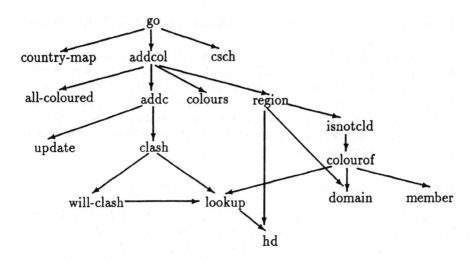

Fig. 5. The dependency graph of the map colouring script.

like feature[3] which analyzes the dependencies between modules and translates any modules which have become out of date. For reasons of efficiency, the tool has been translated into LML [1] which allows compilation into native code, unlike Miranda.

8 Practical Experience with the Distinguished Path Translation Tool

8.1 The LOLITA System

The Artificial Intelligence Systems Research Group at the University of Durham has developed a program for natural language applications. This program, LOLITA[4] [2], consists of approximately 12,000 lines of code[5] distributed between fifty modules and is written entirely in Miranda. In addition, LOLITA incorporates in the region of 450 data files. Initially conceived by Garigliano, there are currently ten people involved in the development and maintenance of the LOLITA source code. As the system increases in size and complexity, it is inevitable that an increased number of errors will be introduced into the program. Debugging methods used with LOLITA at present include a tracing mechanism which makes use of some of the UNIX system interface features of Miranda to produce side-effects which display the functions being used. These tracing functions must be inserted manually into the code, which is clumsy and itself prone

---

[3] This feature was adapted from the lmlmake program by Thomas Hallgren, which is distributed with the source to the Chalmers Lazy ML compiler.

[4] Large-scale Object-based Language Interactor, Translator and Analyser

[5] Not including comments.

to introducing errors. In addition, the information output by the trace is often difficult to interpret.

A rudimentary system for detecting the source of exception errors has also been included in the system. This involves the replacement of each occurrence of the functions which generate exception errors (hd for example) with a unique function which reports its name. This allows for the location of the particular call to the function to be determined, but does not give the full static path which led to the call. The insertion of these new functions is performed manually, which is both cumbersome and time-consuming.

8.2   The Application of the Tool to the LOLITA System

The tool takes approximately ten minutes to translate the whole of the LOLITA system. However, this will not normally be necessary, as the tool will translate only those modules which have been modified since the last translation.

The translated code runs about twenty-five percent slower than the original and uses about thirty percent more memory. This is an acceptable figure, considering that the debugging version is only used when necessary.

The tool has been used successfully to debug exception errors in the LOLITA system.

9   Further Work

9.1   Additional Translation Schemes

A problem at present is that the translation schemes are only of use when a function uses the function **error** to output an error message. Other run-time errors are caught by the implementation (see for example the "missing case" error described in Section 6.1). Translation schemes could be devised in addition to the ones above to handle these other run-time errors.

9.2   Determining why the Error Occurred

These translation schemes help us to find which part of the source code is incorrect. It may also be of use to go a stage further and find out the values of parameters which caused the error. For instance, when an "index out of range" error occurs, it would be helpful to know the value of the index.

Examining the values of parameters introduces several interesting problems. One such problem is in displaying values which may not otherwise be evaluated; this could itself lead to an error. The printing of an arbitrarily large data structure also presents difficulties.

A possible solution to these problems could be to make the display of values interactive; thus the user could choose which values were to be displayed. Of course, the user may choose to display the wrong values, leading to the difficulties listed above; however, the choice is given, which is a considerable improvement on simply displaying the values of all parameters. This interactive approach could not, however, be implemented as part of the source code transformation method; it would have to be built into a language implementation.

A Example Script Before Translation

The dependency graph of this script is given in Figure 5.

```
go = addcol country_map csch

csch=   [(1,'R'), (2,'G'), (3,'B'), (4,'G')]

country_map=[(2,[1,3,6]),(5,[1,4,6]),
            (1,[2,3,4,5,6]),(3,[2,1,6,4]),
            (4,[1,3,6,5]),(6,[1,5,4,3,2])]

colours=['B','G','R','Y']


|| This adds a colour to an uncoloured region.
addcol:: [(*,[*])] -> [(*,char)] ->  [(*,char)]
addcol tab cs
    =cs , if all_coloured tab cs
    =addc (region tab cs) tab cs colours , otherwise
     where
         addc reg t s [] = error "Error!"
         addc reg t s (d:ds)= update s reg d,if ~clash t s d reg
         addc reg t s (d:ds)=addc reg t s ds,otherwise

|| Region finds the first region without a colour
region :: [(*,[*])] -> [(*,char)] -> *
region tab cs = hd [r | r <- domain tab; isnotcld cs r]

|| This returns True if the region is not coloured
isnotcld :: [(*,char)]->*->bool
isnotcld [] r=True
isnotcld clsch r=colourof clsch r = 'U'

|| colourof returns the colour of a region or 'U' if it is
|| not coloured
colourof :: [(*,char)]->*->char
colourof clsch r=lookup clsch r, if  member (domain clsch) r
                ='U', otherwise
```

```
|| This returns True if and only if all regions in a map are
|| coloured.
all_coloured :: [(*,**)] -> [(*,char)] ->bool
all_coloured tab [] = False
all_coloured tab cs = #tab = #cs

domain :: [(*,**)]->[*]
domain table = [k|(k,y)<-table]

clash :: [(*,[**])] -> [(**,***)] -> *** -> * -> bool
clash tab colsc col reg = will_clash (lookup tab reg) colsc col

will_clash :: [**]->[(**,***)]->***->bool
will_clash [] cs c=False
will_clash (n:ns) [] c=False
will_clash (n:ns) cs c = ((lookup cs n=c) \/ (will_clash ns cs c))

|| lookup takes a key and returns the associated
|| value in a lookup table.  The key must be present in the table.
lookup :: [(*,**)] -> * -> **
lookup table x= hd ([y|(z,y)<-table;z=x])

update :: [(*,**)]->*->**->[(*,**)]
update table x y = (x,y):table
```

B   Example Script After Translation

```
%include "stdenv.new"

go = addcol "addcol" country_map csch

csch =   [(1,'R'), (2,'G'), (3,'B'), (4,'G')]

country_map =[(2,[1,3,6]),(5,[1,4,6]),
             (1,[2,3,4,5,6]),(3,[2,1,6,4]),
             (4,[1,3,6,5]),(6,[1,5,4,3,2])]

colours =['B','G','R','Y']

addcol path tab cs
  =cs , if all_coloured (addfunc "all_coloured" path) tab cs
  =addc (addfunc "addc" path)
        (region (addfunc "region" path) tab cs)
```

```
                tab cs colours, otherwise
    where
       addc path reg t s []
           = error ("Error!: path: " ++ path)
       addc path reg t s (d:ds)
           = update (addfunc "update" path) s reg d,
                   if ~clash (addfunc "clash" path) t s d reg
       addc path reg t s (d:ds)=addc path reg t s ds,otherwise


region path tab cs
  = e_hd (addfunc "hd" path)
      [r | r <- domain (addfunc "domain" path) tab;
       isnotcld (addfunc "isnotcld" path) cs r]


isnotcld path [] r=True
isnotcld path clsch r
  = colourof (addfunc "colourof" path) clsch r = 'U'


colourof path clsch r
   = lookup (addfunc "colourof" path) clsch r,
        if member (domain (addfunc "domain" path) clsch) r
   = 'U', otherwise


all_coloured path tab [] = False
all_coloured path tab cs = #tab = #cs


domain path table = [k|(k,y)<-table]


clash path tab colsc col reg
  = will_clash (addfunc "will_clash" path)
     (lookup (addfunc "lookup" path) tab reg) colsc col


will_clash path [] cs c=False
will_clash path (n:ns) [] c=False
will_clash path (n:ns) cs c
   = ((lookup (addfunc "lookup" path) cs n=c)
        \/ (will_clash path ns cs c))


lookup path table x= e_hd (addfunc "hd" path)
                             ([y|(z,y)<-table;z=x])


update path table x y = (x,y):table
```

References

1. L. Augustsson. A compiler for lazy ML. In *Proceedings of the ACM Symposium on Lisp and Functional Programming, Austin*, pages 218—27, August 1984.

2. R. Garigliano, R.G. Morgan, and M.H. Smith. LOLITA: Progress report 1. Technical Report 12/92, Artificial Intelligence Systems Research Group, School of Engineering and Computer Science, University of Durham, Science Laboratories, South Road, Durham DH1 3LE, United Kingdom, 1992.

3. S. Kamin. A debugging environment for functional programming in Centaur. Technical report, INRIA Sophia-Antipolis, 1990.

4. L. Naish. Declarative debugging of lazy functional programs (draft). Technical Report 92/6, Department of Computer Science, University of Melbourne, Parkville, Melbourne, Victoria 3052, Australia, May 1992.

5. H. Nilsson and P. Fritzson. Algorithmic debugging for lazy functional languages. In M. Bruynooghe and M. Wirsing, editors, *Proceedings of the Fourth International Symposium on Programming Language Implementation and Logic Programming*, number 631 in Lecture Notes in Computer Science, pages 385—399, Leuven, Belgium, August 1992. Springer-Verlag.

6. J.T. O'Donnell and C.V. Hall. Debugging in applicative languages. *Lisp and Symbolic Computation*, 1(2):113–145, 1988.

7. E.Y. Shapiro. *Algorithmic Program Debugging*. ACM Distinguished Dissertations. MIT Press, May 1982.

8. R.M. Snyder. Lazy debugging of lazy functional programs. *New Generation Computing*, 8(2):138–161, 1990.

9. I. Toyn and C. Runciman. Adapting combinator and SECD machines to display snapshots of functional computations. *New Generation Computing*, 4(4):339–363, 1986.

10. D.A. Turner. Miranda: a non-strict functional language with polymorphic types. In Jean-Pierre Jouannaud, editor, *Proceedings of the IFIP International Conference on Functional Programming Languages and Computer Architecture*, number 201 in Lecture Notes in Computer Science, pages 1—16, Nancy, France, 1985. Springer-Verlag.

A Generalised Query Minimisation for Program Debugging

Visit Hirunkitti and Christopher J. Hogger

Department of Computing,
Imperial College of Science, Technology and Medicine
University of London
180 Queen's Gate,
London SW7 2BZ, U.K.
e-mail: {vvh, cjh}@doc.ic.ac.uk

Abstract. Shapiro proposed an algorithm called 'Divide-and-Query' which gives a good solution for query minimisation in the context of algorithmic program debugging. His algorithm applies a half-splitting strategy which repeatedly subdivides an AND-tree representing an incorrect computation under the guidance of an oracle until the bug responsible has been localised. His aim was to minimise the number of queries asked of the oracle, and in general his method approximates well to this ideal. There are cases, however, in which it divides the tree suboptimally with the consequence that more queries are posed than are necessary.

This paper explains why the algorithm may have this inefficiency and presents an improved version which, in the average case, overcomes it. We show that the new algorithm is a special case of measurement guidance by minimum entropy technique adapted from fault diagnosis.

1. Introduction

To say that a program contains a bug is taken to mean that there is a discrepancy between the answers computed by the program and the answers intended. The cause of the bug can be sought by consulting an agent called the 'oracle' who possesses an intended model (meaning) **M** for the program against which computed answers may be compared. This requires that the oracle be able to supply **M** on demand, though in practice **M** is unlikely to be held in any complete or explicit form. One may, however, be able to elicit some *part* of **M** by querying the oracle, who may then supply that part as a collection of ground facts. However, if the program has a large computed answer set then it is likely that many such queries will need to be issued, making the diagnostic process very time-consuming and tedious.

We need, therefore, to reduce the number of the queries issued to the oracle. One way of doing this is to allow the oracle to supply other forms of knowledge which represent **M** in ways more concise than sets of ground facts; an example of such a system is that of Drabent et al. [1988], in which the oracle supplies general logical assertions. One can even dispense with the human oracle and instead use a non-human one such as a complete program specification, as proposed by Dershowitz and Lee [1987].

An alternative way of proceeding is that of query minimisation, which seeks to reduce the number of queries issued by trying to discriminate as strongly as possible between subtrees according to the likelihood that they contain the bug. Query minimisation was first investigated by Shapiro [1983] using a very effective *Divide-and-Query* (henceforth "D&Q") algorithm. In this paper we generalise the intuition behind this algorithm with the aim of further improving its effectiveness.

Shapiro's algorithm assigns, to each node of a computation's (AND-)tree, a *weight* which (loosely) represents the likelihood that the (single) bug being sought is contained in the subtree rooted at that node. Using a criterion based on such weights, it then subdivides the tree into two subtrees which are (more or less) equally likely to contain the bug; an oracle decides which of the two does contain it and then proceeds to subdivide this one in turn by the same method. Eventually, the bug is inevitably found.

Presently, we shall show how the D&Q algorithm can in certain cases behave inefficiently, for which we propose a remedy. This remedy in turn suggests a further generalisation of the algorithm equipping it to exploit a given probability that a clause in a diagnosed program is incorrect. An oracle capable of supplying such probabilities reliably will have an enhanced capability for localising bugs.

In what follows we begin with a brief outline of D&Q, and then an example to show how it may divide the tree sub-optimally. We then present an improved heuristic for dividing the tree. The algorithm thereby obtained can be viewed as a special case of measurement guidance by minimum entropy, a general technique employed in many fault diagnosis systems [de Kleer and Williams 1987], [de Kleer 1990], [Pipitone 1986] and [Freitag 1990]. Finally, we show how one might exploit given probabilities. An implementation of the improved algorithm and some debugging sessions using it are given in Appendix A and B respectively. The performances of D&Q and improved algorithms are compared for some programs in Appendix B and C.

2. Shapiro's Query Minimisation

Shapiro's procedure seeks to minimise the number of queries put to an oracle in the course of top-down diagnosis of a faulty computation represented by an (AND-) tree T. Only one bug is sought during the search of T. The search proceeds by identifying in T a node m, referred to as the 'middle node', on the basis of which T is divided into two roughly 'equal' subtrees—one being the subtree T_1 rooted at m and the other T_2 being what remains from T after deleting T_1. The oracle is asked whether m is in M. If the answer is *yes* then the bug is contained in T_2 but otherwise in T_1. The same strategy is then applied recursively to whichever one of T_1 or T_2 contains the bug.

In Shapiro's framework, each node in T is representable as a triple $<p, x, y>$ wherein p names a procedure called on input x which returns output y; such a triple also implicitly denotes the subtree of T that is rooted at that node. It is presupposed that we have some subset $M' \subseteq M$ (possibly empty at first) of nodes already confirmed to be correct. In order to subdivide T systematically, Shapiro devised a measure for each node $<p, x, y>$, relative to M', termed its *weight modulo* M'. [We shall abbreviate this term to 'the weight', leaving the current M' implicit.] It is defined as follows. If the node is in M' then w is 0; otherwise, if it is a leaf then w is 1; otherwise w is 1 plus the sum of the weights of the node's sons. Now suppose that the weight of T's root node is w. Then the *middle node* of T is identified as the *leftmost heaviest* node in T whose weight is less than or equal to $\lceil w/2 \rceil$, where the latter denotes the least integer not less than w/2. The procedure which identifies the middle node in this manner is called *fpm*, and is listed in Appendix A. Given all this, the D&Q algorithm as given by Shapiro [1983] is paraphrased below.

2.1 The Divide-and-Query Algorithm

Input: A procedure **p** in the program **P** and an input x such that **p** called on x succeeds with an output y which is incorrect in **M**, and some **M'⊆M**.

Output: A triple <q, u, v> not in **M** such that **q** *covers* <q, u, v> in **M**—the latter meaning that **M** contains all the immediate descendent nodes of a computation which returns v in response to **q** called on u.

Algorithm:

(i)   Simulate the evaluation of **p** on x that returns y to compute w, the weight of the tree;

(ii) Call a recursive procedure *fp* with <p, x, y>, w and **M'** defined as follows. If w=1 then *fp* returns <p, x, y> and thereby identifies the bug. Otherwise, *fp* finds the heaviest node <q, u, v> in the tree of <p, x, y> whose weight w_q is less than or equal to $\lceil w/2 \rceil$, by using the procedure *fpm*; and then asks the ground oracle whether <q, u, v> is in **M**; if the answer is *yes* then *fp* calls itself recursively with <p, x, y>, w−w_q and **M'**∪{<q, u, v>}, otherwise with <q, u, v>, w_q and **M'**.

Shapiro showed that this algorithm performs at most b*log*n queries in order to find the bug, where b is the branching factor of **T** and n is the number of nodes in **T**.

2.2 Potential for Improving D&Q

For most situations D&Q provides an unbiased way of dividing the tree **T** when there is no information to help us focus upon any particular node, or when there is no reason to partition the nodes in any particular way. However, its commitment always to choose the *leftmost* heaviest node (henceforth denoted by N_L) has the consequence that in some cases the two subtrees obtained by the division of **T** may not be roughly equal. In this event D&Q will perform more subdivisions than necessary to find the bug.

We can, however, subdivide **T** (with respect to some **M'**) in a more discriminating manner. Suppose the weight of **T** (i.e. of its root) is w. We define n_m as the *ideal middle node* of **T** whose weight is *exactly* w/2, as the basis of attaining a more equal subdivision than would be obtained using Shapiro's *fpm*. Note that n_m is an *ideal* node—it may not actually exist in **T**. Then a node n_L whose weight is w_L is defined to be the *leftmost heaviest* node of **T** *with respect to* n_m where $w_L<w/2$. Correspondingly, a node n_R whose weight is w_R is defined to be the *rightmost lightest node* of **T** *with respect to* n_m where $w_R>w/2$. The best node on which to divide **T** is then whichever of n_L and n_R is the *closest* in weight to n_m—for instance, n_R will be the best choice in the case that $(w_R−(w/2))<((w/2)−w_L)$.

Compared with the above, D&Q's *fpm* procedure is less sensitive in that it divides **T** on a node N_L whose weight is less than or equal to $\lceil w/2 \rceil$. Clearly, N_L corresponds to our n_L when n_L is closer to n_m than is n_R, or corresponds to n_m when the ideal middle n_m actually exists in **T**, or even corresponds to n_R when $w_R=\lceil w/2 \rceil$. But whenever n_R is closer to n_m than is n_L and $w_R>\lceil w/2 \rceil$, D&Q fails to choose the better node n_R even though to do so would actually be more consistent with Shapiro's original intuition. The extent to which this distinction affects diagnostic efficiency depends upon the nature of T. In the example which follows we shall see that the distinction is substantial.

3. An Example

This program returns an incorrect answer ('yes') to a call to 'likes(mary, tom)':

likes(mary, X) :- good_personality(X), kind(X), good_in_programming(X).
good_personality(X) :- bold(X), attractive(X), optimist(X),
                    sense_of_humour(X), smart(X).
bold(X) :- not_afraid_of_dog(X), athletic(X).
attractive(X) :- charming(X).
optimist(X) :- thinks_positive(X), compassionate(X).
sense_of_humour(X) :- often_tells_jokes(X).
kind(X) :- likes(X, peace), likes(X, pets), likes(X, children), friendly(X).

not_afraid_of_dog(tom).	athletic(tom).
charming(tom).	thinks_positive(tom).
compassionate(tom).	often_tells_jokes(tom).
likes(tom, peace).	smart(tom).
likes(tom, pets).	friendly(tom).
likes(tom, children).	

good_in_programming(tom). % *This clause is assumed to be incorrect.*

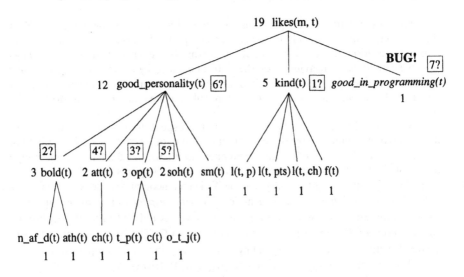

Figure 1. Node choosing strategy by the Divide-and-Query algorithm

Figure 1. sketches the tree **T** for **<likes, (mary, tom), 'yes'>**. Each procedure call represents a node and the number next to it is its weight. A square containing some k? next to a node signifies that D&Q identifies that node as the middle node for the kth subdivision. The fact 'good_in_programming(tom)' is assumed to be the (only) bug. We shall first show how D&Q subdivides this **T** until it finds the bug.

For brevity, let

> **<f>** denotes **<likes**, (mary, tom), 'yes'>
> **<g>** denotes **<good_personality**, tom, 'yes'>
> **<h>** denotes **<kind**, tom, 'yes'>
> **<i>** denotes **<good_in_programming**, tom, 'yes'>

Suppose we have no prior knowledge about this program and thus initially $\mathbf{M'}=\Phi$. Then the weight of **<f>** is w=19. D&Q searches for the leftmost heaviest node of **T** whose weight is $\leqslant \lceil 19/2 \rceil$, that is, ≤ 10. This turns out to be **<h>** whose weight is 5. Asking the oracle whether **<h>** is correct (in **M**) yields *yes*, and so D&Q prunes away the subtree rooted at **<h>**. The process continues in like fashion until it finally localises the bug **<i>**, requiring a total of 7 queries to be posed to the oracle— equivalently, 7 subdivisions of the original tree. Intuitively, however, the best node to have queried first would have been **<g>** (the rightmost lightest node whose weight is 12) rather than **<h>**, since **<g>** is closer than **<h>** to the (hypothetical) ideal middle node whose weight is 9.5. Choosing **<g>** would have divided **T** more equally than would choosing **<h>**. We shall see in due course that our proposed modified algorithm does exactly this, and consequently locates the bug after only 3 subdivisions.

4. The Modified Algorithm

We aim for a modified version of D&Q which considers both the leftmost heaviest node n_L and the rightmost lightest node n_R in order to decide upon which node to divide the tree. In fact, the new algorithm chooses whichever of the leftmost heaviest node n_L and the rightmost lightest node n_R is *closest* to the ideal middle node n_m.

In order to characterise the heuristic identifying this best node, we introduce a term called the *deviation* of a node n from the ideal middle node n_m, denoted by $\delta(n)$. $\delta(n)$ is defined to be the absolute value of the difference between w/2 and the weight w_n of n, i.e. $\delta(n)=|(w/2)-w_n|$. The heuristic is to choose from **T** a node n for which $\delta(n)$ is minimal; this n is bound to be either n_L or n_R. Thus, the weights w_L and w_R of these are computed and hence also their respective deviations $\delta(n_L)$ and $\delta(n_R)$ from n_m. If $\delta(n_L) \leq \delta(n_R)$ then the algorithm will choose n_L, otherwise it will choose n_R.

Modified D&Q Algorithm

Input: A procedure **p** in the program **P** and an input x such that **p** called on x succeeds with an output y which is incorrect in **M**, and some $\mathbf{M'} \subseteq \mathbf{M}$.
Output: A triple **<q**, u, v> not in **M** such that **q** covers **<q**, u, v> in **M**.
Algorithm:
(i)   Simulate the evaluation of **p** on x that returns y to compute w, the weight *modulo* **M'** of the tree;
(ii) Call a recursive procedure *new_fp* with **<p**, x, y>, w and **M'**, defined as follows.

If w=1 then *new_fp* returns **<p, x, y>**. Otherwise, *new_fp* applies aprocedure *new_fpm* (see Appendix A) to compute the deviation of each node from n$_m$, and then finds a node **<q, u, v>** in **T** for which δ(**<q, u, v>**) is minimal:

Then *new_fp* asks the ground oracle whether **<q, u, v>** is in **M**.

If *yes* then *new_fp* calls itself recursively with **<p, x, y>**, w–w$_q$ and **M'∪{<q, u, v>}**, but otherwise with **<q, u, v>**, w$_q$ and **M'**.

The modified algorithm requires, *on average*, that fewer queries be asked of the oracle than does the unmodified D&Q. It carries, of course, an overhead in having to compute and compare n$_L$ and n$_R$ for each subtree divided. Nevertheless, this is outweighed in general by the effort saved in the querying of the oracle. The complexity of the new algorithm remains similar to that of D&Q in requiring at most b*log*n queries to find a counter-example (i.e., a bug).

We sketch below how the modified algorithm deals with the previous example.

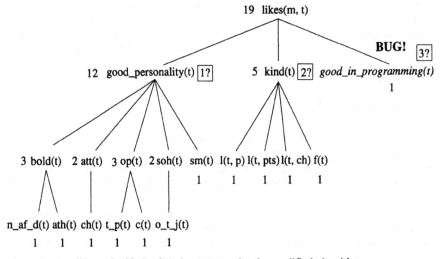

Figure 2. Node choosing strategy by the modified algorithm

In Figure 2. we see the modified algorithm now choosing **<g>** as the first query on which to divide **T** on the basis that δ(**<g>**)=|(19/2)–12|=2.5, an outcome which better fulfils Shapiro's intuition than choosing **<h>** for which δ(**<h>**)=|(19/2)–5|=4.5. After asking the first query, **T** is pruned at **<g>** and the algorithm is re-applied to what remains. Continuing in this fashion we eventually find the bug after posing only 3 queries compared with the 7 posed by D&Q. The performances of the modified and unmodified algorithms are compared for some other programs in Appendix B and C.

5. Query Minimisation Based on Minimum Entropy

The modified algorithm can be interpreted in terms of measurement guidance by minimum entropy, a technique employed in many fault-diagnosis systems such as

GDE [de Kleer 1990], [de Kleer and Williams 1987] and FIS [Pipitone 1986]. These systems apply look-ahead to decide the best measurement to test next, identifying it as whichever one gives *minimum expected entropy*. They can utilise given probabilities that particular components are faulty and can also deal with multiple faults.

Suppose the system under consideration has measurable probe points x_1, x_2, ... For any such point x_i, let $v_{i1},...,v_{im}$ be the possible outcomes of measuring it. Then the *expected entropy* after measuring x_i is given—e.g., see [de Kleer and Williams 1987]—by

$$H_e(x_i) = \sum_{k=1}^{m} p(x_i=v_{ik})H(x_i=v_{ik}) \tag{1}$$

where $p(x_i=v_{ik})$ is the probability that x_i will yield outcome v_{ik}, and $H(x_i=v_{ik})$ is the entropy determined by the diagnosis candidates' probabilities resulting from the hypothesised result $x_i=v_{ik}$.

As shown by de Kleer [1990], the task of minimising $H_e(x_i)$ in the context of fault diagnosis is simplified by assuming that components fail independently and with equal, but small, probabilities, in which case it is sufficient instead to minimise the *scoring function*

$$\$(x_i) = \sum_{k=1}^{m} \frac{c_{ik}}{N}log\frac{c_{ik}}{N}$$

where c_{ik} is the number of diagnoses of any particular size which predict $x_i=v_{ik}$, N is the number of diagnoses altogether of this size and m is the number of possible outcomes that x_i might have. Taking N to be constant, the above can be normalised to a simpler function

$$\$(x_i) = \sum_{k=1}^{m} c_{ik}logc_{ik} \tag{2}$$

This scoring function estimates the expected cost of identifying the actual diagnosis candidate and it is a very good cost function for *the average case*. Entropy minimisation in this context has been explored further by Freitag [1990].

To show how this principle applies to fault diagnosis we consider the following example taken from [de Kleer 1990].

5.1 A Circuit Example

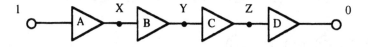

Figure 3. A circuit example

Figure 3. shows a circuit comprising four buffers: A, B, C and D. The input is 1 and gives an *incorrect* output 0. The possible next probe points to be measured are X, Y and Z. Here there are four possible single-fault diagnoses—[A], [B], [C] and [D].

Using a look-ahead strategy we find, for example, that if X is measured to be 0 then the set S of diagnoses will be {[A]} but otherwise {[B], [C], [D]}. Continuing likewise with measurements for the remaining points we obtain altogether the following sets of possible diagnoses:

$$X = 0, \quad S = \{[A]\}; \qquad\qquad X = 1, \quad S = \{[B], [C], [D]\},$$
$$Y = 0, \quad S = \{[A], [B]\}; \qquad Y = 1, \quad S = \{[C], [D]\},$$
$$Z = 0, \quad S = \{[A], [B], [C]\}; \qquad Z = 1, \quad S = \{[D]\}.$$

These sets are then scored as follows:

$$\$(X) = 3log3 + 1log1 = 3.3$$
$$\$(Y) = 2log2 + 2log2 = 2.8$$
$$\$(Z) = 1log1 + 3log3 = 3.3$$

from which it is seen that $\$(Y)$ is the minimum, implying that the next best point to be tested is Y—the same point as would be chosen by a half-split heuristic.

5.2 Minimum Entropy applied to Query Minimisation

The minimum entropy technique as applied to fault diagnosis can be applied also to query minimisation for program debugging. In the absence of any reason to assign particular probabilities to various clause instances used for deriving the tree representing the faulty computation, we assign small but equal probabilities to all of them and treat them as independent. (The clause instances are analogous to system components in fault diagnosis.) The possible outcomes of measurement—that is, of querying any node—are just *yes* and *no*.

We now show how equation (2) can be used for choosing the next best query to be posed at each stage of debugging the program in our earlier example, whose tree is shown in simplified form by Figure 4.

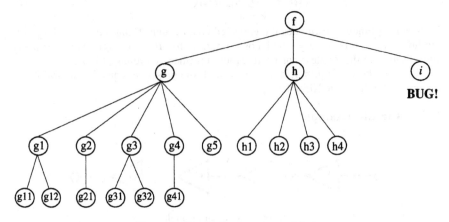

Figure 4. The faulty program revisited

We show only how to calculate $(<g>) and $(<h>) because the calculation of $ for the other nodes is very similar and, in any case, gives values no less than $(<g>) and $(<h>).

?<g> = yes :   S = {[f:-g,h,i], [h:-h1,h2,h3,h4], [h1], [h2], [h3], [h4], [i]}

?<g> = no :   S = {[g:-g1,g2,g3,g4,g5], [g1:-g11,g12], [g11], [g12], [g2:-g21],
        [g21], [g3:-g31,g32], [g31], [g32], [g4:-g41], [g41], [g5]}

?<h> = yes :   S = {[f:-g,h,i], [g:-g1,g2,g3,g4,g5], [g1:-g11,g12], [g11], [g12],
        [g2:-g21], [g21], [g3:-g31,g32], [g31], [g32], [g4:-g41],
        [g41], [g5], [i]}

?<h> = no :   S = {[h:-h1,h2,h3,h4], [h1], [h2], [h3], [h4]}

$$\$(<g>) = 7log7 + 12log12 = 43.44$$
$$\$(<h>) = 14log14 + 5log5 = 44.99$$

This identifies <g> as the next best choice of query, as did our modified D&Q algorithm. It does *not* choose <h>, as does the unmodified D&Q. In the next section we show that the heuristic applied in our algorithm is only a special case derivable from equation (2), and we then prove that, on entropic grounds, it is bound always to choose the next best node. (The interpretation of diagnoses here follows [Pereira et al. 93].)

5.3 Optimal Test for the Half-split Method

Consider equation (2) and assume a program having just one bug (looking for a single bug first)—thus there can be only one counter-example in any T of weight w_n. (However, this technique is also applicable for dealing with multiple bugs.) Since the possible outcomes of measurement (node-querying) are just *yes* and *no*, we have m=2 in (2). If we choose node n as the one to query, this divides the tree (containing all possible diagnoses) into two subtrees (each contains each set of possible diagnoses), having weights w_n and $w-w_n$ respectively. According to (2), we can formulate $(n) as

$$\$(n) = w_n log w_n + (w-w_n) log(w-w_n) \qquad (3)$$

We know that the next best node n to query is that which minimises $(n) and it is trivial to show from the derivative of (3) that $(n) is minimum when $w_n=w/2$. Recall that the node having weight w/2 is the ideal middle node n_m. If n_m actually exists in T then it divides the set of possible diagnoses into two exactly equal sets (two equal subtrees).

Typically the ideal middle node will not actually exist. When this is so, either the leftmost heaviest node n_L or the rightmost lightest node n_R may—depending on the circumstances—be chosen as the next best query, since then either $w_n=w/2-\delta$ (the weight of n_L) or $w_n=w/2+\delta$ (the weight of node n_R) may minimise $(n). Here the number δ is the previously-defined deviation $\delta(n)$ of node n with respect to n_m. The heuristic underlying our modified algorithm—i.e., choose from T the node n for which $\delta(n)=|w/2-w_n|$ is minimum—is thus a special case of equation (2).

Recall that the key case distinguishing our heuristic from that of D&Q occurs when

$$(w_R-w/2)<(w/2-w_L) \text{ and } w_R > \lceil w/2 \rceil$$

When this holds, our algorithm chooses n_R having weight $w/2+\delta$ and this is—entropically—the best choice; by contrast, D&Q chooses instead the node N_L having weight $w/2-\varepsilon$ where $\varepsilon>\delta$. We can prove from (3) that $\$(N_L)>\$(n_R)$, as follows.

Proof

Note—we prove it over reals, hence also for positive integers.

We want to show that $\$(N_L)>\$(n_R)$ whenever $w/2>\varepsilon>\delta> 0$.
Suppose $f(\delta)=(w/2+\delta)log(w/2+\delta)+(w/2-\delta)log(w/2-\delta)$,
Let $\varepsilon=\delta+\Delta$ so that $\Delta>0$. Then

$$\$(n_R)=f(\delta) \text{ and } \$(N_L)=f(\delta+\Delta)$$

so $\quad f(\delta+\Delta) > f(\delta)$

if $\quad f(\delta+\Delta)-f(\delta) > 0$

if $\quad \dfrac{f(\delta+\Delta)-f(\delta)}{\Delta} > 0 \qquad$ since $\Delta>0$

if $\quad \lim_{\Delta\to 0} \dfrac{f(\delta+\Delta)-f(\delta)}{\Delta} > 0$ since the 2nd derivative $f''(\delta)$ is always >0

if $\quad \dfrac{df(\delta)}{d\delta} > 0$

if $\quad log\left(\dfrac{w/2+\delta}{w/2-\delta}\right) > 0$

if $\quad \dfrac{w/2+\delta}{w/2-\delta} > 1$

if $\quad$ true, since $w/2>\delta>0$. $\quad$ **Q.E.D.**

The proven inequality $\$(N_L)>\$(n_R)$ establishes that our method is strictly better on average than D&Q.

5.4 Query Minimisation with Bug Probabilities

Previously we assumed that no particular prior probabilities were assigned to the clause instances, effectively assigning to them equal but small probabilities of magnitude $1/n$ in any tree (having n nodes) already known to contain a single bug. Nevertheless, the number of measurements can be reduced if we can, on whatever basis, assign particular prior probabilities. We can still use equation (2) to determine the next best test.

Consider the following sorting program taken from [Shapiro 83]:

```
C1: isort([X|Xs],Ys) :- isort(Xs,Zs), insert(X,Zs,Ys).
C2: isort([],[]).

C3: insert(X,[Y|Ys],[Y|Zs]) :- Y > X, insert(X,Ys,Zs).
     % The bug!  Y > X must be changed to X > Y.
C4: insert(X,[Y|Ys],[X,Y|Ys]) :- X ≤ Y.
C5: insert(X,[],[X]).
```

From the program listing, Cn names the nth clause. This program returns an incorrect answer *isort([2,1,3],[2,3,1])*. The tree of the computation is illustrated below.

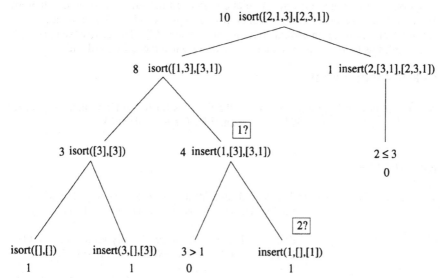

Figure 5. Node choosing strategy when prior bug probabilities are given

In Figure 5, the weights of both $<\leq, (2, 3),$ 'yes'> and <>, (3, 1), 'yes'> are 0, because $\leq$ and > are the predicates (system predicates) which have already been known to be correct with respect to the intended model **M'**. Suppose the oracle supplies the information that "Clause C3 is more likely to be incorrect than the others". This implies that *'insert(1,[3],[3,1]):-3>1, insert(1,[],[1])'*, an instance of clause C3, should be assigned a higher bug probability, Δ/n', than the instances derived from other clauses, which are assigned $1/n'$, where n' is a new weight of the tree and Δ is an integer greater than 1. The new weight of **<insert**, (1, [3]), [3,1]> or any answer derivable from clause C3 can be calculated from the summation of its sons' weights plus Δ; whereas the new weights of the other nodes are still calculated the same way as before, i.e. from the summation of its sons' weights plus 1. The new weight of the root now becomes the new weight of the tree, n'. In this example Δ is assumed to be 3. The higher the number Δ is, the more efficiently the heuristic focuses on an instance of the suspected clause. The weight of **<insert**, (1, [3]), [3,1]> then becomes 4 instead of 2. We can see in Figure 5 that, by applying our heuristic for choosing the next best node, it requires only 2 queries to identify the counter-example *'insert(1,[3],[3,1]) -3>1, insert(1,[],[1])'* rather than 3 as demonstrated in Appendix B.

It can be concluded that, with a prior bug probability being given, the heuristic will choose a node which is closer to an instance of the suspected clause to query next. This may reduce the number of queries required for localising a counter-example.

6. Conclusion

We presented a generalised query minimisation principle for program debugging based on the minimum entropy technique employed in fault diagnosis, and thereby justified a new algorithm which generalises Shapiro's D&Q. The new algorithm performs strictly better in certain circumstances than D&Q. The generalised principle also enables us to accommodate bug probabilities when these are available.

Acknowledgements

We are grateful to Dr. Fariba Sadri and the referees for helpful comments on earlier drafts of the paper, and to the British Council for funding this work.

References

[de Kleer and Williams 87]   de Kleer, J. and Williams, B. C., Diagnosing Multiple Faults, *Artificial Intelligence* **32**, pp. 97-130 (1987).

[de Kleer 90]   de Kleer, J.,Using Crude Probability Estimates to Guide Diagnosis, *Artificial Intelligence* **45**,pp.381-391 (1990).

[Dershowitz and Lee 87]   Dershowitz, N. and Lee, Y., Deductive Debugging, *Proc. of the Symposium on Logic Programming*, San Francisco, pp. 298-306 (1987).

[Drabent et al. 88]   Drabent, W., Nadjm-Tehrani, S. and Maluszynski, J., The Use of Assertions in Algorithmic Debugging, *Proc. of FGCS-88*, pp. 573-581 (1988).

[Freitag 90]   Freitag, H., A Generic Measurement Proposer, *Proc. of the International Workshop on Expert System in Engineering*, Springer-Verlag (1990).

[Pereira et al. 93]   Pereira, L. M., Damásio, C. V. and J. J. Alferes, Debugging by Diagnosing Assumptions, *Proc. of the 1st International Workshop on Automated and Algorithmic Debugging*, Linköping, Sweden, Springer-Verlag (1993).

[Pipitone 86]   Pipitone, F., The FIS electronics troubleshooting system, *IEEE Computer* **19** (7), pp. 68-75 (1986).

[Plaisted 84]   Plaisted, D. A., An Efficient Bug Location Algorithm, *Proc. of the 2nd International Conference on Logic Programming* (1984).

[Shapiro 83]   Shapiro, E. Y., *Algorithmic Program Debugging*, MIT Press (1983).

Appendix A

```
/* An implementation of D&Q algorithm written in Mac Prolog */

fpm(((A,B),Wab),M,W) :-  !, fpm((A,Wa),(Ma,Wma),W),
                fpm((B,Wb),(Mb,Wmb),W), Wab is Wa + Wb,
                ( Wma >= Wmb -> M = (Ma,Wma) ; M = (Mb,Wmb) ).
fpm((A,0),(true,0),W) :-  sdef(A),!,A ; fact(A,true).
                % sdef(A) is equivalent to system(A) in other Prolog.
fpm((A,Wa),M,W) :-   clause(A,B),fpm((B,Wb),Mb,W),
                Wa is Wb + 1, X is W + 1, Y is X / 2,
                ( Wa > Y -> M = Mb ; M = ((A,<-,B),Wa) ).

fp(A,Wa,X) :-    fpm((A,Wa),((P,<-,Q),Wm),Wa),
                ( Wa = 1 -> X = (P,<-,Q) ;
                  query(forall,P,true) -> Wa1 is Wa -Wm,fp(A,Wa1,X) ;
                  fp(P,Wm,X) ),
                retractall(fact(_,true)).

query(forall,P,true) :- ask_yes_or_no(P) -> assert(fact(P,true)) ; fail.
% In Mac Prolog ask_yes_or_no(P) will prompt a yes/no query to the user.

fact([],false). % The declaration of fact/2

/* An implementation of the improved algorithm */

new_fpm(((A,B),Wab),Mab,W) :- !,
                new_fpm((A,Wa),(Ma,Wma),W), new_fpm((B,Wb),(Mb,Wmb),W),
                Wab is Wa + Wb, Wim is W / 2, % the weight of the ideal middle node
                Dist1 is Wim - Wma, abs(Dist1,Dma), % Calculate δ(Ma)
                Dist2 is Wim - Wmb, abs(Dist2,Dmb), % Calculate δ(Mb)
                ( (Dma == Dmb -> (Wmb  < Wma -> Mab = (Mb,Wmb) ; Mab = (Ma,Wma)) ) ;
                  (Dma < Dmb -> Mab = (Ma,Wma) ; Mab = (Mb,Wmb) ) ).
                % choose the node which has δ(n) less than the other
new_fpm((A,0),(true,0),W) :- sdef(A),!,A ; fact(A,true).
new_fpm((A,Wa),M,W) :-
                clause(A,B),new_fpm((B,Wb),(Mb,Wmb),W),
                Wa is Wb + 1, Wim is W / 2, % the weight of the ideal middle node
                Dist1 is Wim - Wa, abs(Dist1,Dma), % Calculate δ(A)
                Dist2 is Wim - Wmb, abs(Dist2,Dmb), % Calculate δ(Mb)
                ( (Dma == Dmb -> (Wb == 0 -> M = ((A,<-,B),Wa) ; M = (Mb,Wmb)) ) ;
                  (Dma < Dmb -> M = ((A,<-,B),Wa) ; M = (Mb,Wmb) ) ).
                % choose the node which has δ(n) less than the other

new_fp(A,Wa,X) :-  new_fpm((A,Wa),((P,<-,Q),Wm),Wa),
                ( Wa = 1 -> X = (P,<-,Q) ;
                  query(forall,P,true) -> Wa1 is Wa - Wm,new_fp(A,Wa1,X) ;
                  new_fp(P,Wm,X) ),
                retractall(fact(_,true)).
```

Appendix B: Demonstration

/* The demonstration for the incorrect program, 'likes(mary,tom)', given earlier */

?fp(likes(mary,tom),19,C).

(1?):	ask_y_or_n(kind(tom))	Oracle: Yes.
(2?):	ask_y_or_n(bold(tom))	Oracle: Yes.
(3?):	ask_y_or_n(optimist(tom))	Oracle: Yes.
(4?):	ask_y_or_n(attractive(tom))	Oracle: Yes.
(5?):	ask_y_or_n(sense_of_humour(tom))	Oracle: Yes.
(6?):	ask_y_or_n(good_personality(tom))	Oracle: Yes.
(7?):	ask_y_or_n(good_in_programming(tom))	Oracle: No.

Debugger: A counter-example C is [good_in_programming(tom) <- true].
The debugger needs 7 queries to localise the counter-example .

?new_fp(likes(mary,tom),19,C).

(1?):	ask_y_or_n(good_personality(tom))	Oracle: Yes.
(2?):	ask_y_or_n(kind(tom))	Oracle: Yes.
(3?):	ask_y_or_n(good_in_programming(tom))	Oracle: No.

Debugger: A counter-example C is [good_in_programming(tom)<- true].
The debugger needs 3 queries to localise the counter-example.
(Note: It gives a better result than D&Q algorithm in this case.)

/* A family program */
uncle(X,Y) :- brother(X,Z), parent(Z,Y).
brother(X,Y) :- male(X), parent(Z,X), parent(Z,Y), X \= Y.
male(jim).
parent(john,frank). % This clause is assumed to be the wrong one.
parent(anne,jim).
parent(anne,john).

?fp(uncle(jim,frank),6,C).

(1?):	ask_y_or_n(male(jim))	Oracle: Yes.
(2?):	ask_y_or_n(brother(jim,john))	Oracle: Yes.
(3?):	ask_y_or_n(parent(john,frank))	Oracle: No.

Debugger: A counter-example C is [parent(john,frank) <- true].
The debugger needs 3 queries to localise the counter-example.

?new_fp(uncle(jim,frank),6,C).

(1?):	ask_y_or_n(brother(jim,john))	Oracle: Yes.
(2?):	ask_y_or_n(parent(john,frank))	Oracle: No.

Debugger: A counter-example C is [parent(john,frank) <- true].
The debugger needs 2 queries to localise the counter-example.

/* An incorrect Quicksort program */
qsort([],[]).
qsort([X|L],L0) :- partition(L,X,L1,L2), qsort(L1,L3), qsort(L2,L4),
                append([X|L3],L4,L0).
% The bug! It must be append(L3,[X|L4],L0).

partition([X|L],Y,[X|L1],L2) :- X < Y, partition(L,Y,L1,L2).
partition([X|L],Y,L1,[X|L2]) :- Y =< X, partition(L,Y,L1,L2).
partition([],X,[],[]).
append([X|L1],L2,[X|L3]) :- append(L1,L2,L3).
append([],L,L).

?fp(qsort([3,1,2],[3,1,2]),21,C).
  (1?):   ask_y_or_n(qsort([2], [2]))   Oracle: Yes.
  (2?):   ask_y_or_n(qsort([1, 2], [1, 2]))   Oracle: Yes.
  (3?):   ask_y_or_n(append([3, 1, 2], [], [3, 1, 2]))   Oracle: Yes.
  (4?):   ask_y_or_n(partition([1, 2], 3, [1, 2], []))   Oracle: Yes.
  (5?):   ask_y_or_n(qsort([], []))   Oracle: Yes.
Debugger: A counter-example C is [qsort([3,1,2],[3,1,2]) <- partition([1,2],3,[1,2],[]),
qsort([1,2],[1,2]),qsort([],[]),append([3,1,2],[],[3,1,2])].
The debugger needs 5 queries to localise the counter-example.

?new_fp(qsort([3,1,2],[3,1,2]),21,C).
  (1?):   ask_y_or_n(qsort([1, 2], [1, 2]))   Oracle: Yes.
  (2?):   ask_y_or_n(append([3, 1, 2], [], [3, 1, 2]))   Oracle: Yes.
  (3?):   ask_y_or_n(partition([2], 3, [2], []))   Oracle: Yes.
  (4?):   ask_y_or_n(partition([1, 2], 3, [1, 2], []))   Oracle: Yes.
  (5?):   ask_y_or_n(qsort([], []))   Oracle: Yes.
Debugger: A counter-example C is [qsort([3,1,2],[3,1,2]) <- partition([1,2],3,[1,2],[]),
qsort([1,2],[1,2]),qsort([],[]),append([3,1,2],[],[3,1,2])].
The debugger needs 5 queries to localise the counter-example.

/* An incorrect Insertion sort program */
isort([X|Xs],Ys) :- isort(Xs,Zs), insert(X,Zs,Ys).
isort([],[]).
insert(X,[Y|Ys],[Y|Zs]) :- Y > X, insert(X,Ys,Zs).
% Y>X is the single bug, it must be X>Y.
insert(X,[Y|Ys],[X,Y|Ys]) :- X =< Y.
insert(X,[],[X]).

?fp(isort([2,1,3],[2,3,1]),8,C).
  (1?):   ask_y_or_n(isort([3], [3]))   Oracle: Yes.
  (2?):   ask_y_or_n(isort([1, 3], [3, 1]))   Oracle: No.
  (3?):   ask_y_or_n(insert(1, [3], [3, 1]))   Oracle: No.
  (4?):   ask_y_or_n(insert(1, [], [1]))   Oracle: Yes.
Debugger: A counter-example C is [insert(1,[3],[3,1])<-3>1,insert(1,[],[1])].
The debugger needs 4 queries to localise the counter-example.

?new_fp(isort([2,1,3],[2,3,1]),8,C).
  (1?):   ask_y_or_n(isort([3], [3]))   Oracle: Yes.
  (2?):   ask_y_or_n(insert(1, [3], [3, 1]))   Oracle: No.
  (3?):   ask_y_or_n(insert(1, [], [1]))   Oracle: Yes.
Debugger: A counter-example C is [insert(1,[3],[3,1])<-3>1,insert(1,[],[1])].
The debugger needs 3 queries to localise the counter-example.

/* An incorrect medical program */
should_take(Person,Symptom) :- has_symptom(Person,Symptom),
                              relieves(Medicine,Symptom).
% the bug! should_take(Person,Symptom) must be should_take(Person,Medicine).

has_symptom(Person,Symptom) :- weak(Person),
                              got_infection(Person,Microorganism),
                              causes(Microorganism,Disease),
                              implies(Symptom,Disease).
weak(john).
got_infection(john,virus).
causes(virus,cold).
implies(running_nose,cold).
relieves(paracetamol,running_nose).

?fp(should_take(john, running_nose), 7, C)
(1?):	ask_y_or_n(weak(john))	Oracle: Yes.
(2?)	ask_y_or_n(got_infection(john, virus))	Oracle: Yes.
(3?)	ask_y_or_n(has_symptom(john, running_nose))	Oracle: Yes.
(4?)	ask_y_or_n(relieves(paracetamol, running_nose))	Oracle: Yes.

Debugger: A counter-example C is [should_take(john,running_nose)<-
has_symptom(john,running_nose),relieves(paracetamol, running_nose)].
The debugger needs 4 queries to localise the counter-example.

?new_fp(should_take(john, running_nose), 7, C)
| (1?): | ask_y_or_n(has_symptom(john, running_nose)) | Oracle: Yes. |
| (2?): | ask_y_or_n(relieves(paracetamol, running_nose)) | Oracle: Yes. |

Debugger: A counter-example C is [should_take(john,running_nose)<-
has_symptom(john,running_nose),relieves(paracetamol, running_nose)].
The debugger needs 2 queries to localise the counter-example.
(Note: In this case the improved algorithm performs better than D&Q algorithm.)

The end of the demonstration.

Appendix C: The comparison between D&Q algorithm and the improved algorithm

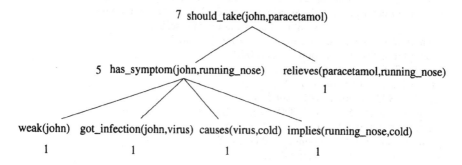

Figure a. The proof tree of the medical program

The table below shows the comparison between the number of queries required by D&Q algorithm and the improved algorithm to identify a counter-example in the medical program given in Appendix B.

An example of counter-example	D&Q algorithm	Improved algorithm
weak(tom)	1	2
got_infection(john,bacteria)	2	3
causes(bacteria,cold)	4	4
implies(stomach_ ache,cold)	5	5
has_symptom(john,cold)	5	5
relieves(penicillin,cold)	4	2
should_take(john,running_nose)	4	2
The number of queries required on average	25/7	23/7

On each row of the table, each clause in the program is assumed to be the incorrect one once. The last row shows that, *on average* the improved algorithm requires less queries to localise a counter-example in the program than D&Q algorithm. Similar comparisons for other programs are given in the following table (in which "Mary likes Tom.", Family and Insertion sort programs have been shown earlier, and Grammar and Arch programs are given at the end of this appendix). The last two columns of the table show number of queries required, on average, by the two algorithms to localise a counter example in each program.

An incorrect program	D&Q algorithm	Improved algorithm
"Mary likes Tom."	94/19	89/19
Family	18/6	17/6
Insertion sort	15/5	15/5
Grammar	99/19	90/19
Arch	55/13	55/13

/* The Grammar program (which assumed to give a wrong answer) */
/* This program returns an incorrect answer 'yes' to a call to 'sentence(1,9)'. */

```
sentence(S0,S) :- noun_phrase(S0,S1), verb(S1,S2), noun_phrase(S2,S).
noun_phrase(S0,S) :- article(S0,S1), adjective(S1,S2), common_noun(S2,S3),
                     preposition(S3,S4), noun_phrase(S4,S).
noun_phrase(S0,S) :- article(S0,S1), common_noun(S1,S).
noun_phrase(S0,S) :- uncount_noun(S0,S).
verb(S0,S) :- connects(S0,stole,S).
article(S0,S) :- connects(S0,a,S).
adjective(S0,S) :- connects(S0,small,S).
uncount_noun(S0,S) :- connects(S0,cheese,S).
common_noun(S0,S) :- connects(S0,piece,S).
common_noun(S0,S) :- connects(S0,mouse,S).
preposition(S0,S) :- connects(S0,of,S).
```

```
connects(1,a,2).
connects(2,mouse,3).
connects(3,stole,4).
connects(4,a,5).
connects(5,small,6).
connects(6,piece,7).
connects(7,of,8).
connects(8,cheese,9).
```

/* The Arch program (which assumed to give a wrong answer) */
/* The program returns an incorrect answer 'yes' to a call to 'arch(a(t(f,t(e,d)),h,g))'.*/

```
arch(a(Y,X,Z)) :- block(X), tower(Y), tower(Z), is_on(X,Y), is_on(X,Z).
tower(X) :- block(X).
tower(t(X,Y)) :- block(X), tower(Y), is_on(X,Y).
is_on(X,t(Y,Z)) :- is_on(X,Y).
```

```
block(d).
block(e).
block(f).
block(g).
block(h).
```

```
is_on(e,d).
is_on(f,e).
is_on(h,f).
is_on(h,g).
```

What's in a Trace: The Box Model Revisited

Gerhard Tobermann[1] and Clemens Beckstein[2]

[1] Bavarian Research Center for Knowledge Based Systems (FORWISS),
Am Weichselgarten 7, 91058 Erlangen, Germany,
Email: toberman@forwiss.uni-erlangen.de
[2] University of Erlangen, IMMD-8 (Computer Science, AI Department),
Am Weichselgarten 9, 91058 Erlangen, Germany,
Email: clemens@immd8.informatik.uni-erlangen.de

Abstract. In this paper we investigate trace protocols of PROLOG programs. We present a precise mathematical specification of the box model for definite programs as it was informally introduced by Byrd. We also give a sketch of how to generalize this specification to normal logic programs.

1 Introduction

The box model as introduced by Byrd (cf. [1, 2]) describes the process of finding an answer to a query wrt a logic program by means of a chronological trace protocol. This protocol contains entries for primitive events associated with the execution of PROLOG procedures. Basic events are `call` (a procedure is being entered), `exit` (a procedure was left signaling a success), `redo` (another solution to the call associated with the procedure is sought for), and `fail` (there is no (other) solution).

Byrd only gives an informal account of how to visualize procedural aspects of the execution of PROLOG programs. He e.g. does not explicitly consider goals with variables and does not show how to keep track of the evolution of bindings during the computation. Therefore it is of no surprise that existing debuggers generate different traces even for simple definite programs like the following (cf. table 1):

```
p(X) :- p1(X), p2(X), p3(X).
p1(a). p1(b).
p2(b).
p3(c).
```

The major reason for this — as we believe — is that he did not introduce the box model along with a formalization. His primary goal apparently was to use the model as a vehicle for teaching and explaining PROLOG.

Our paper is an attempt to fill this gap: we intend to give a precise mathematical specification of PROLOG trace protocols. This reconstruction should explain the differences between the traces (so it can be used as a guide line for a formal description and classification of debugging components of logic programming systems). Additionally our reconstruction should serve as a basis for the

CALL	p(X_g5)	CALL	p(X_g7)	Call: p(_4)	Call	p(X)
UNIFY	p(X_g5)	UNIFY	p(X_g7)	Head [1]: p(_4)	Unify	p(X)
CALL	p1(X_g5)	CALL	p1(X_g7)	Call: p1(_4)	Call	p1(X)
*EXIT	p1(a)	*EXIT	p1(a)	Head [1->2]: p1(_4)	Exit	p1(a)
CALL	p2(a)	CALL	p2(a)	Exit: p1(a)	Call	p2(a)
FAIL	p2(a)	FAIL	p2(a)	Call: p2(a)	Fail	p2(a)
REDO	p1(X_g5)	REDO	p1(X_g7)	Fail: p2(a)	Next	p1(X)
*NEXT	p1(X_g5)	EXIT	p1(b)	Redo: p1(a)	Exit	p1(b)
EXIT	p1(b)	CALL	p2(b)	Head [2]: p1(_4)	Call	p2(b)
CALL	p2(b)	EXIT	p2(b)	Done: p1(b)	Exit	p2(b)
EXIT	p2(b)	CALL	p3(b)	Call: p2(b)	Call	p3(b)
CALL	p3(b)	FAIL	p3(b)	Head [1]: p2(b)	Fail	p3(b)
FAIL	p3(b)	FAIL	p(X_g7)	Done: p2(b)	Nomore	p2()
*REDO	p2/1			Call: p3(b)	Nomore	p1()
*FAIL	p2/1			Fail: p3(b)	Fail	p(X)
*REDO	p1/1			Fail: p(_4)		
*FAIL	p1/1					
FAIL	p(X_g5)					

Table 1. Exhaustive traces for the query $p(X)$ differ in various ways

specification of traces. We believe this is a must have to write portable trace analyzers and to verify trace analyzing algorithms.

2 Trace Graphs and Their Correctness

The central idea of our formalization of the box model is to represent a pair of logic program and query by a unique directed graph that is labeled with logical formulas (corresponding to goals) and to associate paths in this graph with traces of the evaluation of the query wrt the program.

The graph will contain five types of nodes — each corresponding to one of the primitive events happening during the evaluation of a goal: the first attempt to proof a goal, the success or failure of this proof, another attempt to proof the goal and — as an extension to Byrd's model — unifications of the goal with heads of program clauses for the goals predicate.

Definition 1. B-graphs, boxes, and the box graph:

- Let $G = (\mathcal{N}, \mathcal{V})$ be a directed graph. Then G is a *B-graph* iff $\mathcal{N}$ is the disjoint union of the sets $\mathcal{U}, \mathcal{C}, \mathcal{E}, \mathcal{R}, \mathcal{F}$ and we call the sets $\mathcal{U}, \mathcal{C}, \mathcal{E}, \mathcal{R}, \mathcal{F}$ the *types of the nodes in the B-graph G*.
- If $G = (\mathcal{N}, \mathcal{V})$ is a B-graph, then a set of nodes in $B \subseteq \mathcal{N}$ is called a *B-box* in G if the following two properties hold

$$|B \cap \mathcal{C}| = |B \cap \mathcal{E}| = |B \cap \mathcal{R}| = |B \cap \mathcal{F}| = 1 \quad \wedge \quad B \cap \mathcal{U} = \emptyset.$$

We note B-boxes as tuples $B = [c, e, r, f] \in \mathcal{C} \times \mathcal{E} \times \mathcal{R} \times \mathcal{F}$, whenever we want to make explicit the type of the box nodes.

– Let $G = (\mathcal{N}, \mathcal{V})$ be a B-graph and $b : \mathcal{N} \to \mathbb{N}$ and $d : ran(b) \to \mathbb{N}$ be two total functions. Then $G' = (\mathcal{N}, \mathcal{V}, b, d)$ is a *box graph* iff

1. $|\mathcal{C}| = |\mathcal{E}| = |\mathcal{R}| = |\mathcal{F}|$.
2. The function b partitions $\mathcal{N}$ s.t.

$$\exists\, i \in ran(b) : B \subseteq b^{-1}(i) \;\wedge\; b^{-1}(i) - B \subseteq \mathcal{U}.$$

is true for all B-boxes B in G.

In this case we call the B-boxes uniquely determined by b *boxes* of the box graph.

3. The function d determines the *depth* of the nodes in $\mathcal{N}$ s.t.

$$\forall_{n,m \in \mathcal{N}} : b(n) = b(m) \to d(n) = d(m)$$

and only one box (the *root box*) has depth 1.

Hence a box $B \subseteq b^{-1}(i)$ consists of exactly 4 nodes: one of each type $\mathcal{C}, \mathcal{E}, \mathcal{R}$, and $\mathcal{F}$ — its $\mathcal{C}$-, $\mathcal{E}$-, $\mathcal{R}$-, and $\mathcal{F}$-node. Additionally $b^{-1}(i)$ may contain several nodes of type $\mathcal{U}$ which we call the $\mathcal{U}$-nodes of B. Two functions b and d assign the same box number $b(B)$ and depth $d(B)$ to all the nodes of the box.

In a box graph there is no restriction on what edges connect which nodes. Since we are primarily interested in box graphs where paths correspond to PRO-LOG computations we now give definitions of what will serve as building blocks for the correct graph topology (see figures 1 and 2):

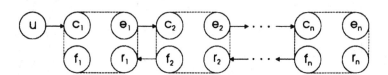

Fig. 1. Row of a boxes

Definition 2. Let $G = (\mathcal{N}, \mathcal{V}, b, d)$ be a box graph, $u \in G$ a node of type $\mathcal{U}$ and $(B_i)_{i \leq n}$ a finite non-empty sequence of pairwise disjoint boxes $B_i = [c_i, e_i, r_i, f_i]$ in G. Then a subgraph $G' = (\mathcal{N}', \mathcal{V}', b', d')$ of G is called the *row* with the nodes u and $B_1, \ldots, B_n$ if the following holds:

1. $\mathcal{N}' := \bigcup_{1 \leq i \leq n} B_i \cup \{u\}$.
2. G' is the subgraph of G induced by the nodes in the set $\mathcal{N}'$.
3. $\mathcal{V}' := \{(u, c_1)\} \cup \{(e_i, c_{i+1}) \mid 1 \leq i < n\} \cup \{(f_{i+1}, r_i) \mid 1 \leq i < n\} \subseteq \mathcal{V}$.
4. $d(B_i) = d(u) + 1$ for all $1 \leq i \leq n$.
5. $b' := b \,|_{\mathcal{N}'}$ and $d' := d \,|_{ran(b')}$
   (the functions b' and d' are restrictions of b and d).

We denote such a row as $R(u, B_1, \ldots, B_n)$ and call the nodes in $\{u, e_n, r_n, f_1\}$ its *pins*.

The following definition of the contents of a box further constrains the number of edges allowed between nodes in the box graph[3] (see figure 2).

(a) true box   (b) fail box

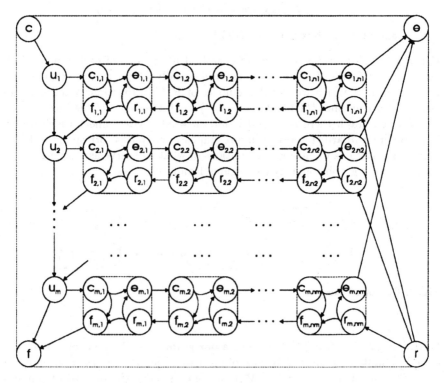

(c) complex box

Fig. 2. Contents of a box; bended arrows indicate possible paths thru a box

Definition 3. Let $G = (\mathcal{N}, \mathcal{V}, b, d)$ be a box graph and $B = [c, e, r, f]$ a box in G. Then the *contents* of B is defined as follows:

---

[3] The name "contents" may suggest that we will use hierarchical graphs (graphs where nodes may contain graphs again) for our formalization. This is not the case.

1. The contents of B is the empty sequence $\emptyset$, if
   - $\{(c, e), (r, f)\} \subseteq \mathcal{V}$ or
   - $(c, f) \in \mathcal{V}$

   is true; in the former case we call B a *true box* in the latter a *fail box*.

2. The contents of B is a non-empty sequence $\left(R(u_i, B_{i,1}, \ldots, B_{i,n_i})\right)_{i \leq m}$, if
   (a) the $R(u_i, B_{i,1}, \ldots, B_{i,n_i})$ with $1 \leq i \leq m$ are rows in G,
   (b) $d(u_i) = d(B) \wedge b(u_i) = b(B)$ for $1 \leq i \leq m$,
   (c) $(\{u, e_{i,n_i}, r_{i,n_i}, f_{i,1}\})_{i \leq m}$ is the sequence of pins belonging to these rows and
   (d) the set

   $$
   \begin{aligned}
   & \{(c, u_1)\} \\
   & \cup \{(u_i, u_{i+1}) \mid 1 \leq i < m\} \cup \{(f_{i,1}, u_{i+1}) \mid 1 \leq i < m\} \\
   & \cup \{(u_m, f)\} \qquad\qquad\qquad \cup \{(f_{m,1}, f)\} \\
   & \cup \{(r, r_{i,n_i}) \mid 1 \leq i \leq m\} \ \cup \{(e_{i,n_i}, e) \mid 1 \leq i \leq m\}
   \end{aligned}
   $$

   is a subset of $\mathcal{V}$.

3. Otherwise the contents of B is the distinguished object $\perp$ (undefined).

True boxes and fail boxes are the *primitive* boxes; boxes that have $\perp$ as their contents are called *invalid*, all other boxes are *complex* boxes.

Using the notions of row and contents we are now ready to define what we mean by the T-graph for a pair consisting of a logic program and a query; in the sequel we represent unit clauses of the program by clauses with the single premise *true* and denote the most general unifier θ for two formulas Q and A by $mgu(Q, A)$.

Definition 4. Let P be a logic program and $Q \equiv (\leftarrow A)$ an atomic goal. Then the *T-graph* for Q and P is a labeled box graph $T(Q, P)$ inductively defined like this:

1. Every node in $T(Q, P)$ is labeled with a literal.
2. The nodes of the *root box* of $T(Q, P)$ are labeled with A.
3. If we look at a box $B = [c, e, r, f]$ in $T(Q, P)$, whose nodes are all labeled with a literal A' then exactly one of the following must be true:
   (a) B is a true box, if $A' \equiv$ *true*.
   (b) B is a fail box, if P does not contain a clause the head of which is unifiable with A'.
   (c) The contents of B is a non-empty sequence I containing a row

   $$R(u, B_1', \ldots, B_n')$$

   iff there is a variant $A \leftarrow B_1, \ldots, B_n$ of a clause $C \in P$ s.t.
   i. A and A' are unifiable,
   ii. u is labeled with A,
   iii. the $B_1', \ldots, B_n'$ are root boxes of the T-graphs for $B_1, \ldots, B_n$ and P, and
   iv. the order of the rows in I is the same as the textual order of the corresponding clauses in P.

The mapping m from nodes to literals is called the *labeling* of the T-graph.

As in Lloyd's definition of SLD resolution (cf. [5]) the variants in condition 3c have to be chosen s.t. they do not have in common any variable with rows residing in the already created part of the T-graph.

Please note that in this definition not all clauses of a predicate p are included in the box for a query Q wrt p. Our definition excludes all clauses that a priori can not be unified with Q. We have also decided not to include the clauses instantiated with the *mgu* of their resp. heads and Q but variants of the clauses themselves. In our opinion this is closer to Byrd's idea.

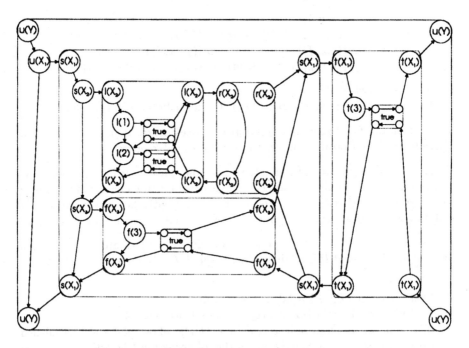

Fig. 3. T-graph for program P and query $u(Y)$

T-graphs only contain primitive and complex boxes but no invalid ones; the contents of a box in the graph is a (in case of primitive boxes empty) sequence of rows (representing clauses unifiable with the label of the enclosing box). As figure 3 shows T-graphs can become quite complex — even for very simple programs like the following program P.

```
u(X) :- s(X),t(X).
s(X) :- l(X),r(X).  s(X) :- f(X).
t(3).
l(1).  l(2).
f(3).
```

Also note that there are simple programs with a finite SLD tree but an infinite T-graph for the same ground query, e.g. the program

```
nat(0).
nat(s(X)) :- nat(X).
```

and the query $nat(s(s(s(0))))$. Although this graph is infinite, we will see later that the only trace path thru the (infinite) trace graph corresponding to this infinite T-graph is of finite length.

Definition 5. Let T be a T-graph. Then a finite path $F = (n_i)_{i \leq k}$ in T with the properties

1. n_1 is the C-node of the root box of T,
2. if there is an edge $(r_2, r_1) \in \mathcal{R}^2$ in F, then F also contains an edge $(e_1, e_2) \in \mathcal{E}^2$ with

$$b(r_1) = b(e_1) \quad \wedge \quad b(r_2) = b(e_2) \quad \wedge \quad e_2 \text{ precedes } r_2 \text{ in } F,$$

is called a C-path in T.

Hence C-paths start at the C-node of the root box and contain the $\mathcal{R}$-node of the last box of a row iff the corresponding $\mathcal{E}$-node was traversed previously in the path. We therefore can state the following proposition:

Proposition 6. Let $T = (\mathcal{N}, \mathcal{V}, b, d)$ be a T-graph and $F = (n_i)_{i \leq k}$ a finite C-path.
Then the following property holds:

$$\forall_{i \leq k} : n_i \notin C \rightarrow \exists_{j < i} : n_j \in C \wedge b(n_j) = b(n_i),$$

Informal proof: C-paths traverse boxes. A box $B = [c, e, r, f]$ can only be entered via the nodes c or r and only be left via e or f since starting from c or r (f or e) there are only edges leading inside (outside) the box (cf. definitions 2 and 3). Hence, maximal paths starting at node c or r and only containing "inner" nodes of B must end in the nodes e or f (in figure 2 these maximal paths are shown as bended arrows). Obviously, c precedes both occurrences of e and f. It remains to show that it also precedes occurrences of r. So let us assume r occurs in the C-path in question. Then because of the definition of C-path the box must have been left before via its $\mathcal{E}$-node. So occurrences of c must precede those of e. If there is no other occurrence of r before e then the proposition follows trivially. Otherwise we know that c must be in the prefix of the C-path before the cycle through e and the proposition follows from the fact that the C-path is finite. $\square$

In other words: if we look at a C-path, then the C-node of a box $B \subseteq b^{-1}(i)$ always precedes all other nodes in $b^{-1}(i)$. We can use this observation to invent a path based version of the function b:

Definition 7. Let $T = (\mathcal{N}, \mathcal{V}, b, d)$ be a T-graph and $F = (n_i)_{i \leq k}$ a C-path in T. Then the *instance number* of a node n in F at position i is uniquely defined by the following recursive function $b' : \{i \mid 1 \leq i \leq k\} \to \mathbb{N}$:

$$b'(i) := \begin{cases} |F_{\leq i}[\mathcal{C}]| & n_i \in \mathcal{C} \\ b'(\max\{j \mid j < i \wedge n_j \in \mathcal{C} \wedge b(n_j) = b(n_i)\}) & \textit{otherwise} \end{cases}$$

The function b' is defined via a course of values recursion (see table 2 at the end of this section for an example):

1. The instance number of the C-node at position i equals the number of C-nodes in the prefix $F_{\leq i}$ of F with length i. The C-node of the root box therefore has instance number 1.
2. Every other node of a box at position i is assigned the instance number of the position j in F, where the C-node of the box occurs last in the prefix of length i. That there actually is such a position is guaranteed by proposition 6.

Hence, given a C-path, the function b' assigns instance numbers to boxes in this path[4]. These numbers are completely determined by the box and the position of the box in the path. Note that the same box may get more than one instance number if it occurs more than once in the C-path. We therefore also speak about "the instance of a box in a C-path" and about "the nodes at position $b'^{-1}(I)$ as belonging to the instance of the box with number I".

It is also evident that the expression $n_j \in \mathcal{C} \wedge b'(n_j) = b'(n_i)$ for a node at position i of a C-path uniquely determines the position $j \leq i$ of the C-node with the same instance number; we will call this node the C-node belonging to n_i and will denote it by $c(n_i)$.

We need one more piece to become able to associate SLD computations with distinguished C-paths: a function that assigns substitutions to positions in C-paths:

Definition 8. Let $T = (\mathcal{N}, \mathcal{V}, b, d)$ be a T-graph with the labeling function m and $F = (n_i)_{i \leq k}$ a C-path in T. Then the function Θ assigns to a node n at position i in path F a *current substitution* as follows:

$$\Theta(n_1) := \emptyset$$

$$\Theta(n_i) := \begin{cases} \Theta(c(n_i)) \circ \theta & n_i \in \mathcal{U} \quad \wedge \quad \theta = mgu(m(c(n_i)) \Theta(c(n_i)), m(n_i)) \\ \Theta(c(n_i)) & n_i \in \mathcal{F} \\ \Theta(n_{i-1}) & \textit{otherwise} \end{cases}$$

(with $c(n_i)$ denoting the C-node belonging to n_i and $\phi \circ \psi$ meaning the application of ψ after ϕ).

The function Θ is also defined via a course of values recursion (see table 2 for an example):

1. The C-node of the root box is assigned the empty substitution.

---

[4] This is what Byrd called the invocation number of a box.

2. A node of type $\mathcal{F}$ is assigned the current substitution of the $\mathcal{C}$-node belonging to it.
3. The current substitution of a $\mathcal{U}$-node u with label A (the head of a program clause) is assigned as follows:
   Let c be the $\mathcal{C}$-node belonging to u, Q the label of c, and σ the current substitution of c. Then if $Q\sigma$ and A are unifiable via θ the current substitution of u is $\sigma \circ \theta$.
   (Please note that the current substitution of a $\mathcal{U}$-node does not depend on the position of the corresponding row in the contents of a box.)
4. In all other cases the node inherits the current substitution of the node immediately preceding it in the path.

With the help of the function Θ we can now characterize the set of paths in the T-graph that correspond to deductions of a SLD proover that utilizes the selection function of PROLOG with depth-first search:

Definition 9. Let $T = (\mathcal{N}, \mathcal{V}, b, d)$ be a T-graph and $F = (n_i)_{i \leq k}$ a $\mathcal{C}$-path in T. Then F is a *T-path* iff it has the following properties:

1. If there is an edge $(r_2, r_1) \in \mathcal{R}^2$ in F, then F also contains an edge $(e_1, e_2) \in \mathcal{E}^2$ with

$$b'(r_1) = b'(e_1) \quad \wedge \quad b'(r_2) = b'(e_2) \quad \wedge \quad e_2 \text{ precedes } r_2 \text{ in } F.$$

2. For every edge $(n_i, n_{i+1}) \in \mathcal{U} \times \mathcal{C}$ in F, if $c(n_i)$ is the $\mathcal{C}$-node belonging to n_i, then $m(c(n_i)) \Theta(c(n_i))$ and $m(n_i)$ are unifiable.

Condition 1 guarantees that upon reentry of a box via its $\mathcal{R}$-node the path is continued in the row that was traversed last (to ensure correct backtracking behavior). Condition 2 makes sure that a row is traversable if the clause corresponding to the row is head-unifiable with the current goal. The definition of T-path does not determine when an edge from a $\mathcal{U}$- to a $\mathcal{C}$-node is part of a T-path: even if the $\mathcal{U}$- and the $\mathcal{C}$-node belonging to it are unifiable, a $\mathcal{U}$-node may be followed by the $\mathcal{U}$-node of the next row or the $\mathcal{F}$-node of the enclosing box in the T-path.

Definition 10. Let $T = T(Q, P)$ be a T-graph with root box $[c, e, r, f]$. Then a T-path $F = (n_i)_{i \leq k}$ in T is called *successful* iff $n_k = e$.

Having attached the label success to distinguished T-paths we will now show correctness (soundness and completeness) wrt to successful T-paths. We will show that every T-path yields a correct answer substitution for the query and program represented by the T-graph. Technically we will do this by showing soundness for distinguished subpaths of successful T-paths:

Definition 11. Let $F = (n_i)_{i \leq k}$ be a successful T-path in the T-graph $T(Q, P)$ and I be an instance number of the box $B = [c, e, r, f]$ in F. Then the *box instance path* for I is the subpath $F[s \leq i \leq t]$ of F with $n_s = c$ and $n_t = e$ for which the following holds:

$$b'(n_s) = b'(n_c) = I \quad \wedge \quad \forall_{1 \leq i \leq k} : i < s \vee t < i \to b'(n_i) \neq I.$$

Successful T-paths therefore are box instance paths for the (unique) instance of the root box of the T-graph.

Theorem 12 Soundness of box instance paths. *Let $F = (n_i)_{i<k}$ be a successful T-path in the T-graph for the program P and the query Q. Then for every box instance path $F[s \leq i \leq t]$ in F the following holds:*

$$P \models \forall(m(n_s) \, \Theta(n_t))$$

Proof: Let $F = (n_i)_{i<k}$ be a successful path in the T-graph $T(Q, P)$. Then for each instance of a box $B = [c, e, r, f]$ with number I in path F there is exactly one box instance path $F' = F[s \leq i \leq t]$ in F. We will show the theorem by induction on the depth $\delta = \max\{d(n_i) \mid n_i \, \epsilon \, F\} - d(B)$ of these subpaths:

- Every box instance path F' with $\delta = 0$ is a path corresponding to a true box with $\Theta(n_t) = \Theta(n_s)$ and we have $P \models true$.
- Induction hypothesis: the theorem holds for box instance paths of depth $\delta < p$.

  Let F' be a box instance path of depth p for box B. If B is a true box, then the theorem must hold for $\delta = p$ as well. Otherwise $B = [c, e, r, f]$ is a complex box with contents $\big(R(u_i, B_{i,1}, \ldots, B_{i,n_i})\big)_{i \leq m}$ and there is a $1 \leq l \leq m$, which uniquely breaks F' into two subpaths. F' starts as

$$\underbrace{(c, u_1, \ldots, f_{1,1},}_{R_1} \underbrace{u_2, \ldots, f_{2,1},}_{R_2} \ldots, \underbrace{u_{l-1}, \ldots, f_{l-1,1},}_{R_{l-1}} u_l)$$

(the subpaths R_j traverse the first $l - 1$ rows — including maybe nodes outside of B) and ends like this:

$$\underbrace{(c_1, \ldots, e_1,}_{F_1'} \underbrace{c_2, \ldots, e_2,}_{F_2'} \ldots, \underbrace{c_{n_l}, \ldots, e_{n_l},}_{F_{n_l}'} e)$$

(the F_i' denote subpaths of depth $\delta < p$ for the boxes $B_{l,i}$). The node u_l therefore is the last $\mathcal{U}$-node of box B that occurs in F' (and therefore in F). From definition 8 then follows

$$\Theta(u_l) = \Theta(c) \circ \theta \qquad \text{with } \theta = mgu(m(c) \, \Theta(c), m(u_l))$$

(the subpaths R_j can be ignored) as well as

$$\forall_{1 \leq i \leq n_l} : \quad \Theta(e_i) = \Theta(c_i)\theta_i$$
$$\forall_{1 \leq i < n_l} : \Theta(c_{i+1}) = \Theta(e_i)$$

and therefore

$$\forall_{1 \leq i \leq n_l} : \Theta(e_i) = \Theta(c) \circ \theta \circ \theta_1 \circ \cdots \circ \theta_i.$$

Because of the induction hypothesis we have

$$\forall_{1 \leq i \leq n_l} : P \models \forall(M_i \, \Theta(c_i) \circ \theta_i),$$

with M_i denoting the label of box $B_{l,i}$ and from this we can conclude

$$\forall_{1 \leq i \leq n_l} : P \models \forall(M_i\, \Theta(e))$$
$$P \models \forall((M_1, \ldots, M_{n_l})\, \Theta(e))$$
$$P \models \forall(m(u_l)\, \Theta(e))$$

and therefore $P \models \forall(m(c)\, \Theta(e))$.

$\square$

In order to prove completeness (that there is a successful T-path for any correct answer substitution) we will use that SLD resolution is complete (cf. [5]):

Definition 13. Let P be a logic program, Q a goal and R a selection function. An SLD deduction from $P \cup \{Q\}$ wrt R then consists of three (maybe infinite) sequences, consisting respectively of

- goals $G_0, \ldots, G_n, \ldots$ with $G_0 = Q$,
- variants $C_1, \ldots, C_n, \ldots$ of program clauses of P and
- most general unifiers $\sigma_1, \ldots, \sigma_n, \ldots$,

where G_{i+1} is the resolvent of G_i and C_{i+1} wrt R and $\sigma_{i+1} = mgu(G_i, C_{i+1})$.

Every goal G_i in a SLD deduction that consists of exactly the literals $L_1, \ldots, L_k$ can therefore be written in the form $G_i = (L'_1, \ldots, L'_k)\sigma_1 \cdots \sigma_i$ (with $L_i = L'_i \sigma_1 \cdots \sigma_i$).

PROLOG's left-most-first selection function is hard-coded in T-graphs. Hence, in the sequel R always will stand for PROLOG's selection function.

Theorem 14 Completeness. *Let P be a logic program and Q a query. Then for every successful SLD deduction from $P \cup \{Q\}$ wrt R there is a T-path $F = (n_i)_{i \leq k}$ in the T-graph $T(Q, P)$ with:*

$$P \cup \{Q\theta\} \vdash_{SLD} \square \;\;\rightarrow\;\; \Theta(n_k) = \theta$$

Before we can prove this theorem we have to define a function ts that assigns *time stamps* to the literals in a SLD deduction $G_0, \ldots, G_n, \ldots$:

- G_0 gets the time stamp 0: $ts(G_0) = 0$.
- If G_{i+1} is the resolvent of G_i and the program clause

$$C_{i+1} \equiv A \leftarrow B_1, \ldots, B_n,$$

then all the new literals $B_1, \ldots, B_n$ of G_{i+1} are time stamped with $i + 1$:

$$ts(B_1) = \cdots = ts(B_n) = i + 1.$$

The time stamp of a literal can therefore be used to identify the program clause that has introduced the literal into the SLD deduction; we call the clause that introduced the literal its parent clause.

The function ts also allows us to formulate the following property: A subgoal $Q = R(G_i)$ of the goal G_i of a SLD deduction *induces* a subgoal Q' of another goal G_j with $i < j$, if $ts(Q') > ts(Q)$ and for every goal G_k $(i < k < j)$ of this SLD deduction we have

$$ts(R(G_k)) > ts(Q).$$

Proof of theorem 14: We will show that for every successful SLD deduction from $P \cup \{Q\}$ wrt R a successful T-path F in the T-graph $T = T(Q, P)$ can be constructed: a step in the SLD deduction will be represented by a corresponding subpath in F.

Let n_c be the last node of the path of F constructed so far. Then the following invariant holds for our incremental construction algorithm:

n_c is the $\mathcal{E}$-node of the root box of T or n_c is the $\mathcal{C}$-node of a box $B = [c, e, r, f]$ in T and $R(G_{i-1})$ is a variant of $m(n_c)\Theta(n_c)$.

Obviously the invariant holds for the first node of F, the $\mathcal{C}$-node of the root box of T, and we will show that the invariant holds again after another construction step is completed.

So let n_c be the last node of F constructed so far and let us assume that the invariant holds. Since $R(G_{i-1})$ and C_i are unifiable via σ_i, so are $m(n_c)\Theta(n_c)$ and C_i. Hence in the contents

$$\left(R(u_l, B_{l,1}, \ldots, B_{l,n_l})\right)_{1 \leq l \leq m}$$

of box B there must be a $1 \leq k \leq m$ s.t. $R(u_k, B_{k,1}, \ldots, B_{k,n_k})$ is the row corresponding to (a variant) of clause C_i (compare def. 4). We now extend F with the following path fragment

$$(u_1, \ldots, u_k, c_{k,1})$$

(here $c_{k,1}$ is the $\mathcal{C}$-node of box $B_{k,1}$); with $\theta_i := mgu(m(n_c)\Theta(n_c), m(u_k))$ we therefore have

$$\Theta(c_{k,1}) = \Theta(u_k) = \Theta(n_c)\theta_i$$

and can proceed doing a case analysis with the form of the clause C_i:

- If C_i is of the form $A \leftarrow true$, then $B_{k,1}$ is a true box and we extend F by $(e_{k,1}, e)$, where $e_{k,1}$ is the $\mathcal{E}$-node of $B_{k,1}$. For the current substitution now holds:

$$\Theta(e) = \Theta(e_{k,1}) = \Theta(c_{k,1}) = \Theta(n_c)\theta_i.$$

So let us look at the sequence of clauses used so far in the SLD deduction. With the abbreviation $\text{last}(A \leftarrow B_1, \ldots, B_n) \equiv B_n$ this sequence can be identified as follows:

$$v_0 := i$$

$$v_{j+1} := \begin{cases} \text{ts}(L_{v_j}) & \text{if } R(G_{v_j-1}) = L_{v_j}\sigma_1 \cdots \sigma_{v_j-1} \\ & \text{and } \text{ts}(L_{v_j}) \neq 0 \text{ and } L_{v_j} = \text{last}(C_{\text{ts}(L_{v_j})}) \\ 0 & \text{otherwise} \end{cases}$$

Thus $p := \min\{j \geq 0 \mid v_{j+1} = 0\}$ defines a (maybe empty) sequence $C_{v_1}, \ldots, C_{v_p}$ of clauses and a sequence $L_{v_0}, \ldots, L_{v_p}$ of literals, where C_{v_j} is the parent clause of $L_{v_{j-1}}$.

Hence for every parent clause C_{v_j} there must be a corresponding row in T that has the following two properties:

1. The box corresponding to (a variant of) $L_{v_{j-1}}$ is the last box of the row.
2. The row is element of the contents of the box labeled with (a variant of) L_{v_j}.

Since e is the $\mathcal{E}$-node of the box for (a variant of) L_{v_0} — L_{v_0} was defined via $R(G_{v_0-1}) = R(G_{i-1})$ — we can extend F with the path consisting of the $\mathcal{E}$-nodes of the boxes for (the variants of) $L_{v_1}, \ldots, L_{v_p}$. If e_p denotes the $\mathcal{E}$- and c_p the $\mathcal{C}$-node of the box for (the variant of) L_{v_p} we therefore have

$$\Theta(e_p) = \Theta(e) = \Theta(c_p)\theta_{v_p} \cdots \theta_i.$$

Because $v_{p+1} = 0$ either $\text{ts}(L_{v_p}) = 0$ or $L_{v_p} \neq \text{last}(C_{\text{ts}(L_{v_j})})$ must hold now. But R always selects the left-most subgoal first and all literals introduced into the SLD deduction by the clauses $C_{v_1}, \ldots, C_{v_p}$ have been processed already. Hence in both cases G_i can't contain a literal induced by L_{v_p}.

- If $\text{ts}(L_{v_p}) = 0$ then $L_{v_p} = Q$ and $v_p = 1$. Therefore $G_i = \square$, c_p is the $\mathcal{C}$-node and e_p is the $\mathcal{E}$-node of the root box of the T-graph and we have

$$\Theta(e_p) = \Theta(c_p)\theta_{v_p} \cdots \theta_i = \theta_1 \cdots \theta_i.$$

Obviously $Q\sigma_1 \cdots \sigma_i$ and $Q\theta_1 \cdots \theta_i$ now are variants of each other.

- If L_{v_p} is not the last literal in its parent clause $C' \equiv A \leftarrow B_1, \ldots, B_n$, i.e. if there is a $1 \leq s < n$ with $L_{v_p} = B_s$, then G_i has to be of the form

$$(B_{s+1}, \ldots, B_n, rest)\sigma_1 \cdots \sigma_i.$$

But there must be a row in T representing C' and the box B' for (a variant of) B_s is a box in this row which is not the last one; hence T contains an edge connecting the $\mathcal{E}$-node of box B' with the $\mathcal{C}$-nodes c_{s+1} of the box for (a variant of) B_{s+1}. We use this edge to extend our T-path and get

$$\Theta(c_{s+1}) = \Theta(e_p) = \Theta(c_p)\theta_{v_p} \cdots \theta_i = \theta_1 \cdots \theta_i.$$

Apparently $R(G_i) = B_{s+1}\sigma_1 \cdots \sigma_i$ again is a variant of $m(c_{s+1})\Theta(c_{s+1})$.

– Otherwise C_i is of form $A \leftarrow B_1, \ldots, B_n$ (different from $A \leftarrow true$). Since $G_{i-1} = R(G_{i-1})$, rest_{i-1} holds, we immediately get

$$G_i = (B_1, \ldots, B_n, \text{rest}_{i-1})\sigma_i.$$

But now, because $m(c_{k,1})$ and B_1 are variants of each other, $R(G_i)$ and $B_1 \Theta(c_{k,1})$ have to be variants of each other as well.

Hence our invariant holds before and after every construction step and the proof is complete. □

We have shown correctness independent of the order of clauses in the program. Since the order of clauses is a crucial factor in the debugging of PROLOG programs we will now further constrain the paths through the T-graph. For this purpose we extend the T-graph to a trace graph.

Definition 15. trace graph and trace path:

– Let P be a logic program, Q an atomic goal, and $T(Q, P)$ be the T-graph for Q and P with root box $[c, e, r, f]$. Then the *trace graph* $T(Q, P)$ for Q and P is the T-graph for Q and P with one additional edge from e to r.
– Let $T = T(Q, P)$ be a trace graph. Then a path F in T is called a *trace path* iff it has the following properties:
  1. n_1 is the C-node of the root box of T.
  2. If there is an edge $(r_2, r_1) \in \mathcal{R}^2$ in F, then F also contains an edge $(e_1, e_2) \in \mathcal{E}^2$ with

$$b'(r_1) = b'(e_1) \quad \wedge \quad b'(r_2) = b'(e_2) \quad \wedge \quad e_2 \text{ precedes } r_2 \text{ in } F.$$

  3. If Q' is the label of the C-node belonging to a node n in the path and $m(n) = A$, then the following must be true:
     (a) If $(n, n') \in \mathcal{U} \times \mathcal{C}$ in F then $Q' \Theta(c(n))$ and A are unifiable.
     (b) If $(n, n') \in \mathcal{U} \times (\mathcal{U} \cup \mathcal{F})$ in F then $Q' \Theta(c(n))$ and A are not unifiable.

Apparently, given a query, a program, and a trace path, then — if it can be extended at all — there is exactly one way to append a node to the path. Trace paths reflect the order of clauses in the program.

Definition 16. Let T be a trace graph with root box $[c, e, r, f]$. Then a trace path $F = (n_i)_{i \le k}$ in T is called *successful* iff $n_k = e$, and *maximal* iff $n_k = f$.

Obviously there can be no "failing" trace paths and successful trace paths have to be sound as a closer inspection of the proof for theorem 12 shows. It is a bit more technically difficult to show the analogon of theorem 14 for successful trace paths. Since trace paths resemble left right depth first traversals of the ordered SLD tree it is clear that trace graphs suffer from the same incompleteness as SLD resolution with PROLOG's computation rule.

All that is left to do is to show how a trace protocol can be obtained from a trace path $F = (n_i)_{i \le k}$; between a node in F and an entry in the trace protocol there is the following one-to-one correspondence:

- position i and the chronological number of the event,
- $b'(i)$ and the invocation number of the goal,
- $d(n_i)$ and the execution depth of the goal,
- the type of the node and the traced port, as well as
- $m(n_i)\,\Theta(n_i)$ and the executed predicate with its arguments

(trace protocol terminology stolen from [3]). For an example see the maximal path in figure 4 and table 2:

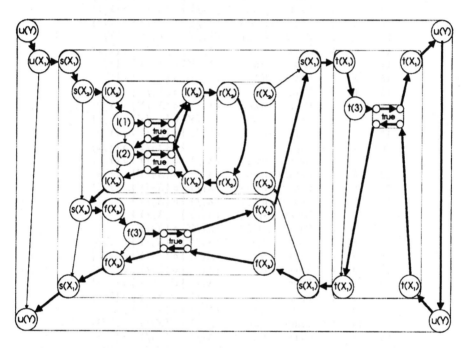

Fig. 4. Maximal trace path in the trace graph $T(u(Y), P)$

3 Conclusion and Future Work

We have presented a precise mathematical specification of trace protocols as they result from the execution of definite logic programs with the PROLOG selection function. The formalization has been shown to be sound and complete wrt the minimal model semantics of logic programs.

We have also extended the formalism to normal logic programs. Figure 5 shows what a trace (sub-)graph for a negative query might look like. Note that in the trace graph the $\mathcal{F}$-node of the !-box does not connect to the $\mathcal{R}$-node of the preceding box in the row but to the $\mathcal{F}$-node of the enclosing box. For the formal

i	$b'(i)$	$d(n_i)$	port	$m(n_i)$	$\Theta(n_i)$
1	1	1	CALL	$u(Y)$	$\emptyset$
2	1	1	UNIFY	$u(X_1)$	$\{X_1/Y\}$
3	2	2	CALL	$s(X_1)$	$\{X_1/Y\}$
4	2	2	UNIFY	$s(X_2)$	$\{X_1/Y\} \circ \{X_2/Y\}$
5	3	3	CALL	$l(X_2)$	$\{X_1/Y\} \circ \{X_2/Y\}$
6	3	3	UNIFY	$l(1)$	$\{X_1/Y\} \circ \{X_2/Y\} \circ \{Y/1\}$
7	4	4	CALL	$true$	$\{X_1/Y\} \circ \{X_2/Y\} \circ \{Y/1\}$
8	4	4	EXIT	$true$	$\{X_1/Y\} \circ \{X_2/Y\} \circ \{Y/1\}$
9	3	3	EXIT	$l(X_2)$	$\{X_1/Y\} \circ \{X_2/Y\} \circ \{Y/1\}$
10	5	3	CALL	$r(X_2)$	$\{X_1/Y\} \circ \{X_2/Y\} \circ \{Y/1\}$
11	5	3	FAIL	$r(X_2)$	$\{X_1/Y\} \circ \{X_2/Y\} \circ \{Y/1\}$
12	3	3	REDO	$l(X_2)$	$\{X_1/Y\} \circ \{X_2/Y\} \circ \{Y/1\}$
13	4	4	REDO	$true$	$\{X_1/Y\} \circ \{X_2/Y\} \circ \{Y/1\}$
14	4	4	FAIL	$true$	$\{X_1/Y\} \circ \{X_2/Y\} \circ \{Y/1\}$
15	3	3	UNIFY	$l(2)$	$\{X_1/Y\} \circ \{X_2/Y\} \circ \{Y/2\}$
16	6	4	CALL	$true$	$\{X_1/Y\} \circ \{X_2/Y\} \circ \{Y/2\}$
17	6	4	EXIT	$true$	$\{X_1/Y\} \circ \{X_2/Y\} \circ \{Y/2\}$
18	3	3	EXIT	$l(X_2)$	$\{X_1/Y\} \circ \{X_2/Y\} \circ \{Y/2\}$
19	7	3	CALL	$r(X_2)$	$\{X_1/Y\} \circ \{X_2/Y\} \circ \{Y/2\}$
20	7	3	FAIL	$r(X_2)$	$\{X_1/Y\} \circ \{X_2/Y\} \circ \{Y/2\}$
21	3	3	REDO	$l(X_2)$	$\{X_1/Y\} \circ \{X_2/Y\} \circ \{Y/2\}$
22	6	4	REDO	$true.$	$\{X_1/Y\} \circ \{X_2/Y\} \circ \{Y/2\}$
23	6	4	FAIL	$true$	$\{X_1/Y\} \circ \{X_2/Y\} \circ \{Y/2\}$
24	3	3	FAIL	$l(X_2)$	$\{X_1/Y\} \circ \{X_2/Y\}$
25	2	2	UNIFY	$s(X_3)$	$\{X_1/Y\} \circ \{X_3/Y\}$
26	8	3	CALL	$f(X_3)$	$\{X_1/Y\} \circ \{X_3/Y\}$
27	8	3	UNIFY	$f(3)$	$\{X_1/Y\} \circ \{X_3/Y\} \circ \{Y/3\}$
28	9	4	CALL	$true$	$\{X_1/Y\} \circ \{X_3/Y\} \circ \{Y/3\}$
29	9	4	EXIT	$true$	$\{X_1/Y\} \circ \{X_3/Y\} \circ \{Y/3\}$
30	8	3	EXIT	$f(X_3)$	$\{X_1/Y\} \circ \{X_3/Y\} \circ \{Y/3\}$
31	2	2	EXIT	$s(X_1)$	$\{X_1/Y\} \circ \{X_3/Y\} \circ \{Y/3\}$
32	10	2	CALL	$t(X_1)$	$\{X_1/Y\} \circ \{X_3/Y\} \circ \{Y/3\}$
33	10	2	UNIFY	$t(3)$	$\{X_1/Y\} \circ \{X_3/Y\} \circ \{Y/3\}$
34	11	3	CALL	$true$	$\{X_1/Y\} \circ \{X_3/Y\} \circ \{Y/3\}$
35	11	3	EXIT	$true$	$\{X_1/Y\} \circ \{X_3/Y\} \circ \{Y/3\}$
36	10	2	EXIT	$t(X_1)$	$\{X_1/Y\} \circ \{X_3/Y\} \circ \{Y/3\}$
37	1	1	EXIT	$u(Y)$	$\{X_1/Y\} \circ \{X_3/Y\} \circ \{Y/3\}$
38	1	1	REDO	$u(Y)$	$\{X_1/Y\} \circ \{X_3/Y\} \circ \{Y/3\}$
39	10	2	REDO	$t(X_1)$	$\{X_1/Y\} \circ \{X_3/Y\} \circ \{Y/3\}$
40	11	3	REDO	$true$	$\{X_1/Y\} \circ \{X_3/Y\} \circ \{Y/3\}$
41	11	3	FAIL	$true$	$\{X_1/Y\} \circ \{X_3/Y\} \circ \{Y/3\}$
42	10	2	FAIL	$t(X_1)$	$\{X_1/Y\} \circ \{X_3/Y\} \circ \{Y/3\}$
43	2	2	REDO	$s(X_1)$	$\{X_1/Y\} \circ \{X_3/Y\} \circ \{Y/3\}$
44	8	3	REDO	$f(X_3)$	$\{X_1/Y\} \circ \{X_3/Y\} \circ \{Y/3\}$
45	9	4	REDO	$true$	$\{X_1/Y\} \circ \{X_3/Y\} \circ \{Y/3\}$
46	9	4	FAIL	$true$	$\{X_1/Y\} \circ \{X_3/Y\} \circ \{Y/3\}$
47	8	3	FAIL	$f(X_3)$	$\{X_1/Y\} \circ \{X_3/Y\}$
48	2	2	FAIL	$s(X_1)$	$\{X_1/Y\}$
49	1	1	CALL	$u(Y)$	$\emptyset$

Table 2. Trace for the query $u(Y)$ and program P

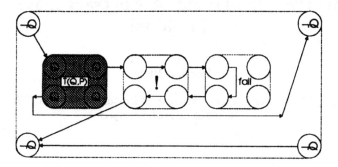

Fig. 5. The trace graph for the negative query $\neg Q$ containing the T-graph for Q

details the reader is referred to a forthcoming technical report that should be available shortly from the authors.

As the proofs show, several aspects of our formalization could be changed without loosing its main soundness and (in-)completeness properties — we did not have to look at the current substitution of $\mathcal{R}$- and $\mathcal{F}$-nodes. Therefore possessing now an answer to the question "What's in a trace?" it is probably time to ask "What should be in a trace?". We strongly believe that the answer to this latter question depends on who is analyzing the trace: man or machine.

Of course, since every node of a trace path appears in a full trace of an SLD computation our formalization can serve as a guide line for the formal description and classification of existing and forthcoming tracers of logic programming systems. But not all this information is psychological adequate for a human trace analyzer nor necessary for trace analyzers like OPIUM (cf. [3]).

Hence psychological research in the spirit of [4] will also be needed to answer questions like: what nodes should be traced in the first place, what current substitution should be assigned to $\mathcal{R}$- and $\mathcal{F}$-nodes, or how variables should be (re-)presented in a trace?

And last but not least it will be interesting to apply our formalization to the verification of trace analyzers like OPIUM [3].

References

1. Byrd, L.: *PROLOG Debugging Facilities*. Technical Report D.A.I. Research Paper 19, Department of Artificial Intelligence, University of Edinburgh, July 1980.
2. Byrd, L.: *Understanding the Control flow of Prolog Programs*. In: *Proceedings of the Logic Programming Workshop, Debrecen*, pages 127–138, 1980.
3. Ducassé, M.: *An Extendable Trace Analyser to Support Automated Debugging*. Ph.D. thesis, University of Rennes, France, June 1992. Report 758.
4. Höök, K.; Taylor, J.; du Boulay, B.: *Redo "Try Once and Pass": the influence of complexity and graphical notation on novices' understanding of Prolog*. *Instructional Science*, 19:337–360, 1990.
5. Lloyd, J.: *Foundations of Logic Programming*. Springer-Verlag, Berlin, 2nd extended edition, 1967.

Declarative Debugging of Abstract Data Types in Gödel

Dominic Binks*

Dept. of Computer Science, University of Bristol, Bristol BS8 1TR, UK
binks@uk.ac.bristol.compsci

Abstract. Modern software engineering uses abstract data types to allow modular programming. When debugging, abstract data types cause problems because the user does not understand the implementation of the type. This is particularly true in declarative debugging where users must determine the validity of an atom. As the user of the type does not know how the type is implemented the user is unable to determine its validity when presented with the implementation. Frequently, the user visualises a structure which the type represents. This *view* can be used when displaying terms of this type during debugging. We introduce the concept of a *representer*, which, establishes an equivalence between a term and this view. During debugging, the representers are used to translate terms to and from their view. When inputting abstract data types, the representer will produce the hidden term from the visible term the user gave. When outputting abstract data types, the representer will produce a visible term from the hidden term. We also extend the idea of representers to be able to handle large data efficiently.

1 Introduction

Abstract data types form a central part of modern software engineering. Using abstract data types, software engineers only need know the interface to a type to use it. This means the implementation can be hidden from them. Abstract data types enforce precisely this separation. In particular, the implementation may be altered without users of the type being aware of the changes.

Hidden data should not be displayed anywhere for three reasons. Firstly, the abstract data type may hide an implementation in the underlying system. Consequently, the implementation may be completely meaningless to the user. Secondly, the user would need to understand how the type is implemented to be able to debug the program. In contrast the user would not need to understand the implementation to write the program. Thirdly, displaying the implementation of an abstract data type violates the type visibility rules.

It is clear, therefore, that hidden terms interfere with declarative debugging when knowledge of the intended interpretation of the buggy program is given by the user. The debugger asks queries of the form "is this particular atom (set

* Supported by SERC grant number 91309576.

of atoms) in the intended interpretation?" The user must answer *yes* or *no* to these queries.

Users, in general, do not know how an abstract data type is implemented, however, they do know what data should be stored in the term. This fact is important when debugging with abstract data types.

For example, consider a balanced binary tree implementation which is made available as an abstract data type. The tree will contain information concerning its balance. The user is unlikely to understand the algorithm used to keep the tree balanced. However, the user knows about the key–value pairs stored in the tree. When debugging the user will want to examine these key–value pairs (to determine validity) without having to understand the algorithm used to balance the tree.[2]

Most work on declarative debugging has been done in Prolog, which does not support abstract data types. Work in other areas includes, for example, lazy functional languages [5], Pascal [6] and concurrent logic languages [3]. There appears to be little consideration for the special treatment of data in any declarative debugging literature, with the exception of [1]. In [1] binding information is used to assist in avoiding irrelevant search. Handling of large terms has been given little consideration explicitly. In Prolog debugging it is assumed that the system will look after displaying large terms by using depth bounds. This is unlikely to prove sufficient for a practical system in which large quantities of data need to be examined. As Prolog has no data hiding mechanisms, this issue has not been researched.

The aim of the current work is to provide a practical declarative debugger for Gödel [2]. As Gödel uses abstract data types extensively, the handling of abstract data types is an important issue for such a system. Furthermore, the use of some of Gödel's abstract data types produce very large terms. The `Program` type, for example, contains data which represents a complete Gödel program which can be very large. Therefore, special consideration must be given to viewing large hidden terms efficiently.

2 Abstract Data Types in Gödel

To understand the techniques proposed in this paper a little examination of Gödel's abstract data type mechanism is required. Since the abstract data type mechanism is based on the module and type systems we must examine how these systems work.

First, we examine Gödel's type system. To understand the type system we need to look at how Gödel is constructed from identifiers, keywords and punctuation. Gödel has a small number of keywords (only 12) which we will discuss

---

[2] It is possible for the implementation to be buggy in a way such that the list of key-value pairs is correct, but the tree is unbalanced. However, throughout this paper we assume such abstract data types have been sufficiently debugged to avoid this problem.

later with reference to the program in the Appendix. Gödel's punctuation symbols are "(),.". Gödel's identifiers can be split into two classes, variables and non-variables. Variables are either an underscore ("_") or begin with a lower case letter. Variables are not declared in Gödel and may be introduced freely at any point. All Gödel's non-variable identifiers, however, must be declared. Non-variable identifiers are characterised by beginning with an upper case letter.

There are two subclasses of non-variable identifier; those belonging to the type system and those belonging to the code. The types of identifiers used in the type system are declared to be either constants (called *bases*) or functions (called *constructors*). Variables can also appear in the type system and are called *parameters* in this context. Through parameters polymorphism is introduced into programs.

The types of identifiers used to construct Gödel code are constants, functions, propositions and predicates. Constants and functions are declared to map to a particular type – the range type. In addition, functions must have their argument types declared. A constant or function can only occur in an argument position of the same type as their range type. As predicates and propositions always map to the Boolean type ({True, False}), the range type of predicates and propositions is not specified. Predicates take a number of arguments each of which must be specified.

The Gödel type checker verifies that all argument positions agree with the types given in the declarations. When arguments are typed by a parameter, as long as all arguments with that parameter have the same type then the formula is type correct. Variables are not explicitly typed but inherit their types from their context. For example, if a variable occurs in an argument position with type t_1 then the variable has type t_1. All other occurrences of this variable will have to occur in positions of type t_1 to be type correct. If all the terms occurring in a formula are typed correctly with respect to their argument positions then the formula is well typed.

Next, we consider Gödel's hierarchical module system. A Gödel module typically consists of two parts; the module interface (*export* part) and the implementation module (*local* part). The export part of a module contains only declarations; the local part of a module contains declarations and code. Both the local and/or the export part can import modules.

When importing a module, the language of the export part and access to the code of the module are imported. The language of a module part is the set of declarations of the given module part combined with any language imported into this module part. If a module is imported into the export part of a module it's language is exported on with the language of the importing module. In contrast if a module is imported into the local part of a module its language is not re-exported with the language of the importing module. The following example illustrates this.

Example. In Fig. 1, the languages of the module parts are labelled with the module name and a letter. The letter indicates whether the set of language declarations is from the export or local part of a module. For example, "Ae"

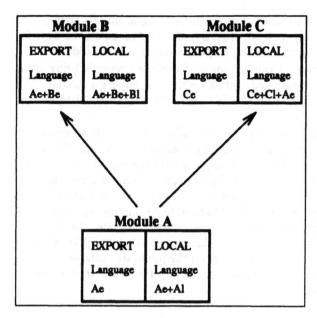

Fig. 1. The Visibility of Module Languages

labels the export language from module A and "Cl" labels the local language from module C. Module B imports module A into its export part and therefore module A's export language is re-exported by module B. Note that the local part of module B has access to the export language of module B. In contrast module C imports module A into its local part. The effect of which is that only the local part of module C has access to the export language of module A. As a result the export language of module A is not re-exported by module C. Neither B or C have access to the local language of module A

Gödel's abstract data types have the interface defined in the export part and the implementation defined in the local part. This way the importing modules can gain no access to the implementation of the hidden terms. In the example, the abstract types of module A are imported into modules B and C. The only access to these types is provided via the predicates declared in the export part of module A.

An Example of Abstract Data Types in Gödel

An example of a Gödel module can be seen in the Appendix. It demonstrates some important aspects of Gödel programming, especially the type system. The module in the Appendix is a top level module, indicated by the keyword **MODULE** at the top. This means that the module does not have an export part. This module then imports the system module **Flocks**. **Flocks** are used for performing manipulation on arbitrary terms. A **flock** is an ordered collection of **Units**; a unit is an identifier with 0 or more arguments. Each argument of a unit is also a unit so units form a very general structure. In fact **Flocks** can be used for doing processing on other programming language source code in Gödel.

Looking at the program we can see some of Gödel's keywords being used; **MODULE** has already been mentioned. **IMPORT** is used to import a module. The only other keyword used in this module is **PREDICATE** which is used to declare predicate symbols.

There are no types declared in this module, although there are several types used. These types have been passed up through the module system. The module **Flocks** declares the type **Flock** and imports **Strings** into its export part. The type **String** is therefore re-exported by **Flocks**. **Strings** declares the type **String** and imports **Lists** into its export part. **Lists** provides a polymorphic type **List(a)**; **a** being a parameter here. **Lists** imports into its export part the module **Integers**. **Integers** declares the type **Integer** and also the standard arithmetic functions (+, -, and so on). All the types used in **FlockTest1** have been passed along this "import chain" as are all the predicate declarations. Any predicates used in the module **FlockTest1** but not declared in it are declared in one of these lower modules.

3 Some Useful Definitions

When considering abstract data types, it is helpful to consider two aspects of a particular hidden term. The first of these is the implementation and the second is the data. The *data* is *what* is stored in the term and the *implementation* is *how* the data is stored in the term.

It is also helpful when working with abstract data types to consider various representations and properties of the data. A *view* is a textual representation of a term which the user understands. This may be the term itself or it may be a new term showing only the data in the term.

It is possible to define certain abstract data types which are *dependent*. Dependent terms are terms which cannot be manipulated without the use of some other term. For example, consider two abstract types α and β. Consider also two terms, s of type α and t of type β. We say t is dependent on s if and only if access to the contents of t is restricted to predicates which require s as an argument. So the type β is dependent on the type α.

The Gödel type **Name** is dependent. A term of type **Name** represents a non-variable identifier (also known as a *symbol name*) at the meta level. As symbol names only have meaning in programs, **Name** terms cannot be decomposed without a **program** term to check **Name** is valid in this program. Most terms, however, do not rely on any other terms and are thus *independent*.

The code which translates between an arbitrary term, which may be hidden, and a view is a *representer*.

For other aspects of logic programming which we refer to throughout the following we use the definitions of [4].

In the following sections we first examine more thoroughly the problems associated with displaying abstract data types. We then propose a method of viewing abstract data types. Following this is a section giving both the motivation for, and the method of, being able to input hidden terms. In order to implement the solutions proposed in this paper certain information is required and these requirements form the subject of the next section. We then discuss an example of the algorithms presented in use. Finally we conclude with a discussion of the limitations of the scheme and directions for future work.

4   Overview of Handling Abstract Data Types

The debugger gains knowledge of the intended interpretation via an oracle. As the role of oracle is frequently performed by the user, the user must answer the queries generated by the debugger. To be able to answer the queries the user must be able to examine the contents of any term including hidden terms.

For example, a program transformer could have a goal `Transform(program1, program2)`, where `program1` and `program2` are ground terms which represent two programs. The result of this call is `program2` which is the transformed `program1`. The user will want to see how `program1` has been changed to produce `program2`.

In other cases, terms may remain constant. For example, an interpreter may not modify the object program so the program term is constant throughout the computation. In this case the user will not need to examine the program. Therefore, we must only translate the term to its view if the user requests it.

When using hidden terms normally, the user is prevented from accessing the implementation of the term. In contrast the debugger has access to the implementation of hidden terms.[3] Since the module system is responsible for hiding the implementation of the abstract data type we cannot ignore module boundaries when debugging.[4]

When using abstract data types the user visualises a structure which models the abstract implementation. The display of abstract data types exploits this user model. The key is to provide a translation procedure to convert between the abstract implementation and the visualised structure. The translation procedure is just a piece of Gödel code. However, the code has the property that it takes two arguments, a hidden term and a visible term and translates between the two. In other words this procedure simply defines a user understood equivalence between two terms.

An outline of the scheme proposed in this paper is: associated with each abstract data type is a translator. When the user asks to examine or instantiate a term, the system uses the translator for this term. If the user is giving an instance, the translator is applied after reading the users input. If the user wishes

---

[3] Note that no access is allowed to some low level system types. Their implementations will remain hidden.

[4] It would be possible to assign a unique naming scheme to the symbols to avoid name clashes across module boundaries. Debugging could then proceed without regard for the module system, but this violates the hiding provided by the module system.

to view a term, the translator is applied before the system displays the term. In either case the user only sees the view and not the hidden term.

For example, a **Program** term might be represented by a set of ASCII files which contain each module part. On the other hand a **Program** term might be represented by a structure which mimics the layout of programs. If the program is represented in this way the user can then select particular aspects of the program to examine by descending the structure's tree.

To output terms the system passes the term as input to its representer. The output of this representer is then displayed. To input hidden terms the system works in much the same way. Initially, the translator is given the term the user input. The translator then uses the abstract data types interface to build a new term. This term has the same type as the argument position of the required variable. The result of the translator is, therefore, an abstract data type with the data the user input stored in it. These translators are referred to (for the purposes of this paper) as representers.

Dependent terms require special consideration in the scheme presented above. Gödel's system modules do declare some dependent types. However, all Gödel's system dependent types have been provided with suitable representers. As a result we avoid the problem of dependent types here. It is envisaged that dependent types are unlikely to occur very often. It is also thought that the existence of dependent types probably suggests a bad organisation of the abstract data type objects.

The proposal above does not say what to do if no representer exists for the given type.[5] When no representer exists for a term we can do one of two things. We could prevent the term being displayed, but this would prevent successful debugging. Alternatively, we could display the implementation. Unfortunately, this violates the visibility rules of the data type, but it will be necessary if programs are to be debugged. We have opted to show the implementation of terms which do not have representers to allow debugging.

Fortunately, representers are usually not hard to write. In practice many abstract data types have convenient representations which can be used for viewing and building terms. Even if the type doesn't have a convenient representation for viewing and building, one can usually be provided without much difficulty. Some complex terms like Gödel's **Program** type do require a lot of work to produce a view from a term.[6] However, terms as complex as this are unlikely to occur often. Most complex terms are likely to be built out of other abstract data types, and thus the translation code need not be complex.

Even though we show the implementation when no representer exists for a given type, this is not a significant weakness in the system. Firstly, for all Gödel system types, suitable representers are provided. Secondly, library module

---

[5] Gödel does not specify that every type must have a representer.

[6] This is because the definition does not require that a **Program** term should mirror the object program. It should merely represent it in some fashion so that access is efficient for operations that are likely to occur often. It should, however, be possible to recreate the original program from the **Program** term (bar comments).

writers are likely to provide representers for their types as a part of writing the code for the library module. Thirdly, if the abstract data type is user defined the user knows the implementation anyway. So, in this case, we do not violate visibility rules. This leaves few cases where displaying the implementation of an abstract type is violating data visibility rules.

Another important aspect to this scheme is the user may define their own representer for any abstract data type. This is the case whether the abstract data type is their own, a library module type, or some Gödel system types. Certain Gödel system types representers require hooks into the system so these representers cannot be changed. Consequently, a user can customise the debugger to their personal use. Users may also tailor the debugger to a particular program. It is this aspect of this scheme which gives it great flexibility.

5 Examining Abstract Data Types

We now discuss how to examine abstract data types in more detail. A diagram of how the algorithm works is given in Fig. 2. If any term in the query is hidden, then the system places the type name in angle brackets in the terms place. The user makes a request to view a particular hidden term (<Type1> in Fig. 2) that occurs in the query. First the system finds out what representer should be used. Next, the system constructs a goal to call which will run the representer. This goal is then run against the representer code. The result of which is a visible term which can be displayed to the user (S in Fig. 2). Note that S is not the same as the term in the query but is a term which represents it. Terms which are visible in the first place have the trivial representer which passes its input to its output. For the sake of convenience, if the term is visible then this is handled automatically in this way.

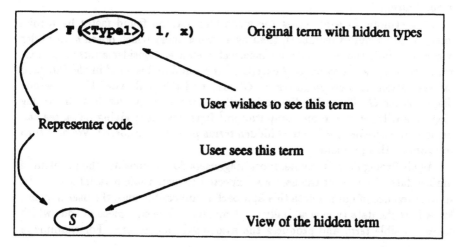

Fig. 2. Diagram of the Examine Algorithm

As we have chosen to display the implementation of terms which do not have representers we must ensure that all symbol names are unique. This prevents confusion between two symbols with the same name but which are declared in different modules. To do this we need to find a representation on a symbol name which ensures that it is unique across modules boundaries.

In Gödel programs every symbol can be uniquely represented by a quadruple <Module, Symbol, Category, Arity>. Here Module is the module the symbol was declared in. Symbol is the symbol name in the context of module Module. Category specifies which part of the language the symbol belongs to. In other words Category indicates whether the symbol is a type symbol, a term symbol, or a predicate symbol. Arity is the arity of the symbol. We can display any term in a form that is based around this representation of symbol names when no other representer is available. We will refer to this form as the quadruple form.

6   Building Abstract Data Types

We now provide motivation for asking instance queries and go on to discuss how we should handle the input of abstract data types.

When using declarative debugging algorithms which require instances the oracle is required to instantiate atoms. Although some algorithms do not need instances, giving instances has two benefits. Firstly, giving instances may reduce the search space and secondly giving instances will give more explicit bug diagnoses. Generally speaking, more information given to the algorithm will help it find the bug faster and more accurately. One example shows that an algorithm working without instances generates 10 times more queries than an algorithm working with instances. Also, the result of non-instance algorithms is in general a non-ground atom. The result of a diagnoser using instance queries is always a ground atom.

Furthermore, in some cases the same bug may be found faster by a miss query, which requires instances, than by a wrong query which doesn't. Consider a goal G which succeeds with an incorrect instance. Consider another goal G' which fails. G' is the same as G except G' is ground and is valid in the intended interpretation. A miss diagnosis on G' may find the goal faster than a wrong diagnosis on G. The miss diagnosis will ask instance queries but the wrong diagnosis will perform more computation.[7] It is clear that giving instances can be helpful, therefore the input of hidden terms must be considered. We now turn to examine this problem.

As all Prolog data is visible, most diagnosers do not consider the problem of hidden data. As a result the user was expected to instantiate a variable directly. In the presence of hidden data this approach is impossible since the user may not know how the data type is actually implemented. We need a piece of code which takes a visible term and produces the associated hidden term. For example, a

---

[7] In fact this is the case with the module given in the appendix.

balanced binary tree implementation might be used and the user may use an association list for viewing and creating a tree.

To input abstract data types we must implement a representer to translate from a visible term to a hidden term. In order to achieve this we can use the algorithm which the diagram in Fig. 3 demonstrates. It is easy to see how it is analogous to the algorithm for examining hidden terms. In fact, in practice these algorithms are combined so that the user may view and construct terms irrespective of the type of query.[8] This way the user need not worry about which algorithm is being used.

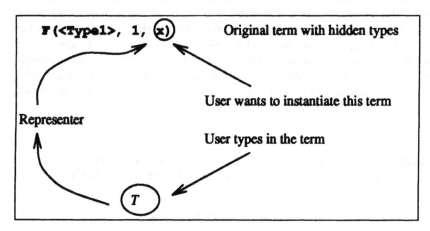

Fig. 3. Diagram of the Construct Algorithm

Note that the term input is not necessarily ground. The user may input non-ground terms to achieve one of the following two aims.

1. The term is large so the user wants to type it in smaller pieces. This is achieved by placing a variable in an argument position and then instantiating later on. The main reason for this is that the type checker can check one level of the structure at a time. This avoids having to type large terms correctly in one go.
2. The term contains hidden terms as subterms. In this case inserting a variable in the argument position allows a different representer to be used on the subterm.

Any abstract data types occurring in the term entered may be input via representers if representers exist for these types.

If no representer is present then the term input by the user is assumed to be in quadruple form as described above. In this case the term is translated by the debugger.

---

[8] When the atom is non-ground, instances may be given.

7 Requirements for Algorithms

We now discuss what information is required by the debugger to use these algorithms. Obviously the debugger needs to know which representers apply to which types. We need to indicate the type this representer refers to and in which direction it is to be used to translate. The direction will be either hidden to view or view to hidden. In order to build the goal we also need to give some other details of the representer. We need to give the order the arguments should appear in the representer call. This will indicate whether the instantiated term should appear in the first or second argument position. We also need to give the name of this binary relation. The name will have two parts, a predicate name and the file in which the code resides. In the case where the predicate is in the module that the type is declared in, then the program name is not be specified. If either or both declarations are empty then the debugger will use the quadruple form. A proposal for a convenient structure for providing the debugger[9] with this information is given in Fig. 4. Note that this data is not in Gödel and would be placed in a file read by the debugger when it is started.

```
REPRESENTER    Flock : ToView : LeftIn : FlockViews,FlockToList;
               Flock : ToHidden : LeftIn : FlockViews,ListToFlock.
```

Fig. 4. Example Term Representer Declarations for Flocks

To explain how the data is used we use the example in Fig. 4. In this example, the representers for the type **Flock** are in a file called **FlockViews** and are called **FlockToList** and **ListToFlock**. The direction in which these should be used is given by the **ToView/ToHidden** argument. The goal is constructed with the input term appearing in the first argument, indicated by **LeftIn**, and the result is returned in the second argument. If the input argument should appear in the second argument position then the symbol here would be **RightIn**. These declarations should not be added to the language as they are not relevant to the language itself. These declarations should be part of a debugger initialisation file.

8 A Small Example

In this section we introduce a small example using the Gödel **Flock** type. The program being debugged simply takes a flock and renames any identifiers in it which match a given string with a new string. The code is given in the Appendix. The debugger uses the predicate **FlockToList** given in Fig. 4 as a representer.

---

[9] The same scheme would be used by Gödel's tracer.

Note that **FlockToList** performs two steps of translation. The first step is from a flock to a list of units and the second is from each unit to a string.

To debug a program we have to give the debugger a goal. For this example the goal

```
<- RenameIdentsInFlock(flock, "world", "newworld", newflock)
```

fails. Here the variable **flock** is bound to the flock formed by flock compiling[10] a file containing the two units **hello** and **world(C,function)**. The variable **newflock** is instantiated to the flock formed by flock compiling a file containing the two units **hello** and **newworld(C,function)**. The query simple renames all the identifiers in the flock with the name **world** to the name **newworld**.

The first query (see Fig. 5) to occur is the failed (ground) atom that initiated the debugging process. All query windows follow a general layout. Along the bottom there are three answer buttons (Yes,No,Abort). There is, also, a possibly empty set of previous replies which will not be displayed if the atom is ground. Compare Fig. 5 with Figs. 8 and 11. Finally the goal is displayed in a browser so that the user can examine the atom. The browser has scroll bars to the right and bottom so that the user can move the atom around in the browser. Also associated with the browser is a menu. This menu allows the user to select terms from the atom to examine. See Fig. 6.

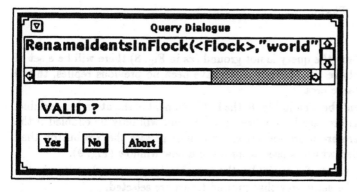

Fig. 5. A Ground Query

When the user selects one of the terms, the selected term is displayed in a separate window. In Fig. 6 the last argument is selected, which is a flock. On displaying the term, the representer is applied if it exists after making sure the term is not visible. See Fig. 7.

Pressing any of the buttons on any window will dismiss the particular window and all its children.

---

[10] This compiles an ASCII file into a flock file which can then be read into the program as a flock.

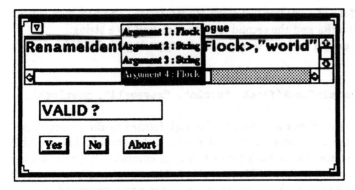

Fig. 6. A Query Menu

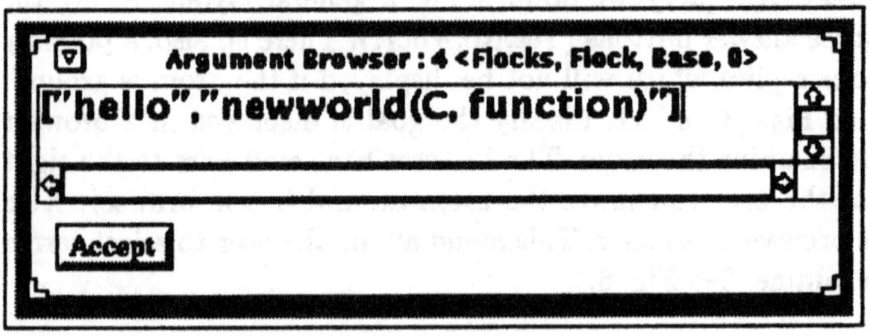

Fig. 7. A View of a Flock

In the case where the query is not ground (as in Fig. 8) there will be a set of previous replies above the atom. If there have been no previous replies, this is indicated in the same area.

Although it can't be seen in Fig. 8, the last argument of the atom is a variable. The menu for this browser hasn't been enabled and will only be enabled if the user indicates there are more solutions. If the user presses the Yes button then the menu is enabled which is used to produce a new window (Fig. 9).

For inputting values for variables the variable terms are selected, via the menu, in exactly the same way that ground terms are selected.

This window is the input window for the term. The Accept button is disabled because the system cannot accept a non-existent term. The user then enters the data as shown in Fig. 10. The response by the debugger is triggered by typing a return in the window. When the term is a valid ground term the window may disappear or the Accept button will become enabled. This depends on whether the input term, when translated, makes any term ground. When a term or atom becomes ground it kills off all it's child windows.

The final example (Fig. 11) is a goal with some previous replies, but none have led to the bug. The window displays several text browsers, with a final slot indicating no more solutions. The browsers of the previous replies have menus which are enabled so that the user can check any of the data already input.

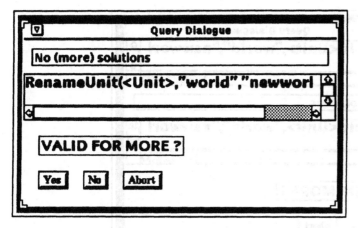

Fig. 8. An Instance Query

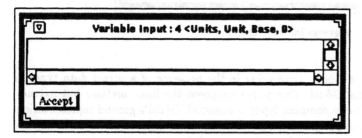

Fig. 9. An Input Window for a Variable

9 Conclusion

The method presented here allows successful declarative debugging of Gödel programs in the barest form. This solution allows the user to debug all abstract data types, even if the implementor has not provided a convenient translation procedure.

This work is part of ongoing research aimed at producing a practical declar-

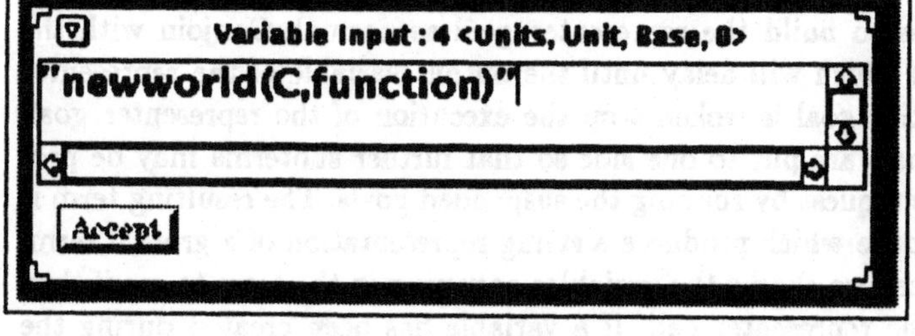

Fig. 10. Data Entered in Input Window

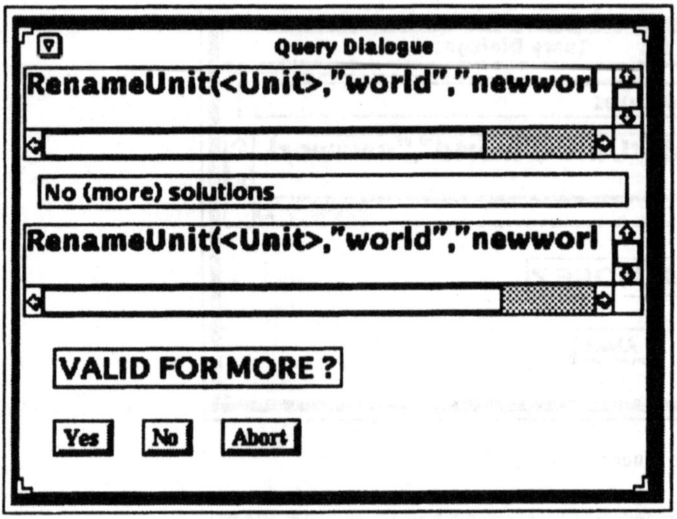

Fig. 11. Query for Previous Instance Query

ative debugger for Gödel. Debugging in the presence of abstract data types is vital to debugging Gödel. This paper proposes the basic method but extending it to handle more complex types is essential. Gödel's ground representation for handling object programs is one such important type. Work is underway on providing an efficient method for viewing such large terms.

It is clear that large terms could be handled by adding a depth bound pretty printer for visible terms. This way the user can perform systematic recursive descent of any term using either menus or a hypertext-like system activated by clicking on terms.

To view large hidden terms we need to avoid passing the whole of the term through the representer as this could take a long time. Ideally we want just the top level function of the term to be translated and then allow the user to work down the structure. For handling large hidden terms we need a lazy representer which will only translate the top level function. It should then work out the types of the subterms and display them as hidden terms. The user can then request to view such terms at which point they will be translated to their view. In this way no more work is done than necessary.

One solution is to build the representer goal as normal. Conjoin with the representer a goal which will delay until the output variable of the representer is bound. When this goal is woken stop the execution of the representer goal. The suspended goals are put to one side so that further subterms may be produced at the users request by running the suspended goals. The resulting term is passed to a procedure which produces a string representation of a ground term. However, the procedure checks the variables occurring in the term to see if they were created in the representer call. If a variable has been created during the representer call it occurs in the string as <<Type>>. When the user selects this term for display the suspended goals are found and then run. This then produces the subterms as they are needed.

There are essentially two problems with this scheme, the first of which is the granularity. The scheme does not allow the user to easily indicate that they wish to view particular terms which may be several levels down. The second is that careful thought should be given to how the suspended goals are stored to avoid unnecessary work. Work which does produce terms other than those the user wants to see should be avoided. It seems likely that an examination of the variables may be sufficient to avoid this problem. However, at this stage it is not yet clear.

One problem that exists with the current implementation is the handling of terms which do not have a representer. As the same method is used for dependent terms the comment applies to these terms as well. The method adopted in this research has been to violate abstract type visibility rules. This compromise has been necessary to permit any form of debugging on such terms. Ideally a solution would protect the visibility rules of the abstract data type. However, further work is needed in both these areas if this goal is to be attained.

We feel that the work described here is a practical contribution to declarative debugging. As this work is also applicable to the display of abstract data types anywhere, it is appropriate for all types of debugging.

References

1. E. Av-Ron. Top-down diagnosis of Prolog programs. Masters Thesis, Weizmann Institute of Science, 1984.
2. P. Hill and J. W. Lloyd. The Gödel programming language. Technical Report CSTR-92-27, University of Bristol, October 1992 (Revised May 1993).
3. Yossi Lichtenstein and Ehud Shapiro. Abstract algorithmic debugging. In Robert A. Kowalski and Kenneth A. Bowen, editors, *Proceedings of the Fifth International Conference and Symposium on Logic Programming*, pages 512–531, Seattle, 1988. ALP, IEEE, The MIT Press.
4. J.W. Lloyd. *Foundations of Logic Programming*. Springer-Verlag, 1987.
5. Lee Naish. Declarative debugging of lazy functional programs. In *Proceedings of the Post Conference Workshop on Logic Programming Environments (Joint International Conference and Symposium on Logic Programming)*, Washington, November 1992.
6. S. Renner. Location of logical errors on Pascal programs with an appendix on implementation problems in Waterloo Prolog/c. Technical Report UIUCDCS-F-82-896, Department of Computer Science, Univeristy of Illinois at Urbana, Champaign-Urbana, Illinois, April 1982.

Appendix

```
MODULE      FlockTest1.

% NOTE: A '%' marks the beginning of a comment line.
```

```
IMPORT    Flocks.

PREDICATE  RenameIdentsInFlock : Flock * String * String * Flock.

RenameIdentsInFlock(flock, string, repstring, newflock) <-
    Extent(flock, n) &
    RenameIdentsInFlockAux(flock, n, string, repstring, newflock).

PREDICATE  RenameIdentsInFlockAux : Flock * Integer * String *
                                    String * Flock.

RenameIdentsInFlockAux(flock, 0, _, _, flock).
RenameIdentsInFlockAux(flock, n, string, newstring, newflock) <-
    n > 0 &
    UnitInFlock(flock, unit, n) &
    RenameUnit(unit, string, newstring, newunit) &
    InsertUnit(flock, unit, n, flocka) &
% Here the programmer inserted a unit when it should have
% been deleted.
    InsertUnit(flocka, newunit, n, flockb) &
    n1 = n-1 &
    RenameIdentsInFlockAux(flockb, n1, string, newstring,
                                                newflock).


PREDICATE  RenameUnit : Unit * String * String * Unit.

RenameUnit(unit, string, newstring, newunit) <-
    UnitParts(unit, ident, args) &
    ( IF    args ~= []
          THEN
                RenameUnitParts(args, string, newstring, newargs)
          ELSE
                newargs = args
    ) &
    ( IF   ident = string
          THEN
                newident = newstring
          ELSE
                newident = ident
    ) &
    UnitParts(newunit, newident, newargs).

PREDICATE  RenameUnitParts : List(Unit) * String * String *
                             List(Unit).
```

```
RenameUnitParts([], _, _, []).
RenameUnitParts([unit|units], string, newstring,
                [newunit|newunits]
            ) <-
    RenameUnit(unit, string, newstring, newunit) &
    RenameUnitParts(units, string, newstring, newunits).
```

Slicing Programs with Arbitrary Control-flow

Thomas Ball and Susan Horwitz

Computer Sciences Department
University of Wisconsin
1210 W. Dayton St.
Madison, WI 53706 USA
e-mail: tom@cs.wisc.edu, horwitz@cs.wisc.edu

Abstract

Program slicing is a program transformation that is useful in program debugging, program maintenance, and other applications that involve understanding program behavior. Given a program point p and a set of variables V, the goal of slicing is to create a *projection* of the program (by eliminating some statements), such that the projection and the original program compute the same values for all variables in V at point p.

This paper addresses the problem of slicing programs with arbitrary control-flow. Previous slicing algorithms do not always form semantically correct program projections when applied to such programs. We give the first algorithm for slicing programs with arbitrary control-flow and a proof of its correctness. Our algorithm works for programs with completely arbitrary control-flow, including irreducible control-flow.

1. Introduction

Program slicing, a program transformation originally defined by Mark Weiser [14], is useful in program debugging [11], program maintenance [7], and other applications that involve understanding program behavior [8]. Given a program point p and a set of variables V, the goal of slicing is to create a *projection* of the program (by eliminating some statements), such that the projection and the original program compute the same values for all variables in V at point p.

Example. The program shown in Figure 1(a) computes the sum and product of the numbers from 1 to N[1]. Figure 1(b) shows the result of slicing the example program with respect to the statement output(*prod*) and the variable *prod*. For any value of N, the example program and the program projection compute the same value for variable *prod* in the output statement. □

---

* This work was supported in part by the National Science Foundation under grant CCR-8958530, by the Defense Advanced Research Projects Agency, monitored by the Office of Naval Research under contract N00014-88-K-0590, as well as by grants from Xerox and 3M.

[1]In the example program, variable N is used without being explicitly initialized. It is assumed that such variables get their values from an initial state on which the program is executed.

begin
  sum := 0
  prod := 1
  i := 0
  while *i* < *N* **do**
    i := *i*+1
    sum := *sum*+*i*
    prod := *prod**i
  od
  output(*sum*)
  output(*prod*)
end
	begin
	  prod := 1
	  i := 0
	  while *i* < *N* **do**
	    i := *i*+1
	
	    prod := *prod**i
	  od
	
	  output(*prod*)
	end

(a) Example Program	(b) Result of slicing with respect to **output**(*prod*)

Figure 1. An example program, and the result of slicing with respect to **output**(*prod*).

This paper addresses a problem that has not been discussed in the literature on program slicing [9, 12-14]. The problem is how to slice programs with unstructured control-flow, *i.e.*, programs that include constructs such as **break**, **continue**, and **goto**. Previous algorithms do not slice such programs correctly. We give a program-slicing algorithm that correctly handles such programs, and we prove that the program projections produced by our algorithm meet the semantic goal of program slicing: Both the original program and the projection compute the same values at the point of the slice. Our algorithm works for programs with completely arbitrary control-flow, including irreducible control-flow [1]. (As given here, our algorithm has a slight technical restriction: A program is sliced with respect to a point p and the set of variables used or defined at p rather than an arbitrary set of variables. Extending the algorithm is straightforward.)

Algorithms for slicing programs with *structured* control-flow have been defined by Weiser [14] and by the Ottensteins [12]. Neither of these algorithms works correctly for programs with unstructured control-flow. We focus on the Ottensteins' algorithm and consider the problems that arise if one tries to apply this algorithm to programs with unstructured control-flow. The Ottensteins' algorithm makes use of two program representations: the control-flow graph [1] and the program dependence graph [5]. Vertices in the control-flow graph represent statements and predicates in the program and edges represent the flow of control in the program. The program dependence graph has the same vertex set as the control-flow graph. Its edge set is defined in terms of relationships in the control-flow graph (control dependences and flow dependences). There are two steps to the algorithm. In Step 1, edges are traversed in the reverse direction in the program dependence graph from the vertex corresponding to program point p (we refer to this step as *backwards-closure*), identifying a set of vertices S in the program dependence graph. Step 2 produces the program projection by eliminating from the original program all components that do not correspond to a vertex in S.

If one uses the standard control-flow graph for programs with unstructured control-flow (*i.e.*, a graph in which a jump gives rise to a single control-flow edge—see Figure 2(b)), the program projections computed by the Ottensteins' algorithm may fail to meet the semantic goal of program slicing; that is, the projections may compute different values than the original program at the point of the slice. The problem is that the algorithm does not correctly detect when unconditional jumps in the program (such as the **break**) are required in the program projection in order to meet the semantic goal of slicing.

Example. Consider the program shown in Figure 2(a). Figure 2(b) shows the standard control-flow graph for this program, and Figure 2(c) shows the program dependence graph of this control-flow graph. In the two graphs, shading is used to indicate the vertices that would be identified by backwards-closure in the program dependence graph with respect to "**output(**prod**)**". Figure 2(d) shows the program projection obtained by eliminating all components not identified by the slicing algorithm. Because the **break** statement is absent from the projection, it does not satisfy the semantic goal (*i.e.*, for some values of *N* and *MAXINT*, different final values of *prod* will be output by the original program and by the projection). A projection that does satisfy the semantic goal (and that would be produced by the slicing algorithm defined in this paper) is shown in Figure 2(e). □

Simply including a vertex for the **break** in the control-flow graph, such that the **break** vertex has a single successor, does not solve the problem. The **break** will still be omitted from the slice because in the program dependence graph there will be no path from the **break** to any other vertex.

The main result of this paper is a slicing algorithm for programs with unstructured control-flow, and a proof of the correctness of this algorithm; that is, we show that the program projections produced by the algorithm have the desired semantic property: Both the original program and the projection compute the same values at the point of the slice. The algorithm is in the style of the Ottensteins' algorithm in that it operates on a program dependence graph representation of a program; however, the program dependence graph is based on a control-flow graph in which a jump is represented as a pseudo-predicate vertex (that always evaluates to *true*). The jump vertex's *true*-successor is the target of the jump, and its *false*-successor is the vertex that represents the jump statement's continuation (that is, the vertex that would be the jump vertex's successor if it were a "no-op" rather than a jump). We are able to prove that by using this augmented control-flow graph, a projection of the program that has the desired semantic property can be formed.

The remainder of the paper is organized as follows. Section 2 provides background material, including a discussion of the language under consideration, and the definitions of control-flow graph and program dependence graph. Section 3 presents our slicing algorithm and gives an outline of its proof of correctness (a full proof can be found in [3]). Section 4 discusses the issues of *minimal* slices. Section 5 reviews related work in the area of slicing and Section 6 summarizes our results.

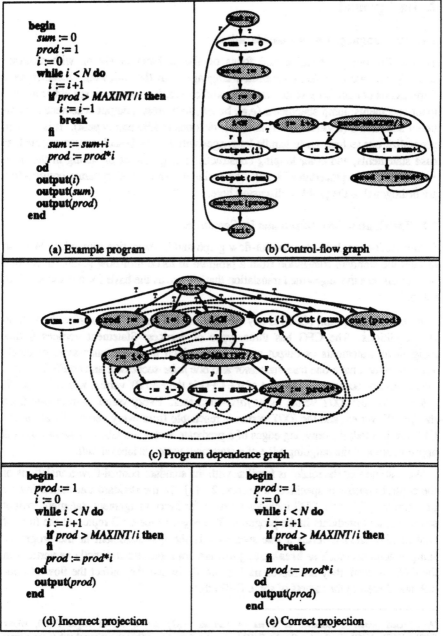

(a) Example program

(b) Control-flow graph

(c) Program dependence graph

(d) Incorrect projection

(e) Correct projection

Figure 2. An example program, its control-flow graph, its program dependence graph (solid arrows are control dependences, dashed arrows are flow dependences), the (incorrect) projection that would be computed using the Ottensteins' algorithm to slice with respect to **output**(*prod*), and the correct projection.

2. Background

2.1. The Language Under Consideration

To simplify our presentation and focus on the problem of slicing with arbitrary control-flow, we consider a simplified language with the following characteristics: Expressions contain only scalar variables and constants; statements are either assignment statements, jump statements (*e.g.*, **break, halt, goto**), output statements, conditional statements (**if-then or if-then-else**), or loops (**while and repeat**). It is easy to generalize our techniques to handle languages with *N*-way branch constructs, such as case statements, and other looping constructs. The problems of slicing in the presence of multiple procedures [9, 10], non-scalar variables, and dynamic control-flow are orthogonal to the problem discussed here.

2.2. The Control-flow Graph and Its Semantics

In this section we define the control-flow graph and its execution semantics. We also discuss the standard translation from a program to its control-flow graph. In Section 3.1, we discuss the *augmented* translation that we use as the basis for our slicing algorithm.

A *control-flow graph* (CFG) is any directed, rooted graph[2] that satisfies the following conditions. The CFG has three types of vertices: Statement vertices (either assignment statements or output statements), which have one successor; predicate vertices, which have one *true*-successor and one *false*-successor; and an *EXIT* vertex, which has no successors. The root of the CFG is the *ENTRY* vertex, which is a predicate that has the *EXIT* vertex as its *false*-successor. Every vertex is reachable from the *ENTRY* vertex, and the *EXIT* vertex is reachable from every vertex. Edges in the CFG are labeled; the outgoing edges of a predicate vertex are labeled *true* or *false* (as appropriate) and the outgoing edge of a statement vertex is labeled *null*.

We assume that the reader is familiar with the standard control-flow translations of the control constructs specified in Section 2.1 [1]. In the standard translation from a program to a CFG, the CFG includes a vertex for every assignment statement, output statement, and predicate in the program. The edges of the CFG represent the flow of control (the *ENTRY* vertex's *true*-successor is the first statement in the program). Jump statements (such as **break** and **goto**) are not represented directly as vertices in the CFG; instead, they are represented indirectly in that they affect the flow of control, and therefore the targets of some CFG edges.

---

[2] A *directed graph* G consists of a set of *vertices* $V(G)$ and a set of *edges* $E(G)$, where $E(G) \subseteq V(G) \times V(G)$. Each edge $(b, c) \in E(G)$ is directed from b to c ($b \rightarrow c$); we say that b is the *source* and c the *target* of the edge.

Example. Figure 2(b) shows the CFG of the program in Figure2(a). □

The operational semantics for the CFG is defined as follows: Execution starts at the *ENTRY* vertex (which always evaluates to *true*), with an initial state σ; at any moment there is a single point of control together with a state mapping variables to values; the execution of each statement or predicate vertex passes control to a single successor. The execution of an assignment statement changes the state. Execution terminates normally if *EXIT* is reached (execution can fail to terminate normally if the program includes an infinite loop or an exception such as division by zero). An execution of CFG G on initial state σ is denoted by $G(\sigma)$.

For an execution $G(\sigma)$, we characterize the *behavior* at a vertex by the sequence of values that arise at that vertex[3]. This is defined as follows: For an assignment statement vertex, the sequence of values assigned to the left-hand-side variable; for an output statement, the sequence of values output; and for a predicate vertex, the sequence of boolean values to which the predicate's boolean expression evaluates. $G(\sigma)(v)$ denotes the sequence of values that arise at vertex v in execution $G(\sigma)$.

The following definition defines what we mean for a vertex in CFG H to replicate the behavior of a vertex in CFG G. Because a CFG includes a vertex for every program component, this definition also makes precise the semantic goal of slicing a program with respect to component c: To create a projection whose behavior at c replicates that of the original program at c. In examining this definition, it is useful to think of CFG H as a slice of CFG G (the vertices in CFG H are a subset of the vertices in CFG G). Because H may not contain vertices present in G, it is impossible to require conditions such as "for all σ, if $H(\sigma)$ terminates normally then $G(\sigma)$ terminates normally". This leads to the asymmetry in the definition.

DEFINITION. Vertex v_H of CFG H *replicates the behavior* of vertex v_G of CFG G iff all the following hold:

- For all σ such that $G(\sigma)$ terminates normally, $H(\sigma)$ terminates normally and $G(\sigma)(v_G) = H(\sigma)(v_H)$.
- For all σ such that $G(\sigma)$ does not terminate normally, $G(\sigma)(v_G)$ is a prefix of $H(\sigma)(v_H)$.[4]

---

[3]Note that our definition of a vertex's behavior differs from the more standard definition, which characterizes a vertex's behavior as the sequence of *states* that arise at that vertex during an execution (where a state associates a value with *every* variable in the program). The standard definition is not suitable for program slicing, since the semantic goal of slicing is *not* to preserve the values of all variables, but only to preserve the values of the variables used or defined at the point with respect to which the slice is taken.

[4]$H(\sigma)$ may or may not terminate normally in this case.

2.3. The Program Dependence Graph

The program dependence graph (PDG) is defined in terms of a program's CFG. The PDG includes the same set of vertices as the CFG, excluding the *EXIT* vertex. The edges of the PDG represent the *control* and *flow* dependences induced by the CFG as follows[5]:

DEFINITION (postdominance). Let v and w be vertices in a CFG. Vertex w *postdominates* vertex v iff $w \neq v$ and w is on every path from v to the *EXIT* vertex. Vertex w *postdominates* the L-branch of predicate vertex v (where L is either *true* or *false*) iff w is the L-successor of v or w postdominates the L-successor of v. While no vertex can postdominate itself, a vertex can postdominate its own L-branch.

DEFINITION (control dependence). Let v and w be vertices in a CFG. Vertex w is directly L-control dependent on v (written $v \rightarrow_c^L w$) iff w postdominates the L-branch of v and w does not postdominate v. A vertex can be directly control dependent on itself. Intuitively, if $v \rightarrow_c^L w$, then whenever v executes and evaluates to L, w will eventually execute, barring abnormal termination. Furthermore, if v executes and does not evaluate to L, w might not execute. In this way, v directly controls whether or not w executes. Note that a vertex with only one successor in the CFG can never be the source of a control dependence edge.

Under the standard definition, there is a *flow dependence* from vertex v to vertex w iff vertex v assigns to variable x, vertex w uses x, and there is a path in the CFG from v to w that does not include an assignment to x (excluding v and w). However, the augmented translation from programs to CFGs that will be introduced in Section 3 causes the CFG to include "dummy" edges; that is, edges that are never traversed in any execution (namely, the *false* edges out of vertices that represent jump statements). Therefore, we use a slightly modified definition of flow dependence:

DEFINITION (flow dependence). Let v and w be vertices in a CFG. There is a *flow dependence* from vertex v to vertex w (written $v \rightarrow_f w$) iff vertex v assigns to variable x, vertex w uses x, and there is a path from v to w that does not include an assignment to x (excluding v and w) and that does not include any "dummy" edge.

Example. Figure 2(c) shows the PDG of the program in Figure2(a). Control dependence edges are shown using solid arrows; flow dependence edges are shown using dashed arrows. □

---

[5] In addition to control and flow dependences, program dependence graphs usually include either def-order dependences [6] or output and anti-dependences [5]. These additional edges are not needed for program slicing, and so are omitted from the definition given here. We also do not need to distinguish between loop-independent and loop-carried dependences (which are ill-defined for irreducible control-flow).

3. Slicing Programs with Arbitrary Control-flow

In this section we present our slicing algorithm and sketch a proof that it produces program projections with the desired semantic property: Given program P and component c, our algorithm, $Slice(P,c)$, produces a projection P' of P such that P' replicates the behavior of P at component c.

3.1. The Slicing Algorithm

Our slicing algorithm is similar to the Ottensteins' algorithm in that it uses a program dependence graph (PDG) to identify the program components in the slice. In particular, given a PDG and a vertex v from which to slice, Step 1 of both the Ottensteins' algorithm and our algorithm identifies the subset of the PDG's vertices from which there is a path along control and/or flow dependence edges to vertex v (i.e., Step 1 computes the backwards reflexive transitive closure with respect to v). Step 2 of both algorithms creates a program projection by eliminating components that do not correspond to the vertices identified in Step 1[6].

The important difference between our algorithm and the Ottensteins' is that we use an *augmented* translation from the program to the control-flow graph (CFG) from which the PDG is built. The translations for all the structured constructs (i.e., **if-then, if-then-else, while,** and **repeat**) remain the same. However, jump statements are explicitly represented in the CFG as pseudo-predicate vertices that always evaluate to *true*. A jump vertex's *true*-successor is the target of the jump; its *false*-successor is the vertex that represents the jump statement's fall-through or continuation (that is, the vertex that would be the jump vertex's successor if it were a "no-op" rather than a jump). The outgoing false edge of a jump vertex is a "dummy" edge that is never actually traversed in an execution.[7] Representing a jump statement this way causes it to be the source of control dependence edges in the PDG. This in turn allows the jump vertex to be correctly included in the backwards-closure in the PDG.

Example. Figure 3(a) repeats the program of Figure 2(a) and shows the program's augmented CFG. Figure 3(b) shows the vertices, control edges, and some of the flow edges of the corresponding PDG (flow edges that are not relevant to the backwards-

---

[6] A precise definition of what it means to eliminate a program component is given in [3]. In short, the elimination operation is defined in terms of the program's abstract-syntax tree; every vertex in the program's PDG corresponds to a node in the abstract-syntax tree. Eliminating the component that corresponds to vertex v means removing the subtree rooted at the tree node that corresponds to v.

[7] It is important to note that representing jump statements this way in the CFG does not change the semantics of the CFG as defined in Section 2.2. In particular, since a jump is treated as a predicate that always evaluates to *true*, and since the jump vertex's *true*-successor is the target of the jump, it is clear that for every vertex v in the standard CFG G and every initial state σ, the behavior at v when G is executed on σ is the same as the behavior at the corresponding vertex when the augmented CFG is executed on σ.

214

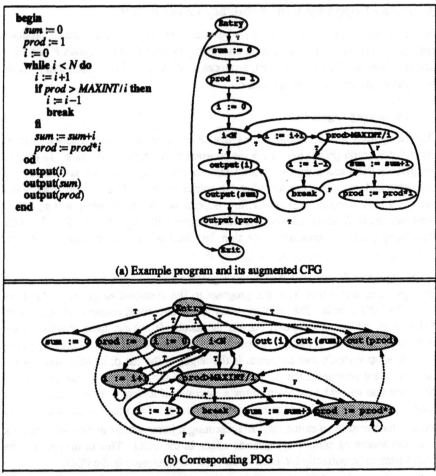

(a) Example program and its augmented CFG

(b) Corresponding PDG

Figure 3. The example program from Figure 2(a), its augmented CFG, and the corresponding PDG. Shading is used to indicate the PDG vertices identified by backwards-closure with respect to "output(*prod*)". Flow edges that are not relevant to the backwards-closure with respect to "output(*prod*)" are omitted.

closure with respect to "**output(*prod*)**" are omitted).

Note that in this PDG, the **break** vertex has three outgoing control dependence edges (which are not in the PDG of Figure 2(c)). These edges are consistent with the intuition behind control dependence: Removing the **break** might change the number of times the assignments to *sum* and *prod* as well as the evaluation of the loop predicate were performed (and therefore there are control dependence edges from the **break** vertex to the vertices that represent these three components). However, in a terminating execution, the presence or absence of the **break** has no effect on whether or not statements outside the loop are executed (and therefore there are no control dependence edges from the **break** vertex to a vertex that represents a statement outside the loop).

In Figure 3(b), shading is used to indicate the PDG vertices that are identified by backwards-closure with respect to "**output(*prod*)**". Note that the shaded vertices correspond to the program components that are included in the correct program projection shown in Figure 2(e). □

3.2. Proof of Correctness

In this section we sketch a proof that our slicing algorithm produces a program projection with the desired semantic property. Because of space limitations, we are unable to give the full proof here. Details of the proof can be found in [3].

A semantics-preserving transformation on CFGs

The first step of the proof is to show that eliminating the vertices not identified by backwards-closure in the PDG with respect to the slicing vertex (Step 1 of the algorithm) is a semantics-preserving transformation on CFGs.[*] In particular, we show that every vertex in the resulting CFG replicates the behavior of the corresponding vertex in the original CFG. This part of the proof does not rely at all on the augmented translation. That is, the results here are for arbitrary CFGs, regardless of the program from which they were derived.

Example. Figure 4 repeats the (augmented) CFG of Figure 3(a) and shows the CFG that results from eliminating the vertices not identified by backwards-closure with respect to "**output(*prod*)**". □

The proof that eliminating the vertices not identified by backwards-closure in the PDG is a semantics-preserving transformation relies on the following definitions and lemmas:

DEFINITION (path-projection). CFG H is a *path-projection* of CFG G iff all of the following hold:

(1) The vertices of H are a subset of the vertices of G.
(2) For every path in G (a sequence of [vertex, edge-label] pairs), if the vertices that are not in H are eliminated along with their outgoing edge labels, then the resulting sequence is a path in H.
(3) For every path PTH in H, there is a path in G whose projection is PTH (as in (2)).

---

[*] To eliminate a vertex x from CFG G: For every vertex a such that there is an edge $a \rightarrow^{L1} x$ and for every vertex b such that there is an edge $x \rightarrow^{L2} b$, remove edges $a \rightarrow^{L1} x$ and $x \rightarrow^{L2} b$; add edge $a \rightarrow^{L1} b$. Remove vertex x.

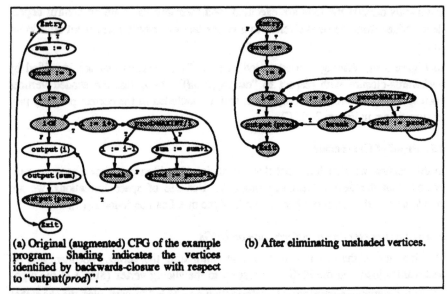

(a) Original (augmented) CFG of the example program. Shading indicates the vertices identified by backwards-closure with respect to "output(*prod*)".

(b) After eliminating unshaded vertices.

Figure 4. Eliminating vertices not in the backwards-closure preserves CFG semantics.

DEFINITION (flow/path-projection). CFG *H* is a *flow/path-projection* of CFG *G* iff both of the following hold:

(1)   *H* is a path-projection of *G*.
(2)   For every vertex *w* ∈ *H*, if *G* induces the flow dependence $v \rightarrow_f w$, then vertex *v* is also in *H*.

Example. Figure 5 shows four CFGs. Both *H* and *J* are path-projections of *G*; however, *K* is not. This is because *G* includes the path ((Entry, T)(*x* >0, F)(*y* :=0, *null*)(output(*y*), *null*), (output(*x*), *null*)(Exit)), but the path ((Entry, T)(Exit)) is not in *K*. *H* is also a flow/path-projection of *G*, but *J* is not. This is because vertex "**output**(*y*)" is in *J*, graph *G* induces a flow dependence from "*y* :=1" to "**output**(*y*)", but vertex "*y* :=1" is not in *J*. □

LEMMA (flow/path-projections preserve CFG semantics). If CFG *H* is a flow/path-projection of CFG *G*, then the behavior of every vertex in *H* replicates the behavior of the corresponding vertex in *G*.

The following lemma shows that backwards-closure in the PDG finds the set of vertices necessary *and* sufficient to form a CFG that is a flow/path-projection of the original CFG.

LEMMA (backwards closure in PDG finds flow/path-projection). Given: CFG *G*, its PDG *D*, and vertex *v*. Eliminating the vertices from *G* that are not in the backwards

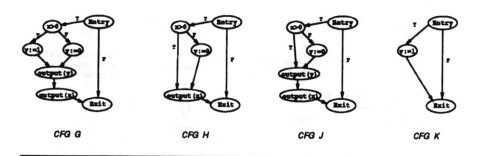

Figure 5. H and J are path-projections of G; K is not. H is also a flow/path-projection of G; J is not.

closure of D with respect to v yields a CFG that is the minimal flow/path-projection of G that contains v.

A semantics-preserving transformation on programs

Recall that the goal of program slicing is to produce a projection of a given *program*, not to produce a projection of a given CFG. As illustrated by the example of Figure 2, under the standard control-flow translation, creating a program projection by eliminating components that do not correspond to the vertices identified by backwards-closure does *not* result in a projection with the desired semantic property.

The second part of the proof of correctness of our algorithm involves showing that under the augmented translation, eliminating program components that do not correspond to the vertices identified by backwards-closure *is* a semantics-preserving transformation on programs (Step 2 of the algorithm). To prove this, we have shown that the relationships pictured in Figure 6(a) hold (see [3] for details). That is, given a program P and a component c, we show that the program Q that results from applying our slicing algorithm to P has a CFG H that is a flow/path-projection of P's CFG G. By the results of the previous section, this means that the vertices of H (in particular, the vertex that corresponds to c) replicate the behaviors of the corresponding vertices of G. This part of the proof relies on several properties relating the abstract syntax of the language to the augmented CFG. Rather than argue directly that H is a flow/path-projection of G, we have shown that H can be obtained from G by eliminating all vertices not identified by backwards-closure, as pictured in Figure 6(b). It then follows from the results of the previous section that H is a flow/path-projection of G.

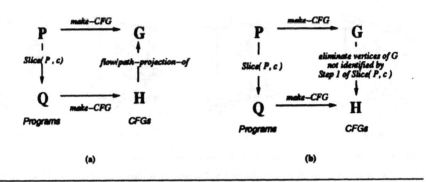

(a)   (b)

Figure 6. Slicing is a semantics-preserving transformation on programs.

4. Slices and Minimality

A slicing algorithm identifies a program projection that behaves identically to the original program at some point of interest. As has been noted before, the usefulness of a slicing algorithm is inversely proportional to the size of the slices it produces. While it is an undecidable problem to find slices of minimal size, it would be possible to employ common compiler optimizations to further reduce the size of slices. For example, copy propagation could be used to prune away copy chains from a slice, as shown below (of course, some renaming may need to be done also):

$$x := x+1; \qquad\qquad x := x+1;$$
$$y := x;$$
$$z := y; \qquad\qquad\quad z := x;$$

We believe that smaller slices are useful, up to a point. In this paper, we have shown that our slicing algorithm based on the program dependence graph produces programs whose CFGs are flow/path-projections of the original program's CFG. That is, they preserve paths of the original program (modulo projection) and the flow of values between components. While these properties are useful for proving the semantic results, they also are intuitively appealing. A slice that does not preserve the paths in a program or the flow of values amongst its components may compute the same result as the original program, but does so in a different way than the programmer originally intended. Flow/path-projections retain the *structure* of the computation as well as its result.

We also have shown that backwards-closure in the PDG identifies the minimal set of vertices needed to form a flow/path-projection of a CFG (that includes a given vertex). In particular, control dependence identifies the vertices that must necessarily be included in a slice in order to form a path-projection. That is, if CFG H is a path-projection of CFG G, w is in H and $v \rightarrow_c w$ is in G's PDG, then v must also be in H.

There are cases where a flow/path-projection that is minimal under the augmented translation is not minimal under the standard translation. In the example below, program Y is the projection that results from slicing program X with respect to C (using the augmented translation). However, under the standard translation, the CFG of program Z is a path-projection of program Y's CFG. Under the standard translation, C is not control dependent on predicate Q (as there is no path from Q to C in the standard CFG). Therefore, Q is not needed in order to form a path-projection including C (under the standard translation). However, under the augmented translation, C is control dependent on Q.

X	Y	Z
If P then	If P then	If P then
If Q then	If Q then	
A		
goto L;	goto L;	
fi	fi	
B		
goto L;	goto L;	goto L;
fi	fi	fi
C	C	C
L: D	L:	L:

It remains an open question whether there is an efficient algorithm for finding a program projection that is the minimal flow/path-projection of the original program under the standard control-flow translation.

We have defined the slice of a program to be a projection of that program. That is, the program slice must be formed by eliminating statements from the original program. Because one of the major applications of slicing is debugging, this is a natural restriction. Presenting the programmer with a slice that does not resemble the original program is clearly unsatisfactory. However, if we drop the requirement that the resulting program be a projection of the original program then it is easy to construct programs that are minimal flow/path-projections with respect to the standard control-flow translation. For example, given a program P with standard CFG G, one could construct the minimal flow/path-projection of G with respect to some vertex (using backwards-closure in the PDG to identify the required vertices) and then synthesize a program from that CFG using a structuring algorithm such as Baker's [2]. However, in a language with unstructured control-flow, there can be many programs with the same CFG. The program that results from such an approach may not be a projection of the original program, even though it meets the semantic goal (because its CFG is a flow/path-projection of the original program's CFG).

5. Related Work

As mentioned previously, Weiser defined the first program slicing algorithm [14]. The Ottensteins defined a more efficient program slicing algorithm using the program dependence graph [12]. Neither algorithm handles unstructured control-flow correctly. Reps and Yang gave the first formal proof that the program slices formed by using the program dependence graph have the desired semantic property [13]. Furthermore, they showed that slicing using the program dependence graph guarantees equivalent behavior at every point in the slice (not just at the slicing vertex). However, they proved this only for programs with structured control-flow. We have shown that the program dependence graph can be used to slice programs with arbitrary control-flow with the guarantee of equivalent behavior at every point (see Section 3.2). We note that Reps and Yang defined a program slice to allow the possible reordering of program statements (including conditionals and loops). Under their definition, the second program shown below is a slice of the first (and vice versa):

a := 1	b := 2
b := 2	a := 1
c := a+b	c := a+b

Although the ordering of statements in the two programs differs, the same sequence of values is computed at each point. Under our framework, neither program's CFG is a path-projection of the other's CFG, so our semantic result about flow/path-projections cannot be applied to compare the programs' behaviors. However, we believe it is possible to extend slicing with reordering even in the presence of arbitrary control-flow.

Choi and Ferrante independently discovered the same problem of slicing programs with arbitrary control-flow [4]. They proposed two solutions to the problem, both based on the program dependence graph. The first uses the idea of an augmented CFG, much the same as ours. The second solution uses the PDG of the program's standard CFG to decide which statements to eliminate. In addition to deleting statements from the original program, their second approach inserts additional gotos to ensure correct control-flow. Thus, the resultant program may not be a projection of the original program. As discussed in Section 4, if it is not necessary to form a program projection, then the PDG of the standard CFG can be used to form a minimal CFG flow/path-projection (with respect to the standard translation). A structuring algorithm can then be used to form a program from the CFG. Structuring algorithms attempt to minimize the number of gotos needed and will probably produce more readable code than the second approach of Choi and Ferrante.

The major difference between our work and the first solution proposed by Choi and Ferrante is the generality of the results. Our algorithm is defined for a language that includes (arbitrarily nested) conditional statements and loops as well as breaks and gotos. In contrast, Choi and Ferrante's first algorithm is defined for a much more limited language in which the only constructs that affect control-flow are conditional and unconditional gotos. As Choi and Ferrante note, any structured control construct (such as an **if-then-else** or a **while** loop) can be synthesized in this simple language. However, as the following example shows, synthesizing control constructs in their simple language can lead to unnecessarily larger slices when the augmented CFG is used. Consider the following structured code and its translation into Choi and Ferrante's language:

```
if P then              if not(P) then goto 1;
   A                      A;
   if Q then              if Q then goto 3;
      halt                goto 2;
   fi                  1: B;
else                   2: C;
   B                   3:
fi
C
```

Under the augmented control-flow translation of the first program, there is no path from predicate Q to statement B, so B cannot be control dependent on Q. However, in the second program, statement B is control dependent on Q because of the edge from "goto 2" to B. Thus, a slice with respect to B in this program picks up predicate Q. One could argue that the statement "goto 2" should not be treated the same as other gotos that are explicitly written by the programmer. However, then one must define some other procedure for determining when these implicit **gotos** are needed in a slice.

6. Conclusions

This paper has addressed the problem of slicing programs with arbitrary control-flow. Previous slicing algorithms do not always form semantically correct program projections when applied to such programs. This is due to the fact that the algorithms do not detect when an unconditional jump such as a **break** is required in a projection. Our work solves this problem by using a program dependence graph defined using an augmented control-flow graph that represents jumps as pseudo-predicates. It remains an open question whether there is an efficient algorithm for finding a program projection that is the minimal flow/path-projection of the original program under the standard control-flow translation.

References

1. A. Aho, R. Scthi, and J. Ullman, *Compilers: Principles, Techniques and Tools,* Addison-Wesley, Reading, MA (1986).

2. B. Baker, "An Algorithm for Structuring Flow Graphs," *J. ACM* 24(1) pp. 98-120 New York, NY, (January 1977).

3. T. Ball and S. Horwitz, "Slicing programs with arbitrary control flow," Technical Report #1128, University of Wisconsin, Madison (December 1992).

4. J. D. Choi and J. Ferrante, "What is in a slice," Unpublished draft, IBM T.J. Watson Research Center (December 1992).

5. J. Ferrante, K. Ottenstein, and J. Warren, "The program dependence graph and its use in optimization," *ACM Transactions on Programming Languages and Systems* 9(5) pp. 319-349 (July 1987).

6. S. Horwitz, J. Prins, and T. Reps, "On the adequacy of program dependence graphs for representing programs," pp. 146-157 in *Conference Record of the 15th ACM Symposium on Principles of Programming Languages,* (San Diego, CA, January 13-15, 1988), ACM, New York (1988).

7. S. Horwitz, J. Prins, and T. Reps, "Integrating non-interfering versions of programs," *ACM Trans. Program. Lang. Syst.* 11(3) pp. 345-387 (July 1989).

8. S. Horwitz, "Identifying the semantic and textual differences between two versions of a program," *Proceedings of the ACM SIGPLAN '90 Conference on Programming Language Design and Implementation (published as SIGPLAN Notices)* 25(6) pp. 234-245 ACM, (June 20-22, 1990).

9. S. Horwitz, T. Reps, and D. Binkley, "Interprocedural slicing using dependence graphs," *ACM Transactions on Programming Languages and Systems* 12(1) pp. 26-60 (January 1990).

10. J. C. Hwang, M. W. Du, and C. R. Chou, "Finding program slices for recursive procedures," *Proceedings of IEEE COMPSAC 88,* (Chicago, IL, Oct. 3-7, 1988), IEEE Computer Society, (1988).

11. B. Korel, "PELAS—Program Error-Locating Assistant System," *IEEE Transactions on Software Engineering* SE-14(9) pp. 1253-1260 (September 1988).

12. K.J. Ottenstein and L.M. Ottenstein, "The program dependence graph in a software development environment," *Proceedings of the ACM SIGSOFT/SIGPLAN Software Engineering Symposium on Practical Software Development Environments,* (Pittsburgh, PA, April 23-25, 1984), ACM SIGPLAN Notices 19(5) pp. 177-184 (May, 1984).

13. T. Reps and W. Yang, "The semantics of program slicing and program integration," in *Proceedings of the Colloquium on Current Issues in Programming Languages,* (Barcelona, Spain, March 13-17, 1989), *Lecture Notes in Computer Science,* Springer-Verlag, New York, NY (March 1989).

14. M. Weiser, "Program slicing," *IEEE Transactions on Software Engineering* SE-10(4) pp. 352-357 (July, 1984).

Slicing Concurrent Programs *
– A Graph-Theoretical Approach

Jingde Cheng

Department of Computer Science and Communication Engineering
Kyushu University
6-10-1 Hakozaki, Fukuoka 812, Japan
cheng@csce.kyushu-u.ac.jp

Abstract. This paper extends the notion of slicing, which was originally proposed and studied for sequential programs, to concurrent programs and presents a graph-theoretical approach to slicing concurrent programs. In addition to the usual control and data dependences proposed and studied for sequential programs, the paper introduces three new types of primary program dependences in concurrent programs, named the selection dependence, synchronization dependence, and communication dependence. The paper also propose a new program representation for concurrent programs, named the Process Dependence Net (PDN), which is an arc-classified digraph to explicitly represent the five types of primary program dependences in the programs. As a result, various notions about slicing concurrent programs can be formally defined based on the representation, and the problem of slicing a concurrent program can be simply reduced to a vertex reachability problem in its PDN representation.

1. Introduction

Debugging is an indispensable step in software development. A program error is a difference between a program's actual behavior and the behavior required by the specification of the program. A "bug" relative to an error is a cause of the error. A bug may cause more than one error, and also, an error may be caused by more than one bug. Debugging a program is the process of locating, analyzing, and ultimately correcting bugs in the program by reasoning about causal relationships between bugs and the errors which have been detected in the program. It begins with some

---

* This work is partly supported by The Ministry of Education, Science and Culture of Japan under Grant-in-Aid for Scientific Research (C) No. 04650319 and by a grant from The Kurata Foundation.

indication of the existence of an error, repeats the process of developing, verifying, and modifying hypotheses about the bug(s) causing the error until the location of the bug(s) is determined and the nature of the bug(s) is understood, then corrects the bug(s), and ends in a verification of the removal of the error [2,19]. In general, about 95% of effort in debugging has to be spent on locating and understanding bug(s) because once a bug is located and its nature is understood, its correction is often easy to do [19]. Therefore, the most important problem in debugging is how to know which statements possibly and/or actually cause the erroneous behavior of a program.

Debugging a concurrent program is more difficult than debugging a sequential program because a concurrent program has multiple control flows, multiple data flows, and interprocess synchronization, communication, and nondeterministic selection. Almost all current debugging methods and tools for concurrent programs only provide programmers with facilities to extract some information from programs and display it in textual form or visual form, but no facilities to support the localization, analysis, and correction of bugs in an automatic or semi-automatic manner. Until now, there is no systematic method proposed and studied for bug location and analysis in debugging concurrent programs [8,11,18]. In order to satisfy the needs from the growing development and use of concurrent systems, it is urgent to establish a systematic and elegant debugging method for concurrent programs.

Program dependences are dependence relationships holding between statements in a program that are determined by control flow and data flow in the program, and therefore, they can be used to represent the program's behavior. In the literature, there are two types of primary program dependences originally proposed and studied for optimization and parallelization of sequential programs, i.e., the control dependence and the data dependence [9,22]. Informally, a statement S is control-dependent on the control predicate C of a conditional branch statement (e.g., an if statement or while statement) if the value of C determines whether S is executed or not. A statement S_2 is data-dependent on a statement S_1 if the value of a variable computed at S_1 directly or indirectly has influence on the value of a variable computed at S_2.

Statically slicing a program on a criterion, originally introduced by Weiser, is a source-to-source transformation method to automatically reduce a program, by analyzing control and data dependences in the program, into a minimal form, which is called a static slice of the original program, such that the reduced program will produce the behavior satisfying the criterion [23,24]. The method is useful in program debugging in the sense that slicing a program can certainly narrow the domain on which reasoning about causal relationship between errors and bugs in the program is performed [13,15,22-24].

Based on Weiser's work, a number of program slicing techniques have been proposed and studied for sequential programs. Ottenstein and Ottenstein showed that once a program is represented by its program dependence graph (PDG for short), which is an arc-classified digraph to explicitly represent control and data dependences in the program [9], the problem of statically slicing the program can be simply reduced to a vertex reachability problem in its PDG representation [20]. Horwitz, Reps, and Binkley introduced a program representation, called the "system dependence graph", for programs with procedures and procedure calls and showed an algorithm for interprocedural static slicing of a program based on its system dependence graph representation [12]. Korel and Laski introduced the notion of a "dynamic slice" and proposed a method to compute a dynamic slice of a program by solving data flow equations over an execution trace of the program [17]. Agrawal and Horgan introduced a program execution trace representation, called dynamic dependence graph, and showed a method to compute a dynamic slice of a program based on its dynamic dependence graph representation [1]. Kamkar, Shahmehri, and Fritzson introduced a program execution trace representation, called the "dynamic dependence summary graph" for programs with procedures and procedure calls, and showed an algorithm for interprocedural dynamic slicing of a program based on its dynamic dependence summary graph representation [14].

However, until recently, there is little program slicing method proposed and studied for concurrent programs. The present author 1991 introduced a program representation, called "Process Dependence Net" for concurrent programs and discussed its various possible applications including slicing concurrent programs [3-5]. This is the first attempt to identify all primary program dependences in concurrent programs and represent them in a digraph for general applications. Duesterwald, Gupta, and Soffa introduced an execution trace representation, called the "distributed dependence graph" for distributed programs, and showed a parallel algorithm to compute dynamic slices of a distributed program based on its distributed dependence graph representation [10]. Korel and Ferguson also proposed a method to compute dynamic slices of a distributed Ada program by analyzing influences in and between multiple executed paths of the program [16].

This paper can be regarded as a further refinement and improvement to the author's some early work. The paper extends the notion of slicing to concurrent programs and presents a graph-theoretical approach to slicing concurrent programs. In addition to the usual control and data dependences proposed and studied for sequential programs, this paper introduces three new types of primary program dependences in concurrent programs, named the "selection dependence", "synchronization dependence", and "communication dependence", and a new program representation for concurrent programs, named the "Process Dependence

Net" (PDN for short), which is an arc-classified digraph to explicitly represent the five types of primary program dependences in the programs. As a result, various notions about slicing concurrent programs can be formally defined based on the representation, and the problem of slicing a concurrent program can be simply reduced to a vertex reachability problem in its PDN representation.

The rest of this paper is organized as follows: Section 2 give some informal definitions about slicing concurrent programs, Section 3 introduces two program representations, named the "nondeterministic parallel control-flow net" and "nondeterministic parallel definition-use net", for representing multiple control flows and multiple data flows in concurrent programs, Section 4 defines the five types of primary program dependences in a concurrent program formally based on its nondeterministic parallel control-flow and/or definition-use nets, Section 5 presents the PDN, defines those notions about slicing concurrent programs formally based on the PDN, and shows applications of the PDN to slicing concurrent programs.

2. Various Slices of Concurrent Programs

A major observation and/or belief underlying the author's work on automated debugging is that if we have sufficient information about a program, its specification, and an execution of it where an error is detected, then, in principle, we should be able to debug the program by analyzing the error and reasoning about bug(s) caused the error based on the information and our knowledge and experiences without totally or partially executing the program time after time. The author considers that there are three key issues in automated debugging : (1) how to acquire, represent, and organize general knowledge about debugging in a general-purpose debugging system, (2) how to identify and capture sufficient information for a debugging problem, and (3) how to effectively and efficiently use the knowledge and information by automated reasoning to find bugs or plausible candidates of bugs.

Based on the above consideration, this paper focuses its attention on whether or not a slice of a concurrent program is adequate to a debugging problem rather than whether or not a slice of a concurrent program is executable.

We give some informal definitions about slicing concurrent programs as follows.

A *static slicing criterion* of a concurrent program is a 2-tuple (s,V), where s is a statement in the program and V is a set of variables used at s. The *static slice* SS(s,V) of a concurrent program on a given static slicing criterion (s,V) consists of all statements in the program that possibly affect the beginning or end of execution of s and/or affect the values of variables in V at s. *Statically slicing* a concurrent program on a given static slicing criterion is to find the static slice of the program with respect to the criterion.

Note that there is a difference between the notion of program slice given above for concurrent programs and that given in the literature for sequential programs, i.e., the above definition includes a condition on the beginning or end of execution of s, and therefore, it is meaningful even if V is the empty set. This makes the notion useful in analysis of synchronization errors in concurrent programs such as deadlocks and livelocks.

A *dynamic slicing criterion* of a concurrent program is a quadruplet (s,V,H,I), where s is a statement in the program, V is a set of variables used at s, and H is a history of an execution of the program with input I. The *dynamic slice* DS(s,V,H,I) of a concurrent program on a given dynamic slicing criterion (s,V,H,I) consists of all statements in the program that actually affected the beginning or end of execution of s and/or affected the values of variables in V at s in the execution with I that produced H. *Dynamically slicing* a concurrent program on a given dynamic slicing criterion is to find the dynamic slice of the program with respect to the criterion.

Note that for a concurrent program, two different executions with the same input may produce different behavior and histories because of unpredictable rates of processes and existence of nondeterministic selection statements in the program [6]. This is the reason why we define the notion of dynamic slicing criterion using a specified execution history H of a concurrent program with an input I.

In debugging a concurrent program, once we found a bug or a plausible candidate of bug, in order to avoid that some new bugs are introduced in debugging the old bug, we often want to know that correcting the bug or candidate will affect which piece of the program, i.e., we want to know which statements in which processes would be affected by a statement if we modify it in debugging. The needs leads us to define some notions about forward-slicing concurrent programs as follows.

A *static forward-slicing criterion* of a concurrent program is a 2-tuple (s,V), where s is a statement in the program and V is a set of variables defined at s. The *static forward-slice* SFS(s,V) of a concurrent program on a given static forward-slicing criterion (s,V) consists of all statements in the program that would be affected by the beginning or end of execution of s and/or affected by the values of variables in V at s. *Statically forward-slicing* a concurrent program on a given static forward-slicing criterion is to find the static forward-slice of the program with respect to the criterion.

A *dynamic forward-slicing criterion* of a concurrent program is a quadruplet (s,V,H,I), where s is a statement in the program, V is a set of variables defined at s, and H is a history of an execution of the program with input I. The *dynamic forward-slice* **DFS(s,V,H,I)** of a concurrent program on a given dynamic forward-slicing criterion (s,V,H,I) consists of all statements in the program that are actually affected by the beginning or end of execution of s and/or affected by the values of variables in V at s in the execution with I that produced H. *Dynamically forward-slicing* a concurrent program on a given dynamic forward-slicing criterion is to find the dynamic forward-slice of the program with respect to the criterion.

3. Nondeterministic Parallel Control-Flow and Definition-Use Nets

We now introduce the nondeterministic parallel control-flow net and nondeterministic parallel definition-use net for representing multiple control flows and multiple data flows in concurrent programs.

Definition 3.1 A *digraph* is an ordered pair (V, A), where V is a finite set of elements, called *vertices*, and A is a finite set of elements of the Cartesian product $V \times V$, called *arcs*, i.e., $A \subseteq V \times V$ is a binary relation on V. For any arc $(v_1, v_2) \in A$, v_1 is called the *initial vertex* of the arc and said to be *adjacent to* v_2, and v_2 is called the *terminal vertex* of the arc and said to be *adjacent from* v_1. A *predecessor* of a vertex v is a vertex adjacent to v, and a *successor* of v is a vertex adjacent from v. The *in-degree* of a vertex v, denoted in-degree(v), is the number of predecessors of v, and the *out-degree* of a vertex v, denoted out-degree(v), is the number of successors of v. A *simple digraph* is a digraph (V, A) such that $(v,v) \notin A$ for any $v \in V$. □

Definition 3.2 An *arc-classified digraph* is an n-tuple $(V, A_1, A_2, ..., A_{n-1})$ such that every (V, A_i) $(i=1, ..., n-1)$ is a digraph and $A_i \cap A_j = \Phi$ for $i=1, 2, ..., n-1$ and $j=1, 2, ..., n-1$. A *simple arc-classified digraph* is an arc-classified digraph $(V, A_1, A_2, ..., A_{n-1})$ such that $(v,v) \notin A_i$ $(i=1, ..., n-1)$ for any $v \in V$. □

Definition 3.3 A *path* in a digraph (V, A) or an arc-classified digraph $(V, A_1, A_2, ..., A_{n-1})$ is a sequence of arcs $(a_1, a_2, ..., a_\ell)$ such that the terminal vertex of a_i is the initial vertex of a_{i+1} for $1 \le i \le \ell-1$, where $a_i \in A$ $(1 \le i \le \ell)$ or $a_i \in A_1 \cup A_2 \cup ... \cup A_{n-1}$ $(1 \le i \le \ell)$, and ℓ $(\ell \ge 1)$ is called the *length* of the path. If the initial vertex of a_1 is v_I and the terminal vertex of a_ℓ is v_T, then the path is called a path from v_I to v_T, or v_I-v_T path for short. □

Definition 3.4 A *nondeterministic parallel control-flow net* (CFN for short) is a 10-tuple $(V, N, P_F, P_J, A_C, A_N, A_{P_F}, A_{P_J}, s, t)$, where $(V, A_C, A_N, A_{P_F}, A_{P_J})$ is a simple arc-classified digraph such that $A_C \subseteq V \times V$, $A_N \subseteq N \times V$, $A_{P_F} \subseteq P_F \times V$, $A_{P_J} \subseteq V \times P_J$, $N \subseteq V$ is a set of elements, called *nondeterministic selection vertices*, $P_F \subseteq V$ $(N \cap P_F = \Phi)$ is a set of elements, called *parallel execution fork vertices*, $P_J \subseteq V$ $(N \cap P_J = \Phi$, and $P_F \cap P_J = \Phi)$ is a set of elements, called *parallel execution join vertices*, $s \in V$ is a unique vertex, called *start vertex*, such that in-degree(s) = 0, $t \in V$ is a unique vertex, called *termination vertex*, such that out-degree(t) = 0 and $t \neq s$, and for any $v \in V$ ($v \neq s$, $v \neq t$), there exists at least one path from s to v and at least one path from v to t. Any arc $(v_1, v_2) \in A_C$ is called a *sequential control arc*, any arc $(v_1, v_2) \in A_N$ is called a *nondeterministic selection arc*, and any arc $(v_1, v_2) \in A_{P_F} \cup A_{P_J}$ is called a *parallel execution arc*. $\square$

A usual (deterministic and sequential) control flow graph can be regarded as a special case of CFN where N, P_F, P_J, A_N, A_{P_F}, and A_{P_J} are the empty set. A CFN can be used to represent the single control flow and/or multiple control flows in a sequential and/or concurrent program written in an imperative programming language such as C, Pascal, Ada, and Occam 2.

Definition 3.5 Let u and v be any two vertices in a CFN. u *forward dominates* v iff every path from v to t contains u; u *properly forward dominates* v iff u forward dominates v and $u \neq v$; u *strongly forward dominates* v iff u forward dominates v and there exists an integer k ($k \geq 1$) such that every path from v to t whose length is greater than or equal to k contains u; u is called the *immediate forward dominator* of v iff u is the first vertex that properly forward dominates v in every path from v to t; u is called the *last continuous forward dominator* of v iff u is the vertex such that any vertex in the path from v to u forward dominates v but a successor of u does not forward dominate v. $\square$

Definition 3.6 A *nondeterministic parallel definition-use net* (DUN for short) is a 7-tuple (N_C, Σ_V, D, U, Σ_C, S, R), where $N_C = (V, N, P_F, P_J, A_C, A_N, A_{P_F}, A_{P_J}, s, t)$ is a CFN, Σ_V is a finite set of symbols, called *variables*, $D: V \rightarrow P(\Sigma_V)$ and $U: V \rightarrow P(\Sigma_V)$ are two partial functions from V to the power set of Σ_V, Σ_C is a finite set of symbols, called *channels*, and $S: V \rightarrow \Sigma_C$ and $R: V \rightarrow \Sigma_C$ are two partial functions from V to Σ_C. $\square$

A usual (deterministic and sequential) definition-use graph can be regarded as a special case of DUN such that N, P_F, P_J, A_N, A_{P_F}, A_{P_J}, Σ_C, S, and R are the empty set. A DUN can be regarded as a CFN with the information concerning definitions and uses of variables and communication channels.

Note that the above definitions of CFN and DUN are graph-theoretical, and therefore, they are independent of any programming language.

We are developing a general-purpose system working on UNIX to compile target programs written in various imperative programming languages (at present, including C, Pascal, Ada, and Occam 2) into their CFN and DUN representations in textual forms [7]. Because of the limitation, here we do not discuss how to transform a program into its CFN and DUN representations.

As an example, Fig. 1 shows a fragment of Occam 2 program and Fig. 2 shows an arc-classified digraph representation of the DUN of the program.

```
1      PAR
2         SEQ
3            input1 ? x; y
4            IF
5               (x<0) OR (y<0)
6                  error1 ! 14 :: "minus operator"
7                  ce ! 0.0
8               y=0
9                  error1 ! 11 :: "zero divide"
10                 ce ! 0.0
11              TRUE
12                 c ! x/y
13        SEQ
14           input2 ? n
15           sum := 0
16           WHILE n<>0
17              input2 ? data
18              sum, n := sum+data, n-1
19           ALT
20              c ? factor
21                 result ! sum*factor
22              ce ? factor
23                 error2 ! 14 :: "invalid factor"
24     STOP
```

Fig. 1 A fragment of Occam 2 program

4. Primary Program Dependences in Concurrent Programs

In general, a concurrent program consists of a number of processes, and therefore, it has multiple control flows and multiple data flows. These control flows and data flows are not independent because of the existence of interprocess synchronization among multiple control flows and interprocess communication among multiple data flows in the program. Moreover, a process in a concurrent program may nondeterministically select a communication partner among a number of processes ready for communication with the process. It is obvious that only using the usual control and data dependences proposed and studied for sequential programs is inadequate for representing the complete behavior of a concurrent program. In order to slice concurrent programs by analyzing various dependences in the programs and construct slices of a concurrent program that includes sufficient information for debugging the program, we must identify all primary program dependences in concurrent programs at first.

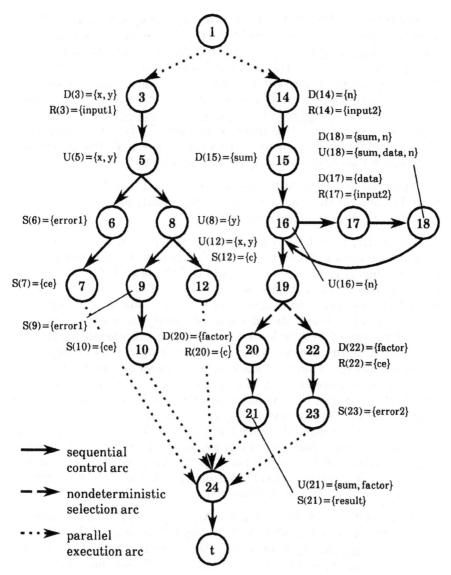

Fig. 2 An arc-classified digraph representation of
the DUN of the program of Fig. 1

In addition to the usual control and data dependences, we now introduce three new types of primary program dependences in concurrent programs, named the *selection dependence*, *synchronization dependence*, and *communication dependence*, which are determined by interaction between multiple control flows and multiple data flows in the programs. Based on the CFN and/or DUN of a concurrent program, we can define various types of primary program dependences in the program as follows.

Definition 4.1 Let $(V, N, P_F, P_J, A_C, A_N, Ap_F, Ap_J, s, t)$ be the CFN of a concurrent program, and $u \in V$, $v \in ((V - (N \cup P_F \cup P_J))$ be any two vertices of the net. u is *directly strongly control-dependent* on v iff there exists a path $P = (v_1 = v, v_2), (v_2, v_3), ..., (v_{n-1}, v_n = u)$ from v to u such that P does not contain the immediate forward dominator of v and there exists no vertex v' in P such that the path from v' to u does not contain the immediate forward dominator of v'. u is *directly weakly control-dependent* on v iff v has two successors v' and v" such that there exists a path $P = (v_1 = v, v_2), (v_2, v_3), ...,$ $(v_{n-1}, v_n = u)$ from v to u and any vertex v_i $(1 < i \leq n)$ in P strongly forward dominates v' but does not strongly forward dominate v". $\square$

Note that according to the above definition, if u is directly strongly control-dependent on v, then u is also directly weakly control-dependent on v, but the converse is not necessarily true.

Informally, if u is directly strongly control-dependent on v, then v must have at least two successors v' and v" such that if the branch from v to v' is executed then u must be executed, while if the branch from v to v" is executed then u may not be executed. If u is directly weakly control-dependent on v, then v must have two successors v' and v" such that if the branch from v to v' is executed then u is necessarily executed within a fixed number of steps, while if the branch from v to v" is executed then u may not be executed or the execution of u may be delayed indefinitely. The difference between strong and weak control dependences is that the latter reflects a dependence between an exit condition of a loop and a statement outside the loop that may be executed after the loop is exited, but the former does not. For example, in Fig. 2, vertices v_6, v_7, and v_8 are directly strongly (weakly) control-dependent on vertex v_5, vertices v_9, v_{10}, and v_{12} are directly strongly (weakly) control-dependent on vertex v_8, vertices v_{17}, v_{18}, and v_{16} are directly strongly (weakly) control-dependent on vertex v_{16}, and vertex v_{19} is directly weakly control-dependent on vertex v_{16} but not directly strongly control-dependent on v_{16}.

Definition 4.2 Let $(V, N, P_F, P_J, A_C, A_N, Ap_F, Ap_J, s, t)$ be the CFN of a concurrent program, and $u \in V$, $v \in N$ be any two vertices of the net. u is *directly selection-dependent* on v iff (1) there exists a path $P = (v_1 = v, v_2)$, $(v_2, v_3), ..., (v_{n-1}, v_n = u)$ from v to u such that P does not contain the immediate forward dominator of v, and (2) there exists no vertex v_i $(1 < i < n)$ in P such that the path from v_i to u does not contain the immediate forward dominator of v_i. $\square$

Informally, if u is directly selection-dependent on v, then v must have some successors such that if the branch from v to one of the successors is executed then u must be executed, while if another branch is executed then u may not be executed. For example, in Fig. 2, vertices $v_{20} \sim v_{23}$ are directly selection-dependent on vertex v_{19}.

The difference between the direct (strong or weak) control dependence and the direct selection dependence is that the former defines a kind of program dependence holding between the control predicate of a conditional branch statement and a statement whether it is executed is determined by the truth value of the control predicate, but the latter defines a kind of program dependence holding between a nondeterministic selection statement and a statement whether it is executed is determined by the nondeterministic selection.

Definition 4.3 Let $(N_C, \Sigma_V, D, U, \Sigma_C, S, R)$ be the DUN of a concurrent program, and u and v be any two vertices of the net. u is _directly data-dependent_ on v iff there is a path $P = (v_1 = v, v_2), (v_2, v_3), ..., (v_{n-1}, v_n = u)$ from v to u such that $(D(v) \cap U(u)) - D(P') \neq \Phi$ where $D(P') = D(v_2) \cup ... \cup D(v_{n-1})$. □

Informally, if u is directly data-dependent on v, then the value of a variable computed at v directly has influence on the value of a variable computed at u. For example, in Fig. 2, vertices v_5, v_8, and v_{12} are directly data-dependent on vertex v_3, vertices v_{16} and v_{18} are directly data-dependent on vertices v_{14} and v_{18}, vertex v_{18} is directly data-dependent on vertices v_{15} and v_{17}, and vertex v_{21} is directly data-dependent on vertices v_{18} and v_{20}.

There are some efficient algorithms to compute the control and data dependences in a sequential program based on the control flow graph of the program [21]. Those algorithms can be modified to compute the control, selection, and data dependences in a concurrent program based on the DUN of the program [7].

Definition 4.4 Let $(N_C, \Sigma_V, D, U, \Sigma_C, S, R)$ be the DUN of a concurrent program, where N_C is the CFN $(V, N, P_F, P_J, A_C, A_N, A_{P_F}, A_{P_J}, s, t)$ of the program, and u and v be any two vertices of the net. u is _directly synchronization-dependent_ on v iff any of the following conditions holds :

1) $(v,u) \in A_{P_F} \cup A_{P_J}$, i.e., (v,u) is a parallel execution arc,

2) $S(v) = R(u)$, or

3) there exists a vertex v' such that v' is directly synchronization-dependent on v, u is the last continuous forward dominator of v', and $S(v'') = \Phi$ and $R(v'') = \Phi$ for any vertex v" (excluding v') in the path from v' to u. □

Informally, if u is directly synchronization-dependent on v, then the start and/or termination of execution of v directly determines whether or not the execution of u starts and/or terminates. For example, in Fig. 2, vertices v_3, v_5, v_{14}, v_{15}, and v_{16} are directly synchronization-dependent on vertex v_1, vertex v_{20} is directly synchronization-dependent on vertex v_{12}, vertex v_{22} is directly synchronization-dependent on vertices v_7 and v_{10}, and vertex v_{24} is directly synchronization-dependent on vertices v_7, v_{10}, v_{12}, v_{21}, and v_{23}.

The difference between the direct (strong or weak) control dependence and the direct synchronization dependence is that the former is irrelevant to the execution timing of a program but the latter is intrinsically relevant to the execution timing.

Definition 4.5 Let $(N_C, \Sigma_V, D, U, \Sigma_C, S, R)$ be the DUN of a concurrent program, and u and v be any two vertices of the net. u is _directly communication-dependent_ on v iff there exist two vertices v' and v" such that u is directly data-dependent on v', $R(v') = S(v")$, and v" is directly data-dependent on v. $\square$

Informally, if u is directly communication-dependent on v, then the value of a variable computed at v directly has influence on the value of a variable computed at u by an interprocess communication. For example, in Fig. 2, vertex v_{21} is directly communication-dependent on vertex v_3.

The difference between the direct data dependence and the direct communication dependence is that the direct data dependence is irrelevant to communication channels of a program but the direct communication dependence is intrinsically relevant to the channels.

5. Process Dependence Net and Concurrent Program Slicing

We now introduce the Process Dependence Net for representing the five types of primary program dependences in concurrent programs.

Definition 5.1 The _Process Dependence Net_ (PDN for short) of a concurrent program is an arc-classified digraph (**V**, **Con**, **Sel**, **Dat**, **Syn**, **Com**), where **V** is the vertex set of the CFN of the program, **Con** is the set of control dependence arcs such that any $(u,v) \in$ **Con** iff u is directly weakly control-dependent on v, **Sel** is the set of selection dependence arcs such that any $(u,v) \in$ **Sel** iff u is directly selection-dependent on v, **Dat** is the set of data dependence arcs such that any $(u,v) \in$ **Dat** iff u is directly data-dependent on v, **Syn** is the set of synchronization-dependent arcs such that any $(u,v) \in$ **Syn** iff u is directly synchronization-dependent on v, and **Com** is the set of communication dependence arcs such that any $(u,v) \in$ **Com** iff u is directly communication-dependent on v. $\square$

A usual program dependence graph for sequential programs can be regarded as a special case of PDN. As an example, Fig. 3 shows an arc-classified digraph representation of the PDN of the Occam 2 program shown in Fig. 1.

Since program dependences in a program are implied by control and data flows in the program, an explicit representation of these program dependences is available only if we have some methods and tools to compute them by analyzing control and data flows in the program and then represent them in some form for general use. We are developing a general-purpose system working on UNIX to compile target programs written in various programming languages (at present, including C, Pascal, Ada, and Occam 2) into their PDN representations in textual forms [7].

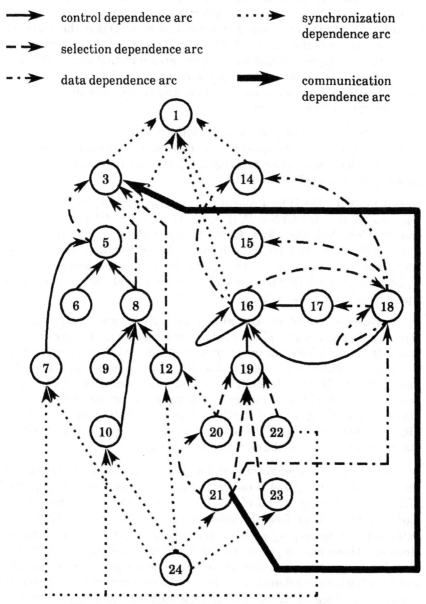

Fig. 3 An arc-classified digraph representation of
the PDN of the program of Fig. 1

We can also consider a representation of a concurrent program, named the "Process Influence Net", as a "reverse" of the PDN of that program.

Definition 5.2 The *Process Influence Net* (PIN for short) of a concurrent program is an arc-classified digraph (**V, Con, Sel, Dat, Syn, Com**), where **V** is the vertex set of the CFN of the program, **Con** is the set of control influence arcs such that any $(u,v) \in$ **Con** iff v is directly weakly control-dependent on u, **Sel** is the set of selection influence arcs such that any $(u,v) \in$ **Sel** iff v is directly selection-dependent on u, **Dat** is the set of data influence arcs such that any $(u,v) \in$ **Dat** iff v is directly data-dependent on u, **Syn** is the set of synchronization influence arcs such that any $(u,v) \in$ **Syn** iff v is directly synchronization-dependent on u, and **Com** is the set of communication influence arcs such that any $(u,v) \in$ **Com** iff v is directly communication-dependent on u. $\square$

In Section 2, we have informally defined some notions about slicing concurrent programs. Now, having the PDN and PIN as dependence-based representations of concurrent programs, we can formally refine those notions based on the PDN and PIN.

Definition 5.3 Let P be a concurrent program, $(V, N, P_F, P_J, A_C, A_N, A_{P_F}, A_{P_J}, s, t)$ be the CFN of P, $(N_C, \Sigma_V, D, U, \Sigma_C, S, R)$ be the DUN of P, and (V, Con, Sel, Dat, Syn, Com) be the PDN of P. A *static slicing criterion* of P is a 2-tuple (s,V) such that $s \in V$ and V = U(s). The *static slice* SS(s,V) of P on a given static slicing criterion (s,V) is a subset of vertices of **V**, SS(s,V)$\subseteq$V, such that for any $v \in V$, $v \in$ SS(s,V) if and only if there exists a path from s to v in the PDN. $\square$

Obviously, based on the above definition, statically slicing a concurrent program on a given static slicing criterion, which is defined as to find the static slice of the program with respect to the criterion, is simply a vertex reachability problem in the PDN of the program. Therefore, having the PDN as a dependence-based representation of concurrent programs, the problem of statically slicing a concurrent program can be easily solved using a usual depth-first or breadth-first graph traversal algorithm to traverse the PDN representation of the program by taking the statement of interest as the start point of traversal.

For a concurrent program P and a given static slicing criterion (s,V), the static slice SS(s,V) of P consists of all statements in P that possibly affect the beginning or end of execution of s and/or affect the values of variables in V. Therefore, the information included in SS(s,V) should be sufficient to a debugging problem concerning s and variables used at s. However, there may be, of course, many statements in SS(s,V) that are completely irrelevant to the error being debugged. For example, a synchronization error detected at s may be independent of those statements included in SS(s,V) as the result of analyzing data dependence. In debugging a concurrent program, having a "partial and/or special" slice of the program rather than a "total and/or general" slice is often more convenient for us to effectively and efficiently debug the program. The above discussion leads us to define some kinds of special static slices of a concurrent program as follows.

Definition 5.4 Let (**V, Con, Sel, Dat, Syn, Com**) be a PDN. A path is called a *control-dependent path* if $(u,v) \in$ **Con** for any arc (u,v) in the path; a path is called a *selection-dependent path* if $(u,v) \in$ **Sel** for any arc (u,v) in the path; a path is called a *data-dependent path* if $(u,v) \in$ **Dat** for any arc (u,v) in the path; a path is called a *synchronization-dependent path* if $(u,v) \in$ **Syn** for any arc (u,v) in the path; a path is called a *communication-dependent path* if $(u,v) \in$ **Com** for any arc (u,v) in the path. $\square$

Definition 5.5 Let P be a concurrent program and (**V, Con, Sel, Dat, Syn, Com**) be the PDN of P. The *control-dependent static slice* **Con-SS**(s,V) of P on a given static slicing criterion (s,V) is a subset of vertices of **V**, **Con-SS**$(s,V) \subseteq V$, such that for any $v \in V$, $v \in$ **Con-SS**(s,V) if and only if there exists a control-dependent path from s to v in the PDN; the *selection-dependent static slice* **Sel-SS**(s,V) of P on a given static slicing criterion (s,V) is a subset of vertices of **V**, **Sel-SS**$(s,V) \subseteq V$, such that for any $v \in V$, $v \in$ **Sel-SS**(s,V) if and only if there exists a selection-dependent path from s to v in the PDN; the *data-dependent static slice* **Dat-SS**(s,V) of P on a given static slicing criterion (s,V) is a subset of vertices of **V**, **Dat-SS**$(s,V) \subseteq V$, such that for any $v \in V$, $v \in$ **Dat-SS**(s,V) if and only if there exists a data-dependent path from s to v in the PDN; the *synchronization-dependent static slice* **Syn-SS**(s,V) of P on a given static slicing criterion (s,V) is a subset of vertices of **V**, **Syn-SS**$(s,V) \subseteq V$, such that for any $v \in V$, $v \in$ **Syn-SS**(s,V) if and only if there exists a synchronization-dependent path from s to v in the PDN; the *communication-dependent static slice* **Com-SS**(s,V) of P on a given static slicing criterion (s,V) is a subset of vertices of **V**, **Com-SS**$(s,V) \subseteq V$, such that for any $v \in V$, $v \in$ **Com-SS**(s,V) if and only if there exists a communication-dependent path from s to v in the PDN. $\square$

Obviously, for any concurrent program and any given static slicing criterion (s,V), the following holds: **SS**$(s,V) =$ **Con-SS**$(s,V) \cup$ **Sel-SS**$(s,V) \cup$ **Dat-SS**$(s,V) \cup$ **Syn-SS**$(s,V) \cup$ **Com-SS**(s,V).

Moreover, some other kinds of special static slices also can be considered. For example, a static slice that is a combination of some kinds of the above special static slices, a static slice that only concerns a subset of variables used at a statement of interest rather than all variables used at the statement, a static slice that only concerns a subset of processes in a program rather than all process in the program, and so on. More detailed discussion on these topics is beyond the scope of this paper.

A dynamic slice of a concurrent program now can be formally defined as a subset of the corresponding static slice of the program as follows.

Definition 5.6 Let P be a concurrent program, $(V, N, P_F, P_J, A_C, A_N, A_{P_F}, A_{P_J}, s, t)$ be the CFN of P, $(N_C, \Sigma_V, D, U, \Sigma_C, S, R)$ be the DUN of P, and $(V, Con, Sel, Dat, Syn, Com)$ be the PDN of P. A *dynamic slicing criterion* of P is a quadruplet (s,V,H,I) such that $s \in V$, $V = U(s)$, and $H \subseteq V$ is a subset of V which includes all actually executed statements in an execution of P with input I. The *dynamic slice* $DS(s,V,H,I)$ of P on a given dynamic slicing criterion (s,V,H,I) is a subset of static slice $SS(s,V)$, $DS(s,V,H,I) \subseteq SS(s,V)$, such that for any $v \in SS(s,V)$, $v \in DS(s,V,H,I)$ if and only if there exists a path from s to v in the PDN and $u \in H$ for any vertex u in the path. $\square$

It is trivial to compute a dynamic slice of a concurrent program based on the corresponding static slice of the program and the program's execution history information that can be collected by an execution monitor.

We can also define various special dynamic slices of a concurrent program similar to those special static slices of the program.

Those notions about statically and dynamically forward-slicing concurrent programs can be formally refined based on the PIN as follows.

Definition 5.7 Let P be a concurrent program, $(V, N, P_F, P_J, A_C, A_N, A_{P_F}, A_{P_J}, s, t)$ be the CFN of P, $(N_C, \Sigma_V, D, U, \Sigma_C, S, R)$ be the DUN of P, and $(V, Con, Sel, Dat, Syn, Com)$ be the PIN of P. A *static forward-slicing criterion* of P is a 2-tuple (s,V) such that $s \in V$ and $V = D(s)$. The *static forward-slice* $SFS(s,V)$ of P on a given static forward-slicing criterion (s,V) is a subset of vertices of V, $SFS(s,V) \subseteq V$, such that for any $v \in V$, $v \in SFS(s,V)$ if and only if there exists a path from s to v in the PIN. $\square$

Definition 5.8 Let P be a concurrent program, $(V, N, P_F, P_J, A_C, A_N, A_{P_F}, A_{P_J}, s, t)$ be the CFN of P, $(N_C, \Sigma_V, D, U, \Sigma_C, S, R)$ be the DUN of P, and $(V, Con, Sel, Dat, Syn, Com)$ be the PIN of P. A *dynamic forward-slicing criterion* of P is a quadruplet (s,V,H,I) such that $s \in V$, $V = D(s)$, and $H \subseteq V$ is a subset of V which includes all actually executed statements in an execution of P with input I. The *dynamic forward-slice* $DFS(s,V,H,I)$ of P on a given dynamic forward-slicing criterion (s,V,H,I) is a subset of static forward-slice $SFS(s,V)$, $DFS(s,V,H,I) \subseteq SFS(s,V)$, such that for any $v \in SFS(s,V)$, $v \in DFS(s,V,H,I)$ if and only if there exists a path from s to v in the PIN and $u \in H$ for any vertex u in the path. $\square$

It is obvious that once a concurrent program is represented by its PIN, the problem of statically forward-slicing the program is simply a vertex reachability problem in the net, which can be easily solved using a usual depth-first or breadth-first graph traversal algorithm to traverse the net by taking the statement of interest as the start point of traversal, and the problem of dynamically forward-slicing the program can be reduced to the vertex reachability problem in the net with the program's execution history information.

6. Concluding Remarks

We have introduced three new types of primary program dependences in concurrent programs and some new program representations for concurrent programs. We also defined some general notions about slicing concurrent programs and showed that once a concurrent program is represented by its dependence-based representations, the problem of slicing the program is simply a vertex reachability problem in the representations which can be easily solved using a usual graph traversal algorithm to traverse the representations by taking the statement of interest as the start point of traversal.

Static and dynamic slicing are useful in debugging concurrent programs because they can be used to find all statements that possibly or actually caused the erroneous behavior of an execution of a concurrent program where an error occurs. A static slice $SS(s,V)$ covers all statements might cause the error occurred at statement s, i.e., all "possible candidates" of bugs. A dynamic slice $DS(s,V,H,I)$ covers all statements actually caused the error occurred at statement s in the execution, i.e., all "actual candidates" of bugs. Therefore, we can say that slicing a concurrent program can certainly narrow the domain on which reasoning about causal relationship between errors and bugs in the program is performed.

However, static and dynamic slices of a concurrent program only cover those "candidates" of bugs but neither locate the bugs nor give some hints on the nature of the bugs. In order to provide programmers with some automatic or semi-automatic manner for bug localization, analysis, and correction in concurrent program debugging, it is necessary to develop more powerful debugging methods and tools.

Acknowledgements

I am grateful to the anonymous referees and Prof. Peter Fritzson for their helpful comments on early drafts of this paper, to Dr. Mariam Kamkar for sending me the paper by Duesterwald, Gupta, and Soffa before this workshop, and to Prof. Bogdan Korel for showing me the paper by himself and Ferguson at the workshop.

References

[1] H. Agrawal and J. R. Horgan, "Dynamic Program Slicing", Proc. ACM SIGPLAN'90, pp.246-256, June 1990.

[2] K. Araki, Z. Furukawa, and J. Cheng, "A General Framework for Debugging", IEEE-CS Software, Vol.8, No.3, pp.14-20, 1991.

[3] J. Cheng, "Process Dependence Net: A Concurrent Program Representation", Proc. JSSST 8th Conference, pp.513-516, September 1991.

[4] J. Cheng, "Task Dependence Net as a Representation for Concurrent Ada Programs", in J. van Katwijk (ed.), "Ada: Moving towards 2000", LNCS, Vol.603, pp.150-164, Springer-Verlag, June 1992.

[5] J. Cheng, "The Tasking Dependence Net in Ada Software Development", ACM Ada Letters, Vol.12, No.4, pp.24-35, 1992.

[6] J. Cheng and K. Ushijima, "Partial Order Transparency as a Tool to Reduce Interference in Monitoring Concurrent Systems", in Y. Ohno (ed.), "Distributed Environments", pp.156-171, Springer-Verlag, 1991.

[7] J. Cheng, Y. Kasahara, M. Kamachi, Y. Nomura, and K. Ushijima, "Compiling Programs to Their Dependence-Based Representations", Proc. 1993 IEEE Region 10 International Conference on Computer, Communication and Automation, to appear, October 1993.

[8] W. H. Cheung, J. P. Black, and E. Manning, "A Framework for Distributed Debugging", IEEE-CS Software, Vol.7, No.1, pp.106-115, 1990.

[9] J. Ferrante, K. J. Ottenstein, and J. D. Warren, "The Program Dependence Graph and Its Use in Optimization", ACM Transactions on Programming Languages and Systems, Vol.9, No.3, pp.319-349, 1987.

[10] E. Duesterwald, R. Gupta, and M. L. Soffa, "Distributed Slicing and Partial Re-execution for Distributed Programs", Proc. 5th Workshop on Languages and Compilers for Parallel Computing, pp.329-337, August 1992.

[11] G. S. Goldszmidt, S. Temini, and S. Katz, "High-Level Language Debugging for Concurrent Programs", ACM Transactions on Computer Systems, Vol.8, No.4, pp.311-336, 1990.

[12] S. Horwitz, T. Reps, and D. Binkley, "Interprocedural Slicing Using Dependence Graphs", ACM Transactions on Programming Languages and Systems, Vol.12, No.1, pp.26-60, 1990.

[13] M. Kamkar, N. Shahmehri, and P. Fritzson, "Bug Localization by Algorithmic Debugging and Program Slicing", Proc. PLILP '90, LNCS, Vol.456, pp.60-74, Springer-Verlag, August 1990.

[14] M. Kamkar, N. Shahmehri, and P. Fritzson, "Interprocedural Dynamic Slicing", Proc. PLILP '92, LNCS, Vol.631, pp.370-371, Springer-Verlag, August 1992.

[15] B. Korel, "PELAS – Program Error-Locating Assistant System", IEEE-CS Transactions on Software Engineering, Vol.14, No.9, pp.1253-1260, 1988.

[16] B. Korel and R. Ferguson, "Dynamic Slicing of Distributed Programs", Appl. Math. and Comp. Sci., Vol.2, No.2, pp.199-215, 1992.

[17] B. Korel and J. Laski, "Dynamic Program Slicing", Information Processing Letters, Vol.29, No.10, pp.155-163, 1988.

[18] C. E. McDowell and D. P. Helmbold, "Debugging Concurrent Programs", ACM Computing Surveys, Vol.21, No.4, pp.593-622, 1989.

[19] G. J. Myers, "The Art of Software Testing", John Wiley & Sons, 1979.

[20] K. J. Ottenstein and L. M. Ottenstein, "The Program Dependence Graph in a Software Development Environment", ACM Software Engineering Notes, Vol.9, No.3, pp.177-184, 1984.

[21] K. J. Ottenstein and S. Ellcey, "Experience Compiling Fortran to Program Dependence Graphs", Software – Practice and Experience, Vol.22, No.1, pp.41-62, 1992.

[22] A. Podgurski and L. A. Clarke, "A Formal Model of Program Dependences and Its Implications for Software Testing, Debugging, and Maintenance", IEEE-CS Transactions on Software Engineering, Vol.16, No.9, pp.965-979, 1990.

[23] M. Weiser, "Programmers Use Slices When Debugging", Communications of ACM, Vol.25, No.7, pp.446-452, 1982.

[24] M. Weiser, "Program Slicing", IEEE-CS Transactions on Software Engineering, Vol.SE-10, No.4, pp.352-357, 1984.

Animators for Generated Programming Environments

Frank Tip*

CWI, P.O. Box 4079, 1009 AB Amsterdam, The Netherlands
tip@cwi.nl

Abstract. Animation of execution is a necessary feature of source-level debuggers. We present a framework where animators are *generated* from existing algebraic specifications of interpreters. To this end, a pattern-matching mechanism is used in conjunction with origin tracking, a generic tracing technique. The generation of animators is illustrated using an example language named CLaX, a Pascal relative. We study how our approach can be extended to the generation of source-level debuggers and algorithmic debuggers from specifications of interpreters.

1 Introduction

We study animators for generated programming environments. An *animator* is a tool which visualizes program execution; typically, it highlights the statement that is currently executing. Animators are especially useful for (automated) debugging and tutoring.

We use the ASF+SDF Meta-environment [14] to generate programming environments, consisting of syntax-directed editors, type-checkers, and interpreters, from algebraic specifications. Specifications are written in the formalism ASF+SDF, a combination of the Algebraic Specification Formalism ASF [4], and the Syntax Definition Formalism SDF [12]. Specifications can be executed in the ASF+SDF Meta-environment as term rewriting systems [15].

Instead of explicitly extending specifications with animation facilities, we *generate* animators from existing specifications of interpreters. We present a generic mechanism for defining animators, consisting of two parts. First, we define the *events* we are interested in. A typical example of such an event is the execution of a statement. Second, the *subjects* of the events, i.e., the language constructs involved, are determined. Events are defined by way of a pattern-matching mechanism. Origin tracking [9] is used for determining the subjects.

We illustrate our techniques using an example language named CLaX, a Pascal relative. In [10], the specification of a programming environment for this language is described in detail.

Finally, we study how our approach can be extended to the generation of source-level debuggers and algorithmic debuggers from specifications of interpreters. It is shown how, for CLaX, several debugger features can be defined.

---

* Partial support received from the European Communities under ESPRIT project 5399: Compiler Generation for Parallel Machines – COMPARE.

2 Related Work

Often, animation is dealt with in an ad-hoc manner, such as keeping track of line-numbers. Below, we discuss some generic approaches.

The program animation system PASTIS [16] allows the animation of Fortran, C, and C++ source code without requiring changes to the program. The system is built as an extension of the GNU source-level debugger, gdb [19]. This debugger sends program data to an animation server. *Visualization scripts* serve to determine which data is to be extracted from the program, and to which animators this data is to be sent. Information is represented by way of a relational model. *Animation scripts* define how information is to be visualized: both textual and graphical display of information is possible. Moreover, several animators can execute in parallel. The main difference with our approach is that PASTIS relies on the ad-hoc extension of a debugger. As a result, only languages that are supported by gdb can be supported by PASTIS. By contrast, we derive animators from specifications. This means that, at least in principle, we can support any language for which a specification is written.

In the context of the PSG system [3], a generator for language-specific debuggers was described in [2]. Language-specific compilers are generated by compiling denotational semantics definitions to a functional language. A standard, language-independent interpreter is used to execute the generated functional language fragments. Correspondences between the abstract syntax tree and the generated fragments are maintained during compilation. To define debuggers, a set of built-in debugging concepts is available. In particular, trace functions are provided for the visualization of execution. Other notions enable one to inspect the state of the interpreter, and to define breakpoints.

Bertot [6] contributes a technique called *subject tracking* to the specification language Typol [7, 13] for animation and debugging purposes. A key property of Typol specifications is that the meaning of a language construct is expressed in terms of its sub-constructs. A special variable, *Subject*, serves to indicate the language construct currently processed. This variable may be manipulated by the specification writer, when different animation or debugging behavior is required.

Berry [5] presents an approach where animators are generated from structured operational semantics definitions. These specifications are augmented with *semantic display rules* which determine how to perform animation when a particular semantic rule is being processed. Various views of the execution of a program can be obtained by defining the appropriate display rules. Static views consist of parts of the abstract syntax tree of a program, and dynamic views are constructed from the program state during execution. As an example of a dynamic view, the evaluation of a control predicate may be visualized as the actual truth value it obtains during execution.

Apart from differences in the underlying specification formalisms, there are two major differences between our approach and Berry's. First, we only consider the highlighting of the language construct which is currently being executed, whereas Berry also considers very advanced animation features such as dynamic call graphs, and reversible execution. The price he pays for this is the fact that he needs to store the entire evaluation history. This contrasts with our method which only involves a small linear run-time space overhead, and no global history at all. Second, Berry's Animator Generator generates animators as stand-alone tools, whereas our animators are smoothly integrated in the programming environments generated by the ASF+SDF system.

3 Specification of an Interpreter

Our example language, CLaX, features the following language concepts: types, type coercion, overloaded operators, arrays, procedures with reference and value parameters, nested scopes, assignment statements, loop statements, conditional statements, and goto statements. In Figure 1, an example of a CLaX program is shown.

```
PROGRAM example;
DECLARE
   i: INTEGER; j: INTEGER;

   PROCEDURE incr(in: INTEGER; VAR out: INTEGER);
   BEGIN { incr }
      out := in + 1;
   END    { incr }

BEGIN { example }
   i := 3;
   incr(i, j)
END.  { example }
```

Fig. 1. Example of a CLaX program.

The interpreter for CLaX is based on the well-known concept of a stack of activation records (see e.g., [1]). This stack contains one record for every procedure that is being executed. Each record contains the code of that procedure, a 'pointer' to the current statement, and a set of (references to) values defined in the procedure. In our specification, two distinct stacks are used to model the stack of activation records, allowing us to separate control flow issues from operations on the data:

- The *code stack* consists of zero or more code records, where each code record is a pair containing the name of the procedure, and a list of statements that remains to be executed.
- The *data stack* consists of zero or more data records, with each data record containing (i) the name of the procedure, (ii) scope information, (iii) label continuations, and (iv) a list of zero or more identifier-value pairs.

As an example, we consider the execution of the CLaX program of Figure 1. When the assignment statement in the procedure body is executed, the state looks as follows:

```
< [ incr, out := in + 1 ] [ example, incr(i, j) ],

  [ incr, 1, in : 3  out: ref(j, ) ]
  [ example, , i : 3  j : 0  incr : ··· ] >
```

The first line shows the code stack, containing two records: one for procedure incr, and one for the main program. The first of these records, [incr, out := in + 1] tells us that the current procedure is named incr, and that the list of statements that remains to be executed consists of the single statement out := in + 1. The second and third line show (parts of) the data stack. The first data record, [incr, 1, in : 3 out: ref(j,)] contains the value 3 for in; moreover, the value for out is a reference to the value of j in the next record.

The CLaX interpreter is invoked by applying a function eval-program to the abstract syntax tree (AST) of a program. First, an initial state is computed; then, a recursive evaluation function eval is repeatedly applied to the state. Applications of eval can be regarded as execution steps of the interpreter. These steps are: (i) the execution of a statement, (ii) the return from a procedure, and (iii) program termination (i.e., extraction of the values of global variables from the final state). The interpreter computes the following list of variable-value pairs for the example program of Figure 1:

```
i : 3   j : 4
```

To give an example of the flavor of the specification, Figure 2 shows equations [ev7] and [ev8] which define the execution of an IF-THEN-ELSE statement. Depending on the result of evaluating the predicate (by way of an auxiliary function eval-predicate, not shown here), the IF statement is replaced by the statements in either the THEN or in the ELSE branch. The complete specification of the CLaX interpreter consists of approximately 200 equations. Basic arithmetic operations and I/O are performed in Lisp.

Algebraic specifications can be executed as term rewriting systems [15]. A term rewriting system (TRS) is obtained from an algebraic specification by orienting the equations from left to right; such an oriented equation is referred to as a *rewrite rule*. Term rewriting is a cyclic process; it consists of the transformation of an initial term (in our setting: a function eval-program applied to the AST of a CLaX program) by repeatedly matching subterms against left-hand sides of rewrite rules. If a match succeeds, a reducible expression (*redex*) is established, and the variables in the rewrite rule obtain a binding. The redex is replaced by the instantiation of the right-hand side of the rewrite-rule, and the term rewriting process proceeds by looking for a new match. A rewriting process terminates when no more redexes can be found, the term is then said to be in *normal form*.

In the case of conditional TRSs, conditions have to be evaluated after a match has been found. A conditional rewrite rule is only applicable if all its conditions

[ev7] `eval-predicate(_Exp, _DStack)` = `TRUE`
===
    `eval( <[_Id, IF _Exp THEN _Stat*' ELSE _Stat*'' END; _Stat*]`
      `_CRec*, _DStack> )` =
    `eval( <[_Id, _Stat*';_Stat*] _CRec*, _DStack> )`

[ev8] `eval-predicate(_Exp, _DStack)` = `FALSE`
===
    `eval( <[_Id, IF _Exp THEN _Stat*' ELSE _Stat*'' END; _Stat*]`
      `_CRec*, _DStack> )` =
    `eval( <[_Id, _Stat*'';_Stat*] _CRec*, _DStack> )`

Fig. 2. Equations defining the execution of an IF-THEN-ELSE statement.

succeed. The evaluation of a condition consists of the instantiation and rewriting of the condition sides, and the comparison of the resulting normal forms.

4 Definition of Events

We mentioned that an application of `eval` corresponds to an execution step of the interpreter. This can be restated as follows: an execution step takes place when a redex *matches* the pattern eval(<[_Id, _Stat*] _CRec*, _DStack>). Here, the variables _Id, _Stat*, _CRec*, and _DStack match any identifier, any list of statements, any list of code records, and any data stack, respectively. Specific applications of `eval` can be recognized by specializations of this pattern. In particular, we propose that an application of `eval` corresponds to:

- *the execution of a statement* if the current code record contains *at least one* more statement which is to be executed. The corresponding pattern, **eval**(<[_Id, _Stat; _Stat*] _CRec*, _DStack>), is obtained by replacing _Stat* by the more specific list _Stat; _Stat* which matches *one* or more statements.
- *the return from a procedure* if the current code record contains no more code to be executed, and there is *more than one* record on the code stack. This event corresponds exactly to a match with the pattern eval(<[_Id,] [_Id', _Stat; _Stat*] _CRec*, _DStack>). Note that the variable _Stat* in the general pattern is replaced by the empty list, and the variable _CRec* by [_Id', _Stat; _Stat*] _CRec*.
- *program termination* if the current code record contains no more code to be executed, and there is *exactly one* record on the code stack. The pattern which describes this event is eval(<[_Id,], _DStack>). This time we have replaced both _Stat* and _CRec* by empty lists.

Table 1 summarizes some events and corresponding patterns for CLaX.

Table 1. Events and corresponding patterns for CLaX.

Event	Pattern
execution of a statement	eval(<[_Id, _Stat; _Stat*] _CRec*, _DStack>)
return from a procedure	eval(<[_Id,] [_Id', _Stat; _Stat*] _CRec*, _DStack>)
evaluation of a predicate	eval-predicate(_Expr, _DStack)
processing of a declaration	init-decls(_Decl; _Decl*, _Stat*, _Path)
processing of a parameter	init-params(_Actual, _Actual*, _Formal; _Formal*, _DStack)

5 Determining Subjects

By matching patterns against redexes, one can determine that a particular program construct is executing. Next, we deal with the remaining question of finding *which* construct is being executed. To this end, we need the following ingredients:

1. A means to trace subterms of redexes back to subterms of the program's abstract syntax tree.
2. A mechanism to indicate subterms of patterns that 'correspond' to subjects.

We use *origin tracking* to deal with the first issue. Informally stated, origin tracking comprises of the following:

- Before the rewriting process is started, each symbol of the initial term is *annotated* with positional information.
- Before the rewriting process is started, a *propagation rule* is derived automatically for each equation of the specification.
- Whenever an equation is applied, positional information *propagated* from the redex to the newly created subterm according to the corresponding propagation rule.

For a formal definition of the origin function, its implementation, and a discussion of its properties, the reader is referred to [9].

For the second issue, we use the well-known notion of *paths* (occurrences). A path is a sequence of natural numbers corresponding to argument positions of function symbols. A path uniquely identifies a function symbol in a term/pattern. As an example, we consider the pattern eval(<[_Id, _Stat; _Stat*] _CRec*, _DStack>), which corresponds to the execution of a statement. Path (1 1 1 2 1) indicates the subterm _Stat, which is matched against the statement that is currently executing. Figure 3 shows the pattern as a tree structure where edges are labeled with argument positions of function symbols. Path (1 1 1 2 1) corresponds to the traversal of this tree from the root to the subterm _Stat.

Table 2 summarizes the paths to the subjects for each of the patterns shown in Table 1.

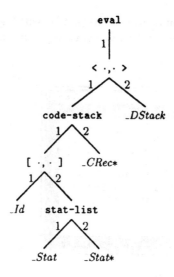

Fig. 3. Pattern eval(<[_Id, _Stat; _Stat*] _CRec*, _DStack>) as a tree structure.

Table 2. Subjects of events. The first column contains paths indicating the subterms of the patterns shown in boxes in the second column. The third column lists the corresponding subjects.

Path(s)	Pattern and subterm(s) indicated by paths	Subject(s)
(1 1 1 2 1)	eval(<[_Id, ⬚_Stat ; _Stat*] _CRec*, _DStack>)	the statement
(1 1 2 2 1)	eval(<[_Id,] [_Id', ⬚_Stat ; _Stat*] _CRec*, _DStack>)	the procedure call
(1)	eval-predicate(⬚_Expr , _DStack)	the predicate
(1 1)	init-decls(⬚_Decl ; _Decl*, _Stat+, _Path)	the declaration
(1 1), (2 1)	init-params(⬚_Actual , _Actual*, ⬚_Formal ; _Formal*, _DStack)	the actual and the formal parameter

6 Example

As an example, we show some snapshots of the animator for CLaX that was generated by the ASF+SDF system. The patterns and paths of Table 2 are used to animate the execution of the program of Figure 1.

First, a match with pattern init-decls(_Decl; _Decl*, _Stat*, _Path) is found. The origin of the subterm at path (1 1), which is matched against variable _Decl is retrieved; the animation of the corresponding declaration is shown in

Figure 4. The next two animation steps (not shown) highlight the declaration of j and the (procedure) declaration of incr, respectively.

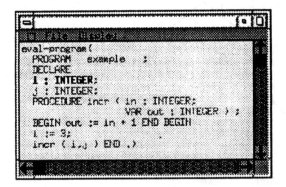

Fig. 4. Animation of the execution of a declaration.

Subsequently, two matches with the 'execute statement' pattern are found, resulting in the animation of the assignment statement of the main program (see Figure 5), followed by the animation of the call statement (not shown).

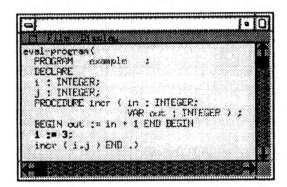

Fig. 5. Animation of the execution of a statement.

Then, the parameters of the procedure call are processed; the first of these two animation steps is shown in Figure 6.

The remaining steps consist of highlighting the statement in the procedure body, followed by the highlighting of the call statement in the main program again. The latter step is due to a match with the 'return from procedure' pattern.

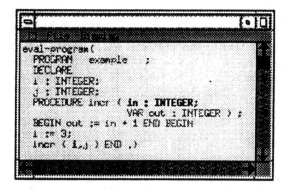

Fig. 6. Animation of formal and actual parameters.

7 Limitations

Experience with our example language CLaX has taught us that our method is in principle suitable for a wide range of programming languages. Nevertheless, there are a few limitations.

The fact that we generate animators from specifications for interpreters implies that we can only perform animations which 'correspond' to execution steps of the interpreter. Moreover, we can only detect events which can be defined as syntactic constraints on redexes. These limitations do not appear to be very restrictive, as is illustrated by the animator we have derived for CLaX.

The use of origin tracking for determining subjects works well for interpreter specifications with a compositional structure, where the execution of a language construct is either expressed in terms of the execution of its sub-constructs, or, recursively, in terms of the execution of the same construct in a modified environment. However, when the execution of a language construct is expressed in terms of the execution of *other* constructs, origin tracking fails to establish relations. As a result, it will not be possible to determine the subject, and animation steps will be missing.

We would like to emphasize that we do not consider this to be a major problem, because most interpreter specifications are – at least to a very large extent – written in a compositional manner. In the case of the CLaX interpreter (which was written before we studied animators), we have changed only 2 equations to obtain the desired animation behavior.

As an example of a problem case, we show an equation which expresses the execution of a REPEAT construct in terms of the execution of a WHILE construct:

```
[evX] eval( <[_Id, REPEAT _Stat* UNTIL _Exp END; _Stat*']
            _CRec*, _DStack> ) =
         eval( <[_Id, _Stat*; WHILE NOT(_Exp) DO _Stat* END; _Stat*']
            _CRec*, _DStack> )
```

Naturally, the problem can be remedied by re-defining the execution of a REPEAT statement in terms of itself and its sub-constructs. We are currently investigating a more appealing solution to this problem, which consists of an extension of the origin function. This would enable us to determine useful subjects in cases such as the one described above. Some ideas in this direction are discussed in [10, 8].

8   Generation of Source-level Debuggers

As an extension of the generation of animators, we are currently investigating the generation of source-level debuggers from specifications of interpreters. Basic debugger features such as single-stepping, breakpoints, state inspection, and providing backtrace information can be expressed in terms of our pattern-matching approach. Below, we discuss how each of these features can be defined for CLaX. For reasons of clarity, we will only pay attention to statement-level debugging features (e.g., breakpoints on statements, single-stepping at statement level). Obviously, each of these features can be defined for all appropriate language constructs. For example, we could define a breakpoint on the 'execution' of a control predicate.

Single Stepping

There is little difference between single-stepping, and the animation steps we have presented earlier. A single CLaX statement is executed by continuing the term rewriting process until the next match with pattern eval(<[_Id, _Stat; _Stat*] _CRec*, _DStack>) is encountered.

Breakpoints

A breakpoint on a CLaX statement can be defined as follows:

1. The user indicates a statement subterm of the AST of the program (e.g., in a syntax-directed editor).

2. The path p from the root of the AST to the designated statement is automatically determined by the debugger.

3. The rewriting process is continued until a match with pattern eval(<[_Id, _Stat; _Stat*] _CRec*, _DStack>) is encountered and the origin of the subterm matched against variable _Stat contains path p.

State Inspection

Using the function eval-exp of the CLaX specification, which computes the value of an expression, the current value of an arbitrary source-level expression can be computed as follows. Suppose that variable _Exp is bound to the expression we want to evaluate. Then, its value can be computed by *rewriting* the (instantiation of the) term eval-exp(_Exp, _DStack), where the binding of variable _DStack is obtained during the last match with pattern eval(<[_Id, _Stat; _Stat*] _CRec*, _DStack>). The rewriting process for the interpreter itself is suspended for the duration of the eval-exp rewriting process.

Backtrace Information

In Section 3, we outlined how an interpreter state contains one code record for each procedure call. Each code record contains a list of statements remaining to be executed in that procedure; the first element of this list is the current statement. All information needed for a backtrace is available, since we can do the following for *each* code record:

- Retrieve the origin of the current statement, and highlight the corresponding subterm of the AST.
- The values of parameters and local variables can be obtained by considering the corresponding record on the data stack.

More advanced features such as watchpoints [19], conditional breakpoints, and breakpoints on a reference to a designated variable can be expressed in similar ways. Moreover, since we operate in an interactive setting, *changing* the values of variables or even the program itself is conceivable. Both of these features can be implemented by physical modification of the interpreter state during the rewriting process.

From the above discussion, we conclude that obtaining the functionality of a source-level debugger is a feasible task. However, before we are able to generate source-level debuggers, more work remains to be done on the development of a formalism to *specify* both the behavior, and the user-interface of a debugger. For example, if one wants to set a breakpoint on a particular language construct, this could be done by selecting that construct in the ASF+SDF system's structure editor. Then, the system could infer the associated pattern from the type of the selected language construct and the debugger specification.

9   Generation of Algorithmic Debuggers

An interesting extension of our work on the generation of conventional source-level debuggers would be the generation of algorithmic debuggers [18, 11]. An algorithmic debugger partially automates the task of localizing a bug by comparing the *intended* program behavior with the *actual* program behavior. The intended behavior is obtained by asking the user whether or not a program unit (e.g., a procedure) behaves correctly. Using the answers given by the user, the location of the bug can be determined at the unit level.

In order to generate algorithmic debuggers from specification of interpreters, the following issues have to be dealt with:

1. The original program has to be transformed into an equivalent, side-effect free program. A possible approach is described in [17]. An extension of the origin function can be used to relate subterms of the ASTs of the original program, and the transformed one.
2. Algorithmic debugging is a post-mortem technique, based on the analysis of the execution tree of a program. Our approach to generate animators and debuggers, on the other hand, can be regarded as interactive debugging. However, patterns could be used to intercept the events when information

(for the execution tree) needs to be stored. This information should include the *origins* of the procedure calls, so as to be able to animate the algorithmic debugging process.

3. A separate algorithmic debugger has to be constructed which interprets the execution tree information, and uses the origins stored in (2) and the relations between the original and the transformed program stored in (1) to animate the algorithmic debugging process.

10 Conclusions and Future Work

We have presented a framework for incorporating animation features in generated programming environments where animators are generated from specifications of interpreters. We have considered simple animators which highlight the language constructs that are currently being executed. Origin tracking and a pattern-matching mechanism are used to define animators. The successful generation of an animator for CLaX shows the feasibility of our approach.

Section 7 describes some limitations, which can be summarized as follows. First, we can only detect events which correspond to syntactic constraints on redexes. Second, the use of origin tracking restricts us to specifications which have a compositional structure. As it turns out, these limitations do not cause much problems.

We claim that our approach for generating animators is suitable for a wide range of imperative programming languages, including realistic languages such as Pascal and C. We will investigate if animators can be generated for languages with parallel and object-oriented features in a similar way. We conjecture that these features will not cause fundamental problems.

A possible criticism is that patterns for defining events may become quite complicated. One should bear in mind, however, that these patterns are similar to the equations of the interpreter specification. We claim, therefore, that the definition of animation features is an easy task for the specification writer.

In Section 8, we have outlined how our approach can be extended to the generation of source-level debuggers, by indicating how various debugger features can be defined for our example language. In Section 9, we have described prerequisites for a further extension to the generation of algorithmic debuggers.

What remains to be developed is a formalism to *specify* animation and debugging features. Such an animator/debugger specification would define both the functionality and the user-interface of the generated tools.

Acknowledgements

I am grateful to Paul Klint, Peter Fritzson, T.B. Dinesh, and the AADEBUG'93 referees for their comments on drafts of this paper.

References

1. Aho, A.V. , Sethi, R., Ullman, J.D.: *Compilers. Principles, Techniques and Tools.* Addison-Wesley, 1986.
2. Bahlke, R., Moritz, B., Snelting, G.: A generator for language-specific debugging systems. In *Proceedings of the ACM SIGPLAN'87 Symposium on Interpreters and Interpretive Techniques*, pages 92–101, 1987. Appeared as SIGPLAN Notices 22(7).
3. Bahlke R., Snelting, G.: The PSG system: from formal language definitions to interactive programming environments. *ACM Transactions on Programming Languages and Systems*, 8(4):547–576, 1986.
4. Bergstra, J.A., Heering, J., Klint, P., Eds.: *Algebraic Specification.* ACM Press Frontier Series. The ACM Press in co-operation with Addison-Wesley, 1989.
5. Berry, D.: *Generating Program Animators from Programming Language Semantics.* PhD thesis, University of Edinburgh, 1991.
6. Bertot, Y.: Occurrences in debugger specifications. In *Proceedings of the ACM SIGPLAN'91 Conference on Programming Language Design and Implementation*, pages 327–337, 1991. Appeared as *SIGPLAN Notices* 26(6).
7. Borras, P., Clément, D., Despeyroux, Th., Incerpi, J., Lang, B., Pascual, V.: Centaur: the system. In *Proceedings of the ACM SIGSOFT/SIGPLAN Software Engineering Symposium on Practical Software Development Environments*, pages 14–24, 1989. Appeared as *SIGPLAN Notices* 14(2).
8. Deursen, A. van: Origin tracking in primitive recursive schemes. Technical report, Centrum voor Wiskunde en Informatica (CWI), 1993. To appear.
9. Deursen, A. van, Klint, P., Tip, F.: Origin tracking. Report CS-R9230, Centrum voor Wiskunde en Informatica (CWI), 1992. To appear in *Journal of Symbolic Computation.*
10. Dinesh, T.B., Tip, F.: Animators and error reporters for generated programming environments. Report CS-R9253, Centrum voor Wiskunde en Informatica (CWI), 1992.
11. Fritzson, P., Gyimothy, T., Kamkar, M., Shahmehri, N.: Generalized algorithmic debugging and testing. In *Proceedings of the ACM SIGPLAN'91 Conference on Programming Language Design and Implementation*, pages 317–326, 1991. Appeared as *SIGPLAN Notices* 26(6).
12. Heering, J., Hendriks, P.R.H., Klint, P., Rekers, J.: The syntax definition formalism SDF - reference manual. *SIGPLAN Notices*, 24(11):43–75, 1989.
13. Kahn, G.: Natural semantics. In Brandenburg, F.J., Vidal-Naquet, G., Wirsing, M., Eds.: *Fourth Annual Symposium on Theoretical Aspects of Computer Science*, volume 247 of *Lecture Notes in Computer Science*, pages 22–39. Springer-Verlag, 1987.
14. Klint, P.: A meta-environment for generating programming environments. *ACM Transactions on Software Engineering Methodology*, 2(2):176–201, 1993.
15. Klop, J.W.: Term rewriting systems. In Abramsky, S., Gabbay, D., Maibaum, T., Eds.: *Handbook of Logic in Computer Science, Vol II.* Oxford University Press, 1991. Also CWI report CS-R9073.
16. Müller, H., Winckler, J., Grzybek, S., Otte, M., Stoll, B., Equoy, F., Higilin, N.: The program animation system PASTIS. Bericht 20, Universität Freibürg, Institut für Informatik, 1990.
17. Shahmehri, N.: *Generalized Algorithmic Debugging.* PhD thesis, Linköping University, 1991.

18. Shapiro E.Y.: *Algorithmic Program Debugging*. MIT Press, 1982.
19. Stallman, R.M., Pesch, R.H.: *Using GDB, A guide to the GNU Source-Level Debugger*. Free Software Foundation/Cygnus Support, 1991. Version 4.0.

Visualization as Debugging: Understanding/Debugging the Warren Abstract Machine*

Julio García-Martín   Juan José Moreno-Navarro

Universidad Politécnica de Madrid **

Abstract. This paper presents a twofold proposal to understand the Warren Abstract Machine. A stepwise definition of the WAM by using abstract data types (for every WAM component) is briefly presented. Furthermore, we describe a visual environment which can be used for the emulation of the Warren Abstract Machine. It has been designed as a high level debugger for object oriented programs, following a methodology sketched in the paper. The tool has the capability to show the user the internal behaviour of the WAM during a program execution by showing its components at the desired level of abstraction. The tool provides an interactive and friendly interface. Configurable tracing and dynamic breakpoint location can be used in a simple and coherent way. All the features included in the tool allow for an easy and powerful examination of the WAM.

1 Introduction

In the last years, the idea that the usual task of a programmer is to develop new programs from scratch has changed. Very often, the programmer needs to modify or maintain an old program or he reuses parts of previous programs. In this situation the programmer needs to understand correctly the behaviour of a program that he did not make (or he did not remember), which could be a non trivial task.

Debugging has been usually considered as the process to find bugs in a program. But it could be also interpreted as a process that tries to understand the (possible incorrect) behaviour of a program. One of the best features of debugging is that program executions can be controlled. This fact could offer us some advantages on the understanding of a program, because it would allow slower computations and more systematic analysis on the execution. Notice that traditional debugging techniques (e.g. tracing, variable watching, breakpoints, etc.) are still valid for the new task.

* This work has been partially supported by the Spanish PRONTIC project TIC93-0737-C02-02

** Departamento LSIIS, Facultad de Informática, Campus de Montegancedo, Boadilla del Monte, 28660 Madrid, Spain, email: {juliog,jjmoreno}@fi.upm.es.

The most interesting way to understand a program is to visualize its internal behaviour. The more flexible and complete is the visualisation, the more helpful is the tool.

In this paper we apply this idea to understand a concrete program: the Warren Abstract Machine (WAM) for PROLOG implementation. It is placed in the field of the technology concerning the development of abstract machines. With all the more reason than other paradigms, abstract machines should be designed with debugging support as a central issue [PW91]: it does hardly complicate the formal specifications and simplifies testing, verification and validation.

One of the most important elements in the success of PROLOG has been the development of efficient implementation techniques. The possibility of compiling PROLOG and getting efficient code was pointed out by Warren [Wa83] with the design of an abstract machine. Due to the high quality of the resulting machine, it is the reference point for PROLOG compilers.

However, besides the success of the WAM, the only way to understand its behaviour is by reading the papers and tutorials devoted to explain how it works. The collection includes the original Warren's work [Wa83], tutorials and descriptions: [GLLO85, MW88, AK91], and formal specifications and verification proofs: [BR91, BR92, Ru89]. Although all of them contain good explanations, specially Aït-Kaci's tutorial and [BR92] formal specification, they solve the problem only partially. On one hand, there are no apparent reasons for many of the decisions on it (at least in the previous papers), and all its descriptions combine implementation tricks with design decisions and there is no way to identify the origin of several behaviours. On the other hand, to fully understand its operation, most of the students of the WAM need to construct their own toy implementation to understand all the details, but this solution implies a great effort.

We think that a complete understanding of the WAM needs more help. Our proposal for a complete understanding of the WAM is twofold:

First, we have developed an abstract view of the WAM by a stepwise formal description. For an abstract view of the WAM we mean a description of the WAM focused in how: a) it implements SLD-resolution with backtracking and b) the main elements of PROLOG (unification and backtracking) can be compiled. We delay implementation details and optimisations as most as possible. Our specification treats each WAM component (heap, trail, stack, registers, etc.) as abstract data types (ADTs). The WAM is derived from SLD-resolution, the operational semantics of PROLOG, in several refinement steps. Moreover, the complete WAM (including optimisations and implementation tricks) can be derived from the abstract WAM by giving efficient implementation of the ADTs in the definition. One interesting point is that both steps are handled in the same framework, with refinements of the data area (in the first step) or with refinements of the implementation of the ADTs.

Second, we have developed a visual implementation of the previous WAM specification. This means that our tool is able to compute PROLOG programs by showing the user all the components of the machine and their evolution. Each element is displayed at the level of abstraction (in the sense of the stepwise specification) the user decides. This tool tries to cover a gap between the pure execution of a PROLOG program and concrete formal descriptions based on WAM specification.

This paper is focused on the visual tool, called Friendly-WAM, and its design and implementation as a high level debugger. For this purpose, we sketch a methodology for debugging object oriented programs (as is our case, because it is based on abstract data types). Our method includes facilities for general tracing in a simple and clean way.

An important problem arises from the combination of two sources of breakpoints during the visualisation/debugging of the WAM. We are interested in giving conditions to examine the program from the WAM definition and also from the original PROLOG program and its execution model (SLD-resolution). The problem is achieved in an uniform way due to the fact that the stepwise description of the WAM contains SLD resolution as the first step.

The final tool combines some mixed characteristics of (semi-automated) debuggers. From this point of view, this paper could be understood as a practical experience of a debugging of an object oriented program.

The rest of the paper is organised as follows: Section 2 presents a more detailed description of the WAM specification and Friendly-WAM. Section 3 sketches our methodology for object oriented programs debugging while Section 4 describes how this methodology is applied in the design and implementation of our tool. Section 5 shows how to use Friendly-WAM. A discussion on related work appears in section 6. Finally, section 7 summarises the conclusion and points to future work.

2 The Starting Point: Stepwise Definition and Computer Visualization of the WAM

As we have said our proposal to understand the WAM consists of a stepwise definition of the machine and an interactive visual tool based on the specification.

This section starts with a brief presentation of our description of the WAM. Next, we establish the requirements for Friendly-WAM.

2.1 Stepwise Description of the WAM

An abstract machine is defined by the following: the *data area* which defines the *configuration* of the machine; the *instruction set* and a *semantic function* for each of its elements (defining the changes on the configuration after executing an instruction); the *transition function* between an initial and a final configuration which is guided by the semantic function of the instruction currently executed; and the *translation function* which compiles a program into machine code. All of these elements can be described formally by using abstract data types (ADTs). The data area is a collection of ADTs. The semantic function is described in terms of the operations of the ADTs.

The derivation of the WAM is carried out in two big steps. The first step is the *derivation of the main elements of the WAM*. We have no space to describe all the refinement steps. We could only mention some important points. The first machine is a stack based description of SLD-resolution solving literals left to right and using the clauses in textual order. The stack contains choice points, representing a resolution step with the current goal (a list of literal starting with a *p* predicate call), the substitution of the resolution step and the next clause for *p* to be used. Goals can be coded into the machine program by changing the goal in choice points by some argument registers and the continuation program label and the next clause by the corresponding program label. Substitutions can be compiled with the help of the heap as a set of pairs (variable name, heap pointer). The variables included in this set are the variables bound during the resolution step represented by the choice point. However, the amount of variables bound in a resolution step is unknown. What is possible to do at compile time is to give names to the local variables of the clause and to collect in a choice point only the bindings to the local variables. A local trail is needed to collect every nonlocal variable binding. It is useful to reconstruct the step substitution. Operationally, the trail is useful to undo variable bindings under backtracking. Furthermore, one could notice that several predicates have only one clause. In this case a full choice point is no longer useful and can be simplified in an environment that contains only the continuation label and the local variables. The environments included in a choice point are collected in a stack. Finally, the parameter passing could be optimised by using specialised machine instructions to construct or unify every component in a term (constant, functor or variable).

After this derivation we get what we call the *Abstract WAM*. We obtain an abstract behaviour of the WAM without knowing implementation details. Due to the lack of space we will concentrate on it. Let us explain how it looks like.

The data area is formed by the *WAM-program, or-stack*, the *argument registers* and the *heap*. The program encompasses a *program counter* and an array of *WAM-instructions*. The or-stack is an instance of the polymorphic ADT *stack* with *choice points* as elements. The ADT choice point contains a copy of the argument registers, the local *trail* (a *set* of variable names), the program address of the next clause and an *and-stack*. The and-stack is another instance of the ADT stack with *environments* as components. An environment contains the continuation label and the *variables*. The ADT variables are defined together with the heap. A variable is a pair (variable name, heap pointer). A heap is a table with a pointer as key and each element is a term: a constant, a constructor with some heap pointers as arguments or a variable name. Finally, the argument registers are an array of heap pointers or variable names.

We do not give details about the elements in the Abstract WAM. Figure 1 collects some examples of the formalisation: An overview of the translation function for clauses (where one can see the instruction set used), the semantic function of a couple of instructions (try_me_else and retry_me_else) and the specifications of the ADTs Trail an instance of a SET) and Environment.

The second main step is the *optimization* of this machine. All the optimisa-

a) Translation function

WAM_Program := *gooltrans* (GOAL)
              proctrans (PROC (p_1))
              . . .
              proctrans (PROC (p_m))

proctrans: Procedure → Wam_Code
proctrans (PROC(p)={C})::=
              clausetrans (C)

proctrans (PROC(p)={C_1,..,C_n})::=

              try_me_else (n, ($label_1$))
              clausetrans (C_1)
   ($label_1$): retry_me_else ($label_2$)
              clausetrans (C_2)
   ($label_2$):   . . .
($label_{n-1}$): trust_me
              clausetrans (C_n)

clausetrans: Clauses → Wam_Code
clausetrans (p(t) :- q_1(s_1),..., q_n(s_n)) :=

   allocate (#Variables (t, s_1,..., s_n))
   unifytrans (t)
   transfertrans (s_1, var (t))
   call ((q_1), arity (q_1))
   transfertrans (s_2, var (t, s_1))
   call ((q_2), arity (q_2))
   . . .
   transfertrans (s_n, var (t, s_1,..., s_{n-1}))
   call ((q_n), arity (q_n))
   deallocate

b) Semantic function

SI: Wam_Inst × Wam_State → Wam_State

SI [try_me_else (L)] wam_state :=
  Next_Instruction
    (Push (wam_state,
        Create-Choice-Point
            (Registers (wam_state), (L),
            Consult_CP (wam_state))))

SI [retry_me_else (L) n] wam_state :=
  Next_Instruction
    (Rewind_Trail
        (Next_Clause
            (wam_state, (L))))

c) Specification of ADT's

adt SET [element] is
  sort set

    op Insert : set element → set
    op Remove : set element → set
    op ∈ : element set → bool
    op ∅ : → set
    operation _⊔_ : set set → set

  axioms
    vars i, j : element
    var S : set
    vars A, B : set

    Insert (Insert (S, i), j) =
        Insert (Insert(S, j), i)   if $i <> j$
    Remove (Insert (S, i), j) = Remove (S, j)
                                     if $i == j$
    Remove (Insert (S, i), j) =
        Insert (Remove(S, j), i) if $i <> j$
    Remove (∅, i) = ∅
    j ∈ Insert (S, i) = ($i == j$) or ($j ∈ S$)
                                     if $i <> j$
    ¬i ∈ ∅
    i ∈ ($A ∪ B$) = ($A ∈ i$) or ($B ∈ i$)
endadt

adt TRAIL is
  extending SET [VAR_NAME] trail
endadt

adt ENVIRONMENT is
  sort environment
  uses VARIABLES WAM_PROGRAM

    op Create : nat prog_addr → environment
    op Modify_CP : environment prog_addr
        → environment
    op Consult_CP : environment → prog_addr
    op Modify_Var : environment nat variable
        → environment
    op Consult_Var : enviroment nat
        → variable

  axioms
    vars *size*, n : nat
    var E : environment
    var CP : prog_addr
    var X : variable

    Consult_CP (Create (*size*, CP)) = CP
    Consult_CP (Modify_CP (E, CP)) = CP
    Consult_Var (Create (*size*, CP)) = Unbound
    Consult_Var (Modify_Var (E, n, X)) = X
endadt

Fig. 1. Examples of the specification

tions are performed similarly as before and the order is (nearly) irrelevant.

- The and-stacks and the or-stack can be implemented as a single one containing both choice points and environments. Two different top pointers are needed.
- It is more efficient to handle a global trail instead of several local ones.
- It is also convenient to implement the heap as a stack of contiguous memory cells.
- The recursive definition of the general unification algorithm can be turned on iteratively by using a new component of the data area (the *push-down list*; PDL for short) that behaves as a stack.
- Semantics of the instructions could also be optimised as in the last call optimisation, environment trimming, indexing of clauses and so on.
- Variable classification allows for a very efficient code. Temporary registers are introduced for this purpose.
- Finally, the data area can be seen as a large stack of memory cells. The correct organisation of the different components helps in the implementation of some operations (i.e. decide if a variable is older than other).

As a result we get a formal description of the WAM, with code area, heap, stack, trail and PDL as components, as described in [AK91].

2.2 Requirements for Friendly-WAM

In order to fully understand the WAM we also want to have a tool/environment suitable to carry out a more controlled execution of WAM programs. Besides this, we were not satisfied with just obtaining the solutions of a program execution. We want to develop a frame where it is possible to carry out progressive analysis and checks during execution. This WAM emulator is designed as an interactive environment with a friendly user interface and it must be strongly related with our stepwise WAM description. We call our tool Friendly-WAM.

The basis of the functionality of Friendly-WAM is the possibility of visualising WAM components as defined in any level of the specification. This means that every ADT can be visualised at the level of abstraction desired by the user. For instance, the trail can be presented as a set of variables inside the and-stack or as a global data with stack structure. All ADTs are viewed by using their own window.

Usually, it is not convenient to show the internal state of the WAM every time a modification in the machine is done. For this reason, the tool presents also some configurable tracing facilities. The user can specify the conditions under which he wants to stop the execution in order to watch the internal state of the WAM.

We have included the PROLOG program as well as the WAM program as a part of the WAM state. It involves that the emulator can show the WAM instruction that is being currently executed, and its PROLOG instruction - clause, goal or predicate- associated. This allows us to trace the execution of the program following the code.

The whole environment looks like a set of windows placed on different positions on the screen. Any investigation about WAM's internal state can be displayed through these windows. In that sense, the emulator is like an X-ray of the WAM. Windows on the emulator are easily configurable with regard to: size, form, frame, mobility, name, etc, and scrolling is possible. The environment can be both mouse-driven or keyboard-driven.

A preliminary version of Friendly-WAM is presented in [GM92]. However, it does not fulfil all the functionality demanded here. The next sections describe how the new version of Friendly-WAM is designed to meet these requirements.

3 Towards a Methodology for Debugging Object Oriented Programs

As debugging is a process that consumes 50-70% of software development time, programs must be designed to facilitate internal manipulation and examination. During the debugging process the programmers have in mind the expected behaviour (or errors) they are aware of. These suppositions are related to the details of the executions and a tracer is required to check them. However, most current tracers show a very poor functionality. The usual kind of features a tracer offers is often fixed (positional breakpoints, variable watching, some simple conditions, etc.), and the functionality is reduced in advance. Therefore tracer commands are not expressive enough, and programmers cannot formulate what they want to check in detail. If we want to obviate this drawback we need to have configurable (or programmable) tracers.

As opposed to the usual *breakpoint* classification: positional class, conditional class and class of asyncronous events[Me89], we have reduced them to only one, the conditional behavioural control. We are certain that all previous cases can be seen as particular conditional case. In adition to this, it allows to maintain a high degree of expressiveness and offers us a single way to automate the debugging activity.

These programmable tracers have been designed for PROLOG ([Du92]) and other languages. One keypoint in this task is to avoid a large number of complicated constructions which are difficult to use. If we leave all the work to the tracer, there is no guarantee that these constructions cover the complete debugging process. The solution used in [Du92] is to integrate trace facilities into the language to be debugged.

In this section we sketch a methodology to introduce configurable trace facilities into an object oriented language. We are interested in static as well as dynamic conditions to enable and disable trace facilities.

We associate the notion of tracing of an object with the visualization of the state of the object in certain moments. We assume that each class has at least one visualization operation.

The tracing (visualization) is activated depending of some debugging conditions. A debugging condition is a boolean class function. Every debugging condition has associated a debugging action. Debugging conditions specify the conditions to stop the normal execution and start debugging actions (which includes visualisation) over the state of the object. The programmer could decide either statically or dynamically which debugging conditions are active. Every time the object is accessed the active debugging conditions are checked. If they are true, the corresponding debugging action is performed.

Let us summarise the method in terms of object oriented programming: Each class has three definition parts: the class interface part, the view part of the class (with the visualisation operations and the part of the state needed to make the visualisation) and the debugging part (with the debugging conditions and actions and possibly adding new state parts to implement them).

The class interface part is the usual definition part of the object (the .hcc file in C++). It contains the operations (*methods* in other terminology) allowed for the object.

The view part contains operations to display the state of the object (as suggested in [Bu91]). It can be developed by the programmer but can also be generated automatically by default. It is easy in a pure object oriented language, provided that primitive objects (numbers, strings, arrays, etc) have their own display operation. Class aggregation means that the visualisation can be done by aggregating the views of the corresponding components. The state of the class could be completed with new elements, for instance a window, a dialogue menu, etc.

The debugging part contains the definition of debugging conditions (boolean functions) as well as debugging actions (operations). The state could be enhanced with new components used by the debugging conditions and actions (for instance, it is possible to check how many times the object is accessed by including a counter in the state).

The active conditions can be defined statically (we can imagine that it is done in the *make file* of the program) or dynamically.

Notice that both the debugging conditions and actions are specified as class operations, so they are coded in the same language as the program.

4 Structure of the program

We have chosen C++ [Str90], an object oriented extension of C, to develop the program. Each abstract data type of the WAM is implemented as a class. Figures 2,3 show the complete hierarchical design of our tool. We draw separately the usage relation (Fig. 2), and inheritance and polymorphism relation (Fig. 3).

In C++ a class has only two sections: the definition part and the implementation one. To manage the view part of a class *class* we generate a new class *class_view* by inheritance. The new class complements the state by including all the elements needed for the visualisation and the displaying operation.

The debugging part is managed in a similar way, inventing the class *class_deb* by inheritance from *class_view*. The state is completed as needed. The operations defined by the user are boolean functions which represent debugging conditions.

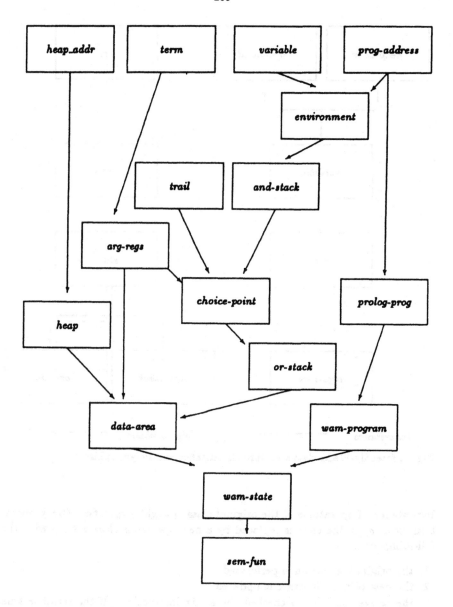

Fig. 2. Abstract WAM class structure

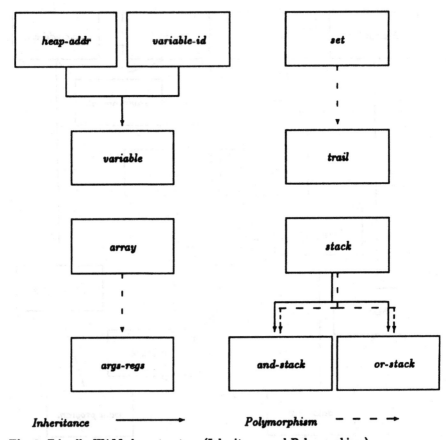

Inheritance ⟶   Polymorphism - - - ⟶

Fig. 3. Friendly-WAM class structure (Inheritance and Polymorphism)

Inheritance of operations of the original class is slightly modified. Every operation *class::op* of the class is replaced by a new operation *class_deb::op* with the following code:

1. the original operation is performed
2. the new part of the state is updated
3. the active condition is checked (by an **if** instruction). If the result is true the object is visualised by a call to the display operation and a debugging action is performed.

Figure 4 shows the structure of classes.

The visualisation class contains only one operation **display**. Each WAM (main) component is showed by using its own window. The initial level of abstraction of the ADT/object is specified as an argument. However, it could be modified by using a dialogue box. The state of the visualisation class contains

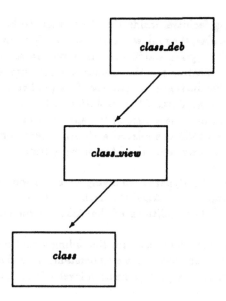

Fig. 4. Structure of a class

the window, the menu and some extra information for helping the reconstruction of the abstract views. For instance, in order to reconstruct the substitution computed in each resolution step the environment needs to know the top of the trail in this moment. This information is not included in the environment but into the environment_view.

The next point to discuss is how to manage active conditions. As we have said, every operation call is followed by an if instruction. The condition of this if is a call to the boolean function pointer class_cond. This function variable can be instantiated statically as a macro by the C preprocessor. The pointer points to a name and the C preprocessor changes this name to a concrete function. In order to specify statically the active condition a simple define instruction is used.

However, it could also be changed dynamically. As class_cond is a variable, an assignment can be done to a concrete function.

Although the user can define his own debugging conditions and actions it is not an easy task in all the cases. For this reason, we have defined a collection of debugging conditions and actions that cover (most of) the user's needs.

The debugging actions included visualisation, watching facilities and delayed or step by step executions of machine instructions. Debugging conditions depend on the particular features of every abstract data types. Among the predefined conditions we can mention:

— stop and visualise after any wam-instruction is executed,
— stop every time the heap is accessed,
— stop every time a choice point is generated,
— stop when something is pushed into the trail (i.e. a goal variable is bound),
  ...

But the tracing facilities inside the WAM that we have described are more powerful. In particular, they allow the user to specify some debugging conditions into the PROLOG program and its execution models. As the PROLOG program is a part of the specification and the visualisation, the user can include debugging conditions on it. For instance, he can specify a predicate, a clause or a specific predicate call as breakpoints. SLD-resolution is the most abstract view of the semantics function, i.e. it is a part of the specification. Therefore, the user can activate debugging conditions related with SLD resolution: for example, we can define a breakpoint every resolution step or every time a non-empty substitution is computed.

A menu allows for dynamic changing of conditions and actions. Usually, changing a condition of an ADT (for instance the *or-stack*) supposes the dynamic changing of the conditions of the ADTs it includes (*and-stack, choice point*, etc.).

Moreover some complete scenarios (including visualisation options) are provided. For a predefined *scenario* we understand a configuration of debugging conditions and actions and a visualisation level setting for all the abstract data types.

Predefined scenarios can be selected before starting the tool (as a parameter of the program) or by using a menu shown at the beginning of the execution. Scenarios avoid incoherent uses of Friendly-WAM facilities.

The whole methodology could lead to a very efficient management of debugging / visualisation features. If the user does not like these facilities, he simply avoids the link of classes class_view and class_deb to the program. Notice that no recompilation is needed.

5 Using Friendly-WAM

In this section some snapshots of a Friendly-WAM session obtained in the execution of a concrete execution example are presented. We will try to give a landscape of the functionality of Friendly- WAM together with making familiar its general aspect. On the other hand, we are interested in showing the large possibilities of the debugging and emulating environments not only in the context of abstract machines, but also in a context of general executions of programs.

Friendly-WAM appears as a set of windows (or icons), each of them representing a WAM component. The *aggregation* relationship of the object oriented paradigm has its correspondence in the visual version on the environment. Every component is represented by a symbolic icon situated inside the window of the object that they are part of. These components are accessed (visualised) by exploiting its icon.

The beginning of the program is carried out in the usual way after debugging conditions have been previously determinated.

At first step of execution, Friendly-WAM presents the aspect showed in figure 5.

The environment is globally managed by an horisontal menu bar placed in the top of the main window. Each of the menu labels has associated a pop-up menu,

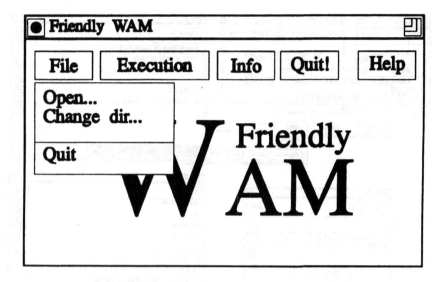

Fig. 5. The Friendly-WAM: A first view

and, among others, the changing of the abstraction level and the debugging
conditions appear as option.

The next snapshot presents a step of the execution. Figure 6 shows how
Friendly-WAM presents a general view of WAM data area, together with other
information about the current program that being executed. It can be seen that
the data area is formed by the *heap* (where terms involved in unifications are
represented), global registers for transferring operations of terms, and the *or-stack*.

At this point, the execution has been stopped because a debugging condition
has been reached: a WAM instruction has accessed the heap. The debugging action is performed: One of the argument registers is inspected and its information
is shown by a dialogue menu.

The next third example of the Friendly-WAM shows a more detailed view of
the WAM (see figure 7). Almost all of the relevant components of the WAM are
presented: *or-stack, trail, argument registers* and the *environments* inside of the
and-stack.

Furthermore, both the PROLOG and the WAM programs show the point
where the execution is going. A menu bar indicates the WAM instruction to
be executed. A debugging condition has been detected trying to carry out an
operation on the *trail*. The WAM instruction inserts the variable into the *trail*
to being unbound later.

More other operations than those presented here could be easily carried out
under Friendly-WAM. During execution a lot of possible checks are possible.

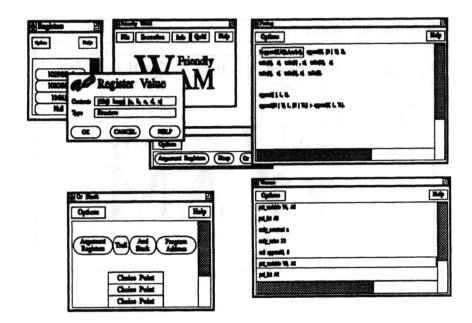

Fig. 6. The Friendly-WAM: Data Area

However, our purpose is not that of giving a lot of concrete descriptions. We hope to succeed in giving a flavour of the power of an environment like Friendly-WAM.

6 Some Related Work

We could discuss two kind of related works: explanations of the WAM and object oriented debugging.

We have mentioned in the introduction the papers devoted to explain how the WAM works. Aït-Kaci's tutorial is a good description of the WAM, but the level of the description is very close to the concrete implementation. The formal description of [BR91] is more close to our work, although its main goal is to provide a formal proof of the correctness of the WAM. We are more focused on the derivation of the WAM from SLD-resolution giving reasons for all the design decisions. [Nils92] completes Kursawe's work [Ku89] on the deduction of an abstract PROLOG machine by partial evaluation, an alternative approach to deduce the WAM specification. It is a very nice and adequate methology to derive the forward behaviour of PROLOG, but efficient backtracking and data representation appear to lead to some difficulties. In all the cases there is no computer support to test the explanations.

We are less familiar with object oriented debugging. [PW91] is a survey of current object oriented debugging tools. The authors establish that *"Debuggers*

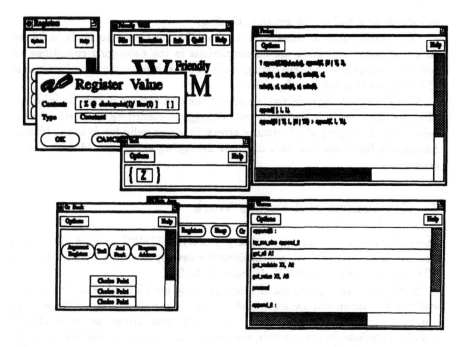

Fig. 7. The Friendly-WAM: Full view

must accentuate the object model of the language around they have been designed. Specifically, object-oriented debuggers should support the concept of debugging at the object level". This means that the particular characteristics of object-oriented programming (i.e. inheritance, polymorphism and dynamic binding) must be taken into account.

There are few existing proposals where the visualisation of their programs is assisted, see [IWCLD88, SM88]). The most successful current tools are GDB ([S88] the gnu C++ debugger), the Smalltalk-80 debugger ([G83]) and Vici ([C88] the Objective-C debugger). They are ordinary imperative debuggers with some special characteristics for object oriented programming. The interface with the user is similar to the interface with the original language (specially in Smalltalk) but the functionality is closed to standard debuggers.

All of them use a tracing language with several commands. The Smalltalk debugger support only positional breakpoints by explicit insertion of *self halt* or *self debug* methods into the program. Vici allows positional and (fixed) conditional breakpoints, but response to breakpoints is not alterable. GDB offers conditional breakpoints that can be associated with one location only. It also allows breakpoints to be dormant until the desired context is established. Moreover, GDB allows the user to define its own tracing commands but in terms of predefined commands.

Notice that none of them give special facilities to debug incorrect inheritance definitions or a bad use of dynamic binding.

Our methodology is more flexible than the mentioned tools. It is focused on visualisation and there are no restrictions in the debugging conditions and actions. They can be changed dynamically (what subsumes dormant breakpoints of GDB) and it is fully configurable.

In our methodology, debugging conditions and actions cannot be inherited. The new class needs to define its own debugging conditions and actions which help in the debugging of inheritance errors. It is also valid for dynamic binding. Ambiguous functions can have different debugging actions, so identification is possible.

7 Conclusions and Future Work

Currently, we have a very preliminary prototype [GM92] running on Personal Computers under DOS. We are finishing the development of a UNIX version for SUN workstations using the X- Windows interface.

Some future enhancements of Friendly-WAM are planned. First, we want to work on the automatic generation of debugging conditions and actions. These can be a part of the specification of the ADTs and written in terms of other ADT's operations. In other words, the user should describe debugging conditions and actions at the level of the specification instead of coding them in C++. The system could generate C++ code for the debugging class automatically. The user should also describe scenarios in this way. We also plan to allow more general debugging conditions at the level of the PROLOG program in the vein of [Du91].

Another point of future work is the formalisation and generalisation of our methodology for object oriented programming debugging. We claim that it is possible to generalise the methodology to get a semi-automated behaviour [3]. The key point is to replace the use of breakpoints (a primitive and restrictive technique) by some formal methods. The notion of *algorithmic debugging* (see [Sha82]) could be useful for this purpose. Although algorithmic debugging has been used mainly in declarative programming (see [Nils92] for the application to a functional language) because of the lack of side effects it could be also applicable to object oriented programming, because the side effects are restricted to the object.

Our methodology also prevents errors caused by a bad use of inheritance and dynamic binding. It seems to useful for all the elements of the taxonomy of object oriented bugs showed in [PW91].

The use of debugging facilities has been a great help during the development of the tool. The debugging facilities are not only useful for visualisation but also for ordinary debugging. The methodology is been used to fix some bugs in the program.

Furthermore, the design of the program has been simplified by distinguishing the debugging, visualisation and interface part of an object. The equation

---

[3] Notice that visualisation of the program should be a fully automated process

understanding & visualizing a program = debugging process seems to be very useful.

Finally, the development of our application has convinced us that tools like the present one offer an adequate way to understand how the WAM works, what are its tricks, and how they could be implemented. The tool is useful not only for students but for people involved on the compilation and implementation of declarative languages.

Acknowledgements

We are grateful to Alvaro Falquina for helping us in the implementation of Friendly-WAM.

References

[AK91]   H. Aït-Kaci: The WAM: A (Real) Tutorial, The MIT Press, 1991.

[BR91]   E. Böerger, D. Rosensweig: WAM Algebras–A Mathematical Study of Implementation, Part I in Proc. CSL'90, Part II in Proc. Russian Conf. on Logic Prog.' 91.

[BR92]   E. Böerger, D. Rosensweig: The WAM–Definition and Compiler Correctness, Technical Report, TR-14/92, Dipartamento di Informatica, Università di Pisa, 1992.

[Bu91]   T. Budd: Object Oriented Programming, Addison Wesley, 1991.

[C88]   B.J. Cox: Objective-C Interpreter version 4.0 User's Reference Manual, Stepstone Inc. Sandy Hook, CT, 1988.

[Du91]   M. Ducasse: Abstract views of PROLOG executions in Opium, Proceedings ISLP'91, The MIT Press 1991, pp. 18-32.

[Du92]   M. Ducasse: A General Trace Query Mechanism Based on PROLOG, Proceedings PLILP'92, Springer LNCS 631, 1992, pp. 400-414.

[GLLO85] J. Gabriel, T. Lindholm, E.L. Lusk, R.A. Overbeck: A Tutorial for the WAM for Computational Logic, ANL-84-84, Argonne Nat. Lab., 1985.

[GM92]   J. García-Martín, J.J. Moreno-Navarro: Friendly-WAM: An Interactive Tool to Understand the Compilation of PROLOG, Proceedings LPAR'92, Springer LNAI 624, Springer Verlag, 1992.

[GM93]   J. García-Martín, J.J. Moreno-Navarro: A Formal Definition of an Abstract PROLOG Compiler, submitted for publication, 1993.

[G83]   A. Goldberg: Smalltalk-80: The Interactive Programming Environment, Addison Wesley, 1983.

[IWCLD88] D. Ingalls, S. Wallace, Y.Y. Chow, F. Ludolph, K. Doyle: Fabrik: a Visual Programming Environment, Proceedings OOPSLA'88, 1988.

[Ku89]   P. Kursawe: How to Invent a PROLOG Machine, New Generation Comp., 5, 1989.

[Me89]   M.G. Menelaou, J.A. Purchase, R.L. Winder: On Debuggers and Debugging Tools and Techniques, UCL Research Note, London, UK, 1989.

[MW88]   D. Maier, D.S. Warren: Computing with Logic: Logic Programming with PROLOG, Ed. Benjamin Cummings, 1988.

[Nils92] U. Nilsson: Towards a Methodology for the Design of Abstract Machines for LP Languages, to appear in The Journal of Logic Programming, vol. 6, num. 1, 1993.

[PW91]   J.A. Purchase, R.L. Winder: Debugging Tools for Object Oriented Programming, Journal of Object Oriented Programming, vol. 4, n. 3, June 1992, pp. 10-27.

[Ru89]   D.M. Russinoff: A Verified PROLOG Compiler for the Warren Abstract Machine, Journal of Logic Programming, vol. 13, n. 4, August 1992, pp. 367-412.

[Sha82] E.Y. Shapiro: Algorithmic Program Debugging, The MIT Press, 1982.

[S88]   R. Stallman: GDB+ Manual, The gnu C++ Debugger, MA, 1988.

[Str90] B. Stroustrup: The Programming Language C++, Addison Wesley, 1987.

[SM88]   P.A. Ssekely, B.A. Myers: A User Interface Toolkit based on Graphical Objects and Constraints, Proceedings OOPSLA'88, 1988.

[Wa83]   D.H.D. Warren: An Abstract Prolog Instruction Set, Technical Note 309, SRI International, Menlo Park, California, October 1983.

Graphical User Interfaces for Algorithmic Debugging

Rickard Westman and Peter Fritzson

Programming Environments Laboratory
Department of Computer and Information Science
Linköping University,S-581 83 Linköping, Sweden
Email: ricwe@ida.liu.se, petfr@ida.liu.se

Abstract. *Algorithmic Debugging* is a method for semi-automatic program debugging, where the debugger incrementally acquires knowledge about the debugged program by interacting with the user. However, a major obstacle that prevents large-scale use of the method is the large number of questions (sometimes hard to answer) put to the user. One important improvement would be to provide a graphical user interface (GUI) for algorithmic debugging that provides *context* and *additional information* that makes it easier for the user to answer questions, and is flexible enough to let the user *postpone answering* certain questions and to a greater extent control where to look for the bug. In this paper we discuss several of these issues, and present a prototype graphical user interface that has been implemented and used as a part of a generalized algorithmic debugger for imperative languages, and recently adapted to an algorithmic debugger for lazy functional languages.

1   Introduction

Algorithmic debugging is a technique for providing automatic computer support for software debugging, first introduced by Shapiro [Sha82]. Initially, the technique was only suitable for side-effect free logic programs, but has later been generalized for programs in other languages, including the debugging of programs written in parallel logic programming languages [LS88], in imperative languages with side-effects and in lazy functional languages. The generalization for imperative languages is known as the *Generalized Algorithmic Debugging Technique* (GADT), which is described in detail in the Ph.D. thesis of Nahid Shahmehri [Sha91] and in [FGKS91], whereas the generalization for lazy functional languages, the *Lazy Algorithmic Debugging Technique* (LADT), is described in a paper by Nilsson and Fritzson [NF92].

However, despite recent improvements in bug location through program slicing and test database lookup, the large number of (sometimes hard to answer) questions to the user in algorithmic debugging remains one of the major obstacles that prevents large scale usage of the method. One important improvement would be to provide a graphical user interface (GUI) for algorithmic debugging that provides *context* and *additional information* that makes it easier for the user to answer questions, and is flexible enough to let the user *postpone answering* certain questions and to a greater extent control where to look for the bug.

As part of the work on GADT, a prototype debugger using that method has been implemented for a subset of Pascal. Initially, a simple TTY-based user interface was used for this implementation, but it was clear that the debugging process would benefit from a more sophisticated, graphical user interface (GUI).

Thus we have implemented a first version of such an interface, which will be described in the following sections of this paper. First, the algorithmic debugging process will be briefly described, from the perspective of the user of the original TTY-based interface. Some inadequacies of this interface will be discussed, and how they can be addressed in a GUI. The features and layout of the current implementation will then be presented, followed by some discussion about implementation issues. Finally, future directions in the development of this interface will be briefly discussed.

2 The Generalized Algorithmic Debugging Tool and the Need for Graphic User Interfaces

The *Generalized Algorithmic Debugging Tool* (GADT) is a prototype implementation of the *Generalized Algorithmic Debugging Technique*. In some contexts, GADT is also used for referring to the technique, but in this paper it only refers to the prototype implementation. Specifically, limitations of GADT should be taken as limitations of the current implementation, not as limitations of the technique per se.

When GADT is used to debug a faulty program, the user will frequently be asked about the *intended behavior* of various parts of the program (currently at the procedure[1] level). Confronted with the actual behavior of the program at a certain point of execution, the user has the option to answer "yes" (the actual behavior was as intended), "no" (the procedure behaved erroneously) or to give an assertion corresponding to the intended behavior.

Figure 1 shows an example of how the user interacts with the debugger, guiding the bug location process in a faulty Pascal program [FAS92]. The algorithmic debugger searches for the bug while posing questions to the user. For example, sorting [2,1,3] in increasing order should yield [1,2,3] and not [3,1]. Therefore, the user answers no – this is incorrect. Sort([1,3])=[3,1] is also incorrect, whereas sort([3])=[3] is correct. Finally the bug is located to within the procedure insert.

---

1. Pascal functions, procedures and program blocks are all referred to as procedures in this paper.

```
sort(in:list=[2,1,3],out:sort=[3,1])?
> no
sort(in:list=[1,3],out:sort=[3,1])?
> no
sort(in: list=[3],out: sort=[3])?
> yes
insert(in: elem=1, in: list=[3],out:insert=[3,1])?
> no
insert(in: elem=1, in: list=[], out: insert=[1])?
> yes
An error has been located inside the body of function insert.
```

Fig. 1. User interaction during bug location.

Even in this small example, it is clear that the user interface leaves a lot to be desired. Considering the debugging of large-scale programs, the problems become even more apparent:

- *Source code browsing*

  There is no way to *view the source code* of the specified procedures from the debugger. Providing automatic lookup of source code (with associated comments), would help the user to answer the questions correctly, and give a better understanding of the execution. Navigating through the source code of a large-scale program manually would be an unnecessary waste of time.

- *Visualization of query context*

  Every question represents a specific node in the execution tree of the program, but it is hard to *visualize the context of the question*, i.e. the structure of this tree, based only on the information presented to the user. For example, from which node in the execution tree is the procedure "insert" invoked, when it fails? In debugging a complex program, the questions asked about it will probably appear to be relatively unrelated to each other: The overall structure of the erroneous execution will most likely be lost from the user's perspective.

- *Saving and restoring debugging context*

  During long debugging sessions, it might be necessary to *save the state* of the debugging session, so that it can be continued later. *Resuming* such a session would be much easier if a graphical representation of the execution tree was available to refresh the user's memory about the current context of debugging.

- *User-tailored control of bug location*

  The user is not at all in *control of the process of debugging*, for better or for worse. This, to some extent, is in the nature of algorithmic debugging, but there is clearly room for improvement. For example, the user interface should be able to support a *flexible starting point* for the debugging process, in contrast to always starting at the beginning of the program execution. Without any way to browse through the execution tree, pointing out the start node would be tricky. Likewise, the user interface should be able to support *skipping parts* of the execution which are known to be correct or irrelevant to the problem. Although GADT does not presently support this kind of operations, the user interface should be designed with such future extensions in mind.

- *Visualization of large data structures*

  The sorted list in the example is very short – the kind of presentation showed in figure 1 would obviously not be suitable if the list contained, for instance, 10000 items. Another example of parameters which would need special treatment is pointer variables, should they be implemented in future versions of GADT. Clearly, a quite flexible mechanism for displaying *large data structures* and *pointer parameters* would have to be included in the user interface, if GADT were to be used for general debugging of "real-world programs."

Many of these reflections are based on the assumption that it is desirable to aid the user in understanding the ongoing debugging process. Certainly, it is possible for the user to answer the questions put to him, without knowing anything at all besides the intended behavior of each procedure and the value of its incoming parameters (supplied in the question). The fault location achieved by GADT would be no less accurate than if the user fully understood each step in the process.

However, this line of reasoning misses one of the currently major problems: it is often hard for the user to answer questions about the correctness of intermediate results from typical programs. If the user has access to information related to the context of the question, has the possibility to browse related source code, can visualize data structures, and is able to ask questions about relevant dependencies in the program (which for example can be computed by program slicing techniques [Wei84] [HRB88] [KL88] [KSF92] [Kam93]), it will become much easier for the user to act as an oracle and provide correct answers to the debugger.

Thus, many of the problems described above could be addressed by graphically presenting the execution tree to the user, and making utility functions (such as source code lookup) available on a per-node basis. The complete execution tree of the sort example is shown in figure 2. In the actual interface, nodes which are not yet visited would, by default, be hidden from view.

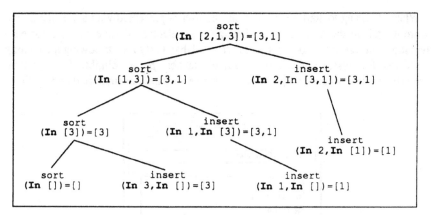

Fig. 2. The execution tree of the function *sort* on input *[2,1,3]*.

3 The Graphical User Interface

Besides the graphic user interfaces of GADT and LADT which are discussed in this paper, we are also aware of a graphic user interface for the *Rational Debugger, RD,* [Per86], which is an algorithmic debugger for Prolog. The user interface for *RD* visualizes the Prolog execution tree during the debugging process. There are several papers on visual user interfaces for conventional debuggers, e.g. [AM86] [ISO87] [Bov87] and [GWM88].

In this section the graphical user interface of GADT, tentatively called *AdView*, will be presented step by step, introducing its elements in the same order as a new GADT user would see them. AdView uses a high resolution display device to present information to the user, and gets feedback through an alphanumeric keyboard and a three-button mouse.

When GADT is started, its control window appears on the screen as shown in figure 3. By clicking on the buttons of the control window, the user can start a **new** debugging session, continue with an **old** one (saved at some previous occasion) or **quit**. Multiple, independent GADT sessions are supported by AdView, each having its own set of windows. The **quit** option exits all GADT sessions in progress.

Fig. 3. The GADT control window

When choosing to start a new session, the user is presented with a file dialog box (figure 4), where the program to be debugged is selected. Various features for easy navigation through the Unix file system are available. Only files following the naming convention for Pascal source code (suffix matches *.p*) are eligible for selection. Currently, programs consisting of multiple source files are not supported by GADT.

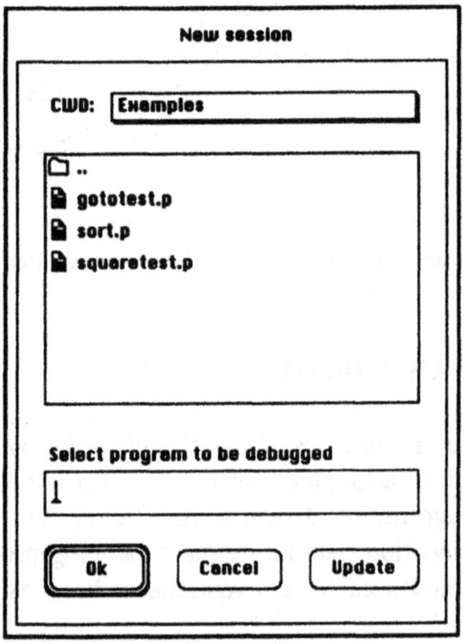

Fig. 4. The file dialog, showing the programs available for debugging

After this selection, algorithmic debugging starts. Whenever the algorithmic debugger needs to know the intended behavior of a procedure, a window showing the execution tree is presented to the user. In figure 5, the question concerns the procedure prepend. In this case, there is only one node of the execution tree labeled prepend, but since this is not always the case, the box representing the node in question is drawn with an emphasized border. The parameters of prepend and relevant global variables, if any, are displayed inside this border. The user answers the question by clicking on the appropriate button (**correct/incorrect**) at the bottom of the window. This process is repeated until the error is located.

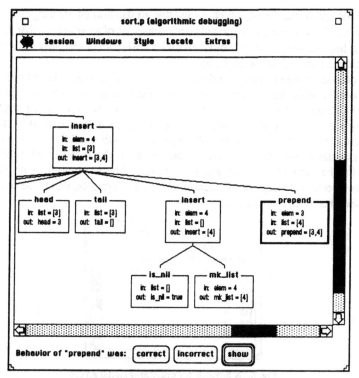

Fig. 5. The algorithmic debugger asks if a procedure behaved correctly.

Note that the execution tree includes all procedure invocations up to the point where the debugger needs user input. Nodes that are executed later are normally hidden. The entire execution up to the current node can be studied by using the scrollbars to the right and the bottom of the display area. Within each level of the tree, the nodes are sorted so that the procedure execution order corresponds to a left-to-right ordering.

Besides providing the user with a view of the execution path followed by the debugger, the tree display can be used as a way to specify execution points when giving commands to the debugger. Since a representation of the actual execution tree is displayed, recursive calls, calls from within loops, etc. can be handled. By pressing the right mouse button over a node, a popup-menu is displayed, showing the actions that can be taken for that node:

- The source code associated with a node can be displayed in a window. As a shortcut, the source code for the current node (the one referred to in the last question) can be shown by clicking at the **show** button at the bottom of the window.
- An **assertion** can be given for the procedure associated with the node, by entering lines of text in a simple text editor.

- A node can be **collapsed**, which means that all its children are temporarily hidden. This mechanism can be used to hide irrelevant parts of a big tree, so that the relevant parts become more visible. Collapsed nodes are drawn in a slightly different way to distinguish them from normal nodes.
- A collapsed node can be **expanded**, reversing the action described above.

In some cases a large parameter value needs special treatment to be displayed, e.g. the 10000 element array discussed earlier. Large array parameters are displayed by showing a moderate number of data items, followed by three trailing dots, signifying that there is more to see. The name of the parameter will also be added to the pop-up menu associated with its node. When selected from the menu, a browser appears, displaying the parameter in a suitable way. Figure 6 shows a browser for displaying the contents of relatively large one-dimensional arrays. Currently, this is the only special case which has been implemented.

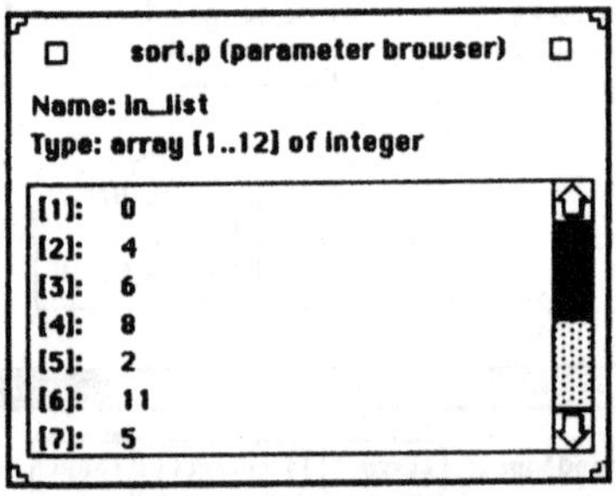

Fig. 6. A browser for one-dimensional arrays

The *execution tree window* is the focus for the algorithmic debugging procedure, but some other structures can also be displayed in tree form by selection in the pull-down menu labeled "Windows" located at the top of the window.

The *static call graph window* shows, for each procedure in the program, any procedures that may directly be invoked from the procedure in question during execution. This window is primarily intended to give an overview of the static program structure, as a complement to the dynamic call graph window. To simplify the display of this graph, it is converted to a tree by breaking up any loops caused by recursive calling structures. This can be seen in figure 7, where the recursive call to the "insert" procedure is indicated by putting the name of the called procedure within parentheses where the loop is broken up. Popup-menus, similar to those attached to the execution tree nodes, are implemented for the nodes in this tree as well.

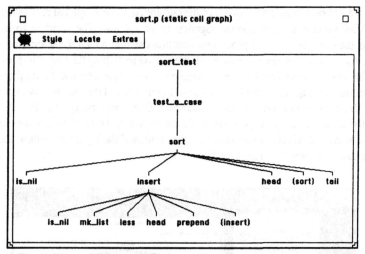

Fig. 7. The static call graph with recursive calls shown in a special way.

Another structure which can be displayed graphically is the program structure with respect to nested procedure definitions. Currently, nested procedure definitions are not included in the Pascal subset implemented in GADT, so all programs have the flat structure shown in figure 8.

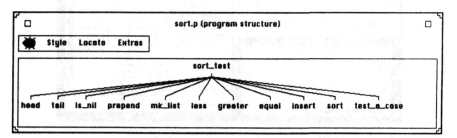

Fig. 8. Program structure with respect to nested definitions

Finally, a window containing the full trace tree (equivalent to the execution tree at the end of execution) can be opened at any time.

In addition to the functions described this far, a number of utility functions for printing, saving debugging sessions, locating nodes by names, changing layout parameters etc. are available from pull-down menus.

Figure 9 shows most components of the current AdView graphical user interface for the GADT system as they appear together in actual use. The window to the right displays the execution tree of procedure/function calls, in which the search for the bug occurs. As we have previously remarked, the reason to display the tree is to provide the user with a better overview when answering questions. The debugger highlights the call which currently is queried (the bold frame to the right), and the user is expected to push one of the buttons labeled correct or incorrect. If the user pushes the button labeled show, the source code of the procedure will be shown in the window at lower left. The window at middle left show the static call structure, and the topmost window shows the nesting structure, mainly to provide better overview.

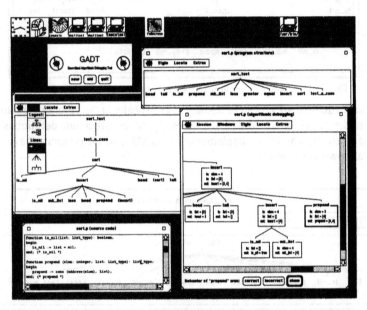

Fig. 9. The current AdView graphical user interface for the GADT system in use on a Sun workstation.

3.1 The LADT Graphical User Interface

As mentioned previously, most of the graphical user interface for GADT could be reused when constructing the graphical user interface for LADT - the Lazy Algorithmic Debugging Tool. The first version of this GUI is shown in figure 10. Some differences are notable. The lazy dynamic execution graph is not displayed since it might be quite complicated in the lazy case. Instead the static call tree is displayed to provide an approximate guidance related to the static program structure, which of course is not as detailed as was the case for the dynamic call graph using GADT. The dialogue window, however, displays the full dynamic sequence of calls up to the current point. Recursive calls in the static call graph window are shown by displaying the name of the function with a recursive call within parentheses. Input/output parameter values are not displayed in the execution tree since they sometimes can be quite big. Instead such values are shown in the interaction window

In addition to buttons for the answers "yes" and "no" there is also a button labeled "maybe". The reason is that there are cases when the user might be unwilling to supply a definite yes or no answer to a question, either because he really does not know the answer, or because the question seems to be large and complicated. Thus, there is an option to answer *maybe* this is correct, I don't know". This effectively lets the user postpone answering the question and get on with the debugging in the hope that a bug is positively identified before he is faced with this question again.

Initially, a "maybe" answer is treated as "no". Thus the children of the current node will be searched. If no bug is found, the algorithm will eventually get back to the node that the user was unsure about, knowing that all its children behaved correctly. At this point, the user is again asked about the node. If he this time indicates that the result is correct, debugging will proceed as usual, the only difference being that the user has had to answer more questions than otherwise would have been the case. If the answer is that the result is incorrect, then there must be a bug in the applied function. However, if the users insists on answering "maybe", the algorithm is forced to conclude that there might be a bug in the function applied. This is reported to the user and the algorithm then continues as if the result was correct, since it is still possible that a more definite bug will be found.

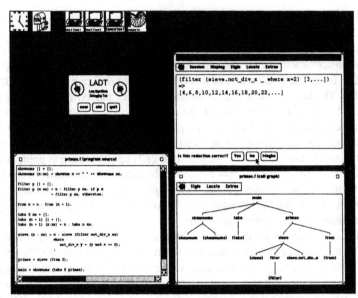

Fig. 10. The graphic user interface for LADT when debugging a small prime number program.

4 Implementation issues

AdView and GADT currently runs under SunOS 4.1.2 on Sun Sparcstations. AdView can be run under most of the popular window systems for this platform – OpenWindows, X11R5 and SunView.

AdView and GADT run as separate processes, communicating through shared data files and a pseudo-terminal (PTY) used by AdView to emulate user input to the underlying TTY-interface. Only slight modifications to GADT have been made, to make it possible to add functionality not present in the original user interface. (Most of the added functionality is contained completely within AdView and does not need support from GADT.)

C++ [ES90] was used as the implementation language for AdView, capitalizing on the object-oriented nature of user interfaces and the availability of powerful application frameworks, in the form of C++ class libraries.

Version 2.2 of the class library ET++ [WGM88] was chosen as a feasible framework for the design of AdView. ET++ contains a very flexible set of user interface classes, such as the **TreeView** class, which allows visualization of tree structures with minimal effort. Also, the ET++ collection classes proved to be very useful for building internal data structures. On the negative side, this version of ET++ contained some quite serious bugs, causing spurious crashes in AdView until they were found and corrected. (Fortunately, ET++ is released with full source code, making such corrections possible.)

5 Future work

Although the current version of AdView seems sufficient for use with GADT, we expect that experience in using algorithmic debugging on more realistic program examples will lead to revisions in the user interface. For example, more powerful browsing capabilities and support for visualizing complex data structures might be needed.

6 Conclusions

Despite recent improvements in bug location, the large number of (sometimes hard to answer) questions to the user in algorithmic debugging remains one of the major obstacles that prevents large scale usage of the method. In this paper we have discussed user interface issues and presented a graphical user interface (GUI) for algorithmic debugging that provides *context* and *additional information* that makes it easier for the user to answer questions, and is flexible enough to let the user *postpone answering* certain questions and to a greater extent control where to look for the bug.

We expect that powerful graphical user interfaces will be a key component in making it feasible to use future algorithmic debuggers on realistic programs.

Acknowledgements

We are grateful to Nahid Shahmehri for suggestions and comments regarding the GUI for GADT and to Henrik Nilsson for similar advice concering the GUI for LADT. This research was supported by NUTEK - the Swedish Board for Industrial and Technical Development. The research was done in part under the GIPE II Esprit II project.

7 Bibliography

[AM86]   E. Adams and S.S. Muchnik, *DBXTool: A Window-Based Symbolic Debugger for Sun Workstations*. Software Practice and Experience, pp. 653-669, July 1986.

[Bov87]   J.D. Bovey, *A Debugger For A Graphical Workstation*, Software Practice and Experience, pp. 647-662, September 1987.

[ES90]   Margarete Ellis and Bjarne Stroustrup. *The Annotated C++ Reference Manual*. Addison-Wesley, 1990.

[FAS92]   Peter Fritzson, Mikhail Auguston and Nahid Shahmehri. *Using Assertions in Declarative and Operational Models for Automated Debugging*. Accepted for publication in the journal Systems and Software 1992.

[FGKS91]   Peter Fritzson, Tibor Gyimothy, Mariam Kamkar and Nahid Shahmehri. *Generalized Algorithmic Debugging and Testing.* Proceedings of the ACM SIGPLAN'91, pp. 317–326, Toronto, Ontario, Canada, June 1991. Also accepted to *LOPLAS*, and as report LiTH-IDA-R-90-42.

[GWM88]   J.H. Griffin, H.J. Wasserman, and L.P. Mcgavran, *A debugger for parallell processes.* Software Practice and Experience, pp. 1179-1190, December 1988.

[HRB88]   Susan Horwitz, Thomas Reps and David Binkley: *Interprocedural Slicing using Dependence Graphs.* ACM Transactions on Programming Languages and Systems, Vol. 12, No. 1, pages 26-61, January 1990.

[ISO87]   Sadahiro Isoda, Takao Shimomura and Yuji Ono. *VIPS: A Visual Debugger.* IEEE Software, pp. 8-19, May 1987.

[KSF92]   Mariam Kamkar, Nahid Shahmehri and Peter Fritzson: *Interprocedural Dynamic Slicing.* In Proc of PLILP'92, August 26-28, 1992. LNCS 631, Springer-Verlag,. Also as research report LiTH-R-91-20.

[Kam92]   Mariam Kamkar: *Interprocedural Dynamic Slicing with Applications to Debugging and Testing.* Ph.D. thesis, Linköping University, April 1993.

[KL88]   Bogdan Korel and Janusz Laski: *Dynamic Program Slicing.* Information Processing Letters, pp 155-163, October 1988.

[LS88]   Yossi Lichtenstein and Ehud Shapiro: *Concurrent Algorithmic Debugging*, In Proc of the ACM Workshop on Parallel and Distributed Debugging, Madison, Wisconsin, May 1998. Proc in SIGPLAN Notices 24:1, Jan 1989.

[NF92]   Henrik Nilsson, Peter Fritzson. *Algorithmic Debugging for Lazy Functional Languages.* In Proc. of PLILP'92 - Symposium on Programming Language Implementation and Logic Programming, Leuven, Belgium August 1992. LNCS 631, Springer Verlag.

[Per86]   Luis Moniz Pereira. *Rational Debugging in Logic Programming.* In Proc. of the Third Logic Programming Conference, pages 203–210, London, England, July 1986

[Sha82]   E.Y.Shapiro. *Algorithmic Program Debugging.* MIT Press, May 1982.

[Sha91]   Nahid Shahmehri. *Generalized Algorithmic Debugging.* Ph.D. thesis, Linköping University, Dec. 1991.

[WGM88]   Andre Weinand, Erich Gamma and Rudolf Marty, *ET++ – An Object-Oriented Application Framework in C++.* In Proc. of OOPSLA'88, pages 46-57, San Diego, California, September 1988.

[Wei84]   Mark Weiser: *Program Slicing.* IEEE Transactions on Software Engineering, Vol. Se-10, No. 4, pages 352-357, July 1984.

Towards a Plan Calculus Based Intelligent Debugging System

Rudi Lutz

School of Cognitive and Computing Sciences, University of Sussex,
Falmer, Brighton, BN1 9QH, England

Email: rudil@cogs.susx.ac.uk

Abstract. When debugging expert programmers seem to use a combination of techniques in order to arrive at an understanding of how a program works. In particular they use a process of programming "cliché" recognition, backed up by a process of general reasoning based on the semantics of the programming constructs used in the program. Other attempts to build knowledge-based debugging systems have used one or other of these techniques, but have not combined them. This paper presents the case for using both these techniques in an integrated way, and argues that the plan calculus is a knowledge representation technique that can facilitate this. An overview of work on an intelligent debugging system for Pascal (IDS) will then be presented.

1 Introduction

In common with many other areas of Artificial Intelligence, automatic debugging shares the property that it is helpful to examine how people perform the task in order to obtain clues as to how best to proceed in trying to automate it. This does not mean that we have to imitate exactly how people do it, since this is beyond the state of the art, and for a domain like automatic debugging may not even be the best way to proceed, since people are not really that good at the task in the first place (probably because programs are complex formal objects, and people are notoriously bad at formal reasoning). However, knowledge of the kinds of strategies people employ can usefully guide the design of the system. This paper will therefore begin with a brief look at the methods used by experienced programmers. It will then briefly survey the main approaches other debugging systems have taken, showing how their strengths result from the attempt to perform one or other of these methods, and their weaknesses result from not applying others. It will then argue that automatic debugging systems need to make *integrated* use of all these methods, and that the plan calculus [19] (a knowledge representation technique for programs and programming knowledge) can facilitate this. This paper will then describe work on a plan calculus based intelligent debugging system (IDS) for Pascal. Although not complete, preliminary results indicate that this approach may enable IDS to progress beyond "toy" programs.

2 Human Debugging Strategies

In order to debug a program, and to explain the program to themselves or others, programmers have to develop an *understanding* of the program. We take this as meaning that the programmer can:

(a)   describe the program in terms of some high-level plan of which the program is an implementation.

(b)   describe how the various parts of the program are implementations of sub-plans.

(c)   describe how these sub-plans interact to achieve the overall goals(plans) of the program.

It is not our intention here to give an account of all the empirical studies on the processes used by programmers when debugging programs. However, such studies (e.g. [28]) have shown that one of the factors which distinguishes expert programmers from novices is their use of programming cliché recognition. If a program is not made up of clichés then programmers find the program much harder to understand and debug, since they then have to fall back on an ability to reason about the program based on their understanding of the semantics of each of the primitive operations in the program. This suggests one possible technique for debugging programs - attempt to understand the program by recognising programming clichés, using reasoning from first principles only when neccessary. If examples of code are found which almost match known plans then an error has possibly been located, particularly if this near-match occurs where there is some inconsistency in the use of known plans. In this case edits can be suggested which would correct the plan. Alternatively a piece of code may be recognised as the implementation of some plan but this plan does not achieve what the program's author says it should. In this case the mismatch can be pointed out, and code which implements the desired plan can possibly be suggested.

Of course, programmers also use various other sources of information available to them e.g. the data input to, and output from, the program, system generated run-time error messages, and trace information. The above debugging method using plan recognition alone is normally only used by programmers on smallish programs. When debugging larger and more complex programs programmers will use the input/output data and trace information together with information from the program's author and/or the run-time error messages to locate the places in the code an error first became apparent. S/he would then attempt to "reason backwards" from this place to the place in the code which originally caused the error. This "reasoning backwards" process is really one of isolating all and only that code which could have affected the place where the error became apparent [34], and one can then reason about this subsection of the code *using all the techniques of plan recognition* etc. Expert programmers will often assume parts of the code to be correct and reason about the rest of the code under these assumptions. Only if the error can't be found, or if some piece of evidence leads to a contradiction will these parts of the code be examined in detail. In addition certain run-time error messages will suggest very specific errors to expert programmers, and they may well just search the code looking for a very specific piece or type of code which their experience tells them is often the cause of the particular run-time error.

It should be clear from the above that the process of program understanding is one of the keys to program debugging (at least as performed by expert programmers), and that two of the processes used by programmers to understand programs are:

(i)   *cliché recognition* - this is the technique where by recognising the form of all or part of a program one can recognise what it does.

(ii)   *general reasoning from first principles about a piece of code* - this involves actually analysing code to see what it does, and arriving at a description (either formal or informal) of its effects. This technique is often used on novel code i.e. code that does not fit any cliché known to the programmer. This situation can occur for two reasons - either the program writer has thought of a new technique (relative to the techniques captured by the cliches known to the debugging programmer) to achieve some standard operation, or they are implementing code corresponding to no known operation but which is essential to achieve some precondition of the code which follows. In the first case, the debugger can compare the effect description she has built up of the code with the effects of known plans. If these are equivalent then effectively the programmer can treat the code as if a known plan had been used in the code instead of the unusual code. One can then say that the expert programmer has again recognised the plan for which this code was an implementation, the only difference being that this time the plan was recognised by reasoning about the code rather than just matching against a library of previously known plans. In this case this can then feed into the process of plan recognition in the code. The second case is more problematical, in that the only description of the unusual code is a symbolic effect description. In this case the best that can be done is to try and show that the effect description does indeed achieve some precondition of the plan(s) it feeds into, in which case the role of this code in the program has been established. Even in the case where two clichés (one of which feeds into the other) have been recognised, but which do not jointly constitute a 'higher-level' cliché, then again some kind of general reasoning will be necessary to show consistency, and establish the roles, of the two plans.

It should also be clear from the above that these two processes are not independent of each other - cliché recognition can provide information for the general reasoning (theorem proving) process, and the general reasoning process can provide information for the cliché recognition process. At present, work on IDS is confined to this program understanding technique. In the future we hope to extend it to include analysis of run-time information etc.

3 Other Automatic Debugging Systems

In this section we will give a brief summary of other attempts to build intelligent debugging systems, concentrating on the two best known of the knowledge-based systems i.e. PROUST and TALUS. Readers interested in a fuller review are referred to [24].

There are several main dimensions along which debugging systems can be classified. The first of these is essentially to do with generality i.e. what range of programs can the system deal with? This issue is related to how much knowledge the systems have to have *in advance* about the problem that the program it is being asked to debug is supposed to solve. Some systems only work on a very narrow range (two or three in some cases) of problems for which the system has extremely detailed knowledge of possible solution strategies (e.g. [21, 22,7]). Other systems only work for problems for which the system already has an example solution (e.g. [1,18]). On the other hand there are systems which attempt to be more general. These essentially fall into three categories - those that require a specification of some type to be submitted along with the program (e.g. PUDSY [11], and MYCROFT [6]), those that simply take a program and attempt to debug it as best they can (e.g. Wertz [37], and IDS itself), and those that take a program and an example of its intended behaviour (an input/output pair) and then attempt to debug it (e.g. Shapiro's Prolog debugger [26]).

The next factor which can be used to differentiate these systems is to do with their use of plan recognition versus their use of general reasoning abilities (e.g. reasoning about the semantics of programs using a theorem prover or symbolic evaluation). Of the systems that work on known problems the two most successful fall at opposite ends of this division. PROUST [7] uses plan recognition alone, while TALUS [18] uses theorem proving alone. As discussed below, both of these systems present problems with respect to trying to increase their domain of applicability. One of the contentions of this paper is that in order to widen the range of programs to which a debugging system can be applied the system will need to use both of these techniques. Lukey's system PUDSY [11] was an early attempt to use both approaches. However, because its plan recognition technique was rather simplistic, it had to fall back on symbolic evaluation much of the time, and this rather limits a system's ability (in particular to cope with larger programs due to problems of scaling).

The systems which make use of theorem proving/symbolic evaluation can be subdivided into two further categories - those which try to show that a program meets a specification (e.g. PUDSY, MYCROFT, and Eisenstadt and Laubsch's SOLO debugger [3]), and those which attempt to show equivalence of a program to a standard reference program (e.g. LAURA [1], and TALUS [18]).

The plan recognition based systems can also be subdivided into two categories - those which essentially use top-down recognition (analysis by synthesis) (e.g. PROUST, Ruth's system [21]), and those which use bottom-up plan recognition (e.g. IDS itself, Wills' system [36, 37, 38], and PUDSY).

There have been a few systems which have tried to use some sort of "reasoning backwards" technique. Weiser's [34] and Kamkar et. al.'s [9] program slicing work, Shapiro's [26] Prolog debugger and Fritzson et. al's [4] work fall into this category, as does Shapiro's SNIFFER system [25]. SNIFFER had three basic components - a primitive "cliche finder", a "time rover" which recorded a program's execution history, and a set of "sniffers" each of which was essentially an 'expert' on a particular type of bug. Each sniffer utilised information from the time rover and from the cliché finder. However, Shapiro concluded that plan diagrams could not be fully effective for debugging programs until a full plan recogniser was available which could cope with such things as plans being spread out over more than one program segment. It would be interesting to re-attempt SNIFFER's approach using the plan recogniser developed for IDS.

Another aspect of these systems which can be used to differentiate them is in the techniques they use for suggesting repairs to programs. In particular, do they use general techniques, or do they make use of a "bug library" ?

3.1 PROUST

The best-known of the plan recognition systems is PROUST, although it has to some extent been superseded by its successor CHIRON. The PROUST system is the work of the Cognition and Programming Project group at Yale University [2, 27, 29, 30, 31, 7], and is an attempt to create a debugging system for Pascal programs. PROUST's knowledge is represented internally in a frame-like formalism orientated very specifically towards Pascal. This knowledge is extremely problem-specific, enabling it to perform reasonably on programs for a few very specific problems. The knowledge is plan based, but the plans are expressed as program schemas (with extra information about preconditions, and about what *goals* the plan can be used to achieve), so the plan matching process is essentially one of matching against the source code. This representation of plans has three main drawbacks:

(i) It makes it difficult to apply to languages other than Pascal, since all the plans would need to translated. This translation may well prove difficult since much Pascal specific knowledge is embedded in them.

(ii) It makes it hard to *verify* plans as reasoning about code fragments is hard, especially as no attempt has been made to really give a semantics to the representation.

(iii) It makes it hard to reason about novel parts of the code that do not match known plans. Of course, if the plans were given a semantics, then whatever underlying programming language semantics one had used could also be used to reason about novel pieces of code.

(iv) The approach is prone to what Wills [37] calls the 'syntactic variability' problem. This is that, once programs start getting more complicated, there are often a very large number of ways in which the syntax of the language will allow the programmer to express a computation. Some of the differences are very superficial e.g. use of different variable names, differing order of statements in cases when the order does not matter, breaking up expressions into sequences of assignments, and so on. However, when combined, these superficial differences can make it very hard for a system based on code template matching to actually find appropriate matches. The solution in PROUST is to have large numbers of templates that attempt to capture all the likely variants. This is only really possible by limiting the system to a few smallish problems. Giving the system general reasoning abilities would enable the system to largely circumvent this problem

Because of the lack of semantics of PROUST's representation methods, it is not really possible for it to recognise inconsistencies in arbitrary programs. Instead, the system has to know in advance what goals have to be achieved by the program (and how these goals inter-relate), and can then check that the program contains plans which achieve all these goals. If a program fails to contain a plan to achieve some goal then a bug has been found. In order to give debugging advice PROUST then makes use of a very large *bug library*. This contains commonly occurring buggy versions of plans, also expressed in the same code template form. If any of these occur in a buggy program, then very specific debugging advice (stored with the bug rules in the library) can be given. This approach enables PROUST to give astonishingly pertinent advice even for some of the truly bizarre errors that novice programmers make. However the price paid is high - the bug catalogue is very large. Even though PROUST can only deal really effectively with one simple programming problem (involving not much more than computing the average of the non-negative numbers read in from a file or terminal), and rather less effectively on a few other simple problems), the PROUST group [8, 32] have catalogued something like 800 different bugs that novices make. This explosion of bug types, and hence in the size of the bug library, make it seem unlikely that this approach can be extended to much larger and more complex programs, let alone arbitrary programs. Furthermore, as yet their system cannot cope with programs involving such things as procedures, or pointer variables, and in order to cope with these it would need a much richer plan representation method allowing both for the fact that plans could be split between procedures, and for reasoning about complex, more abstract, data types.

PROUST's successor, CHIRON [23] goes some of the way towards addressing some of the above deficiencies. It has a similar knowledge base to PROUST, but with much more taxonomic information about the relationships between plans, and with data flow information recorded with the plans. This has resulted in their plan library looking very like a (language specific) subset of the knowledge base developed by Rich [19]. Accordingly it is able to deal with rather more tasks than PROUST. However, to *really* extend the range of programming tasks to which it could be applied would involve first of all giving the representation a semantics, and secondly some way of representing information about implementation techniques for more abstract data types.

If this was done it really would become a language specific version of the plan calculus, and would possibly end up very like IDS.

3.2   TALUS

The best known of the systems based on general reasoning abilities is TALUS [18] (a debugging system for student LISP programs), which has information about tasks students have been set, this time in the form of correct programs. It uses symbolic evaluation and a theorem prover to try and show that its stored program is equivalent to the one the student has submitted. It represents programming knowledge (i.e. common solutions) in a frame-like formalism. TALUS uses program transformation techniques to simplify the student program, and if the program fails on a pre-stored set of example input-output pairs, or if it cannot be proved equivalent to the stored solution program then an error is assumed to be present. In this case the stored, correct program is transformed until it matches the student program as closely as possible, and then this closely matching version is used to suggest repairs. Because TALUS utilises a very general technique it is quite successful on a large variety of problems (18 in all), but cannot cope with global (free) variables in function definitions, or with operations with side-effects (except in special cases). However, despite its claims not to use any plan matching, in essence TALUS uses a very simple form of plan identification, before starting on the process just described. This plan identification is based on extracting a few features from the program being analysed (e.g. recursion type), and these features are then compared against the corresponding features of the known solutions. How well the features match is then used to identify which of the known problems/possible solutions the student program is most likely to be an attempt at. Because this feature matching is quite impoverished the system can get confused. This resulted in TALUS having its own version of error clichés for some problems. These were "solutions" that Murray found students came up with quite often for certain problems (in particular when they had mis-interpreted the problem).

Although highly successful on the problems it knows about, TALUS's approach seems likely to suffer from severe scaling problems as the size of programs increases. Without some kind of plan recognition process (perhaps viewed as the use of pre-proved "lemmas") this problem seems unavoidable.

4   Combining Plan Recognition and Theorem Proving.

Murray [18] makes a very strong case in favour of his program verification approach to program debugging, while Johnson [7] argues equally strongly for plan based program debugging. How can these two viewpoints be reconciled? As discussed earlier, expert programmers use a process of plan recognition, supplemented by general reasoning from first principles. Accordingly, we argue that both techniques will be needed in a debugging system which is intended to be general purpose. Rich's [19] plan calculus is a knowledge representation technique which offers the potential ability to move smoothly between both techniques. Both PROUST and TALUS are tutoring systems. They therefore have available to them a set of possible solutions against which to check the student's program. So in the case of PROUST the system can check that the program contains plans to achieve the same goals as the target program, while TALUS can try to prove equivalence of the student program to the target program. However, in a situation where a target program is not available, the TALUS approach reduces to program verification which is extremely hard and combinatorially explosive, even assuming that a formal specification is available. The problem with a pure plan based approach is that apart from the basic plans needed, one also needs an enormous number (probably combinatorially explosive!) of plans or program transformations to capture minor implementation variants of the same algorithm. The theorem proving approach can get round this because of its generality- these variants can often quite easily be proved equivalent to some standard reference plan. Working within the plan calculus framework we can get the best of both worlds. First of all, we don't necessarily need to know the problem in order to try and understand the program since bottom up plan recognition can lead to an understanding of much of the program. Furthermore, as suggested above, this plan recognition can be viewed as an efficient form of theorem proving. Additionally we can always call on a theorem prover to deal with those parts of the program that do not exactly match known plans. Additionally, it turns out that the near-misses found by the plan recognition process can be regarded as failed attempts to prove some theorem, for which the steps in the proof have been conveniently grouped together. The missing parts of the near-miss can be regarded as telling us how the theorem failed to be proved. Near-miss correction as proposed in this paper can then be viewed as very similar in some sense to Murray's technique of debugging a program by repairing the proof of its equivalence to some reference function.

4.1 The Plan Calculus

The plan calculus is very complex, and we will only briefly summarise its main features. A fuller account can be found in Rich [19] and Lutz [17]. Its main advantages are that it is a (largely) language independent representation, that it has a properly defined semantics enabling reasoning about programs from first principles, even if they operate by side-effect, and that it enables one to reason about programs at different levels of abstraction. Additionally it abstracts away many superficial syntactic differences between programs. Furthermore it provides a formally defined notion of plans, and what it means for a plan to implement some operation. Because plans are defined in a formal, heirarchically structured way, it is possible to verify that they are indeed correct. Although there are other methods for reasoning about programs (e.g. denotational, or structured operational, semantics) none of these have a well-worked out notion of plans, and it is hard to apply them to fragments of programs, especially when the relevant fragments for a plan are widely scattered through the program. Furthermore, the plan calculus gives us a uniform representation for programs, at all levels of description, from the basic representation of programs (the surface plan) to high-level accounts of what they do, thus greatly simplifying the reasoning process. Space does not permit us to give a formal account of the plan calculus here. Readers interested in this are referred to Rich [19] and Lutz [17].

In the plan calculus a program is represented by a *surface plan*. This is a representation of the program as a control and data flow graph. An example, corresponding to the code below:

```
if x<0 then
    z:= -x
else
    z:=x;
```

is shown in Figure 1. Control flow is represented by thick arrows and data flow is represented by thin arrows. Operations such as applying a function (*@function*) are

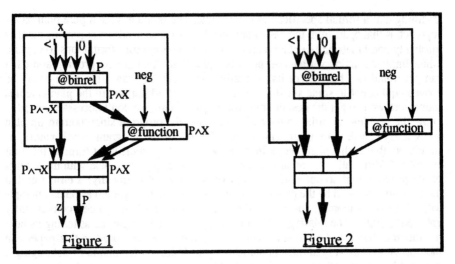

Figure 1   Figure 2

represented by boxes with the appropriate function as one of the inputs. Tests (such as applying a binary relation (*@binrel*)) are shown as boxes, with the relevant relation (e.g. "<") as one of the inputs, and the YES/NO subpartitions of the box indicating which way control flow will go depending on the result of that test. Data flow between two such boxes indicates that data values produced by one are used as inputs to the other. Join boxes are present to reconnect diverging data flows in conditionals, in order to give later operations a single place from which to get their inputs. They can be thought of as transmitting to their output the input value corresponding to whichever control flow input actually activates the join.

The knowledge base (plan library) contains various sorts of information, the most important of which (for our purposes) are definitions of operations, plans (corresponding to "clichéd" patterns of basic operations), and overlays (specifying how a plan can be viewed as implementing some more abstract operation), as well as definitions of primitive functions (e.g. "+") and data types. An example of the definition of an operation is:

```
IOSpec absop /.input(integer) => .output(integer)
Postconditions  .output=absolute-value(.input)
```

where *absolute-value* is defined by:

```
Function absolute-value: integer -> integer
Definition y=absolute-value(x) ↔ [[ge(x,0) ↔ y=x] ∨ [lt(x,0) ↔ y=-x]]
```

A (highly simplified) version[1] of the axiomatisation of the *absop* operation is:

---

[1] The full axiomatisation is actually done in a situational calculus (rather like that of Green [5]). For simplicity, we have omitted the situational arguments, and the related *behaviour functions*, in the axiomatisations we have given, but it should be noted that it is these which ultimately allow a plan calculus based system to reason properly about programs involving side-effects.

$$\forall xy[\ [instance(x, integer) \wedge instance(y, integer) \wedge y=absolute\text{-}value(x)]$$
$$\leftrightarrow\ \exists\alpha[absop(\alpha) \wedge input(\alpha)=x \wedge output(\alpha)=y]\ ]$$

Notice how this enables reasoning in both directions - if we have an occurrence of an *absop* operation in a program then we can deduce the relationship between the inputs and outputs of the operation, and this information can be used by a theorem prover to deduce properties of the program. Alternatively, if we find data values in the program satisfying the right properties, and related to each other in the right way, then we can deduce the existence of an *absop* operation.

Plans and overlays can also be expressed as graphs, and so can be treated as rules of a graph grammar, as described in Wills [36, 37, 38] and Lutz[13, 14, 15]. An example of a plan is *abs-plan* (shown in Figure 2):

Temporal Plan abs-plan
  Roles .if(@binrel) .end(join-output) .action(@function)
  Constraints .if.op=less $\wedge$ .if.two=0 $\wedge$ .action.op=neg $\wedge$ .action.input=.if.one $\wedge$
           .end.fail-input=.if.one $\wedge$ .end.succeed-input=.action.output $\wedge$
           cflow(.if.succeed,.end.succeed) $\wedge$ cflow(.if.fail,.end.fail)

and an example of an overlay is *abs-plan->absop* (shown in Figure 3) which records the system's knowledge that the plan *abs-plan* can be used to implement an *absop* operation:

TemporalOverlay abs-plan->absop
Correspondences absop.input=abs.if.one $\wedge$ absop.output=abs.end.output
        $\wedge$ absop.in=abs.if.in $\wedge$ absop.out=abs.end.out

These too are axiomatised in such a way that if we find an *abs-plan* in a program then we can deduce the existence of an *absop* operation, and hence deduce properties of its

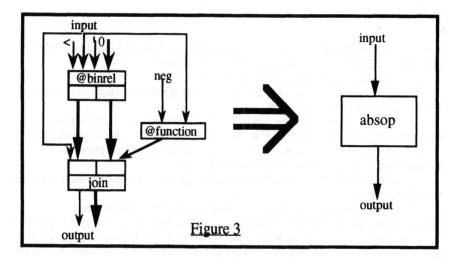

Figure 3

inputs and outputs. However, if the system had not had knowledge of the *abs-plan*, then we could have still deduced the existence of an *absop* in the program. For, suppose the surface plan of a program contained the sub-graph shown in Figure 1. Then from the axiomatisations of *tests* and *joins*, "neg", *@function*, etc we could have deduced that x and z are related by:

$$instance(integer,x) \wedge instance(integer,z) \wedge z=absolute\text{-}value(x)$$

and hence, from the axiom above, deduced the existence of the *absop* operation. This example, although simple (and simplified), illustrates the ability of the plan calculus to compensate for an incomplete plan library by general reasoning (using a theorem prover/symbolic evaluator) from the properties of the basic operations.

The current plan library contains definitions for about 250 plans, data types, operations, and overlays, and is largely based on that in Rich[19], although we have added some new ones of our own. These are organised into a taxonomy whereby plans can be specialisations, or extensions of other plans. For example, a *counting* plan is defined as a specialisation of an *iterative-generation* plan, in which the "generating function" is constrained to be *plus-one*, and the initial value is constrained to be 1. Similarly, operations and data types are also arranged in a taxonomic heirarchy. This enables plans and operations etc. to inherit information and properties from other plans and operations, making the development of the plan library easier, as well as making it easier for a theorem prover to reason about the plans where neccessary. Furthermore, as described in [23], many bugs can be explained by over generalisation of operations, and having taxonomic information easily available should make fixing such bugs easier (as well as making them easier to explain to the user of the system). It should be noted that the current plan library includes most of the plans used by PROUST, expressed in the plan calculus's more general and more principled notation.

One final point should be made here. Although we have not as yet attempted to use Weiser's [34] program slicing technique to reason backwards from the manifestation of an error to its source, the plan calculus/surface plan representation of programs is highly suited to this since it quite explicitly records the data flow information neccessary to perform program slicing.

5 IDS

The overall structure of IDS as finally envisaged is shown in Figure 4. With this architecture IDS's debugging strategy can be summarised as follows:

(a) Translate the program into its surface plan.

(b) Try to understand the program by recognising all occurrences of library plans. Make a note of any "near" matches.

(c) Using a theorem prover derive symbolic descriptions of any remaining (i.e. unrecognised) parts of the surface plan. Note that this could feed back into step (b).

(d) Check for broken preconditions of any of the recognised plans. Where there are such broken preconditions a bug has been located.

(e) Use near match information and broken precondition information to try and repair the program.

(f) Translate the debugged surface plan back into the source language.

Using broken precondition information to locate bugs in this way is similar to Kuper's work [10], in that it makes use of the fact that in a correct program the preconditions for an operation must be set up by the plans and operations which feed into it. If we find an operation in a program whose preconditions are not met then we have located a bug (whatever the purpose of the program).

The translator from Pascal to surface plans is structured in a similar way to a recursive-descent parser, and is similar in many ways to a compiler except that the target language is that of surface plans rather than machine code. This translator can cope with a large subset of Pascal, and the structure is such that it can easily be extended to cope with the rest. As implemented so far it can cope with assignments, procedures and functions, numbers, records and pointers, arrays, if statements, and while statements.

Despite the possiblity offered by the plan calculus to combine both general purpose reasoning using a theorem prover, and graph-based plan recognition, in a syntax independent and language independent manner, when it came to actually trying to use the plan calculus, in particular to do the graph based plan recognition, it became clear that this is an enormously hard problem (reflecting the fact that programs are extremely hard objects to analyse). Therefore the major effort in the IDS project so far has been devoted to developing algorithms for performing this recognition process. As mentioned above the plans and overlays in the library can be regarded as forming the rules of a graph grammar (a flowgraph grammar), and hence the recognition process can be viewed as a form of parsing. Space does not permit a full discussion of the parsing algorithm which is based on a generalisation of traditional chart parsing techniques [33] within a formal framework known as Restricted Structure-Sharing Flowgraph Grammars [13, 14, 17]. For a *fixed* grammar, the algorithm runs in time polynomial in the size of the graph being parsed, and is suitable for both bottom-up and top-down analysis of surface plans. Wills work [38] is heavily based on this algorithm.

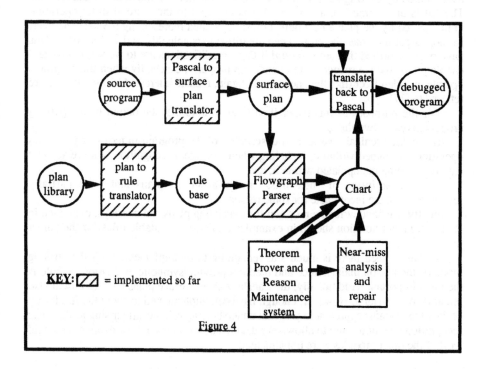

Figure 4

It should be noted that the parsing algorithm really checks for the occurrence of appropriately typed actions with the right data flows between them. Handling the control flows is more complicated since these do not have the same "fixed" nature as the data flows, since parts of a plan can be widely separated in a program. Wills [36, 37, 38] introduced the notion of *control flow environments* to facilitate this. However, although this enabled her to deal with the transitivity of control flow, there is still a problem with recognising plans with non-standard (according to the plan library) patterns of control flow. Dealing with this involves generalising the notion of control flow environments, and checking the control flow constraints now involves checking that a condition, known as the *plan condition*), is satisfiable for the plan. If the plan condition is *true*, then the plan is valid. If the plan condition is *false* then $A_1...A_n$ cannot be the roles of a valid plan. If the plan condition is neither simply *true* or *false*, then we have recognised a plan conditionally, and the plan condition is the condition under which we can say that the plan is present. Most of the time simple propositional reasoning is all that is needed here, and this is all the parser actually performs. Assuming that there is a limit to the depth of nesting of conditional statements in programs, then computing the plan conditions can be done reasonably efficiently. The plan conditions are treated as attributes of the flowgraph grammar, and are propagated during the parsing process. Full details of this, and the parsing mechanism, can be found in [17].

Of course there are various features of the plan calculus that do not exactly fit into the grammatical framework we have developed, in particular, plans involving data plans and data overlays. This is because such plans involve moving up to higher level view of the program. For instance, a plan involving pointers, and record accessing, might be recognised as implementing an operation on a list. The list is not an object manipulated by the original program, which only operates on the pointers and records. The list is an abstraction, and if this list is an input to the more abstract operation implemented by the plan a new object must be created representing the list. The chart parsing algorithm has therefore been modified to enable this, and various new plans have been identified that are *essential* if these modifications are to work properly and enable plans that we recognise to connect up properly, especially when the programs operate by side-effect (like the one above). Again, readers interested in more details are referred to [17].

For the purposes of this paper it suffices to note that the output of the parsing process gives us two things:

(i)   A hierarchically structured description of the program in terms of plans and operations contained within it, including where necessary recognition of more abstract data types being manipulated within it, and

(ii)   A description of "near-miss" information i.e. plans that were partially recognised, but are incomplete for some reason.

Finally, we have written a program for translating plans and overlays, expressed in Rich's compact notation shown in examples earlier, into suitable rules for the parser to use.

As can be seen there is much still remaining to be implemented. Of the missing modules the reason maintenance and theorem proving/symbolic evaluation module is the most important. Additionally, the translator from surface plans back to Pascal also remains to be written. However, enough has been implemented to show the feasibility of the plan calculus approach to program understanding using chart parsing as the basic recognition technique, and to allow very detailed descriptions of how debugging would work if the other modules were implemented.

```
program sort(input,output);
type listelement = record
                          numb : integer;
                          next : ^listelement;
                  end;
          plist = ^listelement;
var head, p : plist;
       n : integer;

procedure addtolist(n : integer; t : plist);
var p : plist;
begin
   new(p);
   p^.numb:=n;
   if t = nil then
      begin
         p^.next := head;
         head:=p;
      end
   else
      begin
/*next two lines are in the wrong order*/
         t^.next:=p;
         p^.next:=t^.next;
      end;
end;
```

```
procedure findplace(n: integer;
                            var p:
plist);
var t : ^listelement;
     found : boolean;
begin
 if head^.numb > n  then
        p:=nil;
 else
      begin
        p:=head;
        t:=p^.next;
        found:=false;
        while not found do
           if t <> nil then
             if t^.numb <= n then
               begin
                 p:=t;
                 t:=t^.next;
               end
             else found:=true
           else found:=true;
      end;
end;

/*main program*/

begin
     head:=nil;
     while not eof do
       begin
              readln(n);
              if head<>nil then
                          findplace(n,p)
              else p:=head;
               addtolist(n,p);
        end;
       p:=head;
       while p<>nil do
         begin
              writeln(p^.numb);
              p:=p^.next;
         end;
end.
```

5.1 An Example

Space does not permit a detailed account of the above process. A full account can be found in [15, 16, 17]. Consider the program shown above. This program is supposed to read in numbers from a file or terminal and output the numbers in ascending order. It does this by use of a linked list which holds the numbers, each new number being stored in the appropriate place in the list. The program contains a couple of user procedures - *findplace*, which finds the correct place in the sorted list where a new number is to go, and *addtolist*, which is supposed to add a new number to the list.

However, there is a bug in this procedure - the two lines responsible for 'splicing in' the new element into the list have been given in the wrong order. Using the flowgraph chart parser IDS is able to recognise that the procedure *findplace* implements an *Internal-Labelled-Thread-Find* operation. This is the plan corresponding to finding an object satisfying some property (in this case being larger than the input number) in a linked list structure. When it tries to analyse *addtolist*, however, it finds various subplans, including a *new-labelled-root* plan. It then tries to understand the main program, by substituting its understanding of the two procedures *findplace* and *addtolist* into the surface plan for the main program. Note that the part of the surface plan for *addtolist* corresponding to the two buggy lines is included in this). It then tries to understand the resulting surface plan, and finds a partial *ordered-labelled-thread-insert* plan, which needs a *labelled-thread-add-after* plan to complete itself. A *labelled-thread-*

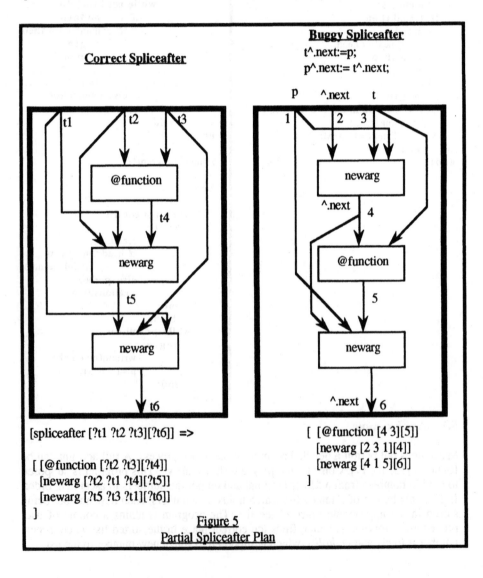

Figure 5
Partial Spliceafter Plan

add-after plan is made up of (amongst other things) a *spliceafter* plan, and indeed there is a partial *spliceafter* plan, corresponding to the two buggy lines. Figure 5 shows the *spliceafter* plan, and the buggy part of the surface plan. The matching (parsing) process gives the best partial match as:

[spliceafter [1 4 3][?t6]] = [[@function [4 3][5]]

                  [newarg [4 1 5][6]]   ]

and needing to find an object matching:

[newarg [6 3 1][?t6]]

to complete the match.By hypothesising that this partial plan should indeed be the *spliceafter* plan obtained by correcting the partial one using the above information, and continuing its analysis, IDS is able eventually to recognise the whole program as performing a *sort* operation on the numbers in the input file. If the theorem proving part of the system had been built, it would have received further confirmation that this is indeed where the bug lies since before correcting the code the preconditions for the *Internal-Labelled-Thread-Find* operation are broken (because, after the first time through the loop, the output from *addtolist* forms the input to *findplace*, which is an *Internal-Labelled-Thread-Find*, and from the axioms for all the operations and plans involved it is easy to show that *findplace*'s preconditions are broken, since the erroneous code can cause a cycle in the thread input to *findplace*, contradicting the definition of a thread). Indeed, it is this broken pre-condition that should alert the system to the presence of a bug. Before actually changing the code the system can query the user about whether the program is indeed trying to sort the numbers in the input file. Note that this bug can be found even if the system does not know what task the program is trying to perform.

5.2 Future Work

Of course much remains to be done to complete this work. In particular it needs the addition of the theorem prover and reason maintenance system, along the lines of Rich's CAKE system [20], and more work needs to be done on heuristics for how to reconnect replacement bug-fixes to the surrounding graph. We are currently working on the use of multiple near-miss information as a guide to this process. For instance, if we know there is a bug at some point in the program, and there is a near-miss to some plan A at that point, and part of what is wrong with A is that it requires a plan B, but cannot find one, and there is also a near-miss to a plan B at that point then this mutual information ought to help both confirm the hypothesis that a B is required, and also to aid the system in working out how to reconnect a repair to B to the surrounding graph. Note that this can help debug programs even if we have no prior knowledge of what the code is supposed to do.

It would also be interesting to look at the various bug classifications, and repair strategies, developed by other researchers to see if these are meaningful in flowgraph terms. If so many of these could perhaps be adopted. In particular, we are working on building a tutoring system (perhaps rather like a combination of PROUST and TALUS) based on this work.

In connection with this suggestion, it should be noted that the system is now almost at a point where it could be given (by a tutor) a solution to a problem students are supposed to be working on. The system could then analyse this in terms of its plan library, and extract a high-level description of what the program does, in terms of high-level operations, and their inter-relationships. This could just be added to the system as a rule, like any other in its plan library. When the system tries to understand student programs, it could then use a combination of top-down and bottom-up recognition to try and recognise the rule. Because of the system's (potential) ability to invoke a theorem prover when confronted with novel code, it should be able to gain some of the strengths of TALUS in being able to deal with programs containing such code. On the other hand, its ability to recognise plans should enable it to deal with much larger and more complex problems than TALUS. Furthermore, it should potentially be able to deal with programs that work by side-effect, and it doesn't take students long before they start using such programming techniques, once they are introduced to almost any kind of data structuring, unless they are severely restricted by the language.

However, tutoring novices is likely to necessitate something like PROUST's approach. In the absence of knowledge about what task the programmer is working on, the approach to debugging that we have adopted requires what we called the Normal Use Heuristic. This is:

If a programmer uses a standard plan in a program then, as a first hypothesis, assume they are using it deliberately in order to achieve the results of operations commonly implemented by that plan, and that therefore the preconditions for these operations should be met.

For more experienced programmers this is probably quite a reasonable assumption. However, for complete novices this almost certainly does not hold. Apart from the fact that novices produce such bizarre code [8, 27] that sometimes, without a deep understanding of the misconceptions underlying the production of such code, it is almost impossible to recognise the intent behind it, they also often misunderstand what a common programming technique actually does, so plans turn up in totally inappropriate places. In this kind of situation, there may be no alternative to some sort of bug catalogue, with appropriate "canned" repairs and advice. On the other hand the approach taken in CHIRON suggests it may be possible to describe bugs in a more principled way, possibly in flowgraph terms. In this case the chart parser can simply use these "bug rules" as yet another set of rules to parse with.

6 Conclusions

The plan calculus seems to offer enormous power to analyse and reason about programs. The ability not only to reason about side effects, but to reason about programs at different levels e.g. to switch from record cells to sets, or to trees, and yet still be able to realise how changes to the structures involved at one level of description affect the other level of description is fundamental to the way in which experienced programmers seem to think about programs. Although we have only so far applied our work to small programs like the one above, Wills [38] has used a variant of our chart parsing algorithm to understand (in the sense described earlier) 1000 line Lisp programs. It is therefore not inconceivable that this approach will be able to scale up to dealing with large realistic programs, although a large knowledge acquisition exercise (to obtain a large enough plan library) would be neccessary first. We therefore hope that the work described here takes us a little closer to actually being able to use the plan calculus as the basis for automated tools to aid programmers in the task of debugging, and ultimately in all aspects of the programming process.

References

1 Adam A., Laurent J. (1980) LAURA A System to Debug Student Programs Artificial Intelligence 15, pp. 75-122.

2 Ehrlich K., Soloway E. (1982) An Empirical Investigation of the Tacit Plan Knowledge in Programming. Research Rep. 236, Yale Univ. Dept. Comp. Sci.

3 Eisenstadt M., Laubsch J. (1981) Domain Specific Debugging Aids for Novice Programmers Proc. 7th Int. Joint Conf. on Artificial Intelligence (IJCAI-81). Vancouver BC, Canada.

4 Fritzson, P., Gyimothy, T., Kamkar, M., and Shahmehri, N. (1991). Generalised Algorithmic Debugging and Testing. Proc. ACM PLDI'91.

5 Green, C. (1969). Theorem Proving by Resolution as a Basis for Question-Answering Systems. Machine Intelligence 4, Michie, D. and Meltzer, B. (eds.) Edinburgh University Press.

6 Goldstein I.P. (1974) Understanding Simple Picture Programs PhD. Thesis MIT AI Lab. Technical Report 294.

7 Johnson, W.L. (1986) Intention-Based Diagnosis of Novice Programming Errors. Pitman(London).

8 Johnson, W.L., Soloway, E., Cutler, B., and Draper, S. (1983) Bug Catalogue I Technical Report YaleU/CSD/RR #286 Dept. Comp. Sci. Yale University.

9 Kamkar, M., Shahmehri, N., and Fritzson, P. (1992). Interprocedural Dynamic Slicing. Proc. PLILP'92, Leuven, Belgium. Lecture Notes in Computer Science 631, Springer-Verlag.

10 Kuper, R.I. (1989) Dependency-Directed Localization of Software Bugs. MIT AI Lab. Technical Report 1053.

11 Lukey F.J. (1978) Understanding and Debugging Simple Computer Programs PhD Thesis, University of Sussex.

12 Lutz, R.K. (1984) Towards an Intelligent Debugging System for Pascal Programs: A Research Proposal. Open University Human Cognition Research Laboratory Technical Report No. 8 April 1984.

13 Lutz, R.K. (1986) Diagram Parsing - A New Technique for Artificial Intelligence. CSRP-054, School of Cognitive and Computing Sciences, University of Sussex.

14 Lutz, R.K. (1989a) Chart Parsing of Flowgraphs. Proc. 11th Joint Int. Conf. on AI. Detroit, USA.

15 Lutz, R.K. (1989b) Debugging Pascal Programs Using a Flowgraph Chart Parser. Proc. 2nd Scandinavian conference on AI, Tampere, Finland.

16 Lutz, R.K. (1992a) Plan Diagrams as the Basis for Understanding and Debugging Pascal Programs. in Eisenstadt, M., Rajan, T., and Keane, M. (Eds.) Novice Programming Environments. London: Lawrence Erlbaum Associates.

17 Lutz, R.K. (1992b) Towards an Intelligent Debugging System for Pascal Programs: On the Theory and Algorithms of Plan Recognition in Rich's Plan Calculus. Ph.D. Thesis, The Open University, Milton Keynes, England.

18 Murray, W.R. (1986) Automatic Program Debugging for Intelligent Tutoring Systems. Doctoral Dissertation, Artificial Intelligence Laboratory, The University of Texas at Austin. June 1986.

19 Rich C. (1981) Inspection Methods in Programming MIT Artificial Intelligence Laboratory AI-TR-604.

20 Rich, C. (1985) The layered architecture of a system for reasoning about programs. Proceedings IJCAI-85, Los Angeles, CA. pp. 540-546.

21 Ruth G.R. (1973) Analysis of Algorithm Implementations PhD Thesis MIT.

22 Ruth G.R. (1976) Intelligent Program Analysis Artificial Intelligence 7, pp. 65-85.

23 Sack, W. and Soloway, E. (1990) From PROUST to CHIRON: ITS Design as Iterative Engineering; Intermediate Results are Important! in Frasson, C. and Gauthier, G. (Eds.) Intellegent Tutoring Systems: At the Crossroads of Artificial Intelligence and Education, Ablex, Norwood, NJ.

24 Seviora, E. R. (1987) Knowledge-Based Program Debugging Systems. IEEE Software. 4(3) : pp. 20-32.

25 Shapiro, D.G. (1978) Sniffer: A System that Understands Bugs. MIT Artificial Intelligence Laboratory. AI Memo 459.

26 Shapiro, E. (1982) Algorithmic Program Debugging. MIT Press, Cambridge, Mass.

27 Soloway E., Bonar J., Woolf B., Barth P., Rubin E., Ehrlich K. (1981) Cognition and Programming: Why Your Students Write Those Crazy Programs Proc. National Educational Computing Conference (NECC-81) pp. 206-219.

28 Soloway, E., and Ehrlich, K. (1984) Empirical Studies of Programming Knowledge. IEEE Trans. on Software Eng., Vol. 10, pp. 595-609

29 Soloway E., Ehrlich K., Bonar J. (1982) Cognitive Strategies and Looping Constructs: An Empirical Study Research Rep. Yale Univ. Dept. Comp. Sci.

30 Soloway E., Ehrlich K., Bonar J., Greenspan J. (1982) What Do Novices Know About Programming Research Rep. No. 218 Yale Univ. Dept. Comp. Sci.

31 Soloway E., Rubin E., Woolf B., Bonar J., Johnson W.L. (1982) MENO-II: An AI-Based Programming Tutor Research Rep. No. 258 Yale Univ. Dept. Comp. Sci.

32 Spohrer, J.C., Pope, E., Lipman, M., Sack, W., Freiman, S., Littman, D., Johnson, L., and Soloway, E. (1985) Bug Catalogue: II, III, IV. Tech. Rep. YaleU/CSD/RR #386. Dept. Comp. Sci. Yale University.

33 Thompson H. and Ritchie, G. (1984) Implementing Natural Language Parsers. Artificial Intelligence: Tools, Techniques, and Applications pp.245-300 (eds. O'Shea, T. and Eisenstadt, M.) Harper and Row.

34 Weiser M. Programmers Use Slices When Debugging (1982) CACM 25, 7.

35 Wertz, H. (1987) Automatic Correction and Improvement of Programs. Ellis Horwood Series in Artificial Intelligence.

36 Wills, L.M. (1986) Automated Program Recognition. MSc Thesis MIT Electrical Engineering and Computer Science.

37 Wills, L.M. (1990) Automated Program Recognition: A Feasibility Demonstration. Artificial Intelligence 45, pp. 113-171.

38 Wills, L.M. (1992) Graph Based Program Understanding. Ph.D. Thesis MIT, Boston, USA

Trace-Based Debugging

Steven P. Reiss

Department of Computer Science

Brown University

Providence, RI 02912

(401)-863-7641, spr@cs.brown.edu

Abstract. This paper describes the beginnings of a research project aimed at trace-based debugging. We plan to build a practical debugger that incorporates the notion of time to allow users to easily navigate over the execution of their systems. Tracing will also provide a framework for integrating intelligent debugging capabilities into the debugger. We have already implemented a mechanism for automatically collecting trace data from an arbitrary binary. This has been used to implement a memory type-state checking tool. We are currently working on efficiently storing and retrieving large trace files and on developing an appropriate debugger user interface.

1. Background

Debugging of procedural programs has not changed significantly in the past twenty-five years. Programmers run their programs inside a debugger. They set breakpoints at various locations, single step the program where appropriate, examine the contents of variables, etc. More importantly, they run their program until a problem is found, set a breakpoint at an earlier location, and run it again, trying to isolate the time and location where the problem occurred. This need to run the program multiple times with the programmer doing all the work of attempting to isolate the problem makes debugging both inefficient and challenging. Moreover, with distributed and parallel systems, such debugging is often impossible since there is no guarantee that two runs of a program will be identical. As our systems become more complex even programs that are traditionally thought of as deterministic and sequential are actually distributed systems since they rely on separate processes such as the windowing system.

Much of the recent work in the area of debugging has been centered around either improving this process, especially for the parallel or distributed case, and on automated debugging. Work for parallel and distributed debugging includes ways of specifying the complex types of conditional breakpoints that are needed to identify error conditions in such systems [4,12]. These typically provide a higher-level language such as path expressions [2] for specifying events or event sequences that should trigger a breakpoint. Work in this area also involves gathering trace information so that the program can be rerun in a deterministic manner [5,9].

Automated debugging involves having the debugger isolate a problem using information from the program, from a program run, and from the user [3]. The debugger builds a model of what the program should be doing by asking the user questions and through analysis of the program code. It takes a program run and looks at information at the procedure-call level to match the actual run against the model of the program to isolate where the execution and the model disagree. Because the specifications can be quite complex, this technique has been limited to relatively small programs where the debugger is assumed to have full knowledge of the program.

We are interested in applying some of the techniques of automated debugging to moderate-to-large existing systems written in a complex object-oriented programming language. Such systems proffer several problems that must be addressed for debugging:

- They are data-oriented rather than procedure-oriented. The organization and design of an object-oriented system centers around its data structures. Similarly, debugging of such systems should center around the use and manipulation of data.

- They make excessive use of pointers. Pointers are used to represent objects either implicitly or explicitly. This makes program analysis quite difficult because of aliasing. It means that most of the data of interest to debugging (i.e. where problems will occur) will be nested deep inside of dynamic data structures and can not be specified by simple variables.

- They are inherently distributed applications. Any program using the X11 windowing system will have potential (if not real) timing dependencies on the windowing environment. Two runs of the same program are not guaranteed to be deterministic. Moreover, because X11 uses the heap, addresses of data, etc. are not even guaranteed to remain the same between runs. The introduction of distributed programming tools such as DCE, ONC or Tooltalk, and of message-based programming as exhibited in FIELD or Softbench, acerbate this problem.

- The debugger does not have knowledge of the complete application. These systems use extensive libraries (such as X11 or Motif) that are not generally available in source form and are compiled without debugging information. These libraries cannot be ignored since they often contain bugs and since problems can occur in the library that are due to the rest of the application misusing the library in some way.

- The systems are inherently large. It is impractical to do a full semantic analysis of a 250,000 line system (much less a million or ten million line one). Similarly, it is impractical to assume that the debugger can build a model of how that system works through interaction with the user.

- The systems are not well understood by the programmer. There is typically no well-defined specification of an existing system. Moreover, any one programmer probably only knows the details of a portion of the system.

We are currently investigating an approach to practical object-oriented debugging based on trace analysis. The basic idea involves gathering large amounts of data while the program is being run and then using this data to allow the programmer to interactively work on isolating the problem without having to rerun the program. By gathering enough trace information, the debugger can answer questions about the state of the program in the past, obviating the need for additional runs. Moreover, the trace information can serve as the basis for analysis-based debugging, for example, allowing the programmer to specify an assertion after the fact and see where that assertion was first violated. While this approach does not achieve all the benefits of automated debugging, it does offer a viable compromise whereby the debugger can offer intelligent assistance throughout the problem isolation process.

2. Gathering Information

Trace-based debugging involves several problems. The first is determining what information should be stored and finding practical ways of gathering and saving that information. Once this is done, the information must be made available to the programmer and used by the debugger in an effective manner.

Since object-oriented programming centers on the manipulation of data structures, generally in the heap, the information that the debugger must gather must include a fairly complete picture of memory. At the same time, procedural issues cannot be ignored so the debugger must also gather information about all procedure calls, parameter values, and return values. Finally, since the debugger can assume no inherent knowledge of the program, it must gather information to model the control flow within the program.

Control flow information can be accumulated by storing information for each entry into a basic block of the program. A basic block is a segment of straight-line code that is executed fully once it is entered. This technique is used in AE [7] for execution monitoring. Basic blocks can be determined either at compile time as in AE, at link time as in Pixie [13], or at run time as we have illustrated in our instruction count profiler for Sparcstations, *iprof*. Additional control flow information is gathered by generating trace information at the entry and exit from each function. While such information can be deduced by considering register values and basic blocks, it is easier to add the relatively small number of trace calls to simplify the trace analysis. About half of the trace messages concern basic block information.

Tracing memory information is the other intensive aspect of the information gathering phase. This is done in both Pixie and AE for performance analysis. Tools such as Traceview [8] or Pixstats (part of Pixie) then provide the user with graphical or textual views of the trace. We want to do full memory tracing to support debugging.

In general, for the debugger to build a model of what was in memory at any particular time, information needs to be saved for every instruction that does a store into memory. On today's RISC machines, this is not that complicated since there are only a small set of instructions that actually store into memory. Moreover, the amount of information that has to be gathered is not as bad as it could be since such machines generally have a large number of registers and the compilers (and programmers) attempt to do as much work in the registers as possible for performance reasons.

While the extensive use of registers in the code will simplify memory tracing, it complicates the overall process of gathering information to enable the debugger to reconstruct the program state at any point in the past. To do this analysis, the debugger must know the values of the registers. It would be impractical to trace every change to a register value. A more reasonable approach is to save the contents of the registers (or at least those that have changed) at the start of each basic block to get an approximation to this. Then, because basic blocks are inherently simple, intermediate values could be computed by the debugger if necessary. This is still a costly operation since there are about twice as many basic block entries as their are writes to memory in a typical unoptimized program.

There are several inherent problems to gathering this much trace information during the execution of a program. The first is that the program can be slowed down to the point where it cannot be used. Our debugging approach assumes the existence of fast machines with large amounts of memory and disk. Our approach to tracing involves instrumenting the object code, either at run time through dynamic patching or after load time ala Pixie. This means that monitoring, while intrusive, can be inherently fast.

Our first use of the trace data is a system that monitors all writes to and loads from memory that is able to run most complex systems with adequate performance. The system is similar in many respects to Purify [6] except that it operates at run time as a debugger would. The slowdown of the monitoring ranges from a factor of ten to one hundred depending on the application. We feel that by optimizing the code in various ways, we can still cut this down considerably. This system does not save the trace information, but instead processes it to detect invalid memory stores and accesses. The processing involved is generally more than the processing that would be involved to pass the information on to another process. Communicating the information to another process efficiently is relatively simple. Using a shared memory protocol, we have demonstrated the capability to send over a hundred thousand messages per second between two processes at a sustained rate on the same machine. By optimizing the protocols here we expect to increase this rate by at least a factor of two.

In addition to this tool, we have implemented a package to do debugger tracing (i.e. all stores, basic blocks with registers, function entry and exit) as well as full tracing (including memory loads and allocation information). This package will either write the trace information out into a file or will send it to an analysis system through a shared memory communications buffer. The shared memory communications link can handle more than a hundred thousand messages a second. This is about the same as the message generation rate in our current, unoptimized, prototype implementation.

The current trace analysis system is a placeholder for the debugger. It is being used to provide a test bed for the tracing package and to perform some incidental services. Currently, analysis options include providing statistics on the traced messages, storing the trace information to disk, and providing a transcript of function entry, basic block entry, and function exit information. Our experience to date has shown that the system is still slower than we would like (by about an order of magnitude), that basic block tracing (and determining what registers were actually used) is one of the principle bottlenecks, and that the amount of trace data is larger than we originally anticipated. The latter is due in part to our getting a faster machine which can generate trace data three times as fast, and in part to the amount of register information that is included with basic blocks as part of the trace data.

A second problem with gathering the trace information involves the large amount of data that is being amassed. This data has to be stored somewhere. With the average message size being around forty bytes, about fifty million messages will fit in two gigabytes of disk space (i.e. on one modern disk). This is sufficient for about a twenty seconds of real execution time. To be practical for debugging the information must be compressed by an order of magnitude or more. This is relatively easy to do since standard compression utilities (GNU gzip, for example) compress the raw file by almost a factor of 20. Additional compression can be achieved by intelligently processing the trace file. For example, local or stack storage information can be compressed or deleted, multiple writes to the same address from within a basic block can be eliminated, or various portions of the program, for example libraries or previously debugged routines, can be declared "safe" and monitoring turned off or ignored for them. If the user has some idea of what the problem is, then tracing can be limited to data structures and routines that affect that particular problem. We have already done some work on using program analysis and slicing to determine potential assignment sites for a complex data structure, for example. Finally, full tracing can be complemented by doing occasional checkpoints. This would only allow the programmer to go back in time to the previous two checkpoints, but would strictly limit the amount of trace data that would be needed.

A third problem involves accessing the data in a meaningful way. We are currently designing a front end to the trace data that will serve as an accessing engine for the debugger and that will allow more complex requests to be processed to allow program analysis questions to be asked directly. This pseudo-database is simplified in that all accesses can be made by memory address and the database knows the fixed finite set of memory addresses and can organize its data structures accordingly. While we have not yet specified the query language, we are planning to use the access engine for other purposes beyond debugging, primarily to provide automatic visualization of user data structures over time.

In general, we feel that our initial experiments have demonstrated that accumulating and saving the massive amount of trace information needed to do trace-based debugging is possible. A slowdown in program execution of one or two orders of magnitude is acceptable for most applications, especially if it only occurs within the context of debugging. We have developed the intrusive monitoring and communications techniques that will be required to support such tracing and are currently using these in example applications in preparation for using them in a debugger.

3. Making Trace Information Available in the Debugger

The easiest way of using this trace information within a debugger is to incorporate a notion of time in the debugger. As a first step toward trace-based debugging we intend to allow the programmer to view the control flow history and to access any memory location at any previous point in the program. Combined with a high-level front end, this will allow the programmer to examine the evolution of each data structure as the program runs.

This approach is similar to incorporating a notion of reverse execution into the debugger, i.e. allowing the debugger to run the program backwards [1,10]. The latter is more general and more flexible, allowing the programmer to see what went wrong and attempt to correct it and continue execution. It is also quite difficult to accomplish in practice because systems, especially complex graphical systems, do not operate in a vacuum, but instead interact with the outside world. It is impossible, for example, to tell the X server to ignore the past k graphic operations. Rather than attempting to synchronize the rest of the world with the notion of time in the application, we just want to give the programmer the ability to view the complete execution history of the program. This is sufficient for the primary task of isolating problems.

Providing trace information through the debugger means that the debugger has to provide the user with a tangible notion of time. While time is continuous, it would not make much sense to the programmer to offer a simple slider for moving time back and forth. Instead, the programmer will want to view the data structure at particular instants in time that seem relevant to the problem at hand, for example, when a routine was last entered or whenever a particular line of code was executed.

We solve this problem by viewing time as a sequence of basic block entries. The programmer will be able to specify points in time by identifying patterns in the overall or hierarchical sequence. The front end to this time specification will concentrate on allowing the user to specify the common cases, for example, the last time execution was at a given line or the Kth previous invocation of a given routine from a second routine. By default, instances of basic blocks will be specified relative to the current time, i.e., fct:line(K) is the Kth previous occurrence of execution at the given line in the given function. A simple, path expression based specification language will be provided for defining more complex patterns. [2]

This will be augmented with a richer event structure that will allow a higher-level specification of time. The basic block sequence decomposes naturally into a hierarchy based on function entry and exit. We will allow the user to specify function events to represent the complete hierarchy (including properly maintaining nesting levels). User-defined events, for example based on the contents of memory, are also desirable. We would like to be able to refer directly to the time of the last write at a given address. Other information, such as the current thread of control in a multi-threaded system, or combinations of events such as a call to a given routine with a certain set of parameters, will be definable as well.

Our first approach to trace-based debugging will use this basic block-based notion of time to augment the standard debugging capabilities. That is, the programmer will be able to specify the current notion of time for examining memory and stack information, and can then use all the standard debugger commands such as expression printing to view variables and data structures. While this is a first step toward a better debugger, more can be accomplished by combining this approach with techniques from automated debugging.

4. Intelligent Debugging

Once the debugger has access to full information about the execution of the program, it is possible to do a lot more. Ideally, one would like the debugger to be told what the problem is and then to automatically identify what portion of the code caused that problem. Because of the complex nature of the systems we want to address and because we can not assume that the debugger or the programmer knows about the whole system, this is not immediately practical. However, we can take large steps in that direction with a minimum of program analysis.

An example of this is the ability to provide a dynamic program slice showing the history of a given value. The key question involving data-centric debugging is how did a particular memory location (identified as part of some data structure) get the incorrect value that it currently holds. A trace-based debugger should be able to provide this information by doing a brief dynamic analysis of basic blocks. The debugger would first identify when the given location was last modified using the trace information. This would identify a particular instruction in a particular basic block. By analyzing the code of that basic block, the debugger could identify the additional variables that were used to derive the incorrect value and could recursively trace each of these. The result would be a dag of value-location pairs that could be presented to the user in an incremental fashion. The analysis that is required here is relatively simple. It could be done as part of the compilation process, but is probably easier to do on the fly by simply understanding the straight-line machine code that comprises the basic block.

Another example of the use of the trace information for analysis would be to allow the programmer to specify assertions about the program. Currently this can be done in the programming language and, in certain cases, in the debugger before a program is run. However, with trace-based debugging, it should be possible for the programmer to specify a simple assertion (i.e. $x > y$ for two locations x and y, or that the value of the left child of a particular tree node is less than the right child) and to have the debugger scan the trace information intelligently to identify when this assertion was invalidated. The programmer should be able to specify multiple assertions dynamically and should be able to incorporate time into the assertions (i.e. x > y during the execution of routine z). This would yield a powerful mechanism whereby the programmer could use the debugger to quickly isolate potential problem sites. The dynamic expression of assertions would also allow the assertions to be made more specific as more is known by the programmer.

For data-centric debugging, this would be more useful if additional information about the contents of memory were available, i.e. if the debugger would know a priori what data structure a given memory address represents. While this is difficult to do when portions of the program are effectively black boxes, it is not impossible for much of the useful data in a program. This can be done in one of two ways. First, in a language like C++, the *new* operator can be enhanced to generate trace information describing the type for most allocations. We already do this in for the FIELD heap visualization tool [11]. Second, the information can be computed. The debugger should have extensive data type information about the system being debugged including descriptions of the internals of each data type and the type of all static and stack storage. By attaching a type to each location as the trace is generated (or after the fact if necessary), it should be possible for the debugger to type much of memory. This would allow queries to be generalized to all instances of a given type, i.e. the left child is less than the right child for all tree nodes.

Such information might not be practical to generate for all of memory without a specific need. However, it can be generated on demand using the information available to the debugger. For a given type, the debugger can find the set of all types that can contain references to the given type. Then the debugger can identify all possible static sources for such references by looking at all variables of those types that are either static or are in an active stack frame. This would then allow the trace information to be scanned to flag only instances of the relevant types rather than attempting to keep track of everything.

These examples only scratch the surface of the possibilities that trace-based debugging will enable. We expect that once we have the basic facilities in place, experience will manifest other uses for the information. By monitoring users of a debugger and attempting to determine what information they would like to have available and what questions they would like to ask, we hope to extend the power of this approach.

5. Current Status

We are really just beginning our work on trace-based debugging for object-oriented programs. We have attempted to lay out a design framework for debugging that will extend automated debugging techniques to large, practical systems. We have attempted to identify the key problems that this framework evokes and have found and, where necessary, implemented, solutions to these problems.

We have a prototype system, *vmon*, that demonstrates the practicality of dynamically finding and modifying the start of basic blocks, all memory loads and stores, and all function entries and exists. This system shows that the initial stage of finding everything is fast and that significant work can be done for each of these cases without slowing the program down by more than two orders of magnitude, and often with much less of an impact. We have also demonstrated that the trace information can be conveyed from the process being traced to a process that is gathering and processing the trace information practically. Modern technology, with processing speed and disk and memory capacity effectively doubling each year or so, provides the power to support practically the techniques needed for trace-based debugging.

We have also done a detailed analysis of how trace based debugging can be incorporated into an existing debugger by identifying the proper notion of time and an appropriate interface for the programmer for this notion. We are currently designing a debugger based on this concept. Finally, we have identified ways in which the technology and concepts of automated debugging can be applied to practical systems using the trace information that is accumulated.

6. References

1.   Marc H. Brown and Steven P. Reiss, "Debugging in the BALSA-PECAN integrated environment," ACM SIGPLAN- SIGSOFT Symposium on Debugging (1983).

2.   Bernd Bruegge and Peter Hibbard, "Generalized path expressions: a high-level debugging mechanism," *Journal of Systems and Software* Vol. 3(4) pp. 265-276 (December 1983).

3.   Peter Fritzson, Tibor Gyimothy, Mariam Kamkar, and Nahid Shahmehri, "Generalized algorithmic debugging and testing," *SIGPLAN Notices* Vol. 26(6) pp. 317-326 (June 1991).

4.   W. Hseush and G. Kaiser, "Data path debugging: Data- orieinted debugging for a concurrent programming language," *SIGPLAN Notices* Vol. 24(1) pp. 236-247 (January 1989).

5.   W. Hseush and G. E. Kaiser, "Modeling concurrency in parallel debugging," *Second ACM SIGPLAN Symp. on PPOPP*, pp. 11-20 (March 1990).

6.   Pure Software Inc., *Purify 2 User's Guide*, Pure Software Inc. (1993).

7.   James R. Larus, "Abstract Execution: A technique for efficiently tracing programs," U. Wisc.-Madison Computer Sci. Dept. TR 912 (February 1990).

8.   A. Malony, D. Hammerslag, and D. Jablonowski, "Traceview: A trace visualization tool," *IEEE Software* Vol. 8(5) pp. 19-28 (September 1991).

9. Robert H.B. Netzer and Barton P. Miller, "Optimal Tracing and Replay for Debugging Message-Passing Parallel Programs," *Supercomputing '92*, Minneapolis, MN, (November 1992).

10. Douglas Z. Pan and Mark A. Linton, "Supporting reverse execution of parallel programs," *SIGPLAN Notices* Vol. 24(1) pp. 124-129 (January 1989).

11. Steven P. Reiss, "Interacting with the FIELD environment," *Software Practice and Experience* Vol. 20(S1) pp. 89-115 (June 1990).

12. Robert V. Rubin, Larry Rudolph, and Dror Zernik, "Debugging parallel programs in parallel," *SIGPLAN Notices* Vol. 24(1) pp. 216-225 (January 1989).

13. MIPS Computer Systems, Inc., *RISCompiler Languages Programmer's Guide*. December 1988.

IDENTIFYING FAULTY MODIFICATIONS IN SOFTWARE MAINTENANCE

Bogdan Korel

Department of Computer Science
Wayne State University
Detroit, MI 48202, USA
E-mail: bmk@cs.wayne.edu

Abstract

Software maintenance involves making changes to a program to correct errors, to improve efficiency, or to extend the program functionality. The existing algorithmic debuggers generally only take into account the modified software, i.e., they do not take into account the original software and modifications being made. However, in software maintenance the original software has been tested and analyzed previously. In software maintenance the goal of debugging is to identify those modifications that cause incorrect program behavior, rather than to identify faulty statements. In this paper we present an approach that uses the information about the original software and determines those modifications that more likely contain fault. In this approach, the modifications that are made to the program are first identified. Then, forward dynamic dependence analysis is used to determine the most suspicious modifications.

1. INTRODUCTION

Software maintenance involves making changes to a program to correct errors, to improve efficiency, or to extend the program functionality. The maintenance phase of the Systems Life Cycle has been estimated to consume 60 to 80 percent of the total life cycle cost of the typical system [Sch87], therefore, developing techniques and tools that enhance the software maintenance phase could be very cost effective. Program debugging involves fault localization and correction. These are time and resource consuming activities; in particular, fault localization itself may constitute 95 percent of the debugging [Mye79]. Traditionally, fault-localization is performed by means of break-and-examine symbolic debuggers. Those debuggers incorporate breakpoint facilities which allow a programmer to specify breakpoints in a program. When a breakpoint is reached, execution is suspended, and then the programmer can then examine various components of the program state and verify its correctness, e.g., the values of program variables. Fault localization requires a good understanding of the program being debugged, however, for a large program developed by a team, it is almost impossible for one programmer to fully understand the program's design. The process of fault localization can become even more aggravating in software maintenance. Here programmers usually debug "someone else's" programs, and they often poorly, or only partially, understand those programs, and debugging of partially understood programs can be exceptionally difficult. Therefore, fault localization is often a hit-and-miss approach. Typically, programmers set breakpoints at arbitrary places and examine arbitrary variables, hoping to find additional incorrect variables (or flow of control) in order to localize the fault.

In algorithmic debugging, program fault localization is facilitated by a systematic search algorithm (e.g., [Ren82, Sha82, Lyl87, Kor88a, Sha90, Fri91]). It usually employs both the program structure and the history of an incorrect program execution. The diagnostic information is derived from the execution trace of the program and is used to formulate hypotheses about the nature of the fault. The existing debugging algorithms for procedural languages (e.g., [Kor88a,Sha90, Kor91,Agr91, Lyl87]) use backward dependence analysis in order to determine the suspect parts of the program and prune away unrelated computations (they are often based on the notion of program slicing [Wei84,Kor88b]). Those algorithms guide the programmer's attention on the suspected parts of the program, i.e., those parts of the program significant to the incorrect computation. A major drawback of algorithmic debugging is a large number of user interactions needed during the debugging process. This is usually caused by the large set of suspects generated by those algorithms. Therefore, it is important to devise methods that will significantly reduce the searching space by concentrating only on the most suspect parts of the program.

In current practice in software maintenance, existing debugging tools and algorithmic debuggers generally assume the modified software, i.e., they do not take into account the original software and modifications being made. However, in software maintenance, the original software has been tested and analyzed previously, and perhaps it produces correct output for the input on which the modified software produces incorrect result. In addition, in software maintenance, the goal of debugging is to localize faulty modifications in the modified program, i.e., to identify those modifications that cause incorrect program behavior. In this paper we present an approach of finding most suspect parts of the modified program. This approach takes into account the original program and is based on forward dynamic dependence analysis. In this approach, modifications to the original program are first identified, and then, based on those modifications, forward dynamic dependence analysis is used to prune away unrelated computations and to determine those modifications that are more likely to contain faults. By taking into account information about the original program, this approach can more efficiently prune away the unrelated computations as opposed to the traditional methods based on backward dynamic dependence analysis.

In the next section, we present basic concepts used in this paper. Section 3 discusses types of program modifications and their influence on the program. In section 4, the approach of finding suspect modifications is presented.

2. BACKGROUND

To facilitate the presentation, we will now define some of the terminology that will be used in this paper. The program structure is represented by a flow graph $G = (N, A, s, e)$ where (1) N is a set of nodes, (2) A, a set of arcs, is a binary relation on N and (3) s and e are, respectively, unique entry and exit nodes. A node in N corresponds to the smallest single-entry single-exit executable part of a statement in the program that cannot be further decomposed. A node can be an assignment statement, an input or output statement, or the predicate of a conditional or loop statement, in which case it is called a *test* node. An arc $(n,m) \in A$ corresponds to a potential transfer of control from node n to node m. A *path* from the entry node s to some node k, $k \in N$, is a sequence $<n_1,n_2,...,n_q>$ of nodes such that $n_1 = s$, $n_q = k$ and $(n_i,n_{i+1}) \in A$, for all n_i, $1 \le i < q$. A path that has actually been executed for some input will be referred to as an *execution trace*. For example, $T_x=<1,2,3,4,5,6,7,8,9,10,12,13,6,14>$ is the execution trace when the program in Figure 1b is executed on the input x: $n=2$, $a=(0,4)$; this execution trace is presented in Figure 2 in a more detail. Notationally, an execution trace is an abstract list (sequence) whose elements are accessed by position in it, e.g., for trace T_x in Figure 2, $T_x(6)=6$, $T_x(11)=12$, etc. Node Y at position p in T_x (i.e., $T_x(p)=Y$) will be written as Y^p and referred to as an *action*. For instance, 6^6 and 6^{13} in trace T_x of Figure 2 are two actions that involve the same node 6. Y^p is a *test* action if Y is a test node. By v^q we denote *variable v at position* q, i.e., variable (object) v before execution of node $T_x(q)$. We want to stress that the notion of execution position is introduced in here only for presentation purposes, i.e., programmers do not identify the execution position of a node in these terms (they usually express the execution position differently, e.g., 6^6 may be expressed as execution of node 6 at the entry to the while loop, and 6^{13} as execution of node 6 after one iteration of the while loop).

Let Y be a node and Y^p be its action. An *use* of variable v is a node Y in which this variable is referenced. A *definition* of variable v is a node Y which assigns a value to that variable. Let $USE(Y)$ be a set of variables that are used in Y and $DEF(Y)$ be a set variables that are defined in Y. Similarly, let $U(Y^p)$ be a set of variables whose values are used in action Y^p and $D(Y^p)$ be a set of variables whose values are defined in Y^p. Sets $U(Y^p)$ and $D(Y^p)$ are determined during program execution, especially for array and pointer variables. Clearly, as it is possible to determine the value of array subscripts during program execution, one can identify the specific array elements that are used or modified by the action. Therefore, for example, array elements can be treated as separate variables that may lead to more precise analysis as opposed to static program analysis.

Dynamic Dependence Concepts

In what follows we review the concepts of dynamic dependence between actions in T_x. Dynamic dependences (e.g., [Kor88b,Choi91]) between actions are captured by two binary relations *Definition-Use* and *Test-Control*, defined over the set $M(T_x)$, where $M(T_x)$ is a set of all actions in a given execution trace T_x, i.e., $M(T_x)=\{Y^p | T_x(p)=Y\}$.

The *DU* (Definition-Use) relation.

The *DU* relation captures the relation where one action assigns a value to an item of data and the other action uses that value. *DU* is a binary relation on $M(T_x)$ defined as follows:

$$Y^p \ DU \ Z^t, p < t, \text{ iff there exists a variable } v \text{ such that: } v \in U(Z^t), v \in D(Y^p),$$
$$\text{and } v \text{ is not modified between } p \text{ and } t \,^{[1)}.$$

For example, in the execution trace of Figure 2 action 2^2 assigns a value to variable *max*, action 8^8 uses *max*, and *max* is not modified between 2^2 and 8^8; consequently, there exists *DU* relation between those actions, i.e., $2^2 \ DU \ 8^8$.

The *TC* (Test-Control) relation.

The *TC* relation captures the dependence between test actions and actions that have been chosen to be executed by these test actions. This relation is based on the notion of control dependence between nodes in a program [Fer87]: Let Y and Z be two nodes and (Y,X) be a branch of Y. Node Z *postdominates* node Y iff Z is on every path from Y to the exit node e. Node Z postdominates branch (Y,X) iff Z is on every path from Y to the exit node e through branch (Y,X). Z is *control dependent* on Y iff Z postdominates one of the branches of Y and Z does not postdominate Y. For example, in the program of Figure 1b node 9 is control dependent on node 8 because node 9 postdominates branch $(8,9)$ and 9 does not postdominate node 8.

Dynamic control dependencies between actions in the execution trace are captured by the *TC* relation defined as follows:

$$Y^p \ TC \ Z^t, p < t, \text{ iff } Z \text{ is control dependent on } Y, \text{ and for all } k, p < k < t,$$
$$T_x(k) \text{ is control dependent on } Y.$$

[1)] Variable v is *not modified between* p *and* t iff for all $k, p < k < t$, there exists W such that $T_x(k)=W, v \notin D(W^k)$.

a. Original Program

```
var
n,max,min,sum,y,i: integer;
a: array [1..20] of integer;
1      input(n,a) ;
2      max := 0 ;
3      min := 100 ;
4      sum := a[1] ;
5      y := a[1];
6      i := 2 ;
7      while i <= n do begin
8,9        if max<=y-1 then max:=y;
10,11      if min>=y then min:=y;
12         sum := sum + y ;
13         i := i + 1 ;
14         y := a[i];
           end ;
15     output(max,min,sum) ;
```

b. Modified Program

```
var
n,max,min,sum,y,i: integer;
a: array [1..20] of integer;
1      input(n,a) ;
2      max := a[1] ;
3      min := a[1] ;
4      sum := a[1] ;
5      i := 2 ;
6      while i <= n do begin
7          y := a[i];
8,9        if max<y then sum:=y;
10,11      if min>y then min:=y;
12         sum := sum + y ;
13         i := i + 1 ;
           end ;
14     output(max,min,sum) ;
```

Node 9 is incorrectly modified.
The correct version: "max := y"

Figure 1. A sample program and its modified version (modified components are highlighted in bold).

1^1	input(n,a)
2^2	max := a[1]
3^3	min := a[1]
4^4	sum := a[1]
5^5	i := 2
6^6	i <= n
7^7	y := a[i]
8^8	max < y
9^9	sum := y
10^{10}	min > y
12^{11}	sum := sum + y
13^{12}	i := i + 1
6^{13}	i <= n
14^{14}	output(max,min,sum)

Figure 2. Execution trace of the modified program of Figure 1b executed on program input: n=2, a=(0,4).

For example, in the execution trace of Figure 2, action 8^8 "influences" the execution of action 9^9; consequently, there exists TC relation between those actions, i.e., 8^8 TC 9^9. However, TC relation does not exist between 8^8 and 10^{10}.

DU and TC relations capture direct dynamic dependences between actions in the execution trace. Indirect dependences between actions can be captured by a closure on the union of both relations, i.e., $(TC \cup DU)^*$. Let Y^p and Z^t be two actions in $M(T_x)$. Z^t is *dependent* on Y^p, $p < t$, iff Y^p $(TC \cup DU)^*$ Z^t. Notice that TC and DU relations can be represented in the form of a dependence graph defined on the execution trace [Kor88a,Cho91].

3. PROGRAM MODIFICATIONS

Let P be an original program and Q its modified version. Modifications can be identified on different level of granuality, for example, modifications can be done on an assignment statement level, a predicate level, if-then-else and while-statement level, procedure level, variable level, etc. In order to identify a modification and its "influence" on the modified program, it is necessary to identify a one-to-one correspondence between components of the original program P and the corresponding modified components in the modified program Q. In this paper the corresponding components are identified on the node level. The correspondence between the nodes of P and Q can be computed, for example, by a program comparison algorithm (algorithms for finding a one-to-one correspondence have been presented in the literature, e.g., [Hor90) or can be determined by the specialized editor during editing of the original program. A one-to-one correspondence algorithm takes as an input control flow graphs of the original program and the modified program and finds points of correspondence between modified nodes in both graphs. Those graphs are usually augmented by inserting dummy nodes that correspond to deletion or insertion operations on nodes. Clearly, if a node (statement) is removed from the original program, the corresponding dummy node is inserted into the graph of the modified program. Similarly, if a node (statement) is inserted then the corresponding dummy node is inserted into the graph of the original program. For example, the augmented programs (with dummy nodes) for programs of Figure 1 are presented in Figure 3. The one-to-one correspondence between modified nodes in those programs is shown in Figure 4. Notice that dummy node $d1$ in the original program is a result of the insertion of node 7 in the modified program. Similarly, dummy nodes $d2$ and $d3$ in the modified program are the result of the deletion of nodes 5 and 14 from the original program, respectively. Notice that dummy nodes are only used by a debugging system and are not displayed to a programmer in the text of the modified program.

a. Original Program

```
var
n,max,min,sum,y,i: integer;
a: array [1..20] of integer;
1      input(n,a) ;
2      max := 0 ;
3      min := 100 ;
4      sum := a[1] ;
5      y := a[1];
6      i := 2 ;
7      while i <= n do begin
dl         y := y ;
8,9        if max<=y-1 then max:=y;
10,11      if  min>=y then min:=y;
12         sum := sum + y ;
13         i := i + 1 ;
14         y := a[i];
           end ;
15     output(max,min,sum) ;
```

b. Modified Program

```
var
n,max,min,sum,y,i: integer;
a: array [1..20] of integer;
1      input(n,a) ;
2      max := a[1] ;
3      min := a[1] ;
4      sum := a[1] ;
d2     y:= y ;
5      i := 2 ;
6      while i <= n do begin
7          y := a[i];
8,9'       if max<y then max:=max
9"                      sum := y ;
10,11      if min>y then min:=y;
12         sum := sum + y ;
13         i := i + 1 ;
d3         y:=y ;
           end ;
14     output(max,min,sum) ;
```

Figure 3.   Augmented original and modified programs of Figure 1 (dummy nodes are shown in italics).

Original program			Modified program		Affected
2	max := 0	---->	2	max := a[1]	*max*
3	min := 100	---->	3	min := a[1]	*min*
5	y := a[1]	---->	*d2*	y := y	*y*
dl	y:=y	---->	7	y := a[i]	*y*
8	max <= y-1	---->	8	max < y	flow of control
9	max := y	---->	9'	*max:=max*	*max*
			9"	sum := y	*sum*
10	min >= y	---->	10	min > y	flow of control
14	y := a[i]	---->	*d3*	y:=y	*y*

Figure 4.   A one-to-one correspondence between modified nodes in programs of Figure 3 and affected variables and control flow.

We informally illustrate the augmentation process for several simple modifications on an assignment-statement level and test-predicate level. Let P be an original program and Q its modified version. Let n be a node in P and n' be the corresponding modified node in Q. Each modification (modified node) may affect directly either a value of a variable or a flow of control at some point in the modified program. Therefore, it is necessary to identify the affected variables or flow of control for each modified node. In what follows we present simple modifications and illustrate the directly affected program elements (variables or control flow) and newly introduced dummy nodes:

a. Modifications of an *Assignment Statement:*
The right hand side of an assignment statement is modified:

Original node	Modified node	Affected
{ n} y := x + z;	{n'} y := x - z;	y

For this modification, variable y is directly affected, i.e., each time when the modified assignment statement is executed in Q the value of y may be different from the value of y in P.

The left hand side of an assignment statement is modified:

Original node	Modified node	Affected
{n} y := x + z;	{n'} y := y (* *dummy node* *)	y
	{n''} v := x + z	v

For this modification, variables y and v are directly affected, i.e., values of those variables in the modified program Q may be different from values in the original program P. In order to capture the direct influence of this modification on variable y, a dummy node "y:=y" is introduced into the modified program. Formally, a modified node should be represented as a "parallel" assignment statement, i.e., (y,v):=(y,x+z). However, for the sake of presentation the parallel assignment node is represented by a sequence of two nodes n' and n''. Notice that the one-to-one correspondence exists between node n in the original program and both nodes n' and n'' in the modified program.

b. Modification of a *Test Predicate*:

Original node	Modified node	Affected
{n} if x < y then z:=1;	{n'} if x <= y then z:=1;	flow of control

For this modification, a flow of control is directly affected, i.e., all nodes that are control dependent on the modified test node are affected by this modification.

c. Insertion
For this modification there is a one-to-one correspondence between a specially introduced dummy node in the original program and the inserted node in the modified program. For example, for the following modification variable y is affected:

Original node	Modified node	Affected
{n} y:= y (*dummy node*)	{n'} y := x + z;	y

d. Deletion

Each deleted node is represented in the modified program by a dummy node in order to capture the effect of deletion in the original program. The variable that is being defined by the deleted node is directly affected by this modification. For example, in the following modification the variable y is affected.

	Original node		Modified node	Affected
$\{n\}$	$y := x + z;$	$\{n'\}$	$y := y;$ (*dummy node *)	y

In summary, each modification can affect directly either variables or a flow of control at some point in the program. When a test node is modified, the control flow at this node may be directly affected. Clearly, if n' is a modified test node in Q, then each time n' is executed it may produce different result (*true* or *false* value) as oppose to n in P; as a result, the flow of control may be different at node n'. On the other hand, when an assignment node is modified, usually one or more variables may directly be affected. For a modified assignment node n', the affected variables are determined by the union of variables defined at n and n', i.e., $DEF(n) \cup DEF(n')$. When the left hand side of an assignment node is modified, a special dummy node(s) is introduced in Q for a variable in $DEF(n)$. A list of modified nodes and affected program components (variables and flow of control) for the program of Figure 1a and its modified version of Figure 1b is shown in Figure 4. The augmented programs of those programs are shown in Figure 3.

4. FINDING SUSPECT MODIFICATIONS

There are significant differences between the debugging of programs during software development and the debugging of programs in software maintenance. For example, in software maintenance there exists a well tested original version of the program, and perhaps this original version works correctly on some program input on which the modified version does not work. In addition, when the modified version of the program does not work as intended, the programmer looks for the faulty modification (as opposed to the faulty statement(s)), i.e., the programmer is interested in finding which modifications caused incorrect program output. We believe that new methods and tools have to be developed that take advantage of the existing information about the original version of the program. Those methods can strengthen the efficiency of debugging as opposed to the traditional methods of debugging.

Let P be an original program and Q be its modified version. When the modified program is executed on input x it produces incorrect output. Let T_x be an execution trace of program Q on input x, and let v^q be a variable whose value is incorrect at execution position q. Usually the original program is modified in several places, therefore, the goal of fault localization is to identify a faulty modification, i.e., the modified node in Q that causes incorrect value of v^q. The major premise is that modified nodes are the most probable cause of incorrect program behavior. In order to identify a faulty "modified" node, it is often necessary to identify the corresponding faulty action; clearly, a faulty node may "behave" correctly many times during its execution, but only one (or few) of its occurrences may cause incorrect program output. Therefore, a faulty occurrence of the modified node (action) that causes incorrect output has to be identified.

Program input: n=3, a=(3,1,4)

affected:

1^1	input(n,a)	
2^2	**max := a[1]**	*max*
3^3	**min := a[1]**	*min*
4^4	sum := a[1]	
$d2^5$	*y:=y;*	*y*
5^6	i := 2	
6^7	i <= n	
7^8	y := a[i]	*y*
8^9	**max < y**	*flow of control*
10^{10}	**min > y**	*flow of control*
11^{11}	min := y	
12^{12}	sum := sum + y	
13^{13}	i := i + 1	
$d3^{14}$	*y:=y*	*y*
6^{15}	i <= n	
7^{16}	y := a[i]	*y*
8^{17}	**max < y**	*flow of control*
$9'^{18}$	*max := max*	*max*
$9''^{19}$	**sum := y**	*sum*
10^{20}	**min > y**	*flow of control*
12^{21}	sum := sum + y	
13^{22}	i := i + 1	
$d3^{23}$	*y:=y*	*y*
6^{24}	i <= n	
14^{25}	output(max,min,sum)	

Figure 5. Execution trace of the program of Figure 3b. The suspect actions are shown in bold.

Let R be a set of modified nodes in Q, and $S(T_\mathbf{x})$ be a set of all actions in $T_\mathbf{x}$ that correspond to the execution of modified nodes, i.e., $S(T_\mathbf{x}) = \{Y^p \in M(T_\mathbf{x})| Y \in R\}$. Set $S(T_\mathbf{x})$ represents a set of all suspect actions in $T_\mathbf{x}$. This set can be used by the algorithmic debugging system in order to guide programmers in the process of debugging, however, for many modified programs this set may be unacceptably large. This can lead to a large number of queries resulting in very inefficient algorithmic debugging.

Consider the program from Figure 1a and its modified version from Figure 1b. The original program and its modified version are supposed to be functionally equivalent, and they are supposed to find the largest and the smallest element of array a and compute the sum of all elements of a. When the modified program is executed on input x: $n=3$, $a=(3,1,4)$, the program produces incorrect value of variable max at the output (the actual value of max is 3; however, the expected value of max is 4). All the remaining outputs, i.e., sum and min, are correct. On the other hand, the original program produces correct output on the given input x. The augmented modified program is presented in Figure 3b, where nine modified nodes are identified, i.e., $R = \{2, 3, d2, 7, 8, 9', 9'', 10, d3\}$. The execution trace of the augmented modified program on input x is presented in Figure 5. The initial set of suspect actions corresponds to all actions of modified nodes from R in the execution trace. For the execution trace of Figure 5, the suspect set is $S(T_\mathbf{x}) = \{2^2, 3^3, d2^5, 7^8, 8^9, 10^{10}, d3^{14}, 7^{16}, 8^{17}, 9'^{18}, 9''^{19}, 10^{20}, d3^{23}\}$.

In order to make the process of algorithmic debugging more efficient, the suspect set has to be computed more precisely. The approach presented in this paper is based on the observation that not all modifications (or their actions) cause incorrect value of v^q. The idea is to prune away those actions from $S(T_\mathbf{x})$ that do not contribute to the computation of the value of v^q. More formally, the problem is stated as follows: Given an execution trace $T_\mathbf{x}$ and an action Y^p in $T_\mathbf{x}$. The goal is to determine whether Y^p may have affected the incorrect value of variable v^q in $T_\mathbf{x}$. When a given action Y^p from $S(T_\mathbf{x})$ does not affect the computation of v^q, it is removed from the suspect set $S(T_\mathbf{x})$.

In order to determine whether a particular action Y^p may affect the value of v^q, we use the dynamic program dependences described in Section 2. The approach is presented for two types of actions: assignment actions and test actions. The following are the conditions to determine whether Y^p may affect the value of v^q:

a. Assignment action

Let Y be a modified assignment node and Y^p be an action of this node in T_x. Additionally, let y be a variable affected by the modified node Y. Action Y^p may affect the incorrect value of v^q iff

   (1) $y = v$, and v is not modified between p and q, or

   (2) there exists action X^k, $p < k < q$, and action Z^t, $k \leq t < q$, such that :

   a. $y \in U(X^k)$, and y is not modified between p and k,

   b. $v \in D(Z^t)$, and v is not modified between t and q, and

   c. $X^k (TC \cup DU)^* Z^t$ or $X^k = Z^t$.

Intuitively, Y^p may affect v^q if there exist two actions X^k and Z^t (in a special case, $X^k = Z^t$) such that the value of a variable defined in Y^p is used in X^k, Z^t is dependent on X^k, and action Z^t assigns the value to v that is not changed along the execution until position q. For example, in the execution trace of Figure 5, action 2^2 may affect the value of max^{25} because $9^{,18}$ uses the value of max defined by 2^2, and $9^{,18}$ assigns a value to max that is not changed until execution reaches node 14.

b. Test action.

Let Y be a modified test node and Y^p be an action of this node. Action Y^p may affect the incorrect value of v^q iff there exist action X^k, $p < k < q$, such that :

   (1) $Y^p (TC \cup DU)^* X^k$, and

   (2) $v \in D(X^k)$, and v is not modified between k and q.

Intuitively, Y^p may affect v^q if there exists action X^k such that X^k is dependent on Y^p, and X^k assigns the value to variable v that is not changed until position q. For example, in the execution trace of Figure 5, test action 8^{17} may affect the value of max^{25} because $9^{,18}$ is control dependent on 8^{17}, and $9^{,18}$ assigns a value to max that is not changed until execution reaches node 14.

After application of the dynamic dependence analysis to the execution trace of Figure 5, the set of suspect actions is reduced to four actions: $S'(T_x) = \{2^2, 7^{16}, 8^{17}, 9^{,18}\}$.

In order to determine whether a particular action may affect an incorrect value of a variable, dynamic program dependences must be computed. One approach is to use backward dynamic analysis, e.g., a method used to compute dynamic program slices [Kor88b,Agr91]. However, methods based on backward dynamic dependence analysis require recording the program execution trace. Dynamic dependences are then computed by tracing the recorded execution trace backwards. For programs with loops, an extremely high volume of information may be recorded during their execution leading to very inefficient analysis.

The alternative approach is to use a forward method for computation of dynamic dependences. The major advantage of the forward approach is that it does not require any recording of the execution trace as opposed to the backward methods. In this paper, we use the forward approach in order to determine whether action Y^p may affect the incorrect value of variable v^q. The approach starts from suspect action Y^p and proceeds "forward" with program execution and determines whether Y^p may affect v^q. In our approach we take advantage of the fact that the initial set of suspect actions can be determined based on the previously identified modified nodes and that this set is usually significantly smaller than the set of all actions of the execution trace.

The algorithm that determines whether an action may affect an incorrect value of a variable is presented in Figure 6. The algorithm starts from a suspect action Y^p and proceeds "forward" with program execution and determines the effect of the suspect action on other program components (actions and variables). The algorithm maintains a set I of affected variables and a set of affected test nodes, i.e., variables and test nodes affected by Y^p. Before execution of each action (step 6), the algorithm determines whether the current action uses an affected variable from set I (step 13). If no affected variable is used at the current action and the current action is not affected by any of the affected test nodes from set C (step 16), a variable defined at the current action is removed from set I (step 19). Otherwise, a defined variable is affected and added into set I (step 14); or if the current action is a test node, it is inserted into set C (because it is affected by Y^p). When the execution reaches position q, it is checked whether v is in the set I of affected variables (steps 28,29).

The space complexity of the algorithm is limited by the size of set I that, in the worst case, corresponds to the number of all variables in the program. Notice that the space complexity for backward dynamic methods is not bounded.

In some debugging situations, it is possible to reduce the set of suspect actions even more. One such debugging situation can be described as follows: the original program works correctly on some input x, but the modified program produces incorrect output on input x. By taking into account the "correct" execution trace of the original program, it is possible to determine more precisely the set of suspect actions.

Let P be an original program and Q its modified version. Program Q produces incorrect output on x; on the other hand, P produces correct output on the same input. Let T'_x be an execution trace of program P and let T_x be an execution trace of program Q on input x. The major idea of this pruning method is to identify only those actions in $S'(T_x)$ that "behave" differently from their counterparts in T'_x. For this purpose, the correspondence between actions in the execution traces has to be identified, i.e., for every action from the suspect set $S'(T_x)$ we have to identify the corresponding action in the execution trace T'_x of the original program.

For example, in the execution traces of programs of Figure 3 (both traces are shown in Figure 7) there exists one-to-one correspondence between action 2^2 in $T_{\mathbf{x}}$ and 2^2 in $T'_{\mathbf{x}}$, and between action 8^{17} in $T_{\mathbf{x}}$ and 8^{17} in $T'_{\mathbf{x}}$. All the remaining correspondences between actions are shown in Figure 7.

Let Y^p be a suspect action in $T_{\mathbf{x}}$, and let Y^t be its corresponding action $T'_{\mathbf{x}}$. Intuitively, if both actions produce the same result, then action Y^p is unlikely to be responsible for the incorrect output in $T_{\mathbf{x}}$. As a result, Y^p can be removed from the suspect set. For example, consider two execution traces from Figure 7. Since action 8^{17} in the new execution trace produces the same result (the result of this predicate is *true*) as the corresponding action 8^{17} in the old execution trace, this suspect action can be removed from the suspect set. Similarly, suspect action 7^{16} can be removed from the suspect set because its corresponding action $d1^{16}$ in the old trace produces the same result, i.e., the value of y equals 4 after execution of both actions. On the other hand, the result of suspect action 2^2 in $T_{\mathbf{x}}$ (*max*=1) and the result of its corresponding action 2^2 in $T'_{\mathbf{x}}$ (*max*=0) are different. Similarly, 9^{18} in $T'_{\mathbf{x}}$ produces different result (*max*=4) from the result produced by $9'^{18}$ in $T_{\mathbf{x}}$ (*max*=4). The final suspect set can now be reduced to the following actions: 2^2 and $9'^{18}$.

The problem of finding the one-to-one correspondence between actions in two execution traces, i.e., the execution trace of the original program and the execution trace of the modified program, is not a trivial problem. There may exist several solutions to the correspondence problem for two execution traces. Presenting the algorithm to find this correspondence is beyond the scope of this paper. We have to indicate however that it is a research challenge to efficiently determine the one-to-one correspondence between two execution traces.

Algorithm DetermineInfluence

The algorithm determines whether an action Y^p may affect the incorrect value of variable v^q.

Input: an action Y^p and variable v^q (p < q)

Output: true, when Y^p may affect v^q

        false, when Y^p does not affect v^q

var

I: a set of variables affected by Y^p.

C: a set of test nodes affected by Y^p.

begin

```
1    if Y is an assignment node then   I := D(Y^p);   C := Ø
2    else I := Ø;  C := {Y}         (* Y is a test node *)
3    endif
4    k:=p;
5    while not ((I = Ø ) and (C = Ø )) and (k < q) do
6         X^k := Execute_Next_Node
7         if X is an assignment node then
8              for each Z ∈ C do
9                   if X is not control dependent on Z then
10                       C := C - {Z}
11                  endif;
12             endfor;
13             if (U(X^k) ∩ I) ≠ Ø then     (* an affected variable is used in X^k *)
14                  I := I ∪ D(X^k)          (* add affected variables *)
15             else
16                  if C ≠ Ø  then
17                       I := I ∪ D(X^k)               (* add affected variables *)
18                  else
19                       I := I - D(X^k)     (* remove variables not affected any more *)
20                  endif
21             endif;
22        else    (* X is a test node *)
23             if (U(X^k) ∩ I) ≠ Ø then     (* an affected variable is used in X^k *)
24                  C := C ∪ {X}
25             endif
26        endif
27   endwhile
28   if v ∈ I    then return (true)          (* Y^p may affect v^q * )
29               else return(false)          (* Y^p does not affect v^q * )
End DetermineInfluence
```

Figure 6.   The DetermineInfluence Algorithm. Function *Execute_Next_Node* executes a current node and returns node id and execution position of the next node that is "about" to be executed.

Old execution trace T'_x				New execution trace T_x
input(n,a)	1^1		1^1	input(n,a)
max:=0	2^2	<------------>	2^2	max := a[1]
min:=100	3^3		3^3	min := a[1]
sum := a[1]	4^4		4^4	sum := a[1]
y := a[1]	5^5		$d2^5$	y:=y
i := 2	6^6		5^6	i := 2
i <= n	7^7		6^7	i <= n
y := y	$d1^8$		7^8	y := a[i]
max<=y-1	8^9		8^9	max < y
min >=y	10^{10}		10^{10}	min > y
min:=y	11^{11}		11^{11}	min:=y
sum := sum + y	12^{12}		12^{12}	sum := sum + y
i := i + 1	13^{13}		13^{13}	i := i + 1
y := a[i]	14^{14}		$d3^{14}$	y := y
i <= n	7^{15}		6^{15}	i <= n
y:=y	$d1^{16}$	<------------>	7^{16}	y := a[i]
max <=y-1	8^{17}	<------------>	8^{17}	max < y
max := y	9^{18}	<------------>	$9'^{18}$	*max := max*
			$9''^{19}$	sum := y
min >=y	10^{19}		10^{20}	min > y
sum := sum + y	12^{20}		12^{21}	sum := sum + y
i := i + 1	13^{21}		13^{22}	i := i + 1
y := a[i]	14^{22}		$d3^{23}$	y:=y
i <= n	7^{23}		6^{24}	i <= n
output(max,min,sum)	15^{24}		14^{25}	output(max,min,sum)

Old execution trace refers to the execution trace of the original program of Figure 3a.
New execution trace refers to the execution trace of the modified program of Figure 3b.
Both programs are executed on input x: n=3, a=(3,1,4)
<------------> indicates the correspondence between actions of both execution traces.

Figure 7. Execution traces of two programs of Figure 1.

5. CONCLUSIONS

In this paper we have presented an approach that computes a set of suspect modifications (actions) in the execution trace of the modified program. This approach is based on the differences between the original program and its modified version and also on forward dynamic dependence analysis. The identified suspect actions may be used by an algorithmic debugging system to guide programmers in the process of fault localization. In particular, a debugging system may direct a programmer's attention to the most suspicious parts of execution that correspond to the identified suspect modifications. It has been shown that the number of generated suspect actions can be significantly reduced by using information about the original program. This type of analysis may speed-up the process of localizing faulty modifications by, for example, reducing number of queries in the debugging algorithm. An experimental prototype of the debugging system is currently under development in which the approach presented in this paper is being implemented as an extension of the algorithmic debugging system PELAS [Kor88a]. We plan to perform a series of experiments in order to determine the efficiency of the approach presented in this paper.

In the related research, backward dependence analysis has been proposed for debugging, e.g., [Kor88a,Sha90, Kor91,Agr91, Lyl87]. Those algorithms use backward dependence analysis in order to prune away unrelated computations (they are mainly based on the notion of program slicing: static slicing [Wei84] and dynamic slicing [Kor88b]). However, one of the problems of program slicing is that faulty nodes may not be included in the derived slice. For example, when a program slice is derived for variable *max* at node 14 for the modified program of Figure 1b, the resulting slice does not contain the faulty node 9 (only nodes 1 and 2 are included). In addition, faulty modifications related to the removal of a statement (e.g., accidental statement removal) will not be detected by slicing (backward dependence methods). This is in contrast to the approach presented in this paper.

An additional advantage of the approach presented in this paper is that no recording is required in order to compute the set of suspect actions since the approach is based on the forward dynamic dependence analysis. On the other hand, methods based on backward dynamic dependence analysis first require the recording of the execution trace, then, after the execution trace of the program is recorded, dynamic dependence relations are computed by tracing the recorded execution trace backwards. However, for large scale programs, an extremely high volume of information may be recorded during their execution leading to inefficient analysis.

REFERENCES

[Agr91]   H. Agrawal, R. DeMillo, E. Spafford, "An execution-backtracking approach to debugging," IEEE Software, May 1991, pp. 21-26.

[Cho91]   J. Choi, B. Miller, R. Netzer, "Techniques for debugging parallel programs with flow back analysis," ACM Tran. on Programming Languages and Systems, vol. 13, No. 4, October 1991, 491-530.

[Fri91]   P. Fritzson, T. Gyimothy, M. Kamkar, N. Shahmehri, "Generalized algorithmic debugging and testing," Conference on Programming Lang., Design, and Implement., June 1991, Toronto, pp. 317-326.

[Gou75]   J. D. Gould, "Some psychological evidence on how people debug computer program," Int. Journal Man-Machine Studies, vol.7, No.2, March 1975, pp. 151-182.

[Kor88a] B. Korel, "PELAS - Program Error Locating Assistant System," IEEE Trans. on Software Engineering, vol. SE-14, No. 9, September 1988, pp. 1253-1260.

[Kor88b] B. Korel, J. Laski, "Dynamic program slicing," Information Processing Letters, vol. 29, No. 3, October 1988, pp. 155-163.

[Kor90]   B. Korel, J. Laski, "Dynamic Slicing in Computer Programs," The Journal of Systems and Software, vol. 13, No. 3, November 1990, pp. 187-195.

[Kor91]   B. Korel, J. Laski, "Algorithmic software fault localization," 24-th Hawaii International Conference on System Sciences, January 1991, vol. II, pp. 246-252.

[Luk80]   F. J. Lukey, "Understanding and debugging programs," Internat. Journal on Man-Machines Studies, vol. 12, February 1990, pp. 189-202.

[Lyl87]   J. Lyle, M. Weiser, "Automatic program bug location by program slicing," 2-nd IEEE Symposium on Computers and Applications, Beijing, China, June 1987, pp. 877-883.

[Mye79]   G. J. Myers, The art of software testing, New York: Wiley-Interscience, 1979.

[Ren82]   S. Renner, "Location of logical errors on Pascal programs," Technical Report UILU-ENG 82 1710, University of Illinois at Urbana-Champaign, Urbana, IL, 1982.

[Sch87]   N. Schneidewind, "The state of software maintenance," IEEE Tran. on Software Engineering, vol. SE-13, No. 3, 1987, pp. 303-310.

[Sha82]   E. Shapiro, "Algorithmic program debugging," Ph.D. Thesis, Department of Computer Science, Yale University, 1982.

[Sha90]   N. Shahmehri, M. Kamkar, P. Fritzson, "Semi-automatic bug localization in software maintenance," Proc. Conference on Software Maintenance, San Diego, Nov. 1990.

[Wei84]   M. Weiser, "Program slicing," IEEE Trans. on Software Engineering, vol. SE-10, No. 4, July 1982, pp. 352-357.

The Application of Formal Specifications to Software Documentation and Debugging

Anoop Goyal*   Sriram Sankar†

Abstract

This paper illustrates the application of formal specifications to software documentation and debugging by presenting a real-life scenario involving the use of a garbage collection package. It illustrates the advantages of using formal specifications over informal documentation. The paper also illustrates the usefulness of run-time checking tools that compares program behavior with their formal specifications.

The scenario presented in this paper goes through a series of steps that include formal specification, run-time checking, and modification of the specification and program based on the results of run-time checking — the typical steps involved in a debugging process, except that this scenario makes use of formal specifications.

Although various research ideas presented in this paper have been published earlier, this paper assimilates all these ideas into a real-life scenario, and illustrates in an easy-to-understand way that these ideas are really useful to software documentation and debugging.

The example has been developed in Ada, and formally specified using the Anna specification language. The tool used in the example is the Anna Run-Time Consistency Checking System developed at Stanford University.

Keywords. algorithmic debugging, Anna, formal specification, formal documentation, run-time consistency checking, software testing.

1 Introduction

Formal specifications have been used in many ways in the software development life-cycle for quite some time. Initially, formal specifications were primarily used for program verification [1, 8], where the goal was to prove that a program would run in a manner consistent with its formal specification. Subsequently, formal specifications have been used for other purposes, such as formal documentation [10, 12], requirements analysis, automatic program generation [3, 7, 16],

---

*Department of Computer Science, Stanford University, Stanford, California 94305. *Phone:* (415)497-7297, *Email:* agoyal@cs.stanford.edu.

†Sun Microsystems Laboratories, Inc., 2550 Garcia Avenue, Mountain View, California 94043. *Phone:* (415)336-6230, *Email:* sriram.sankar@sun.com.

testing (*e.g.*, black-box testing) [2, 6], and run-time monitoring [5, 23]. These applications have resulted in the development of many specification languages such as Anna [10, 12], Larch [4], and Z [22], and tool-sets to support their use.

The Anna specification language was designed by the Program Analysis and Verification Group at Stanford University during the early 80's. The group has also developed a tool-set for Anna that includes a specification analyzer [15] and a run-time monitoring system [17, 19, 20]. We have subsequently worked on a number of applications of Anna and its tool-set which includes: specification methodology and requirements analysis [11, 13]; testing and debugging [9, 18, 21]; and software maintenance [14].

This paper describes a real-life example of the use of the various applications of formal specifications, especially algorithmic debugging [9], described in the earlier publications. In addition, this paper also illustrates the use of formal specifications in software documentation and requirements analysis.

The primary purpose of this paper is to illustrate to the reader that there is a real use for formal methods in the sofware development process. This paper does this by assimilating many of the lessons learned from earlier experiments into this real-life scenario in a simple and easy-to-understand manner.

This example involves the use of a garbage-collection package in a large software project. The garbage collection package was developed in 1985 for use with Ada objects. It has turned out to be very efficient and has been used extensively. However, this package was only informally documented using English comments (*i.e.*, no formal specifications). As the example in this paper will illustrate, the absence of formal specifications turned out to be a serious deficiency in the long run, resulting in wastage of programmer time.

In the example presented in this paper, an application program that uses the garbage collection package was taken through a debugging phase, during which doubts were raised about the correct working of the garbage collection package. Since the application developer did not have a detailed understanding of the implementation of the garbage collection package, and given the large size of the application program, the developer could not narrow down the problem further using traditional debugging techniques. He therefore wrote a formal specification for the garbage collection package in Anna, and used the Anna run-time monitoring system to determine whether or not the implementation of the garbage collection package was consistent with his formal specification. As expected, the run-time monitoring system detected an inconsistency.

This started an interaction between the developer and the implementor of the garbage collection package[1]. The implementor studied the results of the tests conducted by the developer and realized that the formal specification written by the developer did not correctly describe the intended behavior of the garbage

---

[1] For convenience, we shall henceforth use the term "developer" for the person who wrote the application program, and "implementor" for the person who wrote the garbage collection package.

collection package. The implementor, therefore, rewrote the formal specification to reflect more accurately the intended behavior of the garbage collection package. The ramification of this was that *the developer had not understood the proper behavior of the garbage collection package and was therefore using the package wrongly.* Given the size of the application program, the task of correcting the application program was quite large. However, when the application was run with the Anna run-time monitoring system using the revised specification of the garbage collection package, errors were reported that quickly revealed most locations where corrections needed to be made in the application.

A moral of this story is that the early use of formal specifications in documenting software is crucial to the correct understanding of the behavior of various components in the software system. Incorrect assumptions made about some components can cause significant wastage of programmer time. This example indicates that the informal English comments were imprecise — for both the developer's and the implementor's formal specifications were consistent with the English comments, but inconsistent with respect to each other.

This example also illustrates the use of formal specifications as:

- A *requirements analysis* tool. The Anna specification of the garbage collection package acted as a precise communication medium between the developer and implementor. The use of Anna immediately revealed to the implementor the misunderstanding the developer had of the working of the garbage collection package. Informal documentation and informal communication had obviously not worked. Informal interaction between the developer and implementor had failed even after the developer started to suspect a problem with the garbage collection package. This was partly due to the size of the application and the large number of calls it made to the garbage collection package, which resulted in the problem getting concealed in other extraneous details. The use of formal specifications allowed the developer and implementor to organize their thoughts properly and thus have an effective communication.

- A basis to perform *run-time testing and debugging*. In the example presented in this paper, just writing formal specifications may not have sufficed. It was also important to obtain evidence that the implementation of the garbage collection package/application was not behaving consistently with the specifications. This evidence was used in the first phase of this example to convince the implementor that something may be wrong with the implementation of the garbage collection package, and in the second phase to modify the application to correctly use the garbage collection package.

Outline of this paper. The paper proceeds by presenting an overview of the Anna specification language and the run-time monitoring system in Section 2.

Section 3 describes the garbage collection package. The interaction between the developer and the implementor and the detection of various problems in the application and garbage collection package is described in the next three sections — Section 4 describes the developer's attempt at writing a formal specification for the garbage collection package. This is completed by the implementor in Section 5. Section 6 describes how the problem was eventually corrected. Finally, Section 7 concludes the paper.

2   Overview of Anna

Anna [10, 11, 12] (*ANN*otated *A*da) is a language extension of Ada to include facilities for formally specifying the intended behavior of Ada programs. Anna was designed to meet a perceived need to augment Ada with precise machine-processable annotations so that well established formal methods of specification and documentation can be applied to Ada programs.

Anna is based on first-order logic and its syntax is a straightforward extension of the Ada syntax. Anna constructs appear as *formal comments* within the Ada source text (within the Ada comment framework). Anna defines two kinds of formal comments, which are introduced by special comment indicators in order to distinguish them from informal comments. These formal comments are *virtual Ada text*, each line of which begins with the indicator $--:$, and *annotations*, each line of which begins with the indicator $--|$.

2.1   Virtual Ada Text

Virtual Ada text is Ada text appearing as formal comments, but otherwise obeying all of the Ada language rules. Virtual Ada text may refer to the underlying Ada program, but is not allowed to affect its computation. The purpose of virtual Ada text is to define concepts used in annotations, that are not explicitly implemented as part of the program. Virtual Ada text may also be used to compute values that are not computed by the underlying Ada program, but that are useful in specifying the behavior of the program.

2.2   Annotations

Annotations are constraints on the underlying Ada program. They are comprised of expressions that are boolean-valued. The location of an annotation in the Ada program together with its syntactic structure indicates the kind of constraints that the annotation imposes on the underlying program. Anna provides different kinds of annotations, each associated with a particular Ada construct. Some examples of annotations are subtype annotations, object annotations, statement annotations, subprogram annotations, exception propagation annotations, and axiomatic annotations. Subprogram annotations are explained in greater detail because they are used in this paper.

Subprogram Annotations

Subprogram annotations follow Ada subprogram declarations. They are constraints on the formal parameters and results of subprogram calls. They may specify conditions under which exceptions are propagated. A subprogram annotation must be true of every call to the subprogram and it acts as a declarative constraint over the subprogram body. An example follows:

```
procedure Increment(X : in out Integer);
--| where
--|     out (X = in X + 1);
```

In this example, the subprogram annotation of the procedure Increment constrains the value of the parameter X on return to be one greater than its value when called.

2.3   The Anna Run-Time Monitoring System

The Anna run-time monitoring system is a set of programs that convert Anna annotations into run-time checking code. This checking code is inserted into the underlying Ada program. The resulting Ada program is linked to a special *Anna debugger*.

When a *transformed* Anna program is executed, the Anna debugger takes control and provides a top-level interface between the user and the program being tested. Control can be transferred to the underlying program in which case, control returns to the debugger when the program becomes inconsistent with some annotation. The debugger provides the following capabilities:

- *Diagnostics.*
  Provides diagnostic messages when the program becomes inconsistent with an annotation. In this case, the annotation violated and the location of violation is displayed to the programmer.

- *Manipulation of annotations.*
  Annotations can be suppressed or unsuppressed, and their effect when they are violated can be changed. For example, annotations can be completely suppressed, *i.e.*, the program will behave as if the annotations were not present.

3   The Garbage Collection Package

The garbage collection package specification with its original documentation is shown in Figure 1. It is a generic Ada package that is parameterized with two

```
generic
    type Item is limited private;
    type Link is access Item;
package Garbage_Collection is
    procedure Free(Item_Pointer : in out Link);
    --| out (Item_Pointer = null);
    -- If Item_Pointer is null, then do nothing. This procedure
    -- may raise storage_error.
    procedure Get(New_Item_Pointer : in out Link);
    --| out (New_Item_Pointer /= null);
    -- If New_Item_Pointer is not null then do nothing. This
    -- procedure may raise storage_error.
end Garbage_Collection;
```

Fig. 1. The Garbage Collection Package Specification

type parameters — Item and Link. Here Item can be any type, and Link is an access type whose elements are pointers to elements of type Item. The garbage collection package exports two operations — Get and Free.

Ada provides the **new** operation as the only primitive for memory allocation. The language does not guarantee any memory deallocation capabilities. Hence the need for such a package. Get in the garbage collection package has pretty much the same semantics as Ada's **new** operation, and Free is a deallocation operation. If the particular Ada implementation does provide a deallocation operation as a primitive, Free may use it. Otherwise, the garbage collection package may implement a data structure in which it stores free'd items for later reallocation.

Implementation of the garbage collection package. The particular implementation of the garbage collection package that we used in our experiment assumed that the underlying Ada implementation did not provide a deallocation primitive. It therefore collects all free'd items into a data-structure for later reallocation by Get.

Some details of the garbage collection package implementation are mentioned below. This portion may be skipped during the first reading of the paper. The complete garbage collection package implementation is shown in Figure 2.

The garbage collection package maintains two lists: Free_Nodes_With_Free_Items and Free_Nodes_With_No_Items. Free_Nodes_With_Free_Items is a list containing pointers to the items which were allocated at some time but are now free. That is, Free_Nodes_With_Free_Items is a list of pointers. Storing these pointers takes some space. In the program, it is the structure type called Node_Type, which stores these pointers. In further discussion, we will refer to this as the *base* (which can be used to store pointers to items). Free_Nodes_With_No_Items is a list of *base*'s.

```
package body Garbage_Collection is

   type Node_Type;
   type List_Type is access Node_Type;
   type Node_Type is record
      L : Link;
      Next : List_Type;
   end record;
   Free_Nodes_With_No_Items Free_Nodes_With_Free_Items : List_Type;

   procedure Free(Item_Pointer : in out Link) is
      Temp : List_Type;
   begin
      if Item_Pointer /= null then
         if Free_Nodes_With_No_Items = null then
            Temp := new Node_Type;
         else
            Temp := Free_Nodes_With_No_Items;
            Free_Nodes_With_No_Items := Free_Nodes_With_No_Items . Next;
         end if;
         Temp.all := (L => Item_Pointer, Next => Free_Nodes_With_Free_Items);
         Free_Nodes_With_Free_Items := Temp;
         Item_Pointer := null;
      end if;
   end Free;

   procedure Get(New_Item_Pointer : in out Link) is
      Temp : List_Type;
   begin
      if New_Item_Pointer = null then
         if Free_Nodes_With_Free_Items = null then
            New_Item_Pointer := new Item;
         else
            Temp := Free_Nodes_With_Free_Items;
            Free_Nodes_With_Free_Items := Free_Nodes_With_Free_Items . Next;
            New_Item_Pointer := Temp . L;
            Temp . all := (L => null, Next => Free_Nodes_With_No_Items);
            Free_Nodes_With_No_Items := Temp;
         end if;
      end if;
   end Get;

end Garbage_Collection;
```

Fig. 2. Garbage Collection Package Implementation

Initially both the lists are empty. When Get is called, it checks whether Free_
Nodes_With_Free Items is empty. If so, it invokes the Ada **new** operation to
obtain more memory from the operating system. If Free_Nodes_With_Free_Items
is not empty the first pointer to an item is taken from this list and returned to the
user. Also, the *base* storing this pointer is removed from Free_Nodes_With_Free_
Items and added to Free_Nodes_With_No_Items which allows this *base* to be
reused later.

When Free is called, it checks if Free_Nodes_With_No_Items is empty. If so, in
invokes the Ada **new** operation to obtain a new *base* from the operating system.
Otherwise, a *base* is removed from Free_Nodes_With_No_Items and used to store
a pointer to the freed item.

4   Developer's Specification of Garbage Collection Package

The developer had developed an application that made use of the garbage collection package. The garbage collection package was informally specified in English
just as shown in Figure 1. The implementor assumed that the behavior of the
garbage collection package was quite obvious and had therefore not bothered to
specify it in any more detail. And in fact, it had been used for more than six
years in various applications with no problem.

However, the developer's application had a problem that the developer felt may
be due to the garbage collection package. Due to the large size of the application,
and the amount of time it had to be run before the problem showed itself, the
developer found it very difficult to apply traditional debugging techniques. He
therefore wrote a formal specification for what he assumed was the behavior of
the garbage collection package. This specification is shown in Figure 3.

The developer has defined a concept Allocate_Set using virtual Ada text. For
this purpose, the developer has also made use of an off-the-shelf sets package.
Allocate_Set is the set of all items that are currently allocated (*i.e.*, they have not
been freed). The set stores items using pointers to these items, and its initial
value is the empty set since no items are allocated when the program starts
execution.

The specification of Free states that on completion, Item_Pointer will be **null**
and that the item pointed to by the initial value of Item_Pointer is no longer a
member of Allocate_Set.

The specification of Get states that on completion, New_Item_Pointer will not be
null, that New_Item_ Pointer will be a member of Allocate_Set, and finally, that
New_Item_Pointer was not a member of the Allocate_Set when the procedure Get
was called.

The following points should be noted about the above specification:

```
--: with Sets;
generic
   type Item is limited private;
   type Link is access Item;
package Garbage_Collection is

   --: function "<"(X, Y : Link) return Boolean;
   --: package Link_Set is new Sets(Link, "<");
   --: use Link_Set;
   --: Allocate_Set : Set := Init;
   -- Allocate_Set is the set of pointers to all allocated items at
   -- any time.

   procedure Free(Item_Pointer : in out Link);
   --| where
   --|     out (Item_Pointer = null),
   --|     out (not Is_Member(Allocate_Set, in Item_Pointer));

   procedure Get(New_Item_Pointer : in out Link);
   --| where
   --|     out (New_Item_Pointer /= null),
   --|     out (Is_Member(Allocate_Set, New_Item_Pointer)),
   --|     out (not Is_Member(in (Copy(Allocate_Set)), New_Item_Pointer));

end Garbage_Collection;
```

Fig. 3. Developer's Specification

- In the very last line of the specification of **Get**, the function **Copy** has been used. This is because of the ambiguous nature of the expression (**in Allocate_Set**). If **Allocate_Set** is implemented as a pointer-based data structure, (**in Allocate_Set**) basically captures the initial value of only the pointers. If the data being pointed to has been changed during execution of **Get**, (**in Allocate_Set**) also changes value. Hence a fresh copy of **Allocate_Set** (made in the initial state) is used in the specification.

- The specification talks about how **Allocate_Set** changes when **Free** and **Get** are executed. However, **Allocate_Set** is a virtual Ada text entity that the implementation of these procedures has no knowledge of. Therefore, we must insert virtual Ada text into the implementation of these procedures to perform the necessary operations on **Allocate_Set** whenever the "real" allocations and deallocations are performed within the body. Figure 4 shows these virtual Ada text insertions.

- A sets package has been used to obtain all the set concepts. The developer has chosen an off-the-shelf sets package that was developed in 1982 and has been in frequent use since then. The point being that the developer wants to have a very high level of confidence in the correct implementation of the sets package so that he can concentrate his attention on the rest of his code.

```
package body Garbage_Collection is

    . . .

    procedure Free(Item_Pointer : in out Link) is
        Temp : List_Type;
    begin
        if Item_Pointer /= null then
            --: Link_Set . Remove(Allocate_Set, Item_Pointer);
            . . .
        end if;
    end Free;

    procedure Get(New_Item_Pointer : in out Link) is
        Temp : List_Type;
    begin
        if New_Item_Pointer = null then
            . . .
            --: Link_Set . Insert(Allocate_Set, New_Item_Pointer);
        end if;
    end Get;

end Garbage_Collection;
```

Fig. 4. Virtual Ada Text Insertions

Execution with run-time monitoring of specifications. The developer transformed the Anna constructs into checking code using the Anna tools and executed his application. After some time, the following annotation was violated during a call to **Get**:

```
--| out (not Is_Member(in (Copy(Allocate_Set)), New_Item_Pointer))
```

This means that **Get** was returning a value in **New_Item_Pointer** that was already present in **Allocate_Set** — *i.e.*, **Get** was returning an already allocated item[2].

5   Implementor's Specification of Garbage Collection Package

The developer informed the implementor of his findings. When the implementor read the developer's formal specification, he found it to be incomplete. The developer had not specified against possible misuse of the garbage collection

---

[2]There is also the possibility that the sets package has a bug, the Anna specification of the garbage collection package is wrong, or that the virtual Ada code in the body of the procedures has not been inserted correctly. However, the developer has decided to assume (for the time-being) that such problems do not exist.

package. Being the implementor of the garbage collection package, he assumed
that the problem was not in his code! The implementor completed the specification of the garbage collection package as shown in Figure 5.

```
--: with Sets;
generic
   type Item is limited private;
   type Link is access Item;
package Garbage_Collection is

   --: function "<"(X, Y : Link) return Boolean;
   --: package Link_Set is new Sets(Link, "<");
   --: use Link_Set;
   --: Free_Set, Allocate_Set : Set := Init;
   -- The implementor has defined yet another concept —
   -- Free_Set. Free_Set is the set of all items which were some-
   -- time allocated but are currently free.

   procedure Free(Item_Pointer : in out Link);
   --| where
   --|    in (Is_Member(Allocate_Set, Item_Pointer)),
   --|    in (not Is_Member(Free_Set, Item_Pointer)),
   --|    out (Item_Pointer = null),
   --|    out (not Is_Member(Allocate_Set, in Item_Pointer)),
   --|    out (Is_Member(Free_Set, in Item_Pointer));

   procedure Get(New_Item_Pointer : in out Link);
   --| where
   --|    out (New_Item_Pointer /= null),
   --|    out (Is_Member(Allocate_Set, New_Item_Pointer)),
   --|    out (not Is_Member(in (Copy(Allocate_Set)), New_Item_Pointer)),
   --|    out (not Is_Member(Free_Set, New_Item_Pointer)),
   --|    out (in (not Is_Empty(Free_Set)) ->
   --|             (Is_Member(in (Copy(Free_Set)), New_Item_Pointer)));

end Garbage_Collection;
```

Fig. 5. Implementor's Specification

The implementor decided to define another concept using virtual text — the
set **Free_Set**. Free_Set contains all the items that have been allocated at some
earlier time, but are currently free'd. This set is also initialized to be the empty
set.

The implementor has specified two cases of misuse of the garbage collection
package using the two annotations starting with **in** in Free. They state that when
Free is called, the parameter Item_Pointer passed to it must *(1)* be a member of
Allocate_Set, and *(2)* not be a member of Free_Set.

The implementor has .also specified how Free and Get affect Free_Set. The specification states that on return from Free, Item_Pointer must be a member of Free_Set; and that on return from Get, New_Item_Pointer must not be a member of Free_Set and furthermore, if Free_Set was not empty when Get was called, the returned New_Item_Pointer must be from this set.

Here again, the implementation of the garbage collection package has to be instrumented to update Free_Set, just as in the case of Allocate_Set.

Execution with run-time monitoring of specifications. When the transformed version of this program was executed, the following annotation was violated during a call to Free:

$--|$ **in** (Is_Member(Allocate_Set, Item_Pointer))

This means that the item being free'd was not in Allocate_Set. Among other possibilities, this indicated that the developer may be calling Free with an item that was already deallocated. When the implementor informed the developer of this, he said that this was indeed the case and that he (the developer) assumed that the garbage collection package could handle multiple consecutive free requests on the same item just as the corresponding UNIX system call did. The implementor's specification clearly mentions that a free'd item may not be freed a second time. However, he failed to write this down in his initial informal specification of the garbage collection package. This misunderstanding between the implementor and the developer, which caused a lot of wasted effort (there is still the issue of correcting the problem now that it has been detected) could have been avoided by enforcing the use of formal specifications in the first place.

6 Correcting the Problem

There were two alternatives to make the garbage collection package and the program compatible with each other. The first was to tailor the garbage collection package to suit the needs of the program. This was possible with only a few changes in the package implementation, and hence, very tempting. But it would seriously affect the time complexity of garbage collection. The current version of the package had a constant time complexity, whereas the modified package would have a time complexity linear on the number of items allocated. This was deemed undesirable.

The second alternative (which was chosen as the solution to the problem) was to change the application to avoid deallocating the same item twice. This would be difficult to do since deallocations were being performed all over the application in non-trivial ways. Here again, Anna and the Anna run-time monitoring system came to use. The strategy followed by the developer was simple: Execute the application using the garbage collection package specified by the implementor (Figure 5) with the Anna checks enabled. Whenever a deallocation to the same item was repeated, the Anna debugger would report a violation. The location of the violation enabled the developer to fix one particular misuse of the garbage collection package. Repeating this process slowly eliminated most of these problems.

However, after a while, a new problem was encountered. The application would be run for a long time and would run out of memory because the implementation of the sets package did not do its own garbage collection. The implementor remedied this problem by rewriting the specification without using the sets package, but rather using the data structures within the garbage collection package to simulate the required sets. This version of the garbage collection package and its implementation is shown in Appendix A.

With this new version, the developer managed to get rid of all multiple deallocations in a relatively short time.

7 Conclusion

Writing specifications for any program, however trivial it might look at the time, is very important. It is of course best to annotate the program completely, but if that is not feasible, it is good to write at least some annotations. There might not be too much difference between non-rigorous and rigorous specifications, but there is a very large difference between non-rigorous specifications and no specifications at all. Writing specifications is neither difficult nor time-consuming, it is just a matter of habit, which needs to be cultivated, just like good programming style.

8 Acknowledgements

Doug Bryan was the "implementor" and James Vera was the "developer". The authors aided Doug and James in the use of Anna and its tool-set. The Anna project has been led by Prof. David Luckham, who has been a source of inspiration for many of our achievements in the application of formal methods to software develoment.

This work was primarily supported by DARPA through ONR N00014-91-C-0162. During the final phases of this work, Anoop Goyal was supported by the Department of Computer Science at Stanford University and Sriram Sankar was supported by Sun Microsystems Laboratories, Inc.

References

[1] R. W. Floyd. Assigning meanings to programs. In *Proceedings of a Symposium in Applied Mathematics of the American Mathematical Society*, volume 19, pages 19–32. American Mathematical Society, 1967.

[2] J. B. Goodenough and S. L. Gerhart. Towards a theory of test data selection. In *Proceedings of the International Conference on Reliable Software*, pages 493–510, April 1975.

[3] C. Green, D. Luckham, R. Balzer, T. Cheatham, and C. Rich. Report on a knowledge based software assistant. Technical report, Kestrel Institute, 1983.

[4] J. V. Guttag, J. J. Horning, and J. M. Wing. The Larch family of specification languages. *IEEE Software*, 2(5):24–36, September 1985.

[5] D. P. Helmbold and D. C. Luckham. Runtime detection and description of deadness errors in Ada tasking. Technical Report 83-249, Computer Systems Laboratory, Stanford University, November 1983. (Program Analysis and Verification Group Report 22).

[6] W. E. Howden. Algebraic program testing. *Acta Informatica*, 10:53–66, 1978.

[7] B. Krieg-Brückner. Transformation of interface specifications, 1985. PROSPECTRA Study Note M.1.1.S1-SN-2.0.

[8] R. L. London. A view of program verification. In *Proceedings of the International Conference on Reliable Software*, pages 534–545, April 1975.

[9] D. C. Luckham, S. Sankar, and S. Takahashi. Two dimensional pinpointing: An application of formal specification to debugging packages. *IEEE Software*, 8(1):74–84, January 1991. (Also Stanford University Technical Report No. CSL–TR–89–379.).

[10] D. C. Luckham and F. W. von Henke. An overview of Anna, a specification language for Ada. *IEEE Software*, 2(2):9–23, March 1985.

[11] David C. Luckham. *Programming with Specifications: An Introduction to ANNA, A Language for Specifying Ada Programs*. Texts and Monographs in Computer Science. Springer-Verlag, October, 1990.

[12] David C. Luckham, Friedrich W. von Henke, Bernd Krieg-Brückner, and Olaf Owe. *ANNA, A Language for Annotating Ada Programs*, volume 260 of *Lecture Notes in Computer Science*. Springer-Verlag, 1987.

[13] N. Madhav and W. R. Mann. A methodology for formal specification and implementation of Ada packages using Anna. In *Proceedings of the Computer Software and Applications Conference, 1990*, pages 491–496. IEEE

Computer Society Press, 1990. (Also Stanford University Computer Systems Laboratory Technical Report No. 90-438).

[14] N. Madhav and S. Sankar. Application of formal specification to software maintenance. In *Proceedings of the Conference on Software Maintenance*, pages 230–241. IEEE Computer Society Press, November 1990.

[15] Walter Mann. The Anna package specification analyzer user's guide. Technical Note CSL–TN–93–390, Computer Systems Lab, Stanford University, January 1993.

[16] B. Meyer. *Object-Oriented Software Construction*. Prentice-Hall, 1988.

[17] S. Sankar. *Automatic Runtime Consistency Checking and Debugging of Formally Specified Programs*. PhD thesis, Stanford University, August 1989. Also Stanford University Department of Computer Science Technical Report No. STAN–CS–89–1282, and Computer Systems Laboratory Technical Report No. CSL–TR–89–391.

[18] S. Sankar. A note on the detection of an Ada compiler bug while debugging an Anna program. *ACM SIGPLAN Notices*, 24(6):23–31, 1989.

[19] S. Sankar and D. S. Rosenblum. The complete transformation methodology for sequential runtime checking of an Anna subset. Technical Report 86-301, Computer Systems Laboratory, Stanford University, June 1986. (Program Analysis and Verification Group Report 30).

[20] Sriram Sankar. Run-time consistency checking of algebraic specifications. In *Proceedings of the Symposium on Testing, Analysis, and Verification (TAV4)*, pages 123–129, Victoria, Canada, October 1991. ACM Press.

[21] Sriram Sankar, Anoop Goyal, and Prakash Sikchi. Software testing using algebraic specification based test oracles. Forthcoming Stanford University Technical Report, April 1993.

[22] J. M. Spivey. *Understanding Z, A Specification Language and its Formal Semantics*. Cambridge Unversity Press, 1988. Tracts in Theorectical Computer Science, Volume 3.

[23] L. G. Stucki and G. L. Foshee. New assertion concepts for self-metric software validation. In *Proceedings of the International Conference on Reliable Software*, pages 59–65, April 1975.

A Final Version of Garbage Collection Package

```
generic
   type Item is limited private;
   type Link is access Item;
package Garbage_Collection is

   --: function Is_Member(Atom : Link) return Boolean;
   --: function Cardinality return Integer;

   procedure Free(Item_Pointer : in out Link);
   --| where
   --|    in (not Is_Member(Item_Pointer)),
   --|    out (Item_Pointer = null),
   --|    out (Is_Member(in Item_Pointer));

   procedure Get(New_Item_Pointer : in out Link);
   --| where
   --|    out (New_Item_Pointer /= null),
   --|    out ((in(Cardinality) /= 0) -> (Cardinality = in(Cardinality) - 1)),
   --|    out (not Is_Member(New_Item_Pointer));

end Garbage_Collection;

package body Garbage_Collection is

   type Node_Type;
   type List_Type is access Node_Type;
   type Node_Type is record
      L : Link;
      Next : List_Type;
   end record;
   Free_Nodes_With_No_Items, Free_Nodes_With_Free_Items : List_Type;

   --: function Is_Member(Atom : Link) return Boolean is
   --:    Temp : List_Type;
   --: begin
   --:    Temp := Free_Nodes_With_Free_Items;
   --:    while (Temp /= null) loop
   --:       if Temp . L = Atom) then
   --:          return True;
   --:       end if;
   --:       Temp := Temp . Next;
   --:    end loop;
   --:    return False;
   --: end Is_Member;
```

```
--: function Cardinality return Integer is
--:     Temp : List_Type;
--:     Count : Integer := 0;
--: begin
--:     Temp := Free_Nodes_With_Free_Items;
--:     while (Temp /= null) loop
--:        Count := Count + 1;
--:        Temp := Temp . Next;
--:     end loop;
--:     return Count;
--: end Cardinality;


procedure Free(Item_Pointer : in out Link) is
   Temp : List_Type;
begin
   if Item_Pointer /= null then
      if Free_Nodes_With_No_Items = null then
         Temp := new Node_Type;
      else
         Temp := Free_Nodes_With_No_Items;
         Free_Nodes_With_No_Items := Free_Nodes_With_No_Items . Next;
      end if;
      Temp.all := (L=>Item_Pointer,Next=>Free_Nodes_With_Free_Items);
      Free_Nodes_With_Free_Items := Temp;
      Item_Pointer := null;
   end if;
end Free;


procedure Get(New_Item_Pointer : in out Link) is
   Temp : List_Type;
begin
   if New_Item_Pointer = null then
      if Free_Nodes_With_Free_Items = null then
         New_Item_Pointer := new Item;
      else
         Temp := Free_Nodes_With_Free_Items;
         Free_Nodes_With_Free_Items := Free_Nodes_With_Free_Items.Next;
         New_Item_Pointer := Temp . L;
         Temp . all := (L => null, Next => Free_Nodes_With_No_Items);
         Free_Nodes_With_No_Items := Temp;
      end if;
   end if;
end Get;


end Garbage_Collection;
```

Automatic Diagnosis of VLSI Digital Circuits Using Algorithmic Debugging

Krzysztof Kuchcinski, Wlodzimierz Drabent and Jan Maluszynski

Dept. of Computer and Information Science
Linköping University
S-581 83 Linköping, Sweden
e-mail: {kku, wdr, jmz}@ida.liu.se

Abstract. This paper discusses application of the technique of algorithmic debugging, originating from logic programming, to automatic diagnosis of VLSI digital circuits. In particular, the main aim of the presented work is to provide a method for smooth combination of different diagnosis techniques, where the use of logic specifications and algorithmic debugging plays an essential role. Examples of the application of the proposed method to combinational and to sequential circuits are presented.

Keywords: Digital Circuits Diagnosis, Logic Programming, Algorithmic Debugging of Logic Programs, Design Automation

1 Introduction

This paper shows how the concept of algorithmic debugging, originating from logic programming [Sha 82], can be used for diagnosis of digital circuits. The general aim of our work is to create a framework for smooth combination of different diagnosis techniques where the use of logic specifications and algorithmic debugging play an essential role.

Digital circuits are built out of components, each having some input and output ports. Components' ports are connected by connections, let us call them "wires". For our purposes we may assume that a wire can transmit two signals (or have two states): 0 and 1. The structure of a circuit is usually hierarchical: a component is built out of subcomponents, the subcomponents may consist of lower level components, etc. For example, figure 1 represents a full one bit adder component. This component consists of a number of gates which are lower level components in this case.

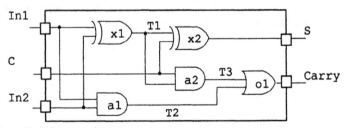

Figure 1 Full one bit adder example

A circuit is usually built according to a detailed, complete design and has some kind of a formal specification describing its behavior. The design is known to be correct with respect to. this specification. This correctness is established by standard methods of electronic engineering. Faults in the circuit are due to technological errors resulting in a discrepancy between the design and the circuit. This in turn results in an incorrect behavior of the circuit.

Diagnosis of a circuit means localizing a fault in it. Example faults are: a faulty elementary (sub)component, a broken connection, an additional incorrect connection ("bridging"). Many faults of elementary components can be modeled as "stuck-at-0" or "stuck-at-1"; a component behaves as if a permanent signal 0 (respectively 1) were present at one of its ports.

Two different kinds of digital circuits, the combinational circuits and the sequential circuits, are often diagnosed by different methods. In a combinational circuit the signals on the output ports can be modeled as a function of the signals on the input ports. A sequential circuit has internal states, so that the output signals are determined not only by the inputs but also by the actual internal state. Thus a sequential circuit can be modeled as a finite automaton. For example, figure 2 represents the decade synchronous counter and its finite automaton.

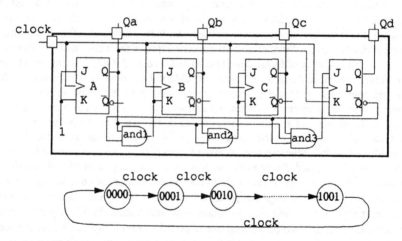

Figure 2 The decade synchronous counter and its finite automaton

The diagnosis problem is important since localization of the fault may make it possible, depending on the technology, to repair the circuit, e.g. by exchanging the faulty component. Even if the circuit cannot be fixed, the diagnosis may indicate the weak points of the design with respect to the technology used, thus giving hints for improvements.

The approaches to circuit diagnosis can be roughly divided as follows:

1. The traditional methods are based usually on fault dictionaries (see e.g. [Lee 76], [Tsu 86]). The fault dictionary for a given circuit is a table whose rows contain all combinations of incorrect input/output values for a selected fault model. For each combination in the table a number of possible faults in the circuit is indicated. A number of tests guided by the fault dictionary may make it

possible to localize a fault in the circuit. This method is conceptually simple but has prohibitive complexity in the case of large circuits. For example, a circuit with 20 input ports and 30 internal lines within the circuit would require a fault dictionary with more than 30.000.000 entries. Moreover, the method is only applicable to combinational circuits. Different extensions and improvements were proposed for this method, however, they do not change the main deficiencies.

2. Diagnosis based on mechanization of expert knowledge. Rule-based diagnosis systems of this kind accumulate the experience of human experts in the form of empirical rules that associate symptoms with underlying faults of the diagnosed device. An example of such a system is presented in [ALP+ 92].

3. Methods using the principle of model-based diagnosis. A model of the circuit gives predictions of the expected behavior. A discrepancy between the observed behavior and the predicted behavior guides a reasoning on the model which results in fault localization hypotheses.

In the approaches mentioned the diagnosed circuit is usually seen as a black-box, where the only observable points are input and output ports.

With the development of VLSI technology, and related complexity of designs which reached more than one million transistors while the number of input/output ports remains limited the classical design methods become very inefficient. For overcoming the complexity barrier the designed circuits are often represented hierarchically using different abstraction models for different design purposes (see e.g. [AR 83]). An important aspect of the design is to make the designed system testable and diagnosable. The measures taken for this purpose (like e.g. including a register scan path) make it possible to observe not only the inputs and the outputs of a circuit, but also some internal wires and components. In such a circuit localization of a faulty component can be facilitated by the observability of some internal points. Clearly, in the search for a faulty component the available observations should be used in a selective way to make the process as efficient as possible. Since the observability is limited, the process can only localize a component with observable faulty behavior. The granularity of the localized component may or may not be satisfactory from the point of view of the diagnosis process. In the latter case a black-box type of diagnosis can be applied to the component to obtain more information. In this paper we propose a framework for such a two-phase diagnosis of partially observable circuits. A common basis for both phases is the assumption that the circuit is described by a logic program, (possibly combined with some functional procedures). The selective use of available observations in the first phase of the diagnosis is achieved by a modification of the idea of algorithmic debugging. An early attempt of using algorithmic debugging for diagnosis of fully observable combinational circuits was described in [Gup 87]. Our approach extends the ideas presented there in different ways. The major extensions are the following:

- A more careful analysis of the basic concepts shows some flaws of Gupta's method and a possibility of different use of algorithmic debugging for diagnosis than the use proposed by Gupta.

- A combination of algorithmic debugging with other diagnosis methods is discussed as a way for dealing with partially observable circuits. The problem of limited observability was pointed out by Gupta as the major obstacle for application of his method.

• Application of algorithmic debugging to diagnosis of sequential circuits.

The second phase of our diagnosis is devoted to the minimal observable faulty subcomponent identified by the algorithmic debugger. For this purpose we use at present a rather restricted version of model-based diagnosis. Extensions and/or combination with traditional methods seems to be possible and will be considered in the future.

The paper is organized as follows. Section 2 surveys some basic ideas: the concept of algorithmic debugging of logic programs and the notion of model-based diagnosis.

Section 3 presents our method. Section 3.1 gives a general presentation of the method. Section 3.2 shows our approach to modeling circuits as logic programs. Section 3.3 discusses applicability of algorithmic debugging for diagnosis of digital circuits with observable components. The differences between algorithmic debugging of logic programs and diagnosis of digital circuits are discussed to indicate modifications of the algorithmic debugger which are necessary for its application to circuit diagnosis.

Section 3.4 presents our approach to black-box diagnosis of the component localized by the algorithmic debugging.

Section 4 shows examples of diagnoses of combinational and sequential circuits using both algorithmic debugging and our black-box diagnosis. The examples have been prepared with the use of our algorithmic debugger [DNM 88a, b], which has not been designed for this application. Section 5 discusses other related papers, presents some conclusions and outlines future work.

2 Preliminaries

2.1 Algorithmic Debugging of Logic Programs.

We assume that the reader is familiar with basic concept of logic programming, or with Prolog. The logic programs used in this paper are mostly definite programs, or definite programs extended with Prolog arithmetic. A definite program is a finite set of definite clauses. Definite programs constitute a proper subset of Prolog and are sometimes called pure Prolog programs.

A logic program describes a family of relations, called its least Herbrand model (see e.g. [Llo 87]). For example the following program:

```
and(0,X,0).
and(1,X,X).
or(0,X,X).
or(1,X,1).
```
describes the finite ternary relations "and" and "or" which characterize the behavior of, respectively, "and" gates and "or" gates. A Prolog system makes it possible to compute elements of the least Herbrand model. This is done selectively by submitting queries, called goals. For example the query

```
?- and(X,1,Y)
```

would produce the answers X=0, Y=0, and X=1,Y=1, thus showing that the atoms and(0,1,0) and and(1,1,1) belong to the least Herbrand model of the program. The least Herbrand model (the actual semantics of the program) may or may not conform to the expectations of the user (the intended semantics), which may be characterized by some independent formal specification. In the case of discrepancy between the least Herbrand model of the program and the specification, the program is said to be faulty. Two kinds of errors can be distinguished:

- *incorrectness*, where the Herbrand model of the program includes some elements not expected by the user. In practice such an error leads to unexpected answers produced by the Prolog system. It can be linked to a clause in the program "responsible" for producing the unexpected answer.

- *insufficiency*, where the Herbrand model of the program does not include some elements expected by the user. In practice such an error leads to missing answers of the computations for some queries. It can be linked to a predicate of the program, whose defining clauses should have characterized the missing element but do not do that.

Algorithmic debugging [Sha 82] is a method of localizing errors in logic programs. By localization of an error we mean indication of the responsible clause in the case of incorrectness and indication of the insufficiently defined predicate in the case of insufficiency. A presence of a bug is determined when, for some input goal, the obtained set of answers differs from the expected one. This demonstrates that the actual semantics of the program differs from its intended semantics. The intended semantics is given by the program's specification and, in practice, such specification is usually informal.

A debugging algorithm localizes a bug in a semi-automatic way. It acquires information about the intended semantics by questioning an oracle. Some formal specification of the intended semantics may be used as the oracle; in practice this role is usually played by the programmer. The kind of questions that can be asked depends on the particular algorithm used. For our purposes it is sufficient to use two kinds of questions [DNM 88a, b]:

1. Is A correct? (in other words is A true in the intended semantics)

2. Is $A_1, ..., A_n$ a complete set of answers for goal A?

where A, $A_1, ..., A_n$ are atoms, i.e. an atomic formulae.

These questions require YES or NO answers. Some algorithms, for example [Sha 82], use questions with more complicated answers.

The existing debugging algorithms have been proved to be correct and complete. The correctness means that the clause, or predicate identified by the algorithm is indeed erroneous in some well defined sense. The completeness means that in every case when the system produces an unexpected (or missing) answer to a given query the algorithm can localize an error. Thus, if the unexpected (or missing) answer is caused by a single error this error will be correctly localized in the program. However, in the case of many errors the algorithm localizes only one of them, which not necessarily fully explains the observed unexpected behavior of the program. The remaining errors will be found by a repeated usage of the algorithm.

An interesting aspect of algorithmic debugging is the assumption of full observability. The localization process is a search through the structure of the program. The search is guided by the comparison of the observed behavior of the program and its subcomponents with the expected behavior, specified by the user either formally or by the answers to the questions posed by the system. Every step of the search starts with a faulty component of the program and attempts to identify a faulty subcomponent of this component. On success the subcomponent becomes the subject of the search. The failure means that all subcomponents of a given faulty component behave correctly on the data at hand, so that the localization process terminates indicating given component as faulty.

2.2 Model-based Diagnosis

As pointed out in Section 1, model-based diagnosis is one of well-established approaches to diagnosis (see e.g. [HCK 92] for a comprehensive survey). In this approach, a model of the diagnosed device is constructed which predicts the behavior of the device. The diagnosis itself is understood as finding the reason of the discrepancy between the observed behavior of the device and the predicted behavior obtained from the model. The diagnosis process consists essentially of three phases: hypothesis generation, hypothesis testing and hypothesis discrimination. The task of hypothesis generation is to determine, based on a given discrepancy, the set of components of the device which might be faulty. The following task of hypothesis testing takes determined components of the previous task and based on the observations of the behavior selects faulty components which could produce the current behavior. Finally, the hypothesis discrimination tries to find out what additional information can be gathered to discriminate between possibly several hypothesis. The method is general and can be applied to many diagnosis problems such as electrical, mechanical or medical.

As pointed out in [HD 88], the general model-based diagnosis should not to be used for problems which are either too hard or too easy. Too hard problems concern diagnosis of the systems which are difficult to model with the current modeling technology. Too easy problems concern diagnosis of the systems for which exhaustive behavior modeling is possible and where the set of faults is well known. It can be noted here that digital circuits have well defined models and faults classes. For simple combinational circuits the traditional diagnosis by fault dictionaries may give good solutions. However, the realistic circuits can hardly be diagnosed in that way. On the other hand, although circuit diagnosis is a favorite source of examples in the papers on domain-based diagnosis, the method does not seem to be widely accepted by industry.

An important subclass of model-based diagnosis is the logic-based approach, where logical formulae represent both the structure and the behavior of the device. It can be further divided into consistency-based and abductive diagnosis. The consistency-based diagnosis assumes correct model described in terms of logic, typically in some variant of first order predicate calculus, specifying the structure and the behavior of the correct device. If the device is faulty its model and current observations are inconsistent. The role of the diagnosis is to find the components which are responsible for this inconsistency. Our approach is similar in that that a circuit is specified by a logic program, which describes the structure and the correct behavior of the circuit.

The abductive diagnosis, on the other hand, works with logical formulas which describe the consequences of faults. Thus, this kind of diagnosis assumes the availability of fault models, that is, knowledge about the possible faults of a component and their behavioral consequences. The second phase of our diagnosis process is similar to abductive diagnosis in that that it also uses logical descriptions of possible faults. However, the difference is that these fault descriptions are combined with the original model of the correct behavior, which plays the essential role also in the second phase of the diagnosis process.

2.3 Is Algorithmic Debugging a Model-Based Diagnosis?

As discussed in [DH 88], model-based diagnosis generates a set of hypotheses and discriminates them afterwards by different means. The paper describes probing as one of the approaches for hypothesis discrimination. In the case of logic programs, probing can be understood as checking the behavior of the components of the program on given data. In algorithmic debugging this behavior is compared with the expected one, which, however, is usually not defined by a formal model, but described in a by-need way by querying the user. Using instead a full formal specification would made the algorithmic debugging closer to model-based diagnosis. However, in algorithmic debugging there is no hypothesis generation and discrimination since the process is controlled by "probing" in the way which guarantees identification of an error. As already pointed out, it is not guaranteed that the identified error fully explains the incorrect behavior of the program which triggered the debugging. There may be other errors which contribute to the incorrect behavior and which are not discovered in the first round. To summarize, the algorithmic debugging is similar to model-based diagnosis in that that it uses a model of "correct expected behavior" of the program. The model is, however, used in the "probing"-controlled search for a faulty component rather than for generation of an exhaustive set of diagnosis hypotheses. The problem of relation between model-based diagnosis and algorithmic debugging is also discussed in [CFT 93].

3 The method

3.1 A General Outline

In this section we propose a method for diagnosis of combinational and sequential circuits, which should be applicable to circuits of realistic size. The method and the supporting tools are under development but first experiments seem to be promising. We adopt the following guidelines:

- The diagnosed circuits should be described in a declarative way. The description language should allow for integration of existing, possibly non-declarative, descriptions of standard components in the declarative top-level description of the diagnosed circuit.
- The system should allow for smooth integration of various diagnosis methods with particular emphasis on using algorithmic debugging for diagnosis of observable subcomponents of the diagnosed circuit.
- The system should provide appropriate degree of automation but it should also allow for user interaction in controlling the search.

To satisfy these requirements we propose the following technical solutions:

- The circuits are to be represented in a hierarchical structural way by logic programs, possibly with external procedures in other languages. Representation of digital circuits as logic programs have been discussed by many authors (see e.g. [Clo 87]) and we use the existing experience. This topic is discussed in the next section. For integration of standard descriptions with logic programs we use results of previous work on logic programs with external procedures ([BM 88], [Bon 92], [MBB+ 93]). The experience with a prototype language based on this theory [KK 91] should be helpful in this work. In the present implementation the C language is supported, however, an extension to VHDL can be considered.

- The process of diagnosis of a faulty circuit is to be divided into two phases. The first phase uses algorithmic debugging for locating a faulty subcomponent. The granularity of the subcomponent depends on the observability characteristics of the circuit. In the worst case the subcomponent is the whole circuit, in the best case a basic faulty subcomponent can be localized, if it is observable. In our previous research we developed a technique of circuit design for testability [GKP 92]. The assumption about using algorithmic debugging for diagnosis allows us to make some design decision in our synthesis method as a trade-off between cost requirement and desired granularity of faulty subcomponents localized by the algorithmic debugging.

In the second phase the localized faulty component is diagnosed using other methods. The solution discussed in this paper is to generate fault descriptions in Prolog. A similar idea can be found in literature, e. g. in [BCM 88]. The logic program obtained in this way is then executed with backtracking, until the results conform to the observed faulty behavior. To reduce the search space we make the single fault assumption. We also propose selective use of fault descriptions restricted to the parts of the subcomponent localized by the dependency analysis of subcomponents and user interactions.

The faulty subcomponent produces incorrect output value on some output port(s) for a given input. For the faulty circuit the search for the faults can be reduced to the subcomponents on which the incorrect output depend. This can be achieved by applying dependency analysis on the component specifications. A concept of dependency relation on proof trees of logic programs was introduced in [DM 85], and [DM 93]. It is expected that the similar method can be developed for our problem. If this restriction is not sufficient another test of the circuit may produce another incorrect output, thus restricting the search to the elements on which both incorrect outputs depend. This resembles to certain extent the use of traditional fault dictionaries, where the dependency information is compiled as possible faults. The difference is that in our case the fault descriptions are generated selectively during the diagnosis. A possibility of a hybrid technique combining incomplete fault dictionaries with reduced fault descriptions may be considered as an alternative.

Clearly, the techniques outlined above are well-known in the field of model-based diagnosis. Our intention is to obtain more experience in their specialization to Prolog with external procedures and in combining them with more traditional methods applied by practitioners.

As the diagnosis problem for single fault is generally NP-complete [Gol 79], it may happen that exhaustive search would still be unrealistic for some circuits. On the other hand, it might be possible for an expert to estimate which elements of a given subcomponent are more likely to be faulty and to enforce appropriate search order. Therefore an interaction with the user should be possible at this phase.

The proposed diagnosis methodology is illustrated in Figure 3. The diagnosis system consists of two parts: algorithmic debugging module and Prolog execution module. The input to the system consists of three items: correct Prolog specification of the diagnosed circuit (possibly with external procedures), actual inputs and outputs of the circuit, and a set of internal, observable lines' values. Based on this information the algorithmic debugging module localizes a minimal observable faulty module. If it is not a basic module the second phase of diagnosis is necessary. As discussed above, a set of descriptions of possible faults is generated and executed in Prolog to localize possible faults. The methodology makes possible user interactions. The user can define faults for the currently diagnosed circuit and can influence the order of the search. In this way his expertise will be used to cut the search space.

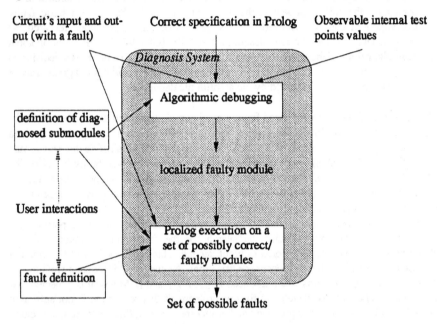

Figure 3 The fault diagnosis methodology

The rest of this section presents some details of the proposed method.

3.2 Modeling circuits as logic programs

3.2.1 Representation of the structure

We consider both combinational and synchronous sequential circuits. The class of synchronous sequential circuits is defined as circuits which can have sequential devices, such as flip-flops and registers, but the state change is only possible at well defined time moments, namely clock ticks. This class of circuits is quite large and includes many industrial examples.

The representation is based on the assumption that every digital circuit's module is represented as a one Prolog procedure. This assumption makes it possible to enforce abstraction and hierarchy. The subcomponents of a complex circuit will be represented by the procedures called from the main procedure representing the circuit. The procedures representing the base components of a circuit may give functional-level, gate-level or transistor-level descriptions. The procedures representing complex circuits may refer to subprocedures using different description levels. This kind of hierarchical description of circuit follows the style of logic programming in a top-down development. On the other hand, it has a clear connection to real designs which have a similar hierarchy. For example, transistors are used to build gates, gates are used to build functional units, registers, etc., printed circuit boards (PCBs) contain functional units, registers, and finally PCBs are used to make a system. The observability of these modules follows similar hierarchy rules.

Combinational circuits are defined by functions between inputs and outputs. For example we can specify a full one bit adder by three different styles represented below (see also figure 1).

Functional definition of 1-bit adder.

```
full_adder_func(Name, In1, In2, C, Carry, Sum) :-
    Sum is (In1+ In2 + C) mod 2,
    Carry is (In1 + In2 + C) div 2.
```

Gate level definition of 1-bit adder

```
full_adder_gates(Name, In1, In2, C, Carry, Sum) :-
    xor(Name/x1, In1, In2, T1),
    and(Name/a1, In1, In2, T2),
    xor(Name/x2, C, T1, Sum),
    and(Name/a2, C, T1, T3),
    or(Name/o1, T2, T3, Carry).
```

Transistor level definition of 1-bit adder (without fault definition)

```
full_adder_tran(Name, A, B, C, SUM, CARRY) :-
    carry_part(Name/cp, A, B, C, NCA, CARRY),
    sum_part(Name/sp, A, B, C, NCA, SUM).


sum_part(Name, A, B, C, NCA, SUM) :-
    ptran(Name/p1, NCA, T1, 1), ptran(Name/p2, C, 1, T5), ptran(Name/p3, B, T1, T5),
    ptran(Name/p4, A, T1, T2), ptran(Name/p5, NCA, T5, T2), ptran(Name/p6, T2, 1, SUM),
    ntran(Name/n1, A, T2, T3), ntran(Name/n2, NCA, T2, T6), ntran(Name/n3, T2, SUM, 0),
    ntran(Name/n4, B, T3, T6), ntran(Name/n5, NCA, T3, 0), ntran(Name/n6, C, T6, 0).

carry_part(Name, A, B, C, NCA, CA) :-
    ptran(Name/p1, A, T1, 1), ptran(Name/p2, B, T1, 1), ptran(Name/p3, A, T2, 1),
    ptran(Name/p4, C, T1, NCA), ptran(Name/p5, B, T2, NCA), ptran(Name/p6, NCA, 1, CA),
    ntran(Name/n1, C, NCA, T3), ntran(Name/n2, B, NCA, T4), ntran(Name/n3, NCA, CA, 0),
    ntran(Name/n4, A, T3, 0), ntran(Name/n5, B, T3, 0), ntran(Name/n6, A, T4, 0).
```

Synchronous sequential circuits are represented in a similar way as combinational circuits but with added state arguments. In addition, a sequential execution model must be defined as recurrently executed procedure over a list of inputs and an initial state. In special cases, finite state machines and data path logic must also be represented for complex digital circuits. Below there is an example of the decade synchronous counter together with its execution model (simulation procedure). The counter is build of J_K flip-flops (defined in the next section) and "and" gates.

```
simulate([], _, []).
simulate([CK|Clock], State, [[Qd,Qc,Qb,Qa]|S]) :-
    counter(DEC, CK, State, NewState),
    NewState = [Qa, _, Qb, _, Qc, _, Qd, _],
    simulate(Clock, NewState,S).

counter(Name, Clock, [Qa, Qabar, Qb, Qbbar, Qc, Qcbar, Qd, Qdbar],
    [QaNew, QabarNew, QbNew, QbbarNew, QcNew, QcbarNew, QdNew, QdbarNew]) :-
    j_k(Name/jkA, 1, 1, Clock, Qa, Qabar, QaNew, QabarNew),
    and(Name/and1, Qa, Qdbar, T1),
    j_k(Name/jkB, T1, T1, Clock, Qb, Qbbar, QbNew, QbbarNew),
    and(Name/and2, Qa, Qb, T2),
    j_k(Name/jkC, T2, T2, Clock, Qc, Qcbar, QcNew, QcbarNew),
    and(Name/and3, Qa, Qb, Qc, T3),
    j_k(Name/jkD, T3, Qa, Clock, Qd, Qdbar, QdNew, QdbarNew).
```

3.2.2 Components Modeling and Fault Models

All components, both combinational and sequential, are modeled by Prolog procedures. For combinational components we will define a function between inputs and outputs. For sequential component an internal state argument will be added both to inputs and outputs. We assume additionally that the delay for output value calculation can be neglected when compared to the clock cycle. This means that the component delays will not be modeled.

For example an, "and" gate is defined in Prolog in a following way.

```
%% correct "and" gate
and(Name, 0, X, 0).
and(Name, 1, X, X).
```

While modeling one bit clocked J-K flip-flop next state argument QNext and QbarNext must be used, as presented below.

```
%% correct clocked J-K flip flop- j_k(Name, J, K, Clock, Q, Qbar, QNext, QbarNext).
j_k(Name, 0, 0, 1, Q, Qbar, Q, Qbar).
j_k(Name, 0, 1, 1, Q, Qbar, 0, 1).
j_k(Name, 1, 0, 1, Q, Qbar, 1, 0).
j_k(Name, 1, 1, 1, Q, Qbar, Qbar, Q).
j_k(Name, J, K, 0, Q, Qbar, Q, Qbar).
```

Since the timing aspect of digital components is not modeled, we restrict ourselves to static fault models. The basic fault model which is used most often in the area of testing and diagnosis is stuck-at-value model which will be our basic fault model. A simple extension to bridging faults is possible.

An example of stuck-at-value fault definitions for "and" gate is following:

```
%% possible s-a-c faults for "and" gate
and(Name, s_a_0, 1, 1, 0).        % stuck-at-0 at one of inputs
and(Name, s_a_1, 0, 1, 1).        % stuck-at-1 at input1
and(Name, s_a_1, 1, 0, 1).        % stuck-at-1 at input2
```

Complex components can get very long Prolog models. However, such components include often standard correct subcomponents, which need not be diagnosed. In this case the subcomponents can be specified by external procedures in procedural languages, such as C, Pascal or even VHDL. The diagnoser uses the specification for simulating the behavior of the subcomponents without diagnosing it. In this way we are able to use existing standard specifications.

3.3 Diagnosis of Circuits by Algorithmic Debugging

This sections discusses the use of algorithmic debugging for fault diagnosis of digital circuits. The idea was first presented by Gupta [Gup 87]. It relies on the use of a (correct) circuit specification represented by a Prolog program, as described in Section 3.2. As algorithmic debugging is able to diagnose only programs, the role of "correct" and "incorrect" is inverted. The actual faulty circuit is assumed correct and the specification incorrect; the circuit is treated as if it were a specification. We are trying to execute the Prolog specification and find out why it does not produce the incorrect results. Algorithmic debugging localizes a procedure of the Prolog specification that is responsible for the discrepancy. In order to make the specification compatible with the circuit, this procedure has to be modified; hence the corresponding component of the circuit has to be modified to make the circuit compatible with the specification. Thus a faulty component has been localized.

As already explained, there are two kinds of errors in logic programs that are subject to algorithmic debugging: *incorrectness* means obtaining an incorrect answer, *insufficiency*- not obtaining some answer (which is required by the intended semantics). Respectively, there are incorrectness diagnosing algorithms and insufficiency diagnosing algorithms.

A discrepancy between a specification and a circuit may be treated both as incorrectness and as insufficiency. In the first case a result produced by the specification is understood to be incorrect with respect to. that given by the actual circuit; in the second case the specification is seen as not able to produce the result given by the circuit. [Gup 87] uses the second approach and does not mention the possibility of the first. The examples presented in the next section have been obtained by using our algorithmic debugger [DNM 88a, b] with the insufficiency approach. It is not yet clear to us, which approach is better/ advantageous.

Consider the example of "and" gate specified in Prolog in Section 3.2.2. An example question asked by the debugger may be: "Is and(a1, 1, 1, 0) correct?". The question is answered by measuring the signals at the ports of the AND gate named a1 in the actual circuit. If the state of the ports is 1,1,0 then the answer is YES; if it is 1,1,1 the answer is NO. However a problem appears which was neglected in the previous work. The first two ports of the gate are inputs and the last one is an output. So if the state of the ports is for example 1,0,0 then the question cannot be answered. We do not now, how the gate would behave if the inputs were 1,1. So the debugging algorithm has to be extended to incorporate DON'T KNOW answers.

This can be done by translating DON'T KNOW into this answer which is given when the related procedure of the program is correct. In the case of incorrectness diagnosers of [Shap 82] and [DNM 88a, b] this means YES, in the case of insufficiency diagnoser of [DNM 88a, b] and "Is A correct?" question this means NO. This solution can be justified as follows. A discrepancy of a component's input signal in the specification and in the circuit means that some other component is faulty or that the connections between the components are incorrect. In both cases the reason of the fault is not the component to which DON'T KNOW answer refers. It seems that [Gup 87] did not encountered this problem, because for the specifications and the insufficiency diagnosing algorithm he used the questions happened to be asked in the order corresponding to the signal flow in the circuit.

To summarize, the algorithmic debugging methods, proposed for Prolog programs, are able to localize incorrect procedures thus finding faulty components represented by them. We use our algorithmic debugger, and the formal specification of the circuit and an observation of incorrect behavior for automatic localization of an incorrect component. The process uses the information about the input stimuli, the real circuit response and the values of its internal lines. This information is obtained by accessing the lines. Since the access is limited, the algorithmic debugging process continues until this information is available and indicates an incorrect procedure at every step of the process. The procedure corresponds to a component of the circuit. Thus, the granularity of the localized faulty component depends on the observability. The module localized is usually compound and other methods are needed to determine a faulty component within this module.

Many current designs use scan path registers to make it possible to control and observe internal points of the design. It is planed to use this technique to get available information regarding internal lines. Our previous work on testability analysis and its improvement (e.g., [GKP 91], [GKP 92]) can be used here to get circuits which are diagnosable.

3.4 Diagnosis of Black-Boxes using Fault Models

The algorithmic debugging process is not able to proceed if we have exhausted information from the real circuit and we still have not localized the fault. In this case we propose to employ a simulation of the module by a Prolog program. The diagnosis finds a modification of the original specification which conforms to the behavior of the faulty module. The modification of the specification is achieved by using, in addition to correct components' declarations, declarations of faulty components as it was discussed in section 3.2.2. The difference between the modified and the original specification describes a possible fault. Since the simulation can produce many possible answers for many combination of faults we limit the number of possible faults in every simulation to one. This reflects the assumption of the existence of one fault and simplifies the simulation. The similar method of simulation based diagnosis was used in [BCM 88], however, it was not combined with an algorithmic debugging. Faults dictionaries can also be used to find a fault if they are available.

As it was already mentioned our black-box diagnosis is similar to the logic-based approach to model-based diagnosis. It is both related to consistency-based diagnosis and abductive diagnosis. By using a formal logical model of a device it is similar to consistency-based diagnosis and by using pre-defined fault models together with their behavioral consequences for a device it has much in common with abductive diagnosis. The main difference is that our method combines both, device and fault models as well as Prolog execution facility to diagnose the device. Prolog is used to find a new specification, consistent with respect to faulty inputs and outputs. This specification is found by replacing correct components by faulty ones, which have defined their fault models.

4 Examples

We illustrate our approach by three examples. The first two of them show the use of algorithmic debugging for diagnosis of, respectively, a combinatorial and a sequential circuit. The examples were run on our algorithmic debugger. The answers to the queries were introduced manually in order to have a better insight of the diagnosis process. A fully automatic execution would be possible by connecting the debugger to a real circuit. The third example illustrates the second, "black-box", phase of the diagnosis.

4.1 One bit adder diagnosis example

The first example is a simple one bit adder discussed also in [Gup 87]. The Prolog program for this adder is included in section 3.2.1. The adder has a stuck-at-1 fault at C input of a2 "and" gate and produces incorrect value for Carry (1 instead of 0). We try to diagnose the circuit by applying an algorithmic debugging program developed in [DNM 88a]. We diagnose why we get an insufficient answer (in fact no answer) from our program for full adder. We answer two questions based on the actual values of the faulty circuit and the diagnosis program finds out an incorrect procedure which represents "and" a2 gate. It is interesting to note that our algorithmic debugging program needed only two questions to find the faulty component while Gupta's solution needed four.

```
| ?- ins(full_adder_gates(fadd, 1, 0, 0, 1, 1)).
Is  or(fadd/o1,0,0,1)  true?  n.
Is the following set of answers INCOMPLETE for the goal:
and(fadd/a2,0,1,B)
answers:
and(fadd/a2,0,1,0)

|: y.
 This atom is not completely covered:
and(fadd/a2,0,1,B)
All matching clauses were invoked
```

The corresponding actual values in the faulty circuit were:

```
xor(fadd/x1, 1, 0, 1),
and(fadd/a1, 1, 0, 0),
xor(fadd/x2, 0, 1, 1),
and(fadd/a2, 0, 1, 1),              %% incorrect value since stuck-at-1 fault occures
```

or(fadd/o1, 0, 1, 1).

The answer for the first question was DON'T KNOW. It was translated manually into NO (see section 3.3) and this answer was given to the algorithmic debugger.

4.2 A decade synchronous counter diagnosis example

The second example is a decade synchronous counter introduced in section 3.2.1. The counter has a stuck-at-0 fault on line Qa which makes that the counter counts only to 3. We diagnose the circuit on the values obtained during first five clock cycles. After eight questions the system finds out the faulty component, the "and2" gate.

|?- ins(simulate([1,1,1,1,1], [0,1,0,1,0,1,0,1], [[0,0,0,1],[0,0,1,0],[0,0,1,1],[0,0,0,0],[0,0,0,1]])).
Is simulate([1,1,1,1],[1,0,0,1,0,1,0,1],[[0,0,1,0],[0,0,1,1],[0,0,0,0],[0,0,0,1]]) true? y.
Is simulate([1,1,1],[0,1,1,0,0,1,0,1],[[0,0,1,1],[0,0,0,0],[0,0,0,1]]) true? y.
Is simulate([1,1],[1,0,1,0,0,1,0,1],[[0,0,0,0],[0,0,0,1]]) true? y.
Is the following set of answers INCOMPLETE for the goal:
counter(B,1,[1,0,1,0,0,1,0,1],C)
answers:
counter(B,1,[1,0,1,0,0,1,0,1],[0,1,0,1,1,0,0,1])
counter(C,1,[1,0,1,0,0,1,0,1],[0,1,0,1,1,0,0,1])

|: y.
Is the following set of answers INCOMPLETE for the goal:
j_k(B/jkD,0,1,1,0,1,C,D)
answers:
j_k(B/jkD,0,1,1,0,1,0,1)

|: n.
Is the following set of answers INCOMPLETE for the goal:
and(B/and3,1,1,0,C)
answers:
and(B/and3,1,1,0,0)
and(C/and3,1,1,0,0)

|: n.
Is the following set of answers INCOMPLETE for the goal:
j_k(B/jkC,1,1,1,0,1,C,D)
answers:
j_k(B/jkC,1,1,1,0,1,1,0)

|: n.
Is the following set of answers INCOMPLETE for the goal:
and(B/and2,1,1,C)
answers:
and(B/and2,1,1,1)

|: y.
 This atom is not completely covered:
and(B/and2,1,1,C)
All matching clauses were invoked

4.3 Black-box diagnosis example

The above examples presented the diagnosis based on algorithmic debugging. As we have pointed out it can be successfully applied only in the case when all internal points in the circuit are accessible. Otherwise we have proposed an additional technique for diagnosis which is based on Prolog simulation in the presence of faulty components. The example below shows which single stuck-at-faults can be diagnosed for the first example when internal points are not accessible. The Prolog execution was done based on the "and" gate faults defined in section 3.2.2.

```
| ?- faults(full_adder(fadd, 1, 0, 0, 1, 1)).

stuck_at_1 at input1 of fadd/o1
stuck_at_1 at input2 of fadd/o1
stuck_at_1 at input1 of fadd/a2
stuck_at_1 at input2 of fadd/a1
```

It can be noted here that even for very simple examples the number of possible faults grows very fast and additional measures must be undertaken. For example, we can run the component on the number of test patterns which will exclude unfeasible faults.

5 Conclusions

We presented a framework which makes it possible to combine different diagnosis techniques, such as algorithmic debugging and model-based diagnosis, for diagnosis of VLSI circuits.

The focus of this paper is on using algorithmic debugging for this purpose. As already mentioned the idea of using algorithmic debugging for digital circuits originates from Gupta [Gup 87]. We extended this work with the objective to diagnose circuits of realistic size. A method similar to algorithmic debugging was also used by [Sim 88] for designing VLSI circuits. It assumed existence of Prolog programs both for implementation and specification of the design circuit. The method was used to find errors in the case when the verification failed. The algorithmic debugging was used only for hierarchical designs and was limited to the first step of the design process.

Our approach has also several advantages over classical diagnosis methods which are usually based on fault dictionaries. First, the method has a well established theory which guarantees to localize a fault. Both algorithmic debugging and Prolog simulation are general techniques which proved to be useful for similar applications. Second, the method is not bounded to any particular fault model. It can be used with stuck-at faults as well as bridging faults, for example. Finally, the method is not restricted to gate level. We can mix gate level and register transfer level descriptions and still be able to perform diagnosis. Moreover, parts of the description can be specified as external functions.

More work is needed to improve some parts of the diagnosis process. For example, Prolog descriptions of circuits are directional and deterministic programs (their arguments can be classified as input or output, the defined relations are functions of the input arguments). This property may be used to specialize and improve diagnosis algorithms. Another important issue is to determine if the circuit diagnosis should be treated as incorrectness or insufficiency diagnosis, and to understand which particular algorithm is most suitable for our purposes.

Acknowledgments

The authors would like to thank Simin Nadjm-Tehrani for the development of the debugger which was used for experiments in this paper.

References

[AR 83]   Abadir, M.S., Reghbati, H.K., *LSI Testing Techniques*, IEEE Micro, February 1983.

[ALP+ 92] Allred, D., Lichtenstein, Y., Preist, Ch., Bennet, M., Gupta, A., *AGATHA: Applying PROLOG to the Test and Diagnosis of Printed Circuit Boards*, Proc. The practical Application of Prolog, April 1-3, 1992, London.

[BM 88]   Bonnier, S., Maluszynski, J., *Towards a Clean Amalgamation of Logic Programs with External Procedures*, LP88, also in Proc. of PLILP '88, LNCS 348, Springer-Verlag, 1989, MIT Press,

[Bon 92]   Bonnier, S., *A Formal Basis for Horn Clause Logic with External Polymorphic Functions*, PhD dissertation, Dept. of Computer and Information Science, Linköping University, May 1992.

[BCM 88] Bosco, P. G., Cecchi, C., Moiso, C., *Exploiting the Full Power of Logic Plus Functional Programming*, Proc. Fifth International Conference and Symposium on Logic Programming, Seattle 1988.

[CFT 93]   Console, L., Friedrich, G., Dupre, D. T., *Model-Based Diagnosis Meets Error Diagnosis in Logic Programs*, in this volume.

[Clo 87]   Clocksin, W. F., *Logic Programming and Digital Circuits Analysis*, J. Logic Programming, 1987:4:59-82.

[DM 85]   Deransart, P. and Maluszynski, J., *Relating Logic Programs and Attribute Grammars*, Journal of Logic Programming, no. 2, vol. 2, 1985, pp. 119-156.

[DM 93]   Deransart, P. and Maluszynski, J., *A Grammatical View of Logic Programming*, The MIT Press, 1993, to appear.

[DNM 88a]Drabent, W., Nadjm-Tehrani, S., Maluszynski, J., *Algorithmic Debugging with Assertions* In H. Abramson and M. Rogers, editors, Meta-Programming in Logic Programming, pp. 501-522, MIT Press, 1989.

[DNM 88b]Drabent, W., Nadjm-Tehrani, S., Maluszynski, J., *The use of Assertions in Algorithmic Debugging*, Proc. of Fifth Generation of Computer Systems 88, Tokyo, Nov.-Dec. 1988.

[Gol 79]   Goldstein, P.P., *Controllability/Observability Analysis of Digital Circuits*, IEEE Trans. on Circuits and Systems, vol. CAS-26, no. 9, September 1979.

[GKP 91] Gu, X., Kuchcinski, K., Peng, Z., *Testability Measure with Reconvergent Fanout Analysis and Its Applications*, The Euromicro Journal, Microprocessing and Microprogramming, nrs 1-5, August, 1991

[GKP 92] Gu, X., Kuchcinski, K., Peng, Z., *An Approach to Testability Analysis and Improvements for VLSI Systems*, to appear The Euromicro Journal, Microprocessing and Microprogramming, nrs 1-5, August, 1992.

[Gup 87] Gupta, A., *Hardware Diagnosis as Program Debugging*, Proc. IJCAI 1987.

[HCK 92] Hamscher, W., Console, L., de Kleer, J., (Editors) *Readings in Model-Based Diagnosis*, Morgan Kaufmann Publishers, San Mateo, CA, 1992.

[HD 88] Davis, R., Hamscher, W., *Model-based reasoning: Troubleshooting*, E. H. Shrobe, editor, Exploring Artificial Intelligence: Survey Talks from the National Conference on Artificial Intelligence, Morgan Kaufman, San Mateo, CA, 1988, also in [HCK 92].

[KK 91] Kågedal, A., Kluzniak, F., *Enriching Prolog with S-Unification*, in PHOENIX Seminar and Workshop on Declarative Programming, 1991, editor John Darlington and Roland Dietrich, series Workshops in Computing, Sasbachwalden, Germany, 18-22 November, pp. 51-65, Springer-Verlag.

[Lee 76] Lee, S. C., *Digital Circuits and Logic Design*, Prentice-Hall, Inc., Englwood Cliffs, N. J., 1976.

[Llo 87] Lloyd, J. W., *Foundations of Logic Programming*, Springer-Verlag, Berlin, second edition, 1987.

[MBB+ 93] Maluszynski, J., Bonnier, S., Boye, J., Kågedal, A., Kluzniak, F., Nilsson, U., *Logic Programs with External Procedures*, in Logic programming languages, constraints, functions and objects, The MIT Press, 1993, editor K.R. Apt, J.W. de Bakker, J.J.M.M. Rutten, pp. 21-48.

[Sha 82] Shapiro, E.Y., *Algorithmic Program Debugging*, MIT Press, Cambridge, Mass. 1982.

[SND 88] Simonis, H., Nguyen, H.N., Dincbas, M., *Verification of Digital Circuits Using CHIP*, Proceedings of the IFIP WG 10.2 International Working Conference on the Fusion of Hardware Design and Verification, Glasgow, Scotland, July, 1988.

[Tsu 86] Tsui, F. F., *LSI/VLSI Testability Design*, McGraw-Hill Inc., 1986.

Author Index

Springer-Verlag
and the Environment

We at Springer-Verlag firmly believe that an international science publisher has a special obligation to the environment, and our corporate policies consistently reflect this conviction.

We also expect our business partners – paper mills, printers, packaging manufacturers, etc. – to commit themselves to using environmentally friendly materials and production processes.

The paper in this book is made from low- or no-chlorine pulp and is acid free, in conformance with international standards for paper permanency.

Lecture Notes in Computer Science

For information about Vols. 1–675
please contact your bookseller or Springer-Verlag

Vol. 712: P. V. Rangan (Ed.), Network and Operating System Support for Digital Audio and Video. Proceedings, 1992. X, 416 pages. 1993.

Vol. 713: G. Gottlob, A. Leitsch, D. Mundici (Eds.), Computational Logic and Proof Theory. Proceedings, 1993. XI, 348 pages. 1993.

Vol. 714: M. Bruynooghe, J. Penjam (Eds.), Programming Language Implementation and Logic Programming. Proceedings, 1993. XI, 421 pages. 1993.

Vol. 715: E. Best (Ed.), CONCUR'93. Proceedings, 1993. IX, 541 pages. 1993.

Vol. 716: A. U. Frank, I. Campari (Eds.), Spatial Information Theory. Proceedings, 1993. XI, 478 pages. 1993.

Vol. 717: I. Sommerville, M. Paul (Eds.), Software Engineering – ESEC '93. Proceedings, 1993. XII, 516 pages. 1993.

Vol. 718: J. Seberry, Y. Zheng (Eds.), Advances in Cryptology – AUSCRYPT '92. Proceedings, 1992. XIII, 543 pages. 1993.

Vol. 719: D. Chetverikov, W.G. Kropatsch (Eds.), Computer Analysis of Images and Patterns. Proceedings, 1993. XVI, 857 pages. 1993.

Vol. 720: V.Mařík, J. Lažanský, R.R. Wagner (Eds.), Database and Expert Systems Applications. Proceedings, 1993. XV, 768 pages. 1993.

Vol. 721: J. Fitch (Ed.), Design and Implementation of Symbolic Computation Systems. Proceedings, 1992. VIII, 215 pages. 1993.

Vol. 722: A. Miola (Ed.), Design and Implementation of Symbolic Computation Systems. Proceedings, 1993. XII, 384 pages. 1993.

Vol. 723: N. Aussenac, G. Boy, B. Gaines, M. Linster, J.-G. Ganascia, Y. Kodratoff (Eds.), Knowledge Acquisition for Knowledge-Based Systems. Proceedings, 1993. XIII, 446 pages. 1993. (Subseries LNAI).

Vol. 724: P. Cousot, M. Falaschi, G. Filè, A. Rauzy (Eds.), Static Analysis. Proceedings, 1993. IX, 283 pages. 1993.

Vol. 725: A. Schiper (Ed.), Distributed Algorithms. Proceedings, 1993. VIII, 325 pages. 1993.

Vol. 726: T. Lengauer (Ed.), Algorithms – ESA '93. Proceedings, 1993. IX, 419 pages. 1993

Vol. 727: M. Filgueiras, L. Damas (Eds.), Progress in Artificial Intelligence. Proceedings, 1993. X, 362 pages. 1993. (Subseries LNAI).

Vol. 728: P. Torasso (Ed.), Advances in Artificial Intelligence. Proceedings, 1993. XI, 336 pages. 1993. (Subseries LNAI).

Vol. 729: L. Donatiello, R. Nelson (Eds.), Performance Evaluation of Computer and Communication Systems. Proceedings, 1993. VIII, 675 pages. 1993.

Vol. 730: D. B. Lomet (Ed.), Foundations of Data Organization and Algorithms. Proceedings, 1993. XII, 412 pages. 1993.

Vol. 731: A. Schill (Ed.), DCE – The OSF Distributed Computing Environment. Proceedings, 1993. VIII, 285 pages. 1993.

Vol. 732: A. Bode, M. Dal Cin (Eds.), Parallel Computer Architectures. IX, 311 pages. 1993.

Vol. 733: Th. Grechenig, M. Tscheligi (Eds.), Human Computer Interaction. Proceedings, 1993. XIV, 450 pages. 1993.

Vol. 734: J. Volkert (Ed.), Parallel Computation. Proceedings, 1993. VIII, 248 pages. 1993.

Vol. 735: D. Bjørner, M. Broy, I. V. Pottosin (Eds.), Formal Methods in Programming and Their Applications. Proceedings, 1993. IX, 434 pages. 1993.

Vol. 736: R. L. Grossman, A. Nerode, A. P. Ravn, H. Rischel (Eds.), Hybrid Systems. VIII, 474 pages. 1993.

Vol. 737: J. Calmet, J. A. Campbell (Eds.), Artificial Intelligence and Symbolic Mathematical Computing. Proceedings, 1992. VIII, 305 pages. 1993.

Vol. 738: M. Weber, M. Simons, Ch. Lafontaine, The Generic Development Language Deva. XI, 246 pages. 1993.

Vol. 739: H. Imai, R. L. Rivest, T. Matsumoto (Eds.), Advances in Cryptology – ASIACRYPT '91. X, 499 pages. 1993.

Vol. 740: E. F. Brickell (Ed.), Advances in Cryptology – CRYPTO '92. Proceedings, 1992. X, 593 pages. 1993.

Vol. 741: B. Preneel, R. Govaerts, J. Vandewalle (Eds.), Computer Security and Industrial Cryptography. Proceedings, 1991. VIII, 275 pages. 1993.

Vol. 742: S. Nishio, A. Yonezawa (Eds.), Object Technologies for Advanced Software. Proceedings, 1993. X, 543 pages. 1993.

Vol. 743: S. Doshita, K. Furukawa, K. P. Jantke, T. Nishida (Eds.), Algorithmic Learning Theory. Proceedings, 1992. X, 260 pages. 1993. (Subseries LNAI)

Vol. 744: K. P. Jantke, T. Yokomori, S. Kobayashi, E. Tomita (Eds.), Algorithmic Learning Theory. Proceedings, 1993. XI, 423 pages. 1993. (Subseries LNAI)

Vol. 745: V. Roberto (Ed.), Intelligent Perceptual Systems. VIII, 378 pages. 1993. (Subseries LNAI)

Vol. 746: A. S. Tanguiane, Artificial Perception and Music Recognition. XV, 210 pages. 1993. (Subseries LNAI)

Vol. 747: M. Clarke, R. Kruse, S. Moral (Eds.), Symbolic and Quantitative Approaches to Reasoning and Uncertainty. Proceedings, 1993. X, 390 pages. 1993.

Vol. 748: R. H. Halstead Jr., T. Ito (Eds.), Parallel Symbolic Computing: Languages, Systems, and Applications. Proceedings, 1992. X, 419 pages. 1993.

Vol. 749: P. A. Fritzson (Ed.), Automated and Algorithmic Debugging. Proceedings, 1993. VIII, 369 pages. 1993.

Vol. 750: J. L. Diaz-Herrera (Ed.), Software Engineering Education. Proceedings, 1994. XII, 601 pages. 1994.

Vol. 751: B. Jähne, Spatio-Temporal Image Processing. XII, 208 pages. 1993.

Vol. 752: T. W. Finin, C. K. Nicholas, Y. Yesha (Eds.), Information and Knowledge Management. Proceedings, 1992. VII, 142 pages. 1993.

Vol. 753: L. J. Bass, J. Gornostaev, C. Unger (Eds.), Human-Computer Interaction. Proceedings, 1993. X, 388 pages. 1993.

Lecture Notes in Computer Science

This series reports new developments in computer science research and teaching, quickly, informally, and at a high level. The timeliness of a manuscript is more important than its form, which may be unfinished or tentative. The type of material considered for publication includes

– drafts of original papers or monographs,

– technical reports of high quality and broad interest,

– advanced-level lectures,

– reports of meetings, provided they are of exceptional interest and focused on a single topic.

Publication of Lecture Notes is intended as a service to the computer science community in that the publisher Springer-Verlag offers global distribution of documents which would otherwise have a restricted readership. Once published and copyrighted they can be cited in the scientific literature.

Manuscripts

Lecture Notes are printed by photo-offset from the master copy delivered in camera-ready form. Manuscripts should be no less than 100 and preferably no more than 500 pages of text. Authors of monographs and editors of proceedings volumes receive 50 free copies of their book. Manuscripts should be printed with a laser or other high-resolution printer onto white paper of reasonable quality. To ensure that the final photo-reduced pages are easily readable, please use one of the following formats:

Font size	Printing area		Final size
(points)	(cm)	(inches)	(%)
10	12.2 x 19.3	4.8 x 7.6	100
12	15.3 x 24.2	6.0 x 9.5	80

On request the publisher will supply a leaflet with more detailed technical instructions or a T_EX macro package for the preparation of manuscripts.

Manuscripts should be sent to one of the series editors or directly to:

Springer-Verlag, Computer Science Editorial I, Tiergartenstr. 17,
D-69121 Heidelberg, Germany

ISBN 3-540-57417-4
ISBN 0-387-57417-4